Teaching and Learning in the Elementary School

Focus on Curriculum

Judy Reinhartz
University of Texas at Arlington

Don M. Beach
Tarleton State University

Merrill,
an imprint of Prentice Hall
Upper Saddle River, New Jersey   *Columbus, Ohio*

Library of Congress Cataloging-in-Publication Data

Reinhartz, Judy.
    Teaching and learning in the elementary school : focus on curriculum / Judy Reinhartz and Don M. Beach.
        p.   cm.
    Includes bibliographical references and index.
    ISBN 0-02-399285-9
    1. Education, Elementary—United States—Curricula. 2. Curriculum planning—United States. 3. Curriculum evaluation—United States. 4. Education, Elementary—United States—History.   I. Beach, Don M.   II. Title.
    LB1570.R3796   1997
    372.19'0973—dc20   96-33011
                                                                                    CIP

Cover art: Rininger, Unicorn Stock Photos
Editor: Debra A. Stollenwerk
Production Editor: Julie Peters
Photo Coordinator: Anthony Magnacca
Design Coordinator: Karrie M. Converse
Text Designer: Mia Saunders
Cover Designer: Rod Harris
Production Manager: Patricia A. Tonneman
Electronic Text Management: Marilyn Wilson Phelps, Matthew Williams, Karen L. Bretz, Tracey Ward
Illustrations: Tom Kennedy
Marketing Manager: Kevin Flanagan
Advertising/Marketing Coordinator: Julie Shough

© 1997 by Prentice-Hall, Inc.
Upper Saddle River, New Jersey 07458

Photo credits: Bettmann Archive, p. 2; Scott Cunningham/Merrill, 68, 98, 149, 195, 218, 326; Anthony Magnacca/Merrill, 26, 123, 170, 271; Barbara Schwartz/Merrill, 49, 246, 298.

Printed in the United States of America

10 9 8 7 6 5 4 3 2

ISBN: 0-02-399285-9

Prentice-Hall International (UK) Limited, *London*
Prentice-Hall of Australia Pty. Limited, *Sydney*
Prentice-Hall of Canada, Inc., *Toronto*
Prentice-Hall Hispanoamericana, S. A., *Mexico*
Prentice-Hall of India Private Limited, *New Delhi*
Prentice-Hall of Japan, Inc., *Tokyo*
Editora Prentice-Hall do Brasil, Ltda., *Rio de Janeiro*

This book is dedicated to teachers, who are the foundation and cornerstone of good teaching, and to two special teachers, our spouses Dennis and Linda, who provided the love, encouragement, patience, and support that made this book possible.

Preface

Educators in the 1990s are rethinking the elementary curriculum. After more than a decade of studying educational issues, teachers and administrators are exploring new ideas and options as they seek to create a coherent and relevant curriculum for the elementary school. Within this context, one critical factor emerges: the elementary school is in transition and will prepare students for a world that is different from the present. As changes continue to occur in family structures, economic conditions, and technological dissemination and retrieval systems, elementary schools and students will be affected by these changes.

It does not take an observer in an elementary school long to recognize that classrooms are complex environments. To function in such complexity, elementary teachers need to understand children and their learning abilities as they relate to the dynamics and demands of society. Such awareness can help teachers develop a coherent educational program that is both meaningful and effective for their students. Elementary teachers should view the curriculum as the primary ingredient for helping all students learn and be successful in a changing world.

Teaching and Learning in the Elementary School: Focus on Curriculum begins by discussing the areas of study that impact curriculum development. To better understand the nature of the elementary curriculum, background information is provided, which includes historical issues and events, social contexts, psychological views and principles, and philosophical views. This information acquaints readers with the elementary school and illustrates the complexity of elementary education, the cultural and ethnic pluralism of classrooms, and the factors that influence learning. Not knowing the sequence of instruction and prior courses readers may have had, we have chosen to provide this overview as a context in which teachers develop and implement curriculum.

PURPOSE OF THE BOOK

The purpose of this book is to provide teachers with the concepts and skills needed to be successful in planning, implementing, and assessing curriculum. The central theme of the book is to give meaning to the very heart of school life—the process of curriculum development which facilitates teaching and learning. To be effective, this process must move from viewing the teacher as a technician to a view of the teacher as a reflective professional who is a part of a collaborative team.

As you read the text you will recognize our appreciation for educational traditions. Such an orientation, we believe, provides the basis for a greater understanding of the elementary school and the curriculum development process. In writing the book, we have maintained an appreciation for the curriculum development process and have integrated the theoretical knowledge base with areas of study to guide educators in planning an effective curriculum for elementary students. It is our belief that, as teachers design a coherent curriculum for their students, they draw upon an understanding of these areas of study to establish theoretical underpinnings and to apply the attendant skills.

Teachers become proficient in planning, implementing, and assessing their curriculum as they construct teaching units, whether topical or thematic. Planning for teaching includes the use of varied curricular designs, resource materials, and educational technology. Implementing lesson plans, or teaching, involves using multiple strategies and procedures. Assessing the curriculum and student learning requires teachers to use a variety of strategies. As teachers select and organize concepts within the subject areas at various grade levels, they construct the scope and sequence of the elementary school.

For us, *planning* the curriculum involves reflection and represents all the deliberations that teachers engage in prior to actual teaching, such as reviewing teacher resource materials, curriculum guides, and available technology, as well as putting the information in a format (e.g., integrated thematic, literature-based) that can be used in the classroom. Teaching is *implementing* the curriculum plans by using a variety of teaching behaviors and strategies that occur along an instructional continuum that ranges from direct instruction to independent study. *Assessing* the curriculum helps to determine the degree to which curriculum planning and implementation have been successful in promoting student learning. Assessment also involves using a variety of strategies, such as portfolios and individual and

small-group assessment, to determine the degree to which students have learned. The chapters focusing on each of the subject areas of the elementary curriculum provide teachers with the general goals and concepts of each subject and serve as a beginning point for constructing a more comprehensive view of the curriculum. A part of the curriculum development process occurs as teachers incorporate the content from each of the subject areas and modify and refine it to meet the learning needs of their students.

ORGANIZATION OF THE TEXT

We have organized the text into three parts. **Part I** provides background information by describing the areas of study that impact in the elementary school. Chapter 1 includes historical background to help the reader understand how contemporary practices developed. Chapter 2 describes the impact of reform efforts on elementary education and provides a profile of the elementary school of today. Chapter 3 presents the social, political, and economic contexts that impact the students, teachers, and school operations. Part I concludes with a discussion in Chapter 4 of elementary school students, with attention given to their physical, cognitive, and moral development.

Part II describes the steps in the process of curriculum development. Chapter 5 discusses the role of educational philosophy and the origins and sources of four philosophies of education. The chapter concludes with a discussion of the relationship of curriculum to teaching, the designs and sources of the curriculum, as well as other aspects of curriculum development. Chapter 6 elaborates on the curriculum planning step by having teachers consider, when planning units and lessons, instructional objectives, domains of learning, student characteristics, teaching strategies, resources and materials, content, and assessment. When considering these items, the subtleties of planning the elementary curriculum become more evident. Chapter 7 describes the implementation of the curriculum, or teaching, step, which includes views of teaching, strategies and delivery systems, and effective teaching behaviors. Teachers have an array of strategies and behaviors from which to select as they accommodate the numerous needs in teaching and learning: developmental levels/needs of students, nature of content, and so on. Chapter 8 discusses the process of curriculum assessment, the levels of assessment, and assessment strategies and procedures (e.g., authentic assessment, tests). Chapter 9 presents a discussion of technology and its impact on the curriculum development process and includes a listing of software resources for each subject area.

Part III examines the various subject areas taught in the elementary school and includes Language Arts, Mathematics, Social Studies, Science, and Physical Education and the Fine Arts. Each chapter presents a general overview of the concepts taught along with program goals, assessment options, and a list of teaching resources and tools. Implicit in presenting the subject areas as isolated chapters is the understanding that this approach does not preclude an integrated thematic design to curriculum development. Theming is not the exclusive domain of any one subject area, but can serve as one mechanism for integrating the elementary classroom. For example, science or social studies concepts can be taught across the curriculum. Even though goals and general concepts for each subject area have been identified, they can still be integrated with other subjects or grouped according to themes and supported by literature. In fact, we have provided an integrated model in Chapter 6 to illustrate an integrated thematic unit.

The Epilogue brings curriculum development to a close by focusing on the role of the classroom teacher in the process, and who, indeed, makes the difference in teaching and learning in the lives of elementary students. This chapter reaffirms the central role of the teacher as the one who engages in the moral profession of teaching. Without teachers, the curriculum would be lifeless.

We have used all of these ideas in some form with our undergraduate and graduate students, so most of the material has been field tested. We also have invited several elementary teachers to review the Table of Contents and chapters and make recommendations to ensure relevancy.

SPECIAL FEATURES

Teachers were invited to submit responses or reactions to instructional situations and lesson/unit plans for various chapters. These "Voice of Experience" pieces are a composite profile of teachers we have worked with and the names for each "Voice of Experience" represent several individuals currently teaching. The classroom descriptions found in the "Voice of Experience" sections provide valuable case knowledge. Teachers have come to value these stories told through the experiences of practicing professionals who have been there!

Each chapter concludes with a section called "Your Turn" in which readers are asked to apply what they have learned from the chapter. As you review the Table of Contents, it is our goal that these topics reinforce the notion that the key to effective teaching and learning in the elementary school is a well-developed curriculum.

This book has evolved from our combined experience of over fifty years in elementary and secondary classrooms, preservice teacher training, and inservice professional development activities. The production of this book has been a labor of love, and the writing has been a collaborative effort in which the authors "speak with one voice." We feel that the result is a unique blend of two viewpoints.

ACKNOWLEDGMENTS

We would like to thank the following individuals who kindly reviewed our manuscript and provided us and our editors with constructive comments: Robert V. Bullough, Jr., University of Utah; Kenneth E. Cypert, Tarleton State University; Russ Firlik, Sacred Heart University; Bernard J. Fleury, Westfield State College; Maureen Gillette, College of St. Rose; Marvin Heller, University of Northern Iowa; Jerry L. Irons, Stephen F. Austin State University; Margaret A. Laughlin, University of Wisconsin, Green Bay; Rena Newson Lott, Alabama A & M University; Rosemary F. Schiavi, Brescia College; Kay W. Terry, Western Kentucky University; Patti Trietsch, Sul Ross State University; Terry L. Wiedmer, Ball State University-Teachers College; Leslie Owen Wilson, University of Wisconsin, Stevens Point.

We would also like to acknowledge the support and interest of the staffs at JoJo's, Borders, and Suzannas for providing a place to think, write, and edit as this book moved from dream to reality.

Finally we would like to thank the staff at Merrill/Prentice Hall, especially Debbie Stollenwerk and Julie Peters, for their encouragement, professional contributions, and their dedication to this project. Thank you!

Brief Contents

Contents

8 Curriculum Assessment **170**

9 Using Technology in the Classroom **195**

PART III
SUBJECT AREAS IN THE
ELEMENTARY SCHOOL
CURRICULUM **217**

10 Curriculum for the Language Arts **218**

11 The Mathematics Curriculum **246**

part one

Areas of Study Impacting Teaching and Learning in the Elementary School

Before beginning the curriculum development process, it is helpful for teachers to investigate the different areas of study that impact teaching and learning in the elementary school. The history of elementary education presented in Chapter 1 provides a tapestry woven of traditions from various time periods against which contemporary practices can be examined.

Chapter 2 discusses the impact of the reform efforts in the 1980s on elementary education and describes the current structure and organization of elementary education by providing a profile of an elementary school. Chapter 3 discusses the implications of the home and family contexts of children and describes the social, pluralistic, and political contexts that influence students, educators, and the operations of the elementary school. Part 1 concludes with Chapter 4, which identifies general principles and views of human development and discusses the physical and cognitive development of elementary students.

chapter 1

The Elementary School:
A History of Change

**AFTER READING THIS CHAPTER, YOU
WILL BE ABLE TO DO THE FOLLOWING:**

- Identify the major historical periods that mark the progress of elementary education in the United States, starting with the Colonial period (1600s) and ending with the Modern Elementary Education period (1980s).

- Describe the special features that characterize each time period and explain how historical events have shaped current views of curriculum and the elementary school.

- Explain the concepts of the common school and the graded school and describe how these concepts impact contemporary school curriculum and practices.

- Describe how Dewey influenced the development of the elementary school.

- Explain how various social and political activities and events influenced the organization, curriculum, and teaching and learning in elementary schools.

- Compare and contrast contemporary definitions of *curriculum*.

- Identify and describe the diverse populations found in elementary schools.

Teachers recognize that the elementary school of today is not the same institution it was in earlier times and that the elementary school of the twenty-first century will not be the same as it is today. As American society changes, so does the nature of the elementary school. In various historical periods, the public has exerted a great deal of pressure on the educational system in order to change school policies and programs. Changes in elementary education often raise questions about the guiding philosophy of the school, the curriculum for elementary students, and the most appropriate or effective organizational plan to accomplish the mission and goals of grades K–6.

Sowards and Scobey (1968) characterize this process as more evolution than revolution, and Fullan and Miles (1992) describe it as crystallizing over time. During the past decade, elementary education has undergone extensive study and scrutiny. The reform and counterreform issues have been generally curricular in nature and focused on the general purposes of elementary education. Many of the recommendations for the improvement of elementary education have centered around predictable issues such as the identification of a common core of learning, the "essentials" versus "frills" (for example, reading and writing versus art and music), literary skills, real-life experiences, and the role of the elementary grades in preparing students for additional education and for their adult roles in society.

To help you better understand current practices and curricular programs, we will review the major historical periods of American education and themes or issues in each period. Today's elementary schools have organizational structures and arrangements that differ from elementary schools of the past. Historically, elementary education has evolved in response to the social, political, and economic pressures within the society at the time, as well as the needs of the students.

In this first chapter and throughout this book, "Voice of Experience" features will highlight the thoughts and experiences of a variety of classroom teachers to illustrate how instructional practices in the elementary school have changed as a result of societal and pedagogical influences. Each teacher represents a collective voice of various teachers we have worked with and interviewed, as well as our own classroom experience.

Depending on the particular circumstances in history, the general purposes of elementary education have focused on such diverse areas as religion, literacy, and nationalism. To illustrate how schools have developed over time in response to social conditions, Figure 1-1 provides a summary of major historical periods, types of schools, and the educational focus or emphasis of the period.

Each period has a unique educational focus established by the prevailing political, social, economic, and historical factors at the time. Present-day curriculum has been influenced not only by previous curricular emphases, but also by current pressures. This historical baggage of ideas and practices provides a legacy from earlier generations that can "help us consider, plan for, and create the next fifty years of curriculum reform" (Schubert, 1993, p. 80).

This chapter sets the stage for understanding elementary education by presenting a historical overview of the development of the elementary school, the evolution or crystallization of the curriculum, and the cultural and historical forces within society that helped to shape curricular programs and practices. This chapter begins with a review of the dame school and the writing

FIGURE 1-1   A Historical Overview of Elementary Education

Period	School Type	Educational Focus/Emphasis
Colonial America (1600s)	Dame school Writing school	Fundamentals of reading and writing, some arithmetic; education seen as way to salvation.
New Nation (1700s)	Combined dame school and writing school to form one-room elementary school	Reading, writing, and arithmetic; religion, important during early period, gave way to patriotic or nationalistic emphasis.
Nineteenth Century (1800s)	Common school and graded (non-sectarian, publicly controlled and supported)	Literacy through reading and writing; character development, citizenship, and social skills through expanded curriculum that also included some social studies.
Early Twentieth Century (1900–1950)	Graded elementary school with multiple levels based on age	Academic skills of reading, writing, and arithmetic linked to child's needs and interests; content areas related to everyday experiences.
Modern (1950–1980)	Multiple age/grade arrangements in an elementary school setting	Meeting diverse student needs from learning-challenged to other-language learners; curriculum includes a wide range from the basics to electives; emphasis on literacy.

school, the dominant forms of education during the early Colonial period (1600s). The early elementary school, which developed during the New Nation period (1700s), illustrates the next step in the evolutionary process. The period of the common school (1800s) is also described, followed by a discussion of elementary education in the early twentieth century (1900s). Finally, the modern elementary school (1950–1980) is examined. (The contemporary elementary school, of the 1980s to the present, is described in detail in Chapter 2.) Chapter 1 concludes with a brief discussion of the various meanings of the term *curriculum* as it as been implemented in elementary schools.

ELEMENTARY EDUCATION IN COLONIAL AMERICA (1600s)

To understand the present nature of the elementary school curriculum, it is helpful to review our Colonial heritage and educational roots. The delivery of curriculum in New England was accomplished almost exclusively through dame schools and writing schools, which were modeled after similar institutions in England that were familiar to the colonists.

Dame schools were run by women in the community who invited children into their homes for teaching and learning, primarily in learning the alphabet and beginning reading. Spelling and moral or religious precepts also were taught, and a few schools included writing and arithmetic as part of their curriculum, but these were generally considered advanced skills. As was the custom of the time, girls seldom advanced beyond their dame school education; instead, they furthered their education by learning domestic skills such as sewing, cooking, knitting, and needlework. Young boys, after they learned the "basics" of words with two or three syllables at the dame school, usually advanced to a writing school in

the community. In describing the education of this period, Small (1914) noted that

> The dame school was a necessity of the times. Boys were not generally admitted to the master's school until they could "stand up and read words of two syllables and keep their places"; girls were not admitted at all. The teaching of simple rudiments was made a family, not a public matter . . . Miss Betty making the figures on the sand[y] floor with her rod, . . . [had] her pupils with their square pieces of birch bark and bits of charcoal, copying the sums she gave them. (pp. 162–164)

From these roots, an elementary education that was devoted to teaching the basics began to take shape. The teacher was paid by the parents for their child's education, and teaching normally occurred in a home, school, church, or town meeting hall. From this beginning, parents have a history of involvement in the education of their children (Walberg, 1984). However, over the years, this parental involvement has generally been limited to middle-income families from the majority (Chavkin, 1993). With the issue of home schooling and school choice as a part of the current national dialogue, it appears that parental involvement, begun in the Colonial period, has become a part of the public agenda, with parents seeking a greater role in the education of their children.

In the Colonies, the emphasis on education and the kinds of schools differed from region to region.

New England Colonies.   In the New England colonies, the first settlers of America conceived the purpose of education as primarily a means to spiritual salvation. The Puritans in New England established an educational program patterned after the English system that had been established for families with money and position. In the New England colonies, an education was viewed as important, but the failure of the colonists to support education on a voluntary basis led to the passage of laws mandating education for children.

The *Massachusetts Law of 1647*, generally known as the Old Deluder Satan Act, is considered to be the first law in this country that supported compulsory education. A section of the law is cited in Figure 1-2.

According to Ikenberry (1974), the opening statement gave the law its name because it noted that the object of "that old deluder Satan" was to keep people ignorant of the scriptures. The law required that every town of 100 households establish a grammar school to instruct youth for the university. Although the education was almost exclusively for males, this law marked the beginning of compulsory schools in America. The education as required by law was not tax supported, and the burden of funding fell to the parents who paid tutors for teaching and learning.

Southern Colonies.   In the Southern colonies, compulsory education was not considered as important. Within the economic and political system of plantation life, the development of public schools on a large scale was hampered, and public schools were therefore very slow to develop. As Sowards and Scobey (1968) note, "a pattern of aristocracy dominated life, and education was no exception; schooling was a private affair" (p. 8). The wealthy plantation owners provided for the education of their own children and a few selected others, but they felt little obligation to provide education for other children.

When viewing educational data today, it is not unusual to find many of the Southern states at the lower end on per-pupil expenditures, teacher salaries, and educational success (Campbell, 1996). The legacy of the earlier educational system, coupled with segregation/integration issues, continues to impact elementary education in the South.

ELEMENTARY SCHOOLS OF THE NEW NATION (1700s)

Because the American society continued to change during the Colonial years and because of the limited curriculum and scope of the dame school, a new type of elementary education emerged that combined the dame school and the writing school. The merger of these schools

FIGURE 1-2   The Massachusetts School Law, 1647 (excerpt)

It being one chief project of that old deluder Satan to keep men from the knowledge of the scriptures, as in former times by keeping them in an unknown tongue, so in these latter times by persuading from the use of tongues, that so at least the true sense and meaning of the original might be clouded by false glosses of saint-seeming deceivers, that learning may not be buried in the grave of our fathers in the church and commonwealth, the Lord assisting our endeavors:

It is therefore ordered, that every township in this jurisdiction, after the Lord hath increased them to the number of fifty householders, shall then forthwith appoint one within their town to teach all such children as shall report to him to write and read, whose wages shall be paid either by the parents or masters of such children, or by the inhabitants in general by way of supply, as the major part of those that order the prudentials of the town shall appoint. Provided, those that send their children be not oppressed by paying much more than they can have them taught for in other towns. And it is further ordered, that where any town shall increase to the number of 100 families or households, they shall set up a grammar school, the master thereof being able to instruct youth so far as they may be fitted for the university. Provided, that if any town neglect the performance hereof above one year, that every such town shall pay five pounds to the next school till they shall perform this order.

established the *one-room school*, which became the early blueprint for the modern elementary school.

Although in this one-room school the focus was on teaching students reading, writing, and the fundamentals of arithmetic, religion was also an important "subject" in the curriculum. Religion was particularly evident in the reading material; Butts (1947) has described this emphasis in the *New England Primer* by saying

> It commonly contained the alphabet in capital and small letters; lists of syllables; and lists of words emphasizing moral concepts. . . . Then came the famous woodcuts illustrating the letters of the alphabet . . . accompanied by religious and moralistic rhymes. . . . The reading material followed, usually under such headings as "The Dutiful Child's Promises," "An alphabet of Lessons for Youth," and included the Lord's Prayer, the Apostles' Creed, the Ten Commandments, . . . and finally the Westminster Catechism. (p. 373)

After the American Revolution, the *New England Primer* contained patriotic sentiments and more secular material. Real-life items of practical value replaced the religious and moral studies of earlier times. Items such as "Whales in the sea, God's voice obey" became "Great Washington brave, His country did save" in the common reading material (Butts, 1947, p. 373). Typically one teacher handled the teaching and learning in the school, with each of the twenty or so pupils on a different level, so teaching and learning tended to be individualized. Recitation was the primary instructional method used, and pupils were called upon one by one to recite their particular learning for the day. Edwards and Richey (1947) provide an excerpt from a diary describing a typical day in the life of an elementary school student after the Revolutionary War:

> I went to the winter school kept by Lewis Olmstead—a man who made a business of plowing, mowing, carting manure, etc., in the summer, and teaching school in the winter. He was a celebrity in ciphering . . . the greatest 'arithmeticker' in Fairfield Country. There was not a grammar, a

geography, or a history of any kind in the school. Reading, writing, and arithmetic were the only things taught, and these very indifferently—not wholly from the stupidity of the teacher, but because he had forty scholars, and the custom of the age required no more than he performed. (p. 117)

This description is further supported by the requirements at this time for teacher preparation at the elementary level, which required the ability to teach reading, writing, and simple arithmetic.

During the later part of the 1700s, the New England colonies remained in the forefront of elementary education, with the Southern colonies lagging behind. In the South, one of the few provisions for public education was set forth by the Society for the Propagation of the Gospel in Foreign Parts, and these were charity schools whose sole purpose was religious training through fundamental skills in reading, writing, and simple arithmetic.

As the nation continued its westward expansion, the one-room school became the primary educational institution in rural areas and continued to focus on the basics of reading, writing, and arithmetic. According to Conrad (1996), the one-room school had

> telltale features: tall windows at either side of a simple, rectangular structure. . . . In the North and West they were built of lumber; in the Southwest, of adobe or hewn stone blocks. Inside, most had a teacher's desk on a platform at the back of the room, slate blackboards, maps of the United States, a picture of George Washington, and a hand-held school-bell. (p. 11)

Students developed just enough competence in each subject in order to function or carry on essential personal or business matters. Teaching in the frontier schools was often difficult because they were remote and provided almost spartan conditions for teaching and learning. Wood (1987), in her book *The Train to Estelline*, provides an excerpt from the diary of Miss Lucy Eliza Richards, a teacher:

This country is more desolate than any place you can imagine. . . . I walked inside [the school] and saw the sun shining through the window . . . and the benches and desks all huddled in one corner. In a minute, I had them all in rows and . . . dusted them off with a wisp of a broom I found. . . . The school is in deplorable condition, dirty and grim. Books, chalk, and erasers—*all* essentials are in short supply or nonexistent, and Mr. Dawson says the woodbox is my responsibility. Much work is needed if school is to begin in two weeks. The building must be cleaned and whitewashed, inside and out. Then the brush must be cleared from the schoolground. (pp. 12–13)

As pioneer teachers prepared their classrooms and taught the children sent to them, they had to accommodate a range of student abilities and attitudes. Older students, who may have had little formal teaching and learning, often had the attitude, "Teach me if you can!" In her diary, Lucy Eliza Richards describes her first day:

On the first day of school eleven students had arrived by eight-thirty. By the time the day was over, . . . I [had] rushed from one to the other, giving each an assignment, and trying to return to check the work by the time it was completed. Most of them tried. Only [one] refused to attempt his assignment. . . . I do not want to be the fourth teacher 'run-off' from White Star. (p. 17)

The sense of dedication, frustration, and commitment expressed by this teacher can be found in today's elementary schools. While the school is no longer one room, the many levels of student ability that the teacher must accommodate may be similar so that the teacher functions in much the same way as Lucy Richards.

ELEMENTARY EDUCATION IN THE NINETEENTH CENTURY (1800s)

The 1800s marked the period when the distinctive form of American public education began to develop and depart from those imported from England and western Europe.

Common School

With the growth of cities and the immigrants from various cultures, the schools had to address a more diverse population. In the middle of the 1800s, vast areas in the West were added as states and territories. With the Emancipation Proclamation and the end of the Civil War, large numbers of African-Americans, who had previously been denied an education as slaves, became part of the school population. And Native Americans came under educational jurisdiction of the Bureau of Indian Affairs. The common elementary school, first established in Massachusetts in 1826, was to provide the new blueprint for elementary schools across the country.

The structure of the *common school* led to the creation of a school board, which included citizens from the community and was responsible for all of the schools in a local area. These common schools experienced a significant enrollment increase in elementary students. As Ornstein and Hunkins (1988) note, "these schools were common, in the sense that they housed youngsters of all socioeconomic and religious backgrounds . . . and were jointly owned, cared for and used by the local community" (p. 63). Some critics would argue that these schools were still very selective, because many minorities and students from lower socioeconomic backgrounds did not attend.

Horace Mann, a Massachusetts legislator and the Massachusetts Commissioner of Education, popularized the concept of the common school by appealing to the various segments of the population for support. Mann believed that an education gained from common schools had market value, that it would create a stable society and a sense of nationalism, and that it would be democratic in nature and a great equalizer of economic differences. Zais (1976) comments on the impact of the common school:

The forces of democracy, industrial development, and nationalism . . . contributed to the establishment of the nonsectarian, publicly controlled and supported common (elementary) school and public high school—a unitary ladder of opportunity specifically adapted to the needs and desires of the American people. (p. 40)

In recognizing the popular appeal and potential social impact of the common school, Spring (1986) further notes that

School reformers placed their hope for a better tomorrow on the growth of the common school. The rhetoric of the nineteenth century . . . was full of promises to end poverty, save democracy, solve social problems, end crime, increase prosperity, and provide for equality of opportunity. (p. 336)

The goals of the elementary school centered on the following components: *literacy*, with the goal that all students would be able to read and write; *moral and character development*, with the hope that children would behave within the accepted guidelines of the time; *citizenship*, with the hope that the students would become participating citizens; and *social and practical skills*, so that the students could become self-sufficient and contributing members of society.

Graded School

As cities continued to grow and America was experiencing urbanization, the first graded school was established in the United States in Boston in 1848. By 1860, the graded school was so widely accepted that it had become the model for elementary schools and continues to dominate the organization of elementary schools. Today, approximately 95 percent of all elementary schools use some form of this plan (Shepherd & Ragan, 1992). The basic characteristics of the graded plan that made it so popular include the following:

■ Using chronological age as the primary basis for entry and grouping as students were placed in grades in a vertical sequence.

■ Assigning and sequencing a specific body of knowledge, skills, and appreciations to each grade, with teaching and learning to last approximately nine months.

■ Developing textbooks for the specific content in each graded sequence.

■ Promoting or moving students to the next grade in the sequence, at the end of a nine-month period when students had completed the work of the preceding grade.

■ Using school organizational patterns that include self-contained classrooms, grade level clusters, or departmentalization.

■ Housing all elementary grades in one building and designating the graded organization with the numbers 1–6.

Gradedness represents a structured system in which specific information or content, skills, and textbooks are "covered" within a set period of time (Tewksbury, 1967).

Factors Influencing the Curriculum

As the 1800s came to a close, there were several major factors, according to Zais (1976), that exerted tremendous influence on the development of the elementary school curriculum.

The Industrial Revolution. The technology and specialization created by industrialization led to the growth of the cities and the need to provide schooling for children who moved to cities with their families. The one-room school of Colonial America gave way to multigraded schools with several teachers in each grade. Urban living in turn impacted family life by creating long hours of work and conditions of relative poverty compared to those of rural life.

Immigration. Toward the end of the 1800s, tremendous numbers of immigrants—mostly from Europe—came to America and expected to create a better life for themselves and their families. They valued education as a means to succeed and wanted a good educational system for their children. Anna, our "Voice of Experience" for this chapter, reflects on her own family's immigrant experience.

 Voice of Experience

Anna remembers stories that her father used to tell about his trip to America. He came to this country from southern Europe as a boy of twelve. His father (Anna's grandfather) had come over earlier, worked, and then sent for his wife and their children. Anna's father had stayed behind with relatives until his family sent for him.

She still remembers the picture he painted of the journey to America. He came over in the hull of a ship with hundreds of other people cramped in very small quarters with no light and amenities. He remembers feeling terribly alone and sick most of the way. There was no parental supervision, and people slept on small pallets or beds that were stacked on top of each other. After days at sea, he remembered arriving at Ellis Island, and as he emerged from the dark hole, he remembered seeing the Statue of Liberty and remembering how large and welcoming she looked. When he left the ship, he had only the clothes on his back and a few personal things in a small case. Before he could be united with his parents, he had to go through a medical examination and was inoculated to make sure that he was "clean." He was quarantined for several days in a cold and impersonal place. He was scared and uncertain about what would happen to him until he saw his parents' faces.

The hope for a better life and the desire to be truly free overwhelmed him as he joined his family in this great land. As he learned a new language in school and left many of the "old ways" behind, he became determined that he and his family would make it in America.

As Anna grew up, it was her father who encouraged her to be a teacher because he believed that teaching was "the noblest of all professions." Anna did, indeed, become a teacher so she could give back some of the things that this country had given her family.

Increase in Information.   Information had increased exponentially, particularly in the areas of science and technology or engineering. Not only did this create new content for the school curriculum, but it also created the need for a more literate society.

Ideas from Abroad.   The work of Johann Heinrich Pestalozzi and Friedrich Froebel greatly influenced the development of the education in this country, from the application of the concept of *readiness* to establishment of kindergartens. Pestalozzi is associated not only with the creation of the modern elementary school but also with his contributions to early childhood education, because he recognized and emphasized that learning was a natural developmental process. Froebel established the kindergarten or "child's garden" and advocated the creation of a specific learning environment (which Montessori later developed into the child's room). Herbart (1894) stressed the importance of moral and intellectual development and was known for his five-step approach to learning, which required preparation, presentation, association, systemization, and application. The practices of these early pioneers in education are still evident in many elementary schools today.

Faculty Psychology.   The faculty psychology view of learning dominated the educational process and led to the practice of rote memorization. Exercising the faculties of the mind—by memorizing facts, numerical operations, spelling lists, and long passages from poetry, speeches, or documents—was designed to enhance learning.

Pluralism in Education

In addition to the factors identified by Zais (1976), other social and cultural events took place that have continued to shape the elementary education experience in America. Although large numbers of European immigrants came to this country in the latter decades of the 1800s, the late nineteenth century and early twentieth century was a time of national transition, as growth and westward expansion further enlarged the pluralistic nature of the society. As Campbell (1996) says, "Since its founding . . . the United States has been a nation of immigrants [but] . . . members of the majority culture have often held xenophobic attitudes toward foreigners, persons who speak other languages, and the native peoples" (p. 61).

During the 1800s, the successive immigrant populations from Asia and Mexico, along with relocation of native peoples and the abolition of slavery, created a more diversified society, rather than, as Appleton (1983) notes, "a nation of one dominant culture" (p. 3). In the early 1800s, all or part of Texas, Utah, Colorado, California, New Mexico, and Nevada were part of Mexico. From 1850 to 1870, large populations of Mexican, Native Americans, and Spanish communities existed in California, Texas, and New Mexico (Campbell, 1996). The education of these groups presented new challenges as language and culture from these groups came together. The issues presented at this time still pose a challenge as elementary schools are confronted with the need to accommodate many languages and cultures.

For Native Americans in other parts of the United States, conditions were no different. Appleton (1983) notes that the Bureau of Indian Affairs (BIA) adopted a position that reflected the educational agenda of the time and supported "Anglo conformity as the ideology that would strongly shape . . . education" on the reservation (p. 5). As Campbell (1996) describes the situation, the BIA permeated the life of the tribes by controlling schools and implementing policies designed to terminate tribes or confine them to reservations on nonproductive lands. Van Til (1974) further comments that, "[o]n the reservations, there was always ambivalence as to whether education should absorb [the Native American] into the American majority patterns or respect his [her] civilization and identity" (p. 296).

Following the Civil War, most African-Americans, especially in the South, lived on farms and as Pinkney (1969) describes the situation,

> few of their children were enrolled in school. Those who were enrolled attended for only short periods. The schools were overcrowded and the buildings were dilapidated. . . . The situation improved little with the turn of the century. It is reported that only 58 percent of the children between the ages of 6 and 14 were enrolled in school as late as 1912. (p. 73)

In his autobiography *Up from Slavery*, Booker T. Washington (1901) describes his yearnings as a young man in wanting to learn to read:

> I induced my mother to get hold of a book for me. How or where she got it I do not know, but in some way she procured an old copy of Webster's 'blue-back' spelling-book, which contained the alphabet, . . . I began at once to devour this book, and I think it was the first one I ever had in my hands. (p. 216)

Although the Civil War ended slavery, it did not provide African-Americans with equal access to American public education in the late 1800s. Campbell (1996) describes the conditions: "legal segregation, inadequate schooling, ideologies of racism . . . and other barriers . . . prevented African Americans from achieving equal opportunity" (p. 57).

Many Chinese people emigrated to the United States because of extreme hardship and violence in their own country. Chinese immigrants located primarily in California as early as the 1840s, and by the end of the gold rush, they represented 10 percent of the population of California (Campbell, 1996). By the late 1800s, the United States government had begun to change its position with regard to immigration. Although immigration from Europe continued until the early 1900s, by the 1880s, the U.S. Congress had legislatively excluded Chinese people from immigrating to the United States.

Changes in Curriculum and School Organization

Perhaps the most significant event of this period was the expansion of the curriculum to include such subjects as spelling, grammar, rhetoric, and composition along with arithmetic, history, and geography. States initially passed laws requiring the teaching of geography; later, government, or civics, was added to the social studies curriculum. Science or nature study was added later to the educational program, and eventually fine arts such as drawing and music were incorporated into the school day.

In addition to an expanded curriculum, the schools grew as a result of the large numbers of children the public schools were educating. Cuban (1983) describes a "day" in the life of an elementary school at the turn of the century:

> Generally, classes were taught in a whole group. Teacher talk dominated verbal expression during class time. . . . Student movement in the classroom occurred only with the teacher's permission, e.g., going to the chalkboard. Classroom activities clustered around teacher lectures, questioning of students, and the class working on textbook assignments. Uniformity in behavior was sought and reflected in classroom after classroom with rows of desks facing the blackboard and teacher's desk. (p. 163)

As Cuban (1983) indicates, the concepts and methods used in the old, one-room schoolhouse were abandoned due to changes in the organization of the elementary school. Teaching assignments began to be made on the basis of a single grade or class, and teachers worked with groups of students of the same age rather than individuals. This arrangement continues to be a characteristic of elementary education in many communities.

In contrast to the elementary school of an earlier time, Reisner (1935) describes the impact of industrialization on the graded elementary school in the late 1800s, which he saw as a "school machine" with specific grade levels and the following characteristics:

> There was a great deal more material included in the graded course of instruction, . . . [but] the quality of teaching and instruction was improved hardly at all. . . . Pupils followed an endless succession of book assignments which they learned . . . to reproduce on call. . . . Pupils master[ed] skills and learn[ed] facts as directed by a teacher who in turn was under the automatic control of a printed course of study, a set of textbooks, and the necessity of preparing her class to pass certain examinations on the contents of a specific number of printed pages. . . . The business of school being what it was, any movement, any conversation, any communication, were out of order. The spirit of control was military and repressive, not constructive and cooperative. (pp. 427-428)

Depending on the purpose or view of education at a particular time, the approach described at the turn of the nineteenth into the twentieth century seems to spiral throughout the succeeding decades. With countermoves of progressivism, there were efforts to prevent gradedness from spreading. (Progressivism will be discussed in more detail later in this chapter.)

With changes in the curriculum and methods of teaching and learning in the elementary school came a new kind of teacher preparation program. The *normal school* was designed to prepare teachers for graded elementary schools and an expanded curriculum that included numerous subjects. The delivery of teaching and learning also changed from individual to group.

As the nineteenth century came to a close, the common school, begun in Massachusetts, had emerged into a graded structure that dominated the organization of elementary education, especially in cities. Society became more stratified as the education of immigrants from non-European cultures as well as African-Americans and Native Americans was being addressed. The curriculum and methods of teaching and learning in the elementary school also changed to fit the new graded school structure.

EARLY TWENTIETH-CENTURY ELEMENTARY EDUCATION (1900–1950)

The early 1900s mark a maturation of elementary education. With the emergence of the science of psychology, the scientific study of children and learning became the basis for curriculum development. The work of Hall (1907) led elementary educators, especially early childhood teachers, to break with Froebel and adopt a more scientific view of children and their learning. Leaders in this field included Anna Bryan, Patty Smith Hill, and Alice Temple (Seefeldt & Barbour, 1994).

Another individual who influenced the way educators view children was Maria Montessori. Her Casa de Bambini opened in Rome in 1907 and attracted many visitors from America who viewed firsthand her curriculum based on her belief that children learn largely through the senses and by remaining engaged in a task (Montessori, 1967). In her monograph *The Child*, Montessori describes the "errors of the past" and the construction of a learning environment designed especially for children.

The work of Dewey and his progressive philosophy was coupled with the emerging scientific study of children and learning. It had a profound impact on the development of the elementary school curriculum in the early twentieth century. According to Zais (1976), the philosophy of progressivism was viewed as "the greatest influence

on the elementary curriculum [for] . . . thirty years following World War I" (p. 59). The basic beliefs of this philosophy can be seen in the curriculum that emphasizes the role of the school in preparing students to be citizens in a democracy. Students are viewed as decision makers as they learn to think and reason for themselves. Dewey (1916) proposed that, through their play and other activities, children interact with their environment, which gives them real-life experiences that help them learn the skills they need to think and problem solve. Such a curricular focus places pupil interest as the basis for learning and recognizes that learning is a social process based on real-life experience for the students involved. Learning is also participatory and interactive as students engage in problem solving.

Dewey's theories on effective educational practices, written more than 100 years ago, are still with us today. Dewey not only blazed the trail, but also he left tools for educators to use in determining what these practices mean to them (Giles, 1987). His innovative ideas still have contemporary value. For example, terms and concepts such as *child-centered curriculum, thematic teaching, applied learning, critical reflection, inquiry using the scientific method, the teacher as artist,* and *the role of experience in constructing knowledge* can be traced to Dewey's theories and found in the many books he wrote.

Dewey's postulation of these ideas predated automation, cybernetic science, Einstein, Freudian psychoanalysis, and German Gestalt psychology. His contemporaries were famous sociologists, philosophers, historians, anthropologists, artists, writers, and architects, including Thorstein Veblen, Franz Boas, Charles Beard, Frank Lloyd Wright, Georgia O'Keefe, Eugene O'Neill, William James, E. L. Thorndike, Alfred Adler, Stanley Hall, and many others. Their contributions, like Dewey's theory building, took place during the first decades of the twentieth century (Rugg, 1924).

In analyzing Dewey's contributions to elementary education, it is helpful to review a time

FIGURE 1-3   Time Line of John Dewey's Life and Accomplishments

1859	Born in Burlington, Vermont; attended University of Vermont, taught two years in high school
1884	Attended Johns Hopkins University, first graduate school modeled after the research institution in Germany; dissertation on Kant's psychology
1894	Served as head of Department of Philosophy, Psychology, and Pedagogy at University of Chicago
1896	Opened the Laboratory School at University of Chicago with his wife, 2 teachers, 16 pupils
1899	Wrote *School and Society*
1904	Left University of Chicago and went to Teacher's College, Columbia University
1916	Wrote *Democracy and Education* (a synthesis of his time spent at the University of Chicago)
1926	Wrote *Experience and Nature*
1927	Wrote *The Public and Its Problems*
1928	Wrote *Progressive Education and School of Education*
1934	Wrote *Art as Experience*
1938	Wrote *Experience and Education*
1939	Wrote *Theory of Inquiry*
1952	Died at the age of 92

line of his career, which spanned nearly six decades. Figure 1-3 provides an overview of Dewey's life and the various educational developments of his career.

Dewey was a prolific writer, as well as an activist throughout his life. His influence on education, which began in 1899 with the publication of his book, *School and Society*, has been significant. Dewey viewed learning as a continuous process that occurs when a child discovers things for himself/herself and reinforces the old adage that "experience is the best teacher." To accomplish such learning, teachers have a key role in making the school curriculum part of the child's total experience. This is done by identifying what the child already knows with respect to the topic under study and linking it to the child's needs and interests (Greene, 1989).

Another critical attribute of an effective teacher, according to Dewey, is the teacher's will-

ingness to share his or her personal experiences with students because the classroom is a place where there is dialogue. Dewey calls this dialogue *conjoint communication*. Communication is an essential component of any classroom because thinking is done singularly and the content of the thought is always social (Greene, 1989).

Dewey's contributions were many and to his credit were many roles:

1. leading interpreter of the doctrine of growth through the personal reconstruction of experience

2. founder of the first laboratory school based upon a theory of human nature, behavior, and knowing, and chief intellectual force in building a new education model

3. pioneer in bringing about two shifts in thought—from the doctrine of authority to the doctrine of experience and from mechan-

ical to organic explanations of the universe, human beings, and their culture

4. clarifier of the social psychology of the human act

5. author of a great library on the scientific method of inquiry and the role of intelligence and problem solving thinking in modern behavior

6. one of the few leaders who succeeded in keeping his balance in the midst of worldwide social hysterics. (Rugg, 1924, pp. 13-14)

The experientialists took Dewey's ideas and advocated "the progressive organization of curriculum by moving from what Dewey called 'the psychological' to what he referred to as 'the logical'" (Schubert, 1993, p. 83). The psychological perspective begins with the interests and concerns of students, and the Deweyian logical curriculum organization includes the relevancy of everyday dilemmas.

This instructional approach to elementary education was a challenge to the tradition of drill and practice. Instead of following a curriculum organized around discrete subjects and "classes," students participated in a variety of classroom experiences designed to integrate the content areas through shared experiences of field trips, story telling, role playing or dramatic presentations, and other forms of creative expression. Jackson (1968) sums up life in such a classroom by suggesting that:

> Learning to live in a classroom involves, among other things, learning to live in a crowd. . . . Most of the things that are done in schools are done with others, or at least in the presence of others, and this fact has profound implications for determining the quality of a student's life. (p. 10)

As a result of the concern for student interest and real-life experiences, the content of the elementary curriculum began to take on a more generic appearance, and the term *language arts* was used as an inclusive subject for reading, writing, speaking, and spelling. Similarly, the term *social studies* was inclusive for history, geography, civics, sociology, and economics. In each of these broad subject areas, real-life problems were addressed as an integral part of the curriculum and terms such as *project-oriented*, *life-centered*, or *child-centered* were used to describe the instructional approach.

As the period of 1900–1950 came to a close, the scientific principles of learning and development continued to influence elementary education. During the first fifty years of the twentieth century, the movement in curriculum reform, aided by Hall, Montessori, and others, went from social behaviorism to progressivism. *Progressive Education at the Crossroads* (Bode, 1938) and *Experience and Education* (Dewey, 1938) were written to undo the misinterpretations surrounding progressivism that had grown in the first three decades of the 1900s (Schubert, 1993).

MODERN ELEMENTARY EDUCATION (1950–1980)

It was not until the post-*Sputnik* period of the 1950s and early 1960s that critics of progressivism were able to turn the tide in favor of a return to the fundamentals of reading, writing, and mathematics—"the basics," as they were called. The fact that the former Soviet Union had won the initial lap of the space race fueled the modern curriculum reform movement in the U.S. and ultimately brought a decline to practices of progressive education. The excesses and abuses the progressives were accused of led many to believe that American public education had failed and that our nation was at risk of losing the Cold War. This concept of "being at-risk" began to appear in response to the United States' place in the global market and the volatility of international relations.

In an effort to regain an advantage in the space race, many elementary schools of the 1950s and 1960s adopted a discipline-centered curriculum, with subject-area teachers for science, mathematics, reading, and social studies. This departmentalization in the elementary school, with self-contained subject classes that began in the 1950s, can still be seen today in the organizational plan of many elementary schools, especially in states where students in the intermediate grades must take mastery and achievement tests in specific subjects.

With the emphasis on the curriculum organized around specific subject areas, the "alphabet soup" movement was born, with numerous curricula named for the instructional program or committee that developed the material. These programs included the Greater Cleveland Math Program (GCMP) or School Mathematics Study Group (SMSG), Man A Course of Study (MACOS), Science A Process Approach (SAPA), and Elementary School Science (ESS). This instructional approach focused on the mastery of a body of knowledge, along with "discovery learning" and laboratory experiences as integral parts of the learning process.

In addition to the curriculum reform, which brought about a change in the content that was taught in the elementary school, Tyler's (1949) *Basic Principles of Curriculum and Instruction* began to impact instructional planning and proposed a different way of structuring the curriculum that would answer the following questions:

1. What educational purposes should the school seek to attain?
2. What educational experiences can be provided that are likely to attain these purposes?
3. How can these experiences be effectively organized?
4. How can we determine whether these purposes are being attained? (pp. 1–2)

The formulation of and answers to these questions led educators to the development of educational objectives that made learner behaviors the primary focus of instructional planning. Because of his impact on curriculum development during this period, Tyler has been called the "father of modern curriculum development." Figure 1-4 provides a summary of his educational contributions.

By the beginning of the 1970s, the discipline-centered approach was being criticized as inappropriate and irrelevant, not related to life away from school and often discriminatory or culturally biased. This curriculum taught children the facts, but many had difficulty integrating this information in a meaningful way. Zais (1976) says that

> Other criticisms of the discipline approach to curriculum . . . pointed to its inherent fragmentation (or lack of integration) of knowledge, its essential elitism in focusing on the college-bound students, and its overemphasis on the rational to the detriment of the aesthetic. Out of this syndrome of reaction was born (or reborn) the humanistic movement in the curriculum. (p. 71)

The humanistic education movement of the 1970s developed partially in response to the great diversity among the student population. When schools began racial integration as a result of the Supreme Court decision in *Brown v. Board of Education*, students with varied backgrounds, cultures, and abilities made up the elementary school population. As Marable (1988) notes, the African-American civil rights movement of the 1950s and 1960s was originally outside each political party, yet the movement produced profound changes in race relations (Omi & Winant, 1994). The social unrest further highlighted the inequalities of opportunity.

Campbell (1996) notes that "Integrationists called for the elimination of structural barriers that prohibited African Americans from full participation in the mainstream of American life" (p. 58). Dr. George Wright recounts his early years growing up in Kentucky and his experiences going to a "black" junior high and a "white" high school (Campbell, 1996). It is a personal response to the changes that were taking place in society as the Kentucky schools became integrated while he was an adolescent. The lessons he learned from his teachers are important and particularly poignant given the context of the 1960s.

In the 1950s and early 1960s, social progress of Mexican-American communities was slowed

FIGURE 1-4   Time Line of Ralph Tyler's Life and Accomplishments

1902	Born to a colonial family and attended schools in Nebraska
1921	Graduated from Doane College in science, mathematics, and philosophy
1921–1922	Taught science in Pierre, South Dakota
1923	Earned a master of arts degree in education at the University of Nebraska—Lincoln
1927	Received his doctorate at the University of Chicago in educational psychology under Charles Hubbard Judd
1927–1929	Was Associate Professor at the University of North Carolina at Chapel Hill where he worked in curriculum
1929–1938	Served as faculty member at Ohio State University as Associate Professor and Research Associate in the Bureau of Educational Research; did pioneering work in testing to assess a broader range of instructional objectives
1934	Became director of the Evaluation Staff of the Eight-Year Study (1933–1941), a national study that measured secondary student achievement outcomes; as part of this study, developed a rationale to guide curriculum development
1938–1953	The University of Chicago
	■ Professor of Education; offered a course, Education 360 in 1940, Basic Principles of Curriculum and Instruction, the syllabus for which was published by the University of Chicago Press as a monograph in 1949. Regarded as a master teacher.
	■ Chairman, Department of Education, 1938–1948
	■ Acting Dean, 1946–1948
	■ 1948–1953, Dean, Division of the Social Sciences; conducted interdisciplinary teaching and collaborative research
1953–1967	Founder and Director of the Center for Advanced Study in the Behavioral Sciences at Stanford
1963–1968	Chair of the Exploratory Committee on assessing the Progress of Education which developed the National Assessment of Educational Progress (NAEP)
1967–1982	Senior Consultant to Science Research Associates
1982–1994	Continued to consult and influence education
1994	Died at age 92

Source: For more information about Ralph Tyler, see H. M. Kolodziey's (1986) *Ralph W. Tyler: A Bibliography 1929–1986.* Washington, DC: National Foundation for the Improvement of Education.

and even set back until 1968, when conditions in Los Angeles schools and other communities led thousands of Mexican-American students to boycott school (Campbell, 1996). In the decades that followed, the numbers of Spanish-speaking children increased steadily to become "the single largest group of limited English students" (Campbell, 1996, p. 18).

At the close of the Vietnam War in the mid-1970s, thousands of Hmong and Mein immigrants from southeast Asia came to the United States. Many of these early immigrants were middle-class, and their children were success- and school-oriented students. As other Asian immigrant groups arrived, they experienced culture shock, and schools often failed to recognize the differences in culture among these groups, thereby exacerbating the difficulties of the newcomers.

With these changes in school populations, the range of individual abilities and interests that each teacher had to address became more diverse. Coleman et al. (1966) found that integration helped low-achieving students and did not detract from the education of high-achieving students. In the 1970s, the call to meet these individual differences through "individualized instruction" led to the creation of educational programs that involved flexible scheduling, learning packets, and learning centers. In addition to the attention given to educational programs that would meet the needs of individual learners, schools also began to experiment with structural changes in school designs, which led to "open-concept" education and included schools without walls. Such designs were based on the belief that children might function at one level in some curricular areas but at a different level in other areas. Therefore, open schools were built to facilitate student movement from one "grade level" to the next as students moved from subject to subject. Teachers were directed to take each learner at his or her level and move each along as far as possible in order to help each attain his or her maximum level or potential.

As the period of 1950–1980 came to a close, elementary schools began to change the instructional program again, as there was movement away from individual concerns in order to achieve greater instructional results and accountability. The period of 1950–1980 witnessed the introduction of social and educational issues in schools that still have not been completely resolved. Public tax support of education, initially questioned in California's Proposition 13 in the 1970s, continues with tax rollback petitions and other election issues. The education of handicapped students initiated by Public Law 94–142 continues to be an issue with concerns for inclusion, as does the education of students for whom English is not a first language. Chapter 2 discusses the most recent developments in elementary education and the issues and concerns that have emerged in the past 15 years.

This discussion of the historical development of elementary education has identified major themes of education and focused on historical events that helped shape the curriculum. From Colonial times to the present, women have played a significant role in the development of education in the United States. Figure 1-5 highlights the accomplishments of some of the women who have provided leadership in education in the U.S. Their contributions have been crucial to the evolution of the mission of schools to educate all children, regardless of race or economic status.

DEFINITION OF *CURRICULUM* AND OTHER KEY TERMS

The social, political, and economic conditions in the U.S. at various times have influenced the ways educators and noneducators alike perceive and have perceived the role and scope of the elementary school and its curriculum. These changing perceptions have contributed to a variety of definitions of the term *curriculum*, based on the mission and goals of the elementary school program at various times in history. Schubert (1993) summarizes the situation succinctly when he says that "the term curriculum is shrouded in definitional controversy" (p. 80).

The earliest use of the term *curriculum* in American education was based on its Latin definition, which is "a course to run or follow." The early use of the term *curriculum*, especially during the for-

FIGURE 1-5   Contributions of Selected Women Leaders in Education

1600s **Anne Hutchinson**—an early social and educational reformer who called for a more humane view of the relationship between God and humanity

1700s **Esther De Berdt Reed and Sarah Franklin Bache**—organized women for relief work and volunteerism

1800s **Susan B. Anthony**—a teacher and administrator in New York who worked to help female teachers gain the same rights and privileges as male teachers and to equalize the inadequate salaries of female teachers

Mary McLeod Bethune—devoted her entire life to the education of African Americans

Charlotte Hawkins Brown—an educational leader who set up a school for poor children and traveled throughout rural North Carolina carrying her educational message

Biddy Mason—a slave who accompanied her master's 300 wagons to California, and when freed settled in Los Angeles where she became wealthy; she was instrumental in purchasing educational and welfare facilities for the poor

Emma Hart Willard—publicly supported higher education for women and founded a ladies seminary that later became the Emma Willard School which has since graduated hundreds of well-educated, progressive women teachers

Frances Wright—a wealthy woman who established a plantation where slaves could be educated and taught a trade to earn their freedom, and campaigned throughout the country for educational facilities for women and free public education for all men and women

1900s **Jane Addams**—Nobel Prize winner and leader in education and social reform who established day-care nurseries and college courses for people of all nations and races

Charl Williams—educational reformer and one of the founders of Delta Kappa Gamma, an honorary education society for women

Ella Flagg Young—teacher and professor who was the first female superintendent in a major city and the first female president of the National Education Association

Source: For more information about women leaders in education, see E. Koontz, (1972), *The Best Kept Secret of the Past 5,000 Years: Women Are Ready for Leadership in Education.* Bloomington, IN: The Phi Delta Kappa Educational Foundation.

mative Colonial period, suggests that this definition represented the dominant view and that, consequently, content became the prescription of what students followed in order to complete a particular program of study. For example, the rigidity of the curriculum in the early dame and writing schools, along with the common and graded schools, allowed little flexibility in course offerings.

Using the historical context and mission of education to help shape the definition of curriculum, Wiles and Bondi (1984, 1993) note that the first modern use of the term occurred in the United States during the 1920s. That definition viewed curriculum as a process rather than a product, and Bobbitt (1924), one of the earliest to propose such a definition, saw curriculum as all of the experiences, both organized and unorganized, that had an educational impact on learners. Other curriculum specialists elaborate on this view and consider curriculum to be all the experiences for children that take place in school under the guidance of the school or teachers.

Planning and process were the central themes of the early definitions of curriculum. A sample of contemporary definitions include the following:

■ all of the learning of students that is planned and directed by the school to attain educational goals (Tyler, 1957)

■ a plan for learning (Taba, 1962, 1973)

■ all planned learning outcomes for which the school is responsible (Popham & Baker, 1970)

■ planned and guided learning experiences with intended learning outcomes produced through knowledge and experience (Tanner & Tanner, 1980, 1995)

■ providing sets of learning opportunities (Saylor, Alexander, & Lewis, 1981)

■ plans for guiding learning and the actualization of those plans (Glatthorn, 1987)

■ a work plan that identifies the content to be taught and the methods used in the process and its purpose is to focus and connect the work of teachers (English, 1992)

■ whatever is advocated for teaching and learning (Schubert, 1993)

The common thread running through these definitions is the idea of planning for teaching and learning. When examining definitions of curriculum, general categories emerge that provide lenses or screens through which curriculum can be viewed as:

■ a series of subjects or content knowledge

■ the experiences (planned or serendipitous) that learners have

■ planned objectives or outcomes (behaviors)

■ planned processes and products that foster learning

Bruner (1966) elaborates on the similarities and the close relationship between curriculum (what is taught) and teaching (how it is taught) by suggesting that

> a curriculum reflects not only the nature of knowledge itself, but also the nature of the knower and the knowledge-getting process . . . where the line between subject matter and methods grows necessarily indistinct. (p. 72)

Using these various definitions as background, we view curriculum as the cornerstone of what happens instructionally in the elementary school because it provides a blueprint for learning. For us, curriculum is planned but flexible enough to meet the needs of individual students and to take into account unplanned, serendipitous, teachable moments. In planning, teachers must consider the factors that impact children as they progress through their school experience. For pre-service (beginning) teachers, the curriculum takes a written form with details such as questions, directions, procedures, and examples. For in-service teachers, the blueprint for learning may be less detailed, because these teachers have a storehouse of past experiences to draw upon as they engage in curriculum development. The plan for teaching and learning can take many forms, but ultimately it represents the educational program that teachers develop and implement in their classrooms based on their experience and the needs of their students.

Curriculum development is similar to the term *curriculum*, but it is a more comprehensive process that involves planning, teaching, and assessment or evaluation. Curriculum development is ongoing as teachers continually monitor their curricular plans in the classroom and as they make decisions to modify those plans for the next day or the next year. *Curriculum planning* involves all of the activities in which the teacher engages prior to teaching and learning, including analysis of content, recognition of student characteristics, and search for possible resources. *Curriculum implementation* involves the actual teaching of the material and interacting with students. *Curriculum assessment*, or *curriculum evaluation*, involves determining the degree to which learning has occurred and to some degree the extent to which the curriculum planning and implementation were successful. Teachers, using their knowledge of the elementary school; the social, political, and economic forces that impact teaching and learning; and the developmental nature of children, organize teaching and learning to meet both the needs of the students and the expectations of society.

In planning, teachers use their knowledge of their students to select not only the appropriate content, based on an examination of the students' abilities, but also to establish appropriate objectives. In planning, teachers consult a number of resources to help them design the most effective units and lessons. As teachers implement their plans, they select a wide variety of strategies, activities, and resources to teach the lesson. Finally, they develop assessment approaches that seek to determine the degree to which students have mastered the objectives and learned the material in a genuine or real situation. Based on the results of the assessment process, modifications may be needed before the next class or unit of instruction. Figure 1-6 provides a conceptual framework of the curriculum development process. (This process is described in greater detail in Chapter 5.)

SUMMARY

This chapter has provided an overview of the major historical periods in the development of elementary education and has presented information regarding the impact of these periods on the curriculum development process. The evolution of elementary education in the United States has departed significantly from European and other models. The dame school was the dominant form of elementary education during the Colonial period (1600–1700). This school was characterized by a limited focus on subject matter and was almost exclusively for the children of the wealthy.

Elementary education in the period of the New Nation (1700s) was characterized by the union of the dame schools and writing schools of earlier times. The focus was on citizenship, fundamental literacy, and the development of moral character. Recitation was an important strategy for teaching this content.

Education in the nineteenth century (1800s) was greatly influenced by the development of the common school, which began to make education available to all children and later became the graded school. Elementary education in the twentieth century has been influenced by events that have taken place outside the school. Psychology and philosophy, the Progressive Education movement, the Soviet launching of *Sputnik* in 1957, and the desegregation order in 1954 have influenced the elementary school curriculum and the teaching–learning process. The development of a pluralistic society has also affected practices in the elementary school. During the past thirty years, many innovations have been attempted as a means of responding to recommendations by lawmakers and voters for elementary education to meet the changing expectations of society.

The chapter concluded with a look at various definitions of the term *curriculum*. A review of the definitions makes it clear that historical events shape our understanding of curriculum at any moment in time. Generally, curriculum can be viewed as subject matter or content, as the experiences the learners have, as the educational objectives and outcomes, and as planned activities for learning. The historical overview, coupled with the various definitions of curriculum, provides a starting point for viewing the elementary school and the curriculum development process.

FIGURE 1-6 The Curriculum Development Process

STEPS IN DEVELOPING THE CURRICULUM

Planning

- Establish goals and objectives.
- Consider characteristics of students.
- Consider teaching strategies.
- Consult resources (i.e., curriculum guide, books).
- Examine the content to be taught.

Implementing

- Determine instructional strategies (continuum).
- Beware of views of teaching.
- Practice effective teaching behaviors.

Assessing

- Utilize formative and summative evaluation procedures.
- Use test and nontest assessment strategies (i.e., portfolio, projects).
- Correlate assessment data with goals, objectives, and methods to modify curriculum and instruction.

Selecting/ Organizing

Subject Areas

- Language arts
- Mathematics
- Social studies
- Science
- Physical education
- Fine arts

The Curriculum Development Process — Setting the Stage
Role of Philosophy, Curricular Designs, Scope, & Sequence

Historical Perspectives

The Elementary School Today

Social Contexts that Shape Elementary Education

Views of Children: Growth and Learning

AREAS OF STUDY

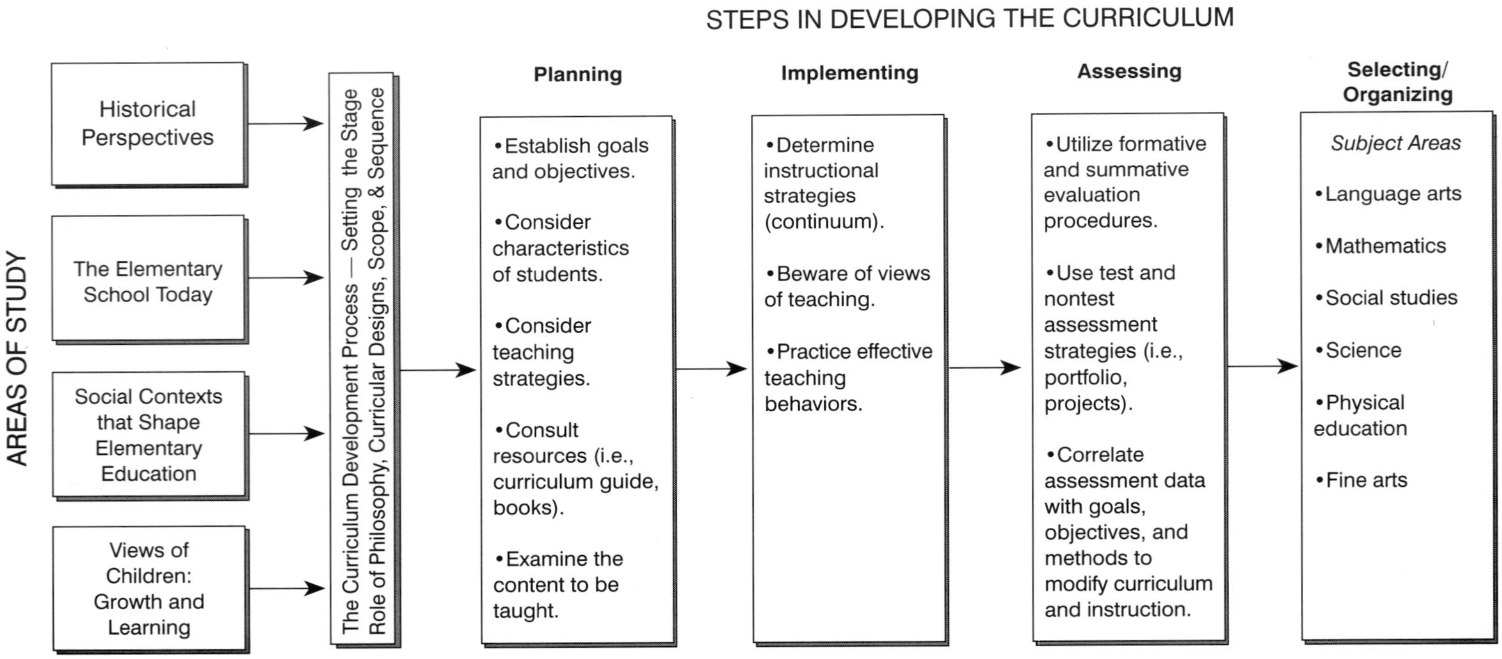

>>
<<<<<<<<<<<<<<<<<<<<<<<<<<<<<<<<<<<<<<<<<<<<<<<<<<<<<<<<<<<<<<<<<<<<<<<<<<<<<<<<<<<<

■ YOUR TURN

1. To prepare for this task, take a moment, close your eyes, and think about an elementary school. Reflect on the time you spent in an elementary school. What do you remember most? What do you wish you could forget? Do you feel that your education in the elementary school was comprehensive and prepared you for continuous learning? Why? Why not? What did or did not make it so?

2. You are going to step back in time to the early 1900s, to serve as a member of a community task force to develop a curriculum for teaching reading. You have been selected as the representative from your school to present its view to the task force. To get started, examine a text written during this time period. What was the composition of the student population? What was the student expected to learn? Does it match the mission and goal statements of the time period? What is the social context? What demands were made on the elementary school and teacher?

3. Review the section on Pluralism in Education. Were you aware of the development of a diverse population in the United States during the 1800s? Can you make parallels with what is happening today in society? If yes, list these parallels. Consult a local school district to find out the demographic breakdown of its student population. Does it have a diverse population? What are some of the challenges teachers face? Interview a teacher to find out.

4. During the twenty-year span from 1950 to 1970, what issues shaped elementary education? How are these issues different in the 1990s? What forces can you project that will impact the elementary curriculum in the year 2010?

5. You are a teacher visiting an elementary campus and have been asked to provide an overview of the elementary education program in your district. Your audience is aware that the elementary schools in the state are not as successful as they could be in enhancing student achievement. The questions you have been asked to address and respond to include the following:

   a. Does the curriculum provide a well-balanced program for all students?

   b. What factors have impacted student success?

   c. By being open to all, aren't your expectations of students somewhat lowered?

6. Obtain an elementary mathematics, science, or social studies textbook and a matching middle-school textbook. Examine the content of each closely. How are they similar? How are they different? What conclusions could you make about learning expectations at the elementary level and at the middle-school level?

■ REFERENCES

Appleton, N. (1983). *Cultural pluralism in education: Theoretical foundations.* New York: Longman.

Bobbitt, F. (1924). *How to make a curriculum.* Boston: Houghton Mifflin.

Bode, B. H. (1938). *Progressive education in the crossroads.* New York: Newson.

Bruner, J. (1966). *Toward a theory of instruction.* Cambridge, MA: Harvard University Press.

Butts, R. F. (1947). *A cultural history of education.* New York: McGraw-Hill.

Campbell, D. E. (1996). *Choosing democracy: A practical guide to multicultural education.* Upper Saddle River, NJ: Merrill/Prentice Hall.

Chavkin, N. F. (1993). *Families and schools in a pluralistic society*. Albany, NY: SUNY Press.

Coleman, J. S., Campbell, E. Q., Hobson, C. J., McPartland, J., Mood, A. M., Weinfield, F. D., & York, R L. (1966). *Equality of educational opportunity*. Washington, DC: Department of Health, Education and Welfare, U.S. Government Printing Office.

Conrad, M. (1996, Spring). The fourth "R"—Schoolhouse "R"cheology. *Mirage, 13*(3), 9–11.

Cuban, L. (1983). How did teachers teach, 1890–1980? *Theory into Practice, 22*, 159–165.

Dewey, J. (1916). *Democracy and education*. Upper Saddle River, NJ: Merrill/Prentice Hall.

Dewey, J. (1938). *Experience and education*. Upper Saddle River, NJ: Merrill/Prentice Hall.

Edwards, F. W., & Richey, H. (1947). *The school in the American social order*. Boston: Houghton Mifflin.

English, F. W. (1992). *Deciding what to teach and test: Developing, aligning and auditing the curriculum*. Newbury Park, CA: Corwin Press.

Fullan, M. G., & Miles, M. B. (1992, June). Getting reform right: What works and what doesn't. *Phi Delta Kappan, 73*(10), 744–752.

Giles, D. E., Jr. (1987). Dewey's theory of experience: Implications for service-learning. *Journal of Cooperative Education, 27*(2), 87–92.

Glatthorn, A. A. (1987). *Curriculum leadership*. Glenview, IL: Scott, Foresman, and Co.

Greene, M. (1989). The teacher in John Dewey's works. In P. W. Jackson and S. Haroutunian-Gordon (Eds.), *From Socrates to software: The teacher as text and the text as teacher. Eighty-Ninth Yearbook of the National Society for the Study of Education. Part I* (pp. 24–35). Chicago: University of Chicago Press.

Hall, G. S. (1907). *The content of children's minds*. Boston: Ginn.

Herbart, J. F. (1894). *Textbook of psychology*. New York: Appleton.

Ikenberry, O. S. (1974). *American education foundations: An introduction*. Upper Saddle River, NJ: Merrill/Prentice Hall.

Jackson, P. W. (1968). *Life in classrooms*. New York: Holt, Rinehart and Winston.

Kolodziey, H. M. (1986). *Ralph W. Tyler: A bibliography 1929–1986*. Washington, DC: National Foundation for the Improvement of Education.

Koontz, E. (1972). *The best kept secret of the past 5,000 years: Women are ready for leadership in education*. Bloomington, IN: Phi Delta Kappa Educational Foundation.

Marable, M. (1988). *Black American politics* (Rev. ed.). New York: Verso.

Montessori, M. (1967). *The child*. Wheaton, IL: The Theosophical Publishing House.

Omi, M., & Winant, H. (1994). *Racial formation in the United States: From the 1960s to the 1990s*. New York & London: Routledge & Kegan Paul.

Ornstein, A. C., & Hunkins, F. P. (1988). *Curriculum: Foundations, principles, and issues*. Upper Saddle River, NJ: Merrill/Prentice Hall.

Pinkney, A. (1969). *Black Americans*. Upper Saddle River, NJ: Merrill/Prentice Hall.

Popham, W. J., & Baker, E. (1970). *Systematic instruction*. Upper Saddle River, NJ: Merrill/Prentice Hall.

Reisner, E. H. (1935). *The evolution of the common school*. Upper Saddle River, NJ: Merrill/Prentice Hall.

Rugg, H. (1924). Dewey and his contemporaries. In A. Stafford Clayton (Ed.), *John Dewey in perspective: Three papers in honor of John Dewey* (pp. 1–14). Bloomington, IN: Indiana University, Division of Research and Field Services.

Saylor, J. G., Alexander, W. M., & Lewis, J. A. (1981). *Curriculum planning for better teaching and learning* (4th ed.). New York: Holt, Rinehart and Winston.

Schubert, W. H. (1993). Curriculum reform. In *Challenges and achievements of American education: The 1993 ASCD yearbook*. Washington, DC: Association for Supervision and Curriculum Development.

Seefeldt, C., & Barbour, N. (1994). *Early childhood education: An introduction* (3rd ed.). Upper Saddle River, NJ: Merrill/Prentice Hall.

Shepherd, G. D., & Ragan, W. B. (1992). *Modern elementary curriculum* (7th ed.). Fort Worth, TX: Harcourt Brace Jovanovich College Publishers.

Small, W. H. (1914). *Early New England schools.* Boston: Ginn and Company.

Sowards, G. W., & Scobey, M. (1968). *The changing curriculum and the elementary teacher* (2nd ed.). Belmont, CA: Wadsworth Publishing Company.

Spring, J. (1986). *The American school.* New York: Longman.

Taba, H. (1962). *Curriculum development: Theory and practice.* New York: Harcourt Brace Jovanovich.

Taba, H. (1973.) *Curriculum development: Theory and practice.* New York: Harcourt, Brace, & World.

Tanner, D., & Tanner, L. (1980). *Curriculum development: Theory into practice* (2nd ed). Upper Saddle River, NJ: Merrill/Prentice Hall.

Tanner, D., & Tanner, L. (1995). *Curriculum development: Theory into practice* (3rd ed). Upper Saddle River, NJ: Merrill/Prentice Hall.

Tewksbury, J. L. (1967). *Nongrading in the elementary school.* Upper Saddle River, NJ: Merrill/Prentice Hall.

Tyler, R. (1949). *Basic principles of curriculum and instruction.* Chicago: University of Chicago Press.

Tyler, R. W. (1957, April). The curriculum then and now. *Elementary School Journal, 57,* 364–374.

Van Til, W. (1974). *Education: A beginning* (2nd ed.). Boston: Houghton Mifflin.

Walberg, H. J. (1984). Improving the productivity of America's schools. *Educational Leadership, 41*(8), 19–27.

Washington, B. T. (1901). *Up from slavery (in African-American literature).* Austin, TX: Holt, Reinhart & Winston.

Wiles, J., & Bondi, J. (1984). *Curriculum development: A guide to practice* (2nd ed). Upper Saddle River, NJ: Merrill/Prentice Hall.

Wiles, J., & Bondi, J. (1993). *Curriculum development: A guide to practice* (4th ed). Upper Saddle River, NJ: Merrill/Prentice Hall.

Wood, J. R. (1987). *The train to Estelline.* New York: Bantam Doubleday Dell Publishing Group, Inc.

Zais, R. S. (1976). *Curriculum principles and foundations.* New York: Thomas Y. Crowell.

chapter 2

The Elementary School Today

AFTER READING THIS CHAPTER, YOU WILL BE ABLE TO DO THE FOLLOWING:

■ Describe the changes in the elementary school in the later part of the twentieth century.

■ Summarize the major points of a variety of reports that offer recommendations for reforming elementary education.

■ Identify the national goals in the America 2000 program as well as the eight Goals 2000: Educate America.

■ Cite examples of room arrangements, school schedule, and the grade organization of the elementary school.

■ Compare and contrast the graded and nongraded arrangements in elementary schools.

■ Explain the difference between the horizontal and vertical school organizational plans.

■ List and provide examples of four challenges that elementary teachers face in the 1990s.

The first chapter chronicled the history and evolution of the instructional program in elementary education. The roots of the modern elementary curriculum began with the contributions of people such as Pestolozzi, Froebel, Montessori, and Dewey, and continue with others who have more recently contributed to our understanding of elementary education. Each historical period has produced a unique perspective for viewing the learners, the curriculum, and the teaching-learning process. Education at the elementary level has undergone a series of changes prompted by the social, political, and economic realities of the time. To illustrate some recent changes in societal views, *CBS News* compared key educational problems reported by people in the 1940s with those reported in 1987 (Seymour & Seymour, 1993). These are as follows:

Then	Now
1. Talking out of turn	1. Drug abuse
2. Chewing gum	2. Alcohol abuse
3. Making noise	3. Pregnancy
4. Running in halls	4. Suicide
5. Cutting in line	5. Rape
6. Robbery	6. Robbery
7. Littering	7. Assault

Just as the issues have changed in the intervening years, so too has the nature of the student population, the way in which subjects are taught, and even the building itself. The changing nature of the learner is described in Chapter 4, and the presentation of subject matter that ranges from the use of interactive video technology to cooperative learning is discussed in greater detail in chapters 7 and 9 and the chapters on elementary subjects (chapters 10-14).

The elementary school has gone through a variety of structured designs from round, open "pods" to multigraded rooms to specialized learning stations. Along with those changes, the curriculum has been revised and modified; more and different subjects are offered and, as our understanding of the world has changed, so has the content to be learned.

The paradox of the elementary school is that in spite of all these changes, elementary education of today is in many ways like the elementary education of earlier times. The school remains a conservative institution of society; therefore, few radical changes in content and delivery have replaced earlier versions. In many ways, elementary students still focus on the "basics" of reading, writing, and mathematics. When changes are implemented, they often are "window dressing" with little permanent impact on the actual teaching-learning process.

Goodlad (1984), in his longitudinal study of schooling, notes the sameness of instruction that exists among schools, regardless of size and location. For example, the different languages children speak have been a continuing issue in the elementary school. Whether referring to the 1900s when there was a high influx of immigrants from eastern and southern Europe to the United States or to the 1990s with new immigrant groups, the concern over non-English-speaking students is not new. The issue of teaching students who are not fluent in English is the same; what is different is the number of languages spoken in any given school. In an elementary school in Arlington, Virginia, for example, more than 15 languages are spoken, including Arabic, Amharic, Japanese, Ga, Thai, Twi, Vietnamese, and many others (Seymour & Seymour, 1993).

In the 1870s, teachers were expected to engage in noninstructional tasks such as filling the lamps, cleaning the chimneys, trimming the wicks, bringing in water, and scuttling coal. Today, noninstructional tasks are still part of teachers' duties and responsibilities and include completing paperwork mandated by the district, state, and/or federal government, ensuring the learning environment is rich with print materials and resources, spending part of their lunch monitoring students in the cafeteria, and/or supervising bus activities. The nature of the tasks may have changed over the past one hundred years,

but teachers are still required to engage in noninstructional activities.

During the past decade, the elementary school has been a focus of review. Prompted by the numerous reports chronicling the ineffectiveness of public education—*A Nation at Risk* (National Commission on Excellence in Education, 1983), *Everybody Counts* (National Research Council, 1989), *Holmes Report* (Holmes Group, 1986), *First Lessons* (Bennett, 1986)—numerous public task forces and virtually all professional educational organizations have examined the entire elementary school program. Reports of declining academic ability as measured on standardized tests have caused state legislatures and voters to begin a process of reform that has taken more than a decade to complete. In the search for ways to improve the elementary school, much rhetoric has focused on the need for student mastery of basic skills of reading, writing, and mathematics, or the "essentials." Regardless of the time frame, these "essentials" seem to form the common core of the elementary school curriculum.

This chapter describes the current status of elementary education by describing the contemporary school of the 1980s and 1990s, after a decade of reform reports and studies of the educational process. It also provides a profile of an elementary school today, including an overview of the general characteristics, the mission and goals, and the organizational patterns. The chapter concludes with a look at some of the issues and challenges that educators at the elementary level face and will face in the years ahead. The purpose of this chapter is to present the culture and ecology of the elementary school as a safe and nurturing environment for all children and as a robust institution that has many different facets.

ELEMENTARY EDUCATION AND THE DECADE OF REFORM (1980s)

In the early 1980s, the perceived picture of student achievement as presented in the media was rather dismal. The year 1983 is considered a benchmark for the reform reports that followed the release of *A Nation at Risk* (National Commission on Excellence in Education, 1983). This publication signaled a new round of challenges and changes for American public education as it analyzed the "quality of education in America" (p. iii) and established the tone of what was to come by declaring that, "Our nation is at risk [because] . . . the average graduate of our schools . . . today is not as well educated as the average graduate of 25 or 35 years ago" (pp. 5, 11). The report also documented the following findings:

■ When comparing student achievement internationally, on 19 academic tests, students from the United States scored last on seven tests and never first or second in contrast with students from other industrialized nations.

■ Achievement in science declined steadily as measured by national assessments in 1969, 1973, and 1977.

■ Institutions of higher learning witnessed a 72-percent increase in remedial mathematics courses over a five-year period (1975–80).

■ It was estimated that 23 million adults in the United States were functionally illiterate when asked to demonstrate everyday tasks of reading, writing, and computation.

In light of these findings, it is no wonder that there was cynicism regarding the effectiveness of the educational system in America. Educators, feeling pressure from politicians and members of the community, became frantic to improve the quality of instruction in the nation's schools. Figure 2-1 presents examples of recommendations from several of the reports published in the early 1980s. These recommendations served as pathways for solving many educational problems, ranging from more community involvement at the local level to specific actions at the state and national levels for improving student learning.

After the release of *A Nation at Risk* and later reports, several concerns emerged, along with sets of prescriptions. As these reports were published and disseminated, various states attempted to respond to the concerns raised by formulating new educational policies, which included the following:

■ reducing the student-teacher ratio (Ohio, Arkansas)

■ expanding the professional development opportunities for faculty and staff (Massachusetts, Tennessee)

■ raising graduation requirements (Florida, Ohio)

■ above all, increasing local and state expenditures to compensate for the decrease in the contributions of the federal government (Ohio, Tennessee, Arkansas)

■ comprehensive testing (Arkansas)

In California, the Mathematics, Engineering, and Science Achievement (MESA) program was established to increase the number of minorities in the areas of mathematics and science.

Along with this preoccupation with educational excellence there has been a proliferation of test development and an increase in the testing of elementary students. The results from the tests have been mixed, and whether there have been significant gains in achievement for all students—and especially for students who are challenged physically, mentally, and linguistically—is not clear. There has been a tendency to overgeneralize what students are learning when using only test measures to assess achievement.

Using paper-and-pencil assessment often creates a curriculum misalignment because the goals stated in the lesson do not match how the curriculum is implemented nor the measures used to assess the results of these goals. Paper-and-pencil assessment is more compatible with directive teaching strategies. When teachers utilize manipulatives as instructional aids, then assessment should occur through the use of hands-on materials to solve problems. That kind of assessment aligns the goals of the curriculum with instruction and measurement of student

FIGURE 2-1 Recommendations of Selected Reports on Education

Report	Recommendations
Time for Reform (Council for Basic Education, 1982)	▪ educational goals and standards should be established by parents and community members ▪ federal government to provide liberal education with an emphasis on science ▪ increasing learning time in schools ▪ strengthening overall academic standards
Making the Grade (Twentieth Century, 1983)	▪ federal government to provide increased special programs for minorities, immigrants, and students with disabilities ▪ educational program to emphasize science, to promote scientific literacy among citizens ▪ focus on improving language, science, and math skills ▪ voucher system for disadvantaged students
Educating Americans for the 21st Century (National Science Foundation, 1983)	▪ national system for measuring student achievement ▪ federal government to have a role in developing national goals ▪ increasing the school day and/or school year (specifically including one hour per day for mathematics and thirty minutes per day for science, for students in grades K-6)
Action for Excellence (Education Commission of the United States, 1983)	▪ developing partnerships between business and education with the federal government to provide funds to support education ▪ emphasis on increased academic standards—periodic testing, higher expectations in an environment that is organized and disciplined ▪ minimum competencies in the basics—reading, writing, and speaking—as well as in economics and reasoning skills
A Nation at Risk (National Commission on Excellence in Education, 1983)	▪ federal and state government to cooperatively finance education of students with special needs—handicapped, disadvantaged, minority, bilingual, gifted ▪ national testing ▪ expanded school time: seven-hour school day; two hundred days per year; more homework ▪ grouping students by performance (rather than age) ▪ performance: periodic testing, increased grading standards, increased graduation requirements (English, mathematics, science, social studies, computer science—the new basics) ▪ courses in vocational education

Source: Information from "The National Reports on Education: Implications for Directions and Aims" by A. Ornstein (1985), *Kappa Delta Pi Record*, 21(2), 58-64.

learning. With regard to higher cognitive skills (such as critical thinking and problem solving), there is often a mismatch between the goals and mission of education and the type of measurement used to determine whether what was taught has been learned. For example, one of the goals for teaching mathematics is to use a concrete-to-abstract approach (manipulatives followed by written exercises); assessment involves using everyday situations.

Many of the reports have focused on school expenditures (e.g., cost per student, teacher salaries, and role of governmental agencies in funding programs). The issue of school funding and equity has also surfaced, with courts ruling that states must develop a funded educational system that is equitable and accessible. Several court cases (including *Brown v. Board of Education* in 1954), Title VI of the Civil Rights Act of 1964, Title IX of the Education Amendments of 1972, and other laws have addressed the issues of equal access and funding equity.

The status of the teaching profession was scrutinized in the reports as well. As a result, restructuring education and teacher empowerment became the focus for school faculties. Establishing partnerships with local school districts, businesses, and universities has led to professional development schools (PDS). (PDSs are discussed later in this chapter.) These restructuring efforts have introduced an entirely new vocabulary and new ways of operating schools. Figure 2-2 presents a list of some of these new buzzwords in education.

Review the words and phrases listed in Figure 2-2, and see how many you have heard recently. Not only new terms and phrases have been introduced into the educational language, but also, with them, a rethinking of the elementary school—its mission and curriculum; the role of teachers, administrators, parents, business leaders, and members of the community; the educational results of, decision making for, and management of the school; proficiency levels of students; and student grouping patterns.

FIGURE 2-2   The New Language of Educators: Do These Words and Phrases Sound Familiar?

Accelerated schools
Action research/teacher as researcher
Authentic assessment
Collaborative/collaboration
Cooperative learning
Thematic integrated curriculum
Mentors/coaches
National certification
Paradigm
Performance assessment
Restructuring
Site-based management
Student portfolios
Systematic approach
Teacher empowerment
Thematic teaching
TQM (Total Quality Management)
Ungraded schools

Note: For more information, see "Are We Still a Nation at Risk?" *NEA Today*, April 1993, p. 5.

In addition to the changes in schools created by all of these efforts, the composition of the student population today differs substantially from that of twenty years ago, and these demographic changes have received national attention. Today, there are more youngsters living in one-parent homes (in 1970, it was 12 percent; in 1989, it was 25 percent), more who are abused (a 259 percent increase from 1976 to 1989), and more who live in poverty (13 million, with an increase of 2 million over the past decade) (Berliner, 1993a). The Norman Rockwell family of an earlier time, in which there is a father working and a mother taking care of the two small children (a boy and a girl) of school age "constitutes only 6% of U.S. households" (Hodgkinson, 1991, p. 9).

This nostalgic view of the family unit is being replaced by single parents whose income averaged about $11,000 at the end of the 1980s; in fact, according to Hodgkinson (1991), "at least two million school-age children have no adult supervision at all after school. Two million more are being reared by neither parent" (p. 9). A common phrase used today to describe these students in the elementary school is "latchkey kids"—those who are left alone unsupervised while their parent(s) or guardian(s) is working. Self-care often has a negative connotation, but this is the reality for many of today's elementary-school-age children. The situation seems even worse when estimates suggest that 50,000 to 200,000 children are without homes to go to on any given day; this fact is borne out when reviewing the statistics from 1988, which show that 40 percent of those who were in shelters were families with elementary-school-age children (Hodgkinson, 1991). (The issue of latchkey children is presented in greater detail in Chapter 3.)

About one third of our children are at risk and are headed for failure because circumstances are stacked against them: they are poor, neglected, sick, have handicapping conditions, and lack the nurturing and protection they need. According to Hodgkinson (1991), educators can't fix the "leaky roof" over *all* children, but they can become part of the network of health and social service agencies to help keep the roof from completely coming down.

When a profile is generated to describe the students in today's elementary school, the response is certainly not a homogeneous one. The current student population comes in many different sizes, with varying developmental, cultural, and social needs and characteristics. (The nature of the elementary student is described in greater detail in Chapter 4.)

GOALS AND NEW INITIATIVES FOR THE ELEMENTARY SCHOOL TODAY

In its effort to address the needs of today's elementary students, America 2000 is a program that has generated national attention. It was launched in September 1989 by President Bush, with the support of the 50 state governors, at a national conference to improve public school education. Six national goals were formulated and became the national agenda for education to help make America all that it can and should be. These national goals are as follows:

1. All children in America will start school ready to learn.

2. The high school graduation rate will increase to at least 90 percent.

3. American students will leave grades four, eight, and twelve having demonstrated competency in challenging subject matter including English, mathematics, science, history, and geography; and every school in America will ensure that all students learn to use their minds well, so they may be prepared for responsible citizenship, further learning, and productive employment in our modern economy.

4. U.S. students will be first in the world in science and mathematics achievement.

5. Every adult American will be literate and will possess the knowledge and skills necessary to compete in a global economy and exercise the rights and responsibilities of citizenship.

6. Every school in America will be free of drugs and violence and will offer a disciplined environment conducive to learning. (U.S. Department of Education, 1991)

In the spring of 1994, Congress passed President Clinton's plan to reform education; the bill was called Goals 2000: Educate America Act. The America 2000 goals became the backbone of Goals 2000: Educate America Act (Public Law 103–227). This act established for the first time a national mission statement for public schools in America (Weiss, 1994). The act increased the goals to eight (goals four and eight were added by Congress). The Goals 2000: Educate America Act includes the following:

1. All children in America will start school ready to learn.

2. The high school graduation rate will increase to at least 90 percent.

3. All students will leave grades 4, 8, and 12 having demonstrated competency over all challenging subject matter . . . , and [all students will be] prepared for responsible citizenship, further learning, and productive employment.

4. The nation's teaching force will have access to programs for the continued improvement of professional skills.

5. United States students will be the first in the world in mathematics and science achievement.

6. Every adult American will be literate.

7. Every school in America will be free of drugs and violence and will offer a disciplined environment conducive to learning.

8. Every school and home will engage in partnerships that will increase parental involvement and participation in promoting the social, emotional, and academic growth of children.

The purpose of Goals 2000 is to set national standards for student achievement in the core curriculum (math, science, history, geography, and language arts). Much of the work has to be done at the state and local levels. With the enactment of this legislation came $105 million to create model programs. By setting standards, the federal government establishes its role in helping states, local agencies, and individual schools define quality education, but participation remains entirely voluntary (Earley, 1994).

In the intervening years, between the beginning of the reform reports and the establishment of national educational goals, schools continued to work to improve student achievement. The insistence on "back to the basics" so that Johnny and Sarah could read was accomplished to a limited degree. With this encouragement came the trend in requiring more writing, math, and science instruction in the elementary school. But Anrig and Lapointe (1989) asked the pertinent question, "What don't students know?" They

sought to answer the question and found the following answers:

■ In reading, 94 percent of the students were reading at "grade level" while 210,000 nine-year-olds could not read nor understand the textbooks they were using. By the time they reached the seventh and eighth grades, 40 percent of them continued to have difficulty understanding and comprehending. Little improvement was noted, especially among minority students in higher-order skills. Moreover, these students had "lost" the interest in reading.

■ Achievement in mathematics was better than it had been five years before but not as good as it had been fifteen years before. By age nine, 74 percent of the students in the third and fourth grades performed at grade level, which means they could add and subtract problems with two-digit numbers. However, of the high school students who graduated, almost half of them had not mastered eighth-grade math.

■ In science, students were doing better but not as well as their counterparts twenty years ago. For example, half of the seventh and eighth graders did not understand the fundamentals of life and physical sciences.

■ In writing, student performance overall had improved, with more students writing grammatically correct prose and more minority students achieving. Only 28 percent of seventeen-year-olds were able to write an essay using imagination, and only 25 percent could write an analytic paper.

In 1993, ten years after the publication of *A Nation at Risk*, there are those who said that our nation was still at risk educationally.

The state of Kentucky took these earlier concerns seriously and proposed what some have called the most ambitious state educational reform program, with the passage of the Kentucky Education Reform Act (KERA) of 1990 on

April 11. KERA targets primary-grade children and a curriculum that is age- and individually-developmentally appropriate. This legislation required each elementary school in the state to implement an ungraded primary (K-3) program during or before the 1992-1993 school year. This ungraded program was to include the following:

■ Educational practices that are developmentally appropriate, to include an integrated curriculum, active student and teacher interaction, the use of manipulatives, varied instructional procedures, and flexibility in student groupings

■ Classrooms composed of multi-age/multi-ability family groupings, ranges in ages, and heterogeneous groups

■ Continuous progress in school that is supported by the use of observations, anecdotal records, portfolios, and videos

■ Authentic assessment strategies used in all curriculum areas

■ Qualitative reporting that describes how students are progressing within the system

■ Professional teamwork and planning that involves teachers working together to develop curriculum plans

■ Increased parental involvement with continuous communication with the school (Cantrell, 1994)

The KERA ungraded primary program also funded risk programs for three- and four-year-olds. To ensure help for the entire family, resource centers were established as part of the KERA program as well, to provide social welfare benefits. KERA is an innovative program that can serve as a model for schools across the nation for initiating social change in schools by linking the community with the schools (Family Resource and Youth Service Centers and the Housing and Neighborhood Development Strategies—HANDS) and by developing a curriculum that meets the needs of all children—the gifted, the talented, the learning challenged, and those in the middle (Murray, 1993).

The results of the KERA program to date suggest that while test scores are not soaring, children are improving when compared to themselves (Cantrell, 1994). The KERA program has been instrumental in motivating children, parents, and teachers to move away from a highly structured school approach to one that is flexible and starts where the students are. Such an approach is based on learner goals and a belief that social problems can be solved educationally. Those less convinced about the success of the KERA programs find it difficult to accept goals for schooling that cannot be measured (e.g., becoming a responsible member of a family and work community), and worry that there is too little testing. Some critics think the KERA program is costing too much money for the results that are being produced. Given time to follow those students in the program, using a longitudinal study will help to document the success for individuals as well as the entire KERA program.

PROFILE OF AN ELEMENTARY SCHOOL

After all the attention focused on education during the 1980s, what does a day in an elementary school look like in the 1990s? In many ways, the daily schedules of elementary schools remain very much the same. A day in an elementary school—whether in Palm Springs or Harlem—has a schedule similar to other schools. The schools begin at approximately the same time (taking into account the different time zones), have similar ways of getting the day started (announcements, birthday notations, awards/recognitions, Pledge of Allegiance), start lunch at midmorning (often beginning with primary grades), and make every effort to have language arts and mathematics instruction sometime during the morning.

Goodlad (1984) documented this sameness and found that schools were much more alike than different:

> It has been said that a school is a school is a school and if you've seen one, you've seen them all. To the extent that the schools we studied are representative of many more schools, there is truth in that observation. . . . We . . . have seen the extraordinary sameness of instructional practices in the more than 1,000 classrooms observed. (p. 246)

Goodlad continues by saying that schools are different in more elusive ways, such as the ways students and teachers relate to each other, the schools' academic orientation, the degree of autonomy of students and faculty, and the kind of peer pressure exerted in the student interactions. Schools may differ, but schooling across the United States is much the same. "Schools differ in the way they conduct their business and the way the people in them relate to one another in conducting that business. But the business of schooling is everywhere very much the same" (Goodlad, 1984, p. 264).

To illustrate the sameness of the classrooms, Kidder (1989) describes the beginning of school for Chris Zajac. If Goodlad's data are correct, then this scene gets acted out across the United States each fall. Kidder describes that process this way:

> When Chris had first walked into her room in late August, it felt like an attic. The chalkboards and bulletin boards were covered up with newspaper, and the bright colors of the plastic chairs seemed calculated to force cheerfulness upon her. . . . She looked around her empty classroom. It was fairly small as classrooms go, about twenty-five by thirty-six feet. . . . She put up her bulletin board displays, scouted up pencils and many kinds of paper—crayons hadn't yet arrived; [she] made a red paper apple for the door, and moved the desks around into the layout she had settled on in her first years of teaching. . . . Her desk was already where she wanted it, in a corner by the window. . . . Over there in the corner, her desk would not get in her way. And she could retire to

> it between lessons, a little distance from the children, and still see down the hallway between her door and the boys' room—a strategic piece of real estate—and also keep an eye on all the children at their desks. . . . [W]hen the room was arranged to her liking, she went home to the last days of summer. (pp. 12-13)

This scenario represents the beginning of elementary schools each fall and illustrates what one would find in visiting classrooms before the first day of class anywhere in the United States.

With these similarities in mind, it might be tempting to think that teaching in the elementary school is simple, but it is the subtle differences in the way teachers plan and implement the curriculum and the way they relate to each other and to their students that make teaching in the elementary school complex. The chapters that follow are designed to provide insights into understanding many of these subtleties in planning and delivering the curriculum. In the sections that follow, some of the subtleties of elementary schools will be discussed.

Classroom Arrangement

Various room arrangements are developed by teachers not only to match their personal style and preference, but also to maximize control and management and minimize distractions and misbehavior. Figure 2-3 provides one example of an elementary classroom arrangement.

On the first day, the teacher gets acquainted with his or her new students and establishes rules for conduct and work, and students begin the task of learning the daily routine. Elementary teachers may read the story "My First Day of School" by P. K. Hallinan. During the first weeks of school, teachers learn about their students' "unique traits that combine to make [a] class a lively, diverse group" (*Instructor*, 1993, p. 53).

With some variations, elementary students start school at about 8:00 A.M. and are dismissed at approximately 3:30 P.M. In the intervening hours, the schedule typically is packed full of

FIGURE 2-3   An Example of an Elementary Classroom

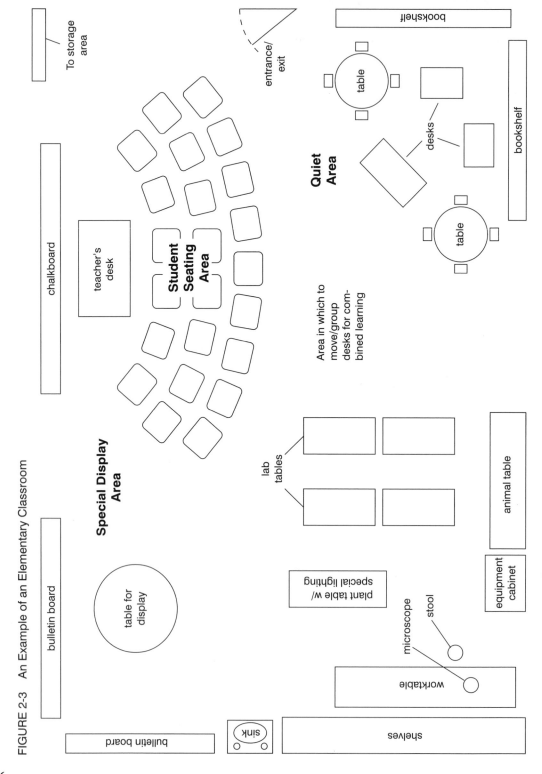

learning activities (curriculum). An example of a first-grade elementary schedule looks something like this:

8:05–8:30	Arrival/Pledge of Allegiance
8:30–10:20	Language arts
10:20–11:10	PE/Music/Computers
11:10–11:30	Language arts
11:30–12:00	Lunch
12:00–12:30	Language arts
12:30–1:30	Mathematics
1:30–2:00	Recess
2:00–3:20	Science/Health/Social studies
3:20–3:30	Dismissal

A schedule for grades 3 and 4 has generally the following components:

8:00	Arrival
8:05	Tardy bell, classes begin
8:10	Pledge of Allegiance, announcements for the day
8:15	Mathematics
9:10	Reading
10:05	Recess
10:25	Language arts
11:20	Art/Music
12:05	Lunch
12:40	Social studies
1:35	Physical education
2:30	Science
3:25	Cleanup
3:30	Dismissal

Within the framework of these schedules, students experience the elementary curriculum for approximately 180 teaching days a year.

Elementary School Organizational Patterns

The historical roots for the organization of elementary education can be traced from colonial times, when children attended dame schools and, later, writing schools, before going to grammar schools and then to graded schools, the first of which was established in Boston in 1848.

The Graded School.   The elementary school curriculum has typically been organized by the age of the children served. The assigning of students to different "positions" or levels is called the *graded arrangement.*

The movement of students from grade to grade according to age is referred to as the *vertical organizational plan.* The vertical plan provides a beginning and ending as students move to higher curricular areas. Within this view of the elementary school, students enter kindergarten at age five and leave the elementary school between ages eleven and twelve, when they have completed grade six. As Tewksbury (1967) notes,

> The . . . work of an elementary school is divided into six levels, more commonly referred to as grades. The work in each grade is clearly designated . . . [and] usually consists of specific skills, topics, and textbooks to be covered. All boys and girls in a given grade are expected to do only that work reserved for that grade. (p. 2)

An example of the age-grade organization is illustrated in the following.

Age	*Grade Level*
11	6
10	5
9	4
8	3
7	2
6	1
5	K

Most states determine the age for entry into elementary school, and it is common to expect a child who will be six on or before September 1 to enter first grade. States also established upper age limits for elementary students, recognizing the need for older students (12–14 years) to be in middle school or junior high school. With the advent of the middle-school movement, many school districts reorganized the elementary school to include grades five and sometimes six in the middle school. The middle-school movement recognizes the unique developmental characteristics of preadolescent students who range in age from eleven through fourteen. The middle school provides a transitional educational program between elementary school and high school. In many states, middle school teachers receive a separate certification or use the secondary certification process.

In grouping kindergarten with the six elementary grades, communities have established a variety of patterns, frequently determined by the facilities available. A common arrangement is to have a school that begins with kindergarten and ends with grade 6 (K–6). However, some communities have primary (K–3) and intermediate (4–6) campuses. Other communities may have a K–2 campus, a 3–4 campus, and a 5–6 campus. Even though kindergarten may be included in the organizational structure of the elementary school, kindergarten teachers normally have additional training in early childhood education and additional licensing requirements.

The basic features of the vertical organizational graded plan, according to Shepherd and Ragan (1992), includes assignment to grade based on chronological age, a specific body of knowledge and skills to be learned in each grade, and movement from one grade or level to the next (promotion) predicated on completion of all work at a satisfactory level. There are limitations of the graded arrangement, as cited by Smith (1987), which include "locking students into certain groups, regardless of ability levels and encouraging teachers to teach to the group with a rigid curriculum" (p. 105). Anderson (1993) goes on to say that the graded school has an overloaded, textbook-dominated curriculum and it is built on "primitive assumptions about human development and learning" (p. 10).

The Nongraded School.   The flip side of the graded arrangement is *nongraded*; the major aim of the nongraded organizational pattern is continuous progress. To overcome locking students into certain groups, this system allows students to progress through the curriculum at their own pace. Goodlad and Anderson in 1959 highlighted the ineffectiveness of tracking in their book *The Nongraded Elementary School.*

The graded system "ignores the social and emotional needs of students" (Calkins, 1992, p. 10). O. V. Wheeler, principal of Ridgeway Elementary School, says that "grade levels and kids don't always match up" (Willis, 1991, p. 1). In the nongraded system, "progress is reported in terms of tasks completed and the manner of learning, not by grades or rating systems" and "the continuous progress is reflected in students' growth of knowledge, skills, and understanding, not movement through a predetermined sequence of curriculum levels" (Pavan, 1992, p. 22). Pavan goes on to cite the results from several research studies on nongraded programs, which include the following:

■ When comparing the two arrangements—the graded and the nongraded—the results tend to favor nongradedness.

■ On measures of academic achievement, the nongraded groups performed better (58%) than graded groups.

■ The benefits of nongradedness increase the longer the students have nongraded experiences.

■ Certain at-risk students (African-American boys, those at a low socioeconomic level, and underachievers) do better when they have nongraded experiences.

Although there may be disagreement regarding the methods employed, Pavan (1992) believes that the nongraded arrangement definitely "produces positive results for children" (p. 25). Kentucky has acted on this belief and has implemented the nongraded/continuous progress arrangements statewide.

Self-contained Classrooms.   The *horizontal organizational pattern* places the students into groups for instructional purposes. *Self-contained classrooms* and *departmentalization* are the two basic approaches to horizontal organization. The self-contained classroom remains the most popular approach, particularly in grades 1–3; in such a classroom, students spend the day primarily with one teacher learning concepts in language arts, mathematics, social studies, and science. Many teachers prefer this approach because they are not tied to specific time units and can be flexible in spending more time on topics when necessary. Second, the classroom teacher can plan units and lessons that integrate the curriculum more effectively. Nevertheless, Smith (1987) cites several shortcomings of the self-contained approach:

■ Pupils and teachers are isolated from other students and teachers.

■ Students are primarily forced to interact with students in the same classroom.

■ Cliques are easily established.

■ Many teachers are not capable of teaching all subject areas.

■ Leaders remain leaders and followers remain followers. (p. 106)

Departmentalization.   By contrast with the self-contained classroom pattern, in a school with departmentalization, the teacher is considered a specialist in one or two curriculum areas. Some teachers favor the departmental approach because it reduces the need to plan lessons in all the major subjects of the curriculum. On the downside, teachers using this approach do not have an opportunity to get to know their students as well as teachers can in a self-contained classroom.

MEETING THE CHALLENGES

In many respects, the 1990s reflect what occurred in the 1980s to a great degree. This section identifies and examines briefly several key challenges that educators will face in the coming decade. These challenges are varied and need actions that

go beyond mere tinkering and rhetoric (Tye, 1992).

The particular challenges for elementary teachers discussed in this section include creating family, school, community, and university partnerships; teaching *all* students, with emphasis on inclusion; and reasserting the importance of universal public education. These and other challenges will form part of the agenda for elementary educators in the years ahead.

Partnerships

A primary challenge for educators is establishing *partnerships*. There must be a clear connection between the family, the school, and the community. Without this connection, schools cannot be effective because they are isolated from "the familial, cultural, and community context" (Stevens & Price, 1992, p. 23). As the twentieth century draws to a close, we must reframe relations between the home and the school and take seriously an old African saying: "The whole village educates the child" (Edwards & Young, 1992, p. 80). Research suggests that when parents are involved, they can play a significant role in increasing their child's success in school, in the areas of student behavior, grades, scores on tests, and attitudes (Henderson, 1988). Having parents making learning a part of a child's daily activities (i.e., having a science box at home with a funnel, measuring tape, film canister, magnet; collecting articles on favorite subjects; and writing down messages, for example) can translate into a successful school year. Many communities establish informal links with parents and local business leaders who volunteer and serve as tutors before and after school. Some volunteers even present lessons on specialized topics.

Universities should be a part of this partnership as well. Preparing teachers for the teaching profession requires a close collaborative relationship; such a relationship is critical if teacher education is going to be successful in preparing teachers well for the next twenty-five years. With a better-prepared teaching force, schools can become better places for America's youth to learn (Brennan & Simpson, 1993). The schools should serve as the laboratories where pre-service teachers work side-by-side with in-service teachers and university professors to learn the theoretical as well as the practical dimensions of the teaching and learning process (Reinhartz, 1996). In professional development schools (PDSs), university and school personnel share the responsibility for the preparation of teachers; these PDSs are examples of partnerships that are being forged across the United States. "The key to PDSs is collaboration; collaboration among all the participants—university faculty, classroom teachers, their students, district administrators, staff, and the teacher education students" (Reinhartz, 1996).

Figure 2-4 illustrates how public schools and colleges of education are collaborating in the preparation of teachers; with such structure, university-based coursework is no longer the norm. The new model continues to evolve as the participants collaborate in determining ways to main-tain the coherence and integrity of preparing teachers for the next decades.

As demonstrated in Figure 2-4, the new model makes possible learning experiences that are relevant to teachers in training, because these experiences take place in "real" elementary (or secondary) school classrooms. The term being used to characterize this new model is a *seamless web* of experiences, taking the best available from the university, schools, community, and business and weaving it into a quality teacher preparation program.

Inclusion

A second challenge for elementary teachers is *inclusion*—a philosophy that embodies the notion that there is an "abiding commitment to providing educational opportunity to *all* our citizens" (Tye, 1992, p. 10). The restructuring needed to accomplish this goal is contrary to the historical trend. For example, from the beginning, education in the United States was designed for boys

FIGURE 2-4   Collaboration Between Public Schools and Colleges of Teacher Education

Old Model	New Model
Instruction and practice based at university with limited interaction with public school students and teachers	Instruction and practice based at school sites with classrooms serving as laboratories with diverse and differentiated field experiences
University courses taught in isolation with content overlapping, little team planning/teaching	Courses as integrated blocks to reduce repetition; planned and taught by instructional teams
Lecturing and individual testing, primary mode of instruction and evaluation	Delivery of instruction varied with emphasis on cooperative/team/individual performance-based proficiency assessment
Course content and experiences not necessarily developmentally paced	Instructional and field experiences are geared to preservice teacher's level of readiness
Limited support system while in teacher education	Institutionalized network involving an instructional team of educators
Staff development for teachers: short-term and lacks continuity	Staff development determined by teachers: long-term and continuous; individualized

only; it gradually changed, and education was extended to girls (Tye, 1992). But gender inclusion is only the beginning.

In recent years, educators have faced the challenge of "making schools more inclusive" (Willis, 1994, p. 1). What does it mean to make a school more inclusive? Or, more importantly, what is inclusion and what are the implications for students and educators? How do educators go about creating classrooms in which "all children are accepted and included"? (Gross & Ortiz, 1994, p. 32). With the passage of the Education for All Handicapped Children Act, Public Law 94–142, nearly 20 years ago, "the rights of all . . . children to a free and appropriate public school education" were affirmed (Vann, 1994, p. 39). The amended Public Law 94–142 is known as the Individuals with Disabilities Education Act (IDEA). School districts have responded in a number of different ways, often along a continuum of services with the least restrictive environment being the regular classroom, moving to a resource room, and then to a self-contained special education classroom. The latter options, providing resource classrooms and/or special education classrooms, are the most common models educators have selected when considering ways to meet individual student needs.

In the first model, students with special needs are pulled out of their regular classes during the school day for several hours per week to work with specially trained teachers in resource classrooms. When students need more supervision, the second model, which places them in special education classrooms with special education teachers, is implemented (Vann, 1994). The third model is *inclusion.*

Inclusion differs from mainstreaming. *Mainstreaming* refers to the placement of special education students in regular education classes for specific areas of study, such as science, health, and social studies. These classes are heterogeneously grouped. Mainstreaming is closely linked to the traditional special education delivery system. Unlike mainstreaming, inclusion brings the services to students with a commitment to educate them in a school and classroom they would regularly attend (Rogers, 1993). The term *inclusion* is used to describe a movement of individuals who seek to "create schools and other social institutions that are based on acceptance, belonging, and community" (Salend, 1994, p. 49). Salend goes on to say that inclusionary schools acknowledge and affirm the rights of all students and educate them in regular classrooms that are age-appropriate to the maximum extent. The inclusion philosophy supports a system of education that does not segregate students who challenge the system (Falvey, Givner, & Kimm, 1995).

The following principles can help guide educators as they make a significant effort to provide instructional and technological supports to accommodate all students (Flynn & Kowalczyk-McPhee, 1989; Stainback, Stainback, & Bunch, 1989; Salend, 1994):

■ All students should be educated in the regular classroom regardless of race, linguistic ability, economic status, gender, age, ability, ethnicity, religion, or sexual orientation.

■ All students are capable of learning and becoming contributing members of society.

■ All students are entitled to quality services that allow them to be successful in school.

■ All students have access to services to meet their individual needs.

■ All students have opportunities to play and work together.

■ All students are taught to appreciate and value human diversity and similarities.

■ All professionals, parents, and community agencies work collaboratively to share skills, talents, and resources and are involved in the educational process.

Inclusive programs reject the teaching of students with disabilities in self-contained special education classrooms.

Such terms as *inclusion*, *full inclusion*, and *regular education initiatives* are used; they are not a part of the federal law, but Rogers (1993) emphasizes that all of these terms "have been used to express varying beliefs about what the law means [or] should mean" (p. 1). Even though these terms are not in the law, the regulations make it clear that schools must find an inclusive solution for each student. Currently, an inclusive solution means placing each student in the "regular" classroom with supplementary services and materials (Willis, 1994).

Many people ask, why must an inclusive solution be developed, and why must an inclusive philosophy be embraced? First, it is important to recognize that nearly one tenth of all the six- to twelve-year-olds in the U.S. receive special services and about half of that tenth have learning disabilities related to speech or language impairments (Willis, 1994). Willis goes on to say that the rest of this group are mentally retarded and/or have hearing, visual, orthopedic, and/or other health impairments. According to Rogers (1993), there are two schools of thought for supporting an inclusive solution philosophy:

■ Lack of inclusion segregates students and is a violation of the students' civil rights.

■ Special education programs have not been successful in terms of developing academic, social, and vocational skills.

Many inclusion advocates believe that the educational focus in special classrooms is myopic and concentrates too much on the child and not enough on changing the learning environment (Willis, 1994). Research findings seem to suggest that "students who are not pulled out do better than those who are segregated . . . and despite increases in spending, children . . . have not shown the growth that was predicted" (Van Dyke, Stallings, & Colley, 1995, p. 476). The Dowling Urban Environment Learning Center in Minneapolis is one of the success stories; it "changed from a special school for disabled students to a fully inclusive, racially mixed, general education magnet school for grades K–6" (Raison et al., 1995).

Having inclusive schools does not mean eliminating special education costs. It does mean reconceptualizing the way services are delivered to students. Effective inclusion is characterized by schools that implement such practices as "heterogeneous grouping, peer tutoring, multi-age classes, middle school structures, 'no-cut' athletic policies, cooperative learning, and development of school media centers which stimulate students' electronic access to extensive databases for their own research" (Rogers, 1993, p. 4). The benefits from these educational practices include holding students to higher expectations, exposing them to content that is more challenging, and modeling different appropriate social behaviors (Willis, 1994). When more special educational services are moved to the regular classroom, a range of options are provided to accommodate all students.

The debate about inclusion will continue, but attitudes are changing. What is less clear is the precise path to take to achieve full inclusion. Vann (1994) reminds us that "a meaningful dialogue between . . . [and among] educators [at all levels] could go a long way toward improving the chances for successful implementation in our classrooms—for the benefits of all children" (p. 40).

Universality of Public Education

Another challenge, according to Tye (1992), is the "reaffirmation of the importance and *universality of public education*" (p. 13). Tye emphasizes that it is crucial that all educational, business, community, and national leaders recognize that providing the best education for all the children of the United States—rich, poor, majority, minority, with and without learning limitations—is in the interest of our country. It is clear that "educators alone cannot 'fix' the problems of education because dealing with the root causes of poverty must involve health-care, housing, transportation, job-training, and social welfare bureaucracies" (Hodgkinson, 1991, p. 16). A commitment to the common good needs to be rekindled.

One current challenge to providing a quality education to all students is the use of *vouchers* or *schools of choice*. Results from the 27th Annual Phi Delta Kappa Gallup Poll (Elam, Rose, & Gallup, 1995) indicate that two thirds of the American population oppose "choice whereby students attend private schools at public expense" (p. 42) even though they support "giving parents choice of the public school their children attend, regardless of where they live" (p. 45).

The idea of vouchers first appeared in the literature about 1983, and polls have consistently shown that the trends in opinion oppose the use of vouchers for private or church-related schools. The topic of school choice resurfaced when President Bush in 1988 made it the centerpiece of his education reform initiative. "Thirteen states and many more school districts have adopted some kind of choice plan involving public schools . . . in the past five years" (Elam, Rose, & Gallup, 1992, p. 48). California, Pennsylvania, and Colorado have said no to voucher plans that would serve to reinforce choice. *School Choice* (Boyer, 1992), a recent study conducted by the Carnegie Foundation for the Advancement of Teaching, found that the claimed benefits of school choice have not matched the current evidence. Foundation President Ernest Boyer (1992) suggests that few parents of public school children are interested in choice, as evidenced by the fact that less than 2 percent of the parents eligible have opted to participate.

This report is not without its critics. On the editorial page of *The Dallas Morning News* (August 11, 1994), the headlines tell a different story: "School Choice: It Makes Sense to Provide Options." The editorial goes on to say that Dallas along with eleven other cities nationwide have become "part of a national private initiative to give low-income families that option." Allen (1992) agrees with the idea of choice as the key to

better schools. Although individual choice appears consistent with American thought, it does not necessarily result in improved schools.

Other options that have surfaced for improving the performance of public schools are *charter schools* and *home rule*. Charter schools are found in seven states (Colorado, Massachusetts, Wisconsin, New Mexico, Minnesota, Georgia, and California) and Stefonek (in Cole & Schlechty, 1992) identified the following common attributes:

1. choice within the public schools
2. contractual relationships with the school's operator
3. site-based management
4. district becomes the purchaser, rather than provider, of services
5. parental and community support
6. innovative programming
7. exemption from various educational statutes
8. performance-based learning (p. 9)

Bierlein and Mulholland (1994) point out that a charter school in its purest form

> is an autonomous educational entity operating under a contract negotiated between the organizers who manage the school (teachers, parents, or others from the public or private sector), and the sponsors who oversee the provisions of the charter (local school boards, state education boards, or some other public authority). (p. 34)

They go on to say that an approved charter school becomes a recognized legal entity that can hire, fire, sue, and be sued, as well as control its own finances. Funding is based on enrollment, and the educational focus is on business outcomes.

Home rule has been dubbed radical because it goes beyond the concept of charter schools. The common denominator of both systems, charter schools and home rule, is the degree of local control. The driving force of home rule is to move the control of education from "the statehouse to the schoolhouse" (Baker, 1994). Within this con-

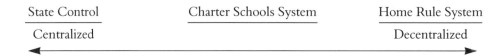

State Control	Charter Schools System	Home Rule System
Centralized		Decentralized

text, all decisions except those involving desegregation laws rest with the districts and school boards and are free from state education rules and regulations. School districts and individual schools have been given the opportunity to shape teaching methods, staffing, use of technology, and governance in the direction that they feel is needed. The major difference between charter schools and home rule is that in the former system, school districts agree to meet state-imposed standards for student performance, student-teacher ratios, teacher certification, desegregation, and safety. In the home rule districts, only the laws governing desegregation are operative. In the graphic shown on this page, the charter school system represents a compromise between total centralization (state bureaucracy) and a totally decentralized system.

Both charter schools and home rule offer a significant departure from how school districts have been managed, both help to cut down on government bureaucracy, and, according to supporters, these systems provide greater choice and a different view of school governance. It is still too early to determine the benefits of each.

SUMMARY

Concerns for academic excellence continue to raise expectations, and the demand for quality instruction continues to serve as the catalyst for reforming elementary education. There have been countless school reform initiatives at various levels in the past two decades. These initiatives have heightened public interest, which has resulted in a rich discussion of what the issues in education are, with many state governments becoming involved in the educational improvement process.

As the twenty-first century approaches, the scrutiny of elementary education and the mandate to restructure elementary schools will continue to escalate, because, for many, the school is not the solution but a part of the problem. The challenge for educators is to rethink the elementary school curriculum and the teaching-learning process in ways that are consistent with the recommendations made by scholars in the disciplines, current research, and the fact that the U.S. is moving increasingly toward being an information society. As the times have changed, other institutions such as hospitals have changed while schools have remained basically the same. Cole and Schlechty (1992) point out that

the knotty problem confronting schools is that they are like they used to be, while other societal institutions have changed dramatically. Thus the current concern with the restructuring of schools contains an implicit concern for the development of new models of leadership within these restructured schools. (p. 135)

There is some movement to reconceptualize the elementary school from a self-contained system to one that is described as a community of learners—students, parents, teachers, business leaders, and members of the local community learning together. As the 1990s come to a close, it is an exciting time for those associated with educating students at the elementary level. Chapter 2 included a description of the major organizational arrangements in the elementary school; these arrangements include the vertical and horizontal patterns.

The best way to describe this period of the 1980s and 1990s is metaphorical: the leaky roof on our educational house needs our attention.

Just doing repairs will cause the whole house to come down (Hodgkinson, 1991). What is needed is not only a new roof but also an entirely new and different foundation and structure—one that is strong enough to hold the students and what they need to be literate for the next several decades. The challenges facing educators include establishing partnerships, teaching for inclusiveness, and reasserting a commitment to the universality of education. The time for rhetoric is over, and the time for action to deal with these changes is now.

This chapter included the mission of the elementary school that centered around the six national goals of America 2000. These goals will provide the focus for schooling as the twenty-first century approaches. When President Bush looked at education in America, he called for a "revolution" in schooling. He went on to say that rather than having more reports, there is a need to get on with the business of reinventing the classroom (Leonard, 1992). In 1994, the Goals 2000: Educate America Act was passed, which increased the national goals to eight.

■ YOUR TURN

1. Make an appointment to visit a local elementary school. On your visit look for the following things:

   a. *Structure of the school*—old or new; graded or nongraded; departmental or self-contained.

   b. *Student–teacher ratio*; types of interaction.

   c. *Student–student* interaction.

   d. *Instructional materials* (e.g., types of textbooks, computers, maps, science laboratory equipment, manipulatives).

   Keep notes/reactions to what you observe in your journal. When you have a quiet moment, review your comments and consider visiting another school if you still have questions or want to experience another elementary school.

2. You have been asked to address the members of the parent-teacher association and your topic is, "Looking Back After Ten Years—*The Nation at Risk*."

To get ready, review Figure 2-1 and the recommendations. To help you prepare for your presentation and make a "T" chart. Label the left column *Reform Reports and Recommendations* and the right *Current Responses*. After listing the recommendations and analyzing them, determine the status of the recommendations and make a judgment about how successful each recommendation has been in the last ten years.

Offer three recommendations of your own to help the "reinventing process" move forward.

3. Spend some time in an elementary school by making arrangements with the district office or individual school campus. Make an appointment to visit with the principal and/or a classroom teacher. During your conference, ask the following questions:

   a. What are the major problems, concerns, and/or issues that teachers are dealing with?

   b. What efforts are being taken to empower teachers and manage the school at the campus level?

c. What are the concerns of parents? What are they doing to address these concerns?

d. What organizational plans are found in your school? Why?

e. Does the school have a nongraded/continuous progress approach? Why? Why not?

4. Obtain the most recent *Phi Delta Kappa Gallup Poll* and two older ones, one from five and one from twenty years ago. Review the top ten issues/problems. Find the ones common to all three and those that are different. Which issues are persisting, and why?

5. David Berliner (1993b), in "Mythology and the American System of Education," identified 13 myths. Review some of the following myths and in your journal react to each of these.

a. *Myth 1*: Today's youths do not seem as smart as they used to be.

b. *Myth 2*: Today's youths cannot think as well as they used to.

c. *Myth 5*: The bottom students now score better on achievement tests, but the performance of the better students has declined. Our top students are not as good as they were.

d. *Myth 6*: The performance of American students on standardized achievement tests reveals gross inadequacies.

e. *Myth 7*: Money is unrelated to the outcomes of schooling.

f. *Myth 8*: The American public school system is a bloated bureaucracy, top-heavy in administrators and administrative costs.

g. *Myth 9:* American productivity has fallen, and a major factor in that decline is the poorer education of the work force.

■ REFERENCES

Allen, J. (1992, May). Choice is key to better schools. *The World & I*. Washington, DC: Times Corporation.

Anderson, R. H. (1993). The return of the nongraded classroom. *Principal*, 72(3), 9–12.

Anrig, G. R., & Lapointe, A. E. (1989). What we know about what students don't know. *Educational Leadership*, 47(3), 4–9.

Baker, M. B. (1994, February 20). Bush suggests local control for schools. *Fort Worth Star-Telegram*, Section A, 22.

Bennett, W. J. (1986). *First lessons: A report on elementary education in America*. Washington, DC: U. S. Department of Education.

Berliner, D. C. (1993a, June/July). Are our schools really failing? *Advocate*, 12(8), 12–16.

Berliner, D. C. (1993b, April). Mythology and the American system of education. *Phi Delta Kappan*, 74(8), 632–640.

Bierlein, L. A., & Mulholland, L. A. (1994). The promise of charter schools. *Educational Leadership*, 52(1), 34–40.

Boyer, E. L. (1992). *School Choice*. Princeton, NJ: The Carnegie Foundation for the Advancement of Teaching.

Brennan, S., & Simpson, D. (1993, Summer). The professional development school: Lessons from the past, prospects for the future. *Action in Teacher Education*, XV(2), 9–17.

Cantrell, M. (Fall, 1994). Kentucky Education Reform Act: A state's efforts. *Contemporary Education*, 66(1), 40–42.

Calkins, T. (1992). The track: Children thrive in ungraded primary schools. *The School Administrator*, 49, 5, 8–13.

Cole, R. W., & Schlechty, P. C. (1992). Teachers as trailblazers. *Educational Horizons*, 70(3), 135–137.

Earley, P. M. (1994, April 11). Goals 2000 legislation is passed in Senate. *AACTE Briefs*, 15(7), 1, 7.

Edwards, P. A., & Young, L. S. J. (1992). Beyond parents: Family, community, and school involvement. *Phi Delta Kappan, 74*(1), 72–80.

Elam, S. M., Rose, L. C., & Gallup, A. M. (1992). Gallup/Phi Delta Kappa poll, 24th annual. *Phi Delta Kappan, 74*(1), 41–53.

Elam, S. M., Rose, L. C., & Gallup, A. M. (1995). Gallup/Phi Delta Kappa poll, 27th annual. *Phi Delta Kappan, 77*(1), 41–53.

Falvey, M. A., Givner, C. C., & Kimm, C. (1995). What is an inclusive school? In R. A. Villa & J. S. Thousand (Eds.), *Creating an inclusive school*. Alexandria, CA: Association for Supervision and Curriculum Development.

Flynn, G., & Kowalczyk-McPhee, B. (1989). A school system in transition. In S. Stainback, W. Stainback, & M. Forest (Eds.), *Educating all students in the mainstream of regular education* (pp. 29–41). Baltimore: Paul H. Brookes.

Goodlad, J. (1984). *A place called school*. New York: McGraw-Hill.

Goodlad, J., & Anderson, R. H. (1959). *The nongraded elementary school*. New York: Harcourt.

Gross, A. L., & Ortiz, L. W. (1994, March). Using children's literature to facilitate inclusion in kindergarten and the primary grades. *Young Children*.

Hallinan, P. K. (1987). *My first day of school*. Nashville, TN: Ideals Publishing.

Henderson, A. T. (1988, October). Parents are a school's best friends. *Phi Delta Kappan, 70*(2), 148–153.

Hodgkinson, H. (1991, September). Reform versus reality. *Phi Delta Kappan, 73*(1), 9–16.

Holmes Group. (1986). *Tomorrow's school*. East Lansing, MI: Holmes Group.

Instructor. (1993, September). Getting help for children in need: A guide to early diagnosis and referral. *130*(2), 53–56.

Kidder, T. (1989). *Among school children*. New York: Avon.

Leonard, G. (1992, May). The end of school. *The Atlantic, 24*(26), 28, 32.

Murray, G. J. (1993). KERA and community linkages. *Equity & Excellence in Education, 26*(3), 65–67.

National Commission on Excellence in Education. (1983). *A nation at risk: The imperative for education reform*. Washington, DC: U.S. Department of Education.

National Research Council. (1989). *Everybody counts: A report to the nation on the future of mathematics education*. Washington, DC: National Academy Press.

Ornstein, A. (1985). The national reports on education: Implications for directions and aims. *Kappa Delta Pi Record, 21*(2), 58–64.

Pavan, B. N. (1992). The benefits of nongraded schools. *Educational Leadership, 50*(2), 22–25.

Raison, J., Hanson, L. A., Hall, C., & Reynolds, M. C. (1995, February). Another school's reality. *Phi Delta Kappan, 76*(6), 480–482.

Reinhartz, J. (1996). A view from within the new PDS paradigm: A teacher educator's perspective. *Texas Teacher Education Forum, 21*, 33–42.

Rogers, J. (1993, May). The inclusion revolution. *Research Bulletin No. 11*. Bloomington, IN: *Phi Delta Kappa*, Center for Evaluation, Development, and Research.

Salend, S. J. (1994). *Effective mainstreaming: Creative inclusive classrooms* (2nd ed.). Upper Saddle River, NJ: Merrill/Prentice Hall.

School choice: It makes sense to provide options. (1994, August 11). *The Dallas Morning News*. p. 24A.

Seymour, D., & Seymour, T. (1993). *America's best classrooms*. Princeton, NJ: Peterson's Guides.

Shepherd, G. D., & Ragan, W. B. (1992). *Modern elementary curriculum* (7th ed.). Ft. Worth, TX: Harcourt Brace Jovanovich College Publishers.

Smith, T. E. C. (1987). *Introduction to education*. St. Paul, MN: West Publishing Company.

Stainback, W., Stainback, S., & Bunch, G. (1989). A rationale for the merger of regular and special education. In S. Stainback, W. Stainback, & M. Forest (Eds.), *Educating all students in the mainstream of regular education* (pp. 15–26). Baltimore: Paul H. Brookes.

Stevens, L. J., & Price, M. (1992, September). Meeting the challenge of educating children at risk. *Phi Delta Kappan, 74*(1), 18–23.

Tewksbury, J. L. (1967). *Nongrading in the elementary school*. Upper Saddle River, NJ: Merrill/ Prentice Hall.

Tye, K. A. (1992, September). Restructuring our schools: Beyond the rhetoric. *Phi Delta Kappan, 74*(1), 8–14.

U.S. Department of Education. (1991). *America 2000: An education strategy*. Washington, DC: U.S. Government Printing Office.

Van Dyke, R., Stallings, M. A., & Colley, K. (1995, February). How to build an inclusive school community: A success story. *Phi Delta Kappa, 76*(6), 475–479.

Vann, A. S. (1994, May). Inclusion: Who gains and who loses? *Principal, 73*(5), 39–40.

Weiss, S. (1994, May). Goals 2000. *NEA Today, 12*(9), 3.

Willis, S. (1991, March). Breaking down grade barriers: Interest in nongraded classrooms on the rise. *Curriculum Update, 33*(3), 1,4.

Willis, S. (1994, October). Making schools more inclusive: Teaching children with disabilities in regular classrooms. *Curriculum Update* 1–8.

chapter 3

Social Contexts of Elementary Education

AFTER READING THIS CHAPTER, YOU WILL BE ABLE TO DO THE FOLLOWING:

- Identify the four social contexts that influence the education of children.

- Describe the prevalent home and family contexts of children and the problems encountered by latchkey children.

- Explain the nature of pluralism in society and its impact on elementary children.

- Describe the degree to which children are vulnerable to violence and crime in society.

- Discuss the role of federal and state governments in providing for education.

- Provide a representative list of legislation that has influenced elementary education.

- Cite examples of landmark court cases that have impacted the elementary education program (the instructional program, the curriculum, the separation of church and state issues, and students' rights).

The instructional program of the elementary school does not develop in a vacuum, nor does education develop autonomously. As Ravitch (1993) notes, it "tends to mirror society and is seldom at the cutting edge of social change" (p. 43). There are forces at work in society that shape the educational process and provide a context in which schools carry out their mission. These social and cultural forces also influence the public's perception of the educative process and its involvement with schools and children.

Ravitch (1993), in noting these forces that impact education, suggests that "the future of education will be shaped not by educators, but by changes in demography, technology, and the family" (p. 43). To realize the impact of these forces of change, think of a clock ticking: the following statistics from a 1989 Children's Defense Fund document tell the story of what will happen within the next twenty-four hours to children age eighteen and under in our country:

2,740 teenagers will get pregnant

1,105 teenagers will have abortions

1,293 teenagers will give birth

700 babies will be born with low birth weight

69 babies will die before one month of life

107 babies will die before their first birthday

27 children will die because of poverty

9 children will die from guns

6 teenagers will commit suicide

1,375 teenagers will drop out of high school

1,849 children will be abused

3,288 children will run away from home

2,987 children will see their parents divorced

135,000 children will arrive at school with a gun (Children's Defense Fund, 1989)

The problems inherent in society also affect lives of children. As the clock ticks away, it is evident that

Changes in the social structure . . . have an impact [on] educational systems [which] are integral parts of the broader social system. . . . If the larger social system experiences fundamental change, this is reflected in the curricula and other aspects of the educational systems. ("A Look to the Future," 1989/90, p. 222)

Many educators are predicting that there will be an increase in the number of elementary students who will have special learning needs because they are increasingly coming from homes with serious abuse or drug addiction problems. As Coontz (1995) notes, "Educators often see firsthand the fallout from the rapid economic, social and demographic changes America has experienced over the last quarter century" (p. K1). Schools must anticipate these changing needs and modify their curriculum and staffing patterns accordingly.

How society values and views its children determines the kind (or lack) of education they receive. According to Morrison (1993), the conditions children face say a great deal about society's support and priority for the education of its citizens. These conditions also reveal a great deal about the forces that impact elementary children and the curricular program. As society changes, so do the educational programs that determine what children experience and learn.

Hodgkinson (1991) compares the state of American education to a house that was once well cared for, but it has deteriorated over time to the point where the roof leaks and water has entered the attic and trickled down to the first floor. Now, with buckled floors, broken windows, and a faulty electrical system, the owners have returned and started to fix up the house, which has been neglected for too long. This analogy illustrates that even with the recent reform efforts discussed in Chapter 2, the fixing up process of the educational house has had limited success. And the roof still leaks because

spectacular changes . . . have occurred in the nature of the children who come to school [and] until we pay attention to these changes, our tin-

kering with the rest of the house will continue to produce no important results. (Hodgkinson, 1991, p. 9)

Children are shaped by environmental, social, political, and economic conditions, as well as by their own biological development. The children did not cause the current conditions; nevertheless, the conditions need to be understood, addressed, and dealt with before the roof is repaired.

Educators alone cannot fix the leaky roof of the educational house. They need help from health and social welfare agencies, community members, parents, and leaders in business and politics. Corrigan (1990) contends that part of the reform movement in education involves forging a collaborative health/education service delivery system for children and their families to help ensure that all children have opportunities to learn and be successful. There is no time to waste in assigning blame, because without action, the house continues to deteriorate and America and its children become the losers.

This chapter discusses some of the social forces that impact children and affect their chances for success in school: the social contexts of the home and family environment, the ethnic composition of the community, the presence of violence and crime, and the political nature of education.

INFLUENCES OF HOME AND FAMILY ON EDUCATION

Several factors can put children at risk in school, and their home environment is one of the most critical. Educators need to be aware of the primary home and family contexts into which their students are born and raised. According to *The Dallas Morning News* ("Study Says," 1995), the American family is in an unprecedented state of flux and the 1990s may be the toughest decade ever for children, as the family of *Leave It to Beaver* gives way to the family of *Murphy Brown*. Citing a recent Rand study, the newspaper article notes that "the traditional American family, while still alive, is no longer the predominant social institution. Rather, it has become one of several household models" ("Study Says," 1995, p. 2C).

Households in the U.S. have changed. For example, between 1980 and 1990 the number of single-female-headed households increased to 35.6 percent of the total and single-male-headed households increased to 29.1 percent (Hodgkinson, 1991). Most revealing is the statistic that according to Coontz (1995), "In the real world of 1994, only 50.8% of all youths live with both biological parents" (p. K13). These changes in the family structure impact the educational process in many ways. For example, schools have taken on many responsibilities of the family by providing qualified elementary students breakfast and lunch, as well as by being the location for after-school supervision.

The school is no longer the place where children go from 8:00 A.M. to 3:00 P.M.; they come to school sometimes as early as 7:00 A.M. and remain in programs after school as late as 6:00 P.M., when a parent or other adult picks them up. Other children who leave school at 3:00 or 3:30 P.M. often arrive home when there is no one to supervise them. These students are described as *latchkey children* because they have a key on a string around their neck (or in their pocket) to let themselves in at home. These children are responsible for themselves until an adult arrives.

These children can be at risk for physical danger without adult supervision (Salkind, 1994), and the number of latchkey children is escalating each year, as more parents and caregivers work and leave their dependents without adult supervision. According to Salkind, as of 1994, 15 percent of children ages 6–9 and 45 percent of those ages 9–12 were latchkey children. Salkind (1994) further notes that in addition to being left unsupervised, these children lack a sense of being loved and nurtured.

As these data suggest, the concept of the two-parent, nuclear family is not as great a factor in shaping the lives of children as it once was. Many children cannot expect the support and nurturance of both parents; nonrelatives, teachers, counselors, and principals often become the primary adult support system for these children. These changes in the composition of the family have implications for teaching and what happens in school. For one, teachers' communication with parents is different: requesting to see a child's parent, requesting a signature on a note sent home, or addressing the parents in a conference may involve any number of configurations. In addition, the amount of adult supervision present in the home has become minimal for many children, which means that no one is available to monitor homework. As a result, many schools have had to rethink their homework policies in response to this situation.

Even when children live in a home with both biological parents, the family relationships are in a state of flux because of the increase in the number of two-career families. In 1970, only 30 percent of mothers were working; by 1980, the percentage had increased to 50 percent; by 1990, the percentage had increased to 60 percent (Olson, 1990). The implications of two-career families on child care and education are great. The consequences of not having family members talking, reading, and interacting with their children are most frequently seen in the area of language development. The number of preschool programs for children who are experiencing delayed social, physical, and language development has significantly increased.

As Ryan and Cooper (1993) note, in the past "teachers could count on sure support from families; now teachers often find it difficult to even get in contact with many parents" (p. 355). Teachers in the elementary school have to increase their efforts to establish a school-home link that increases the chances for success in learning and in school. As Coontz (1995) suggests, if we are to help children and their families be successful in the 1990s, we have to abandon the myths of how families have functioned in the past. To deal with these changes in family structure, strategies such as those used by Parents Anonymous of Connecticut (a group that helps parents make decisions), The Grandmother Hotline (which links children with older adults), and Phoenix Mutual Life Insurance Companies (which offers a course that provides parents with information to ease their anxiety) need to be continued and expanded (Salkind, 1994).

The current nature of the family has become the focus of several conservative groups who have sought to promote a view of the family and the adoption of an agenda that many consider to be extremist in its position (Wiley, 1995). Figure 3-1 provides a summary of these groups and their goals.

Public schools have been criticized as promoting views that are antagonistic to those held by various conservative organizations. As these groups seek greater control of the educational process, not only at the local level, but also at state and national levels, their focus on schools may intensify.

EFFECTS OF PLURALISM IN SOCIETY ON EDUCATION

The composition of the student population in public schools is changing and demographic studies predict an even greater degree of change in the future. Ryan and Cooper (1993) describe this change in the makeup of the student population:

> Today, . . . about 20 percent of children under seventeen are minorities, including African-Americans, Hispanic-Americans, and Asian-Americans. By the year 2000, over one-third of all school-age children, and by 2020, nearly half, will fall into this category. (pp. 349-350)

As Hodgkinson notes, as a nation we should value all of our children and ensure that they

FIGURE 3-1   Conservative Groups and Their Goals

Organization	Goals
The Christian Coalition Headed by Pat Robertson	Opposes feminist agenda and works to elect Christian candidates to political office.
Eagle Forum Headed by Phyllis Shlafly	Promotes conservative agenda and opposes sex education in school curricula and resource materials.
Focus on the Family Headed by James Dobson	Opposes sex education in curricula and monitors proposed legislative efforts.
Concerned Women for America Headed by Beverly LeHaye	Opposes sex education and programs that threaten the values of the traditional family.
Citizens for Excellence in Education Headed by Rev. Robert Simonds	Advocates Christian control of public schools.

Source: For more information, see *Unmasking Religious Right Extremism* (pp. 1–6) by the American Association of University Women, 1994, Washington, DC.

become productive and contributing members of society. To achieve these goals, Willis (1993) says, we can begin by "building commitment to the American ideals of pluralism and democracy, and spurring action to make those ideas a reality" (p. 1). The idea of the pluralistic nature of American society was also discussed in Chapter 1.

Meeting the challenge of a pluralistic society will require addressing the following questions (Willis, 1993):

■   How can teachers ensure the academic success of all students, including various ethnic populations?

■   How can teachers address the needs of all children in the classroom?

Educators must begin by developing an ethnically sensitive and balanced curriculum which, according to Cortes (1990a), represents the following groups in some way: Native Americans, African-Americans, Latinos, Asians, and Europeans. To be effective, elementary teachers must be prepared to address the need for and value of ethnically diverse classrooms and find ways to reinforce multicultural contributions within the elementary school curriculum.

Many children come to school with a family background that involves more than one ethnic heritage. Elementary teachers need to help students "see historical events from a variety of perspectives . . . and [recast] the traditional curriculum" (Willis, 1993, p. 2). In reporting on conversations with teachers, Willis (1993) notes that they feel that it is important that both the "good and the bad" dimensions of U.S. history are presented. Toward that end, teachers can discuss with students some of the ways historical material has been interpreted. For example, few elementary texts discuss the kinds of advanced economic and political systems that were part of Native American culture. In fact, many textbooks give the impression that Native Americans did not exist until they were "discovered" and "conquered." A Native American colleague of mine

has pointed out that Columbus Day is not a celebration for her. Another example for discussion is Thomas Jefferson: as a leader during the making of our nation, he owned slaves and at the same time made many national decisions about slavery.

Teachers have to walk a fine line between overgeneralizing about groups of people and stereotyping and presenting misleading information (Cortes, 1990b). Many textbooks now present information about the important contributions minority groups and individuals have made to our total society. Therefore, as teachers present information in class, it is important to balance the portrayals of contributions of various groups to society to broaden students' cultural awareness.

EFFECTS OF VIOLENCE AND CRIME ON EDUCATION

Another social factor that affects children is the amount of violence and crime to which they are exposed. Violence has become a way of life in many communities, homes, and schools across America. Many children grow up in violent communities or dysfunctional families. Studies have shown that children who grow up exposed to violence, especially in the family, have difficulty establishing trust, autonomy, and social competency (Wallach, 1993). As Corrigan (1990) has observed,

> Children learn what they live. If a child is beaten at home and lives in a trash heap, how will he or she learn to develop a sense of optimism about the future if not in school? The school must reverse the spiral toward futility for many young people. If we ever needed a kinder, gentler America, it is now. (p. 2)

The amount of violence to which children are exposed is pervasive. Kotulak (1990) and Bell (1991) found that 74 percent of the 1000 children they interviewed in Chicago reported witnessing a murder, shooting, stabbing, or robbery. Even more revealing is the fact that 47 percent of these incidences of violence involved friends or family members. The violence is not limited to one geographic region; Zinsmeister (1990) found a similar situation in Baltimore, as did Pynoos and Eth (1985) in Los Angeles.

The kinds of violence children are exposed to each day put them at risk for danger and brutality; the psychological toll they pay for living under these situations is immeasurable. According to Wallach (1993)

> when children have to defend themselves constantly from inside and outside dangers, their energies are not available for other . . . tasks, such as learning to read and write and do arithmetic and learning about geography and history, and science. (p. 6)

There are data to suggest that cognitive abilities are also affected (Terr, 1981). The scenario depicted in Figure 3-2 illustrates the impact of violence on the play of young children. As seen in this interaction, the impact of violence in the world of children has far-reaching effects.

One indicator of the strength of the connection between education and crime is the fact that more than 80 percent of the prisoners in the jails of Texas, for example, are high-school dropouts. Each prisoner costs the taxpayers more than $20,000 per year to maintain; by contrast, it only costs the taxpayers approximately $3,300 per year to keep a child in school (Hodgkinson, 1991). The investment to educate an individual produces a greater return on the dollar than the return on money allotted for incarceration.

The roots of violence reach far beyond the schools. Teachers, along with support service providers, must work toward long-term solutions. Together, as they work with elementary students, they need to do the following things (Wallach, 1993):

■ Provide opportunities for children to develop meaningful relationships with caring and knowledgeable adults.

■ Organize their schedules so that adults spend as much time with these children as possible.

■ Provide children with clear expectations, and establish limits.

■ Provide experiences that encourage children to express themselves.

■ Keep children safe and help them learn that retaliation is not the way to settle disputes.

FIGURE 3-2   Violence at Play

A kindergarten teacher in a Chicago public school was discussing her dilemma concerning two boys in her classroom. All of the children were at their tables, engaged in drawing, when the teacher noticed these boys crawling under the tables, pretending to have guns. When one of the boys saw the teacher watching them, he reassured her, "Don't worry, we're just playing breaking into an apartment." The teacher questioned whether she should let the play continue or offer a more socially acceptable view of behavior. How should she react? A Head Start teacher in the group said that the boy who was taking the lead in this game had been in her class the year before, and that his family's apartment had been burglarized. The boy had been very frightened and, after that experience, had changed from a confident, outgoing youngster to a quiet and withdrawn child. Here it was a year later, and he was just beginning to play out his experience. He was becoming the aggressor in the play instead of the helpless victim. And he was regaining some of his old confidence. (Wallach, 1993, p. 7)

To help students deal with conflict, Carlsson-Paige and Levin (1993) offer a "constructivist approach" that includes "defining the problem, brainstorming, using negotiation skills, and choosing solutions that satisfy both sides" (p. 10). Many teachers have already implemented these and other strategies in their classrooms, but more needs to be done. As children deal with crime and violence in their homes and communities, they need safe zones created by the schools to provide a place for them to learn alternatives to violence as a means of solving problems.

Classroom practices that emphasize a "carry a big stick" approach have not worked; new ones that emphasize problem solving need to be developed. Teachers must be aware of their responsibilities with regard to violence directed toward children. Many states require that teachers, as well as other adults, report any suspected case of child abuse to the appropriate authorities. In addition, teachers must work to establish a classroom environment that is safe and secure for children and model a problem-solving approach to conflicts and misunderstandings.

THE POLITICAL CONTEXT OF EDUCATION

When the word *politics* comes up, an argument or a great silence often follows. The role of politics—state and federal—in education varies depending on the times and is often associated with the economic climate and with the power of political parties, various lobbying groups, and agencies. For many teachers, this factor may seem remote and unrelated to teaching and learning, yet it is vital because teachers are personally affected by decisions made by others regarding finances, salaries, programs, and governance.

Role of the Federal Government

The federal government's role in education in this country has historically been controversial.

Part of the controversy can be attributed to the United States Constitution and its Tenth Amendment, which delegates the responsibility for public education to the states. Because of the Tenth Amendment, education has been viewed as a state function (Smith, 1990), and it would seem that the debate over the role of the federal government and who legally governs public education should be a moot point, but it is not.

In reality, each of the three branches of the federal government plays a role in setting the education agenda in the United States. Although the federal government provides less money for public schools than do state and local governments, federal dollars play a strategic role in education (Ryan & Cooper, 1995). In addition to funding initiatives, the federal government also establishes educational programs through laws or court decisions. Even the executive branch has some prerogatives over education with regard to funds and enforcement procedures. The legislative branch has become increasingly involved in education over the past 200 years, as described in the following section.

Legislative Branch. With the passage of the Land Ordinance Act of 1785 requiring townships to establish public schools, the first piece of federal education legislation was passed. From this beginning point, many other laws that have affected public education were enacted. The following list provides a representative sample:

■ The Northwest Ordinance of 1787 affirmed the federal government's commitment to education.

■ The Morrill Land Grant Act of 1862 gave states federal land to construct land grant colleges.

■ The Smith-Hughes Act of 1917 provided public schools with federal funds for vocational education programs.

■ The Lanham Act of 1941 provided federal funds to school districts for dependents of military personnel.

■ The National Defense Education Act
(NDEA) of 1958 provided federal funds for
improving science, mathematics, and foreign
language education.

Legislation earmarked funds for other educational purposes in the following acts:

■ Manpower Development Training Act of
1962

■ Vocational Education Act of 1963

■ Economic Opportunity Act of 1965

■ Higher Education Act of 1965

■ Elementary and Secondary Education Act
(ESEA) of 1965

■ Bilingual Education Act of 1968

■ Rehabilitation Act of 1973

■ Education for Handicapped Children Act of
1975 (amended in 1991 to become Individuals with Disabilities Education Act [IDEA])

Additionally, the following pieces of legislation related to civil rights also have affected education (Smith, 1990):

■ Titles VI and VII of the Civil Rights Act of
1964

■ Title IX of the Education Amendments of
1972

■ Rehabilitation Act of 1973

All of this is ample evidence that the legislative branch of the federal government has been directly involved in education by providing funds to support different types of programs.

Judicial Branch.   In the past fifty years, the courts have become increasingly engaged in all aspects of education—racial discrimination, students' rights, compulsory school attendance, sex discrimination, collective bargaining, school finance, curriculum materials, and the rights of teachers, handicapped students, and students who are not English speakers. Landmark court cases have impacted instructional programs in the areas of race, sex discrimination, and language;

curriculum; separation of church and state; and students' rights.

Race, Sex Discrimination, and Language

■ *Brown v. Board of Education, Topeka, Kansas,*
1954: Children going to public school could
not be denied admission on the basis of race;
the court ruled that segregated public schools
are unconstitutional (Zirkel, 1978).

■ *Green v. County School Board,* 1968: The court
required that a plan for desegregation be
developed and implemented (Zirkel, 1978).

■ *Swann v. Charlotte-Mechlenburg Board of Education,* 1971: The court ruled that busing was a
legitimate means for achieving desegregation
in the schools, and it gave district courts
great discretion in addressing the longstanding school systems that were segregated
(Zirkel, 1978).

■ *San Antonio Independent School District v.
Rodriguez,* 1973: The state funding model
was upheld in which local property taxes are
used to fund a minimum educational program for students (Zirkel, 1978).

■ *Plyler v. Doe,* 1982: The court "held that
Texas violated the equal protection clause by
authorizing school districts to deny an education to children not legally admitted to the
country" (Simpson, 1995, p. 77).

Curriculum

■ *West Virginia State Board of Education v.
Burnette,* 1943: The court prohibited schools
from requiring that students participate in
flag salutes or other patriotic ceremonies as a
part of the school curriculum (Imber & Van
Geel, 1995).

■ *Board of Education v. Pico,* 1981: The court
agreed that there are constitutional limitations on a school board's authority to censor
textbooks (Imber & Van Geel, 1995).

■ *Virgil v. School Board of Columbia County,*
1989: The court upheld the decision of the
school board to remove from the curriculum

an anthology that had been used as a text-book, because of its sexually explicit and vulgar content (Imber & Van Geel, 1995).

■ *Board of Education of the Westside Community Schools v. Mergens*, 1990: The court defined a non-curriculum-related student group and ruled that denial of recognition to a student-initiated Christian Club violated the Equal Access Act (Imber & Van Geel, 1995).

Separation of Church and State

■ *Abington School District v. Schempp; Murray v. Curlett*, 1963: The court "ruled that the required reading of ten Bible verses and reciting the Lord's prayer during the school day, on school grounds, or conducted by school personnel is unconstitutional" (Zirkel, 1978).

■ *Epperson v. Arkansas*, 1968: The court ruled a "law forbidding the teaching of evolution . . . unconstitutional" (Zirkel, 1978).

■ *Sloan v. Lemon*, 1973: A law allowing for reimbursement by the state to parents who paid for tuition for their children who attended private schools was ruled unconstitutional by the Supreme Court (Zirkel, 1978).

Students' Rights

■ *Tinker v. Des Moines Independent Community School District*, 1969: The court ruled that it was unconstitutional to suspend a student for wearing an arm band or other symbolic expressions if it does not interfere with school (Zirkel, 1978).

Executive Branch. The executive branch of the federal government has been and continues to be involved in public education. The federal Department of Education, established in 1867, had a limited impact, as did the United States Office of Education. In 1979, the U.S. Department of Education was elevated to cabinet status in President Carter's administration and was charged with the following tasks:

1. Ensuring equal educational opportunities for all citizens.

2. Strengthening the federal commitment to support state and local efforts to meet educational needs.

3. Encouraging increased involvement of the public, parents, and students in federal education programs.

4. Promoting improvements in the quality of education through research, evaluation, and information sharing.

5. Improving coordination, management, and accountability of federal education programs. (Neill, 1980, p. 701)

To accomplish these lofty goals, various organizational units were established.

Over the years, many presidents have convened task forces to study various educational issues. Eisenhower established a White House Conference on Education. Reagan formed the committee that issued the *A Nation at Risk* report. Bush worked with governors from the 50 states to establish an educational agenda called America 2000, which has been modified by Clinton into Goals 2000.

Role of State Governments

Unlike the federal government, state governments have exerted a great deal of pressure and influence on education. According to Saylor (1982), the states do four things that impact education:

■ Provide in their constitutions for funding and organizing education.

■ Enact laws that govern curriculum and educational practices.

■ Hear court cases and render decisions which impact instructional programs and funding.

■ Grant power to the state department and state boards of education to enforce laws, accredit and standardize the schools, prescribe and/or influence the textbook selection process, recommend a state curriculum and other guidelines, and require competency examinations.

The governance system at the state level varies from state to state, but there are some common elements that help to answer the question "Who governs/controls education?" Each state constitution provides the legal basis for education in that state. As discussed in Chapter 2, Kentucky has become a prime example of states taking the initiative to improve the education of children. The Kentucky Education Reform Act (KERA) of 1990 has provided a prototype for other states to follow as they seek to restructure their educational processes. Along with the governor and the state legislature, the state courts are the fundamental components of a typical state school system.

In most states, the next levels of governance include the state board of education, the state superintendent or commissioner of education, the state department of education, local school districts along with school boards that represent the local community as elected members, local superintendents, local school principals, teachers, and students (Ryan & Cooper, 1993). Figure 3-3 provides an overview of the role of a state school board member in this process. As you read "A View from the Inside," you will notice the number of decisions that board members must make in the course of fulfilling their responsibilities.

Figure 3-4 identifies the typical educational hierarchy in a school district, with the representative lines of authority and the titles of people who are charged with making decisions at each level regarding the educational program. The number of directors or other members of the hierarchy included depends on the size of the district.

A review of the structure in Figure 3-4 reveals that it is not always easy to discern exactly who is involved in governing education. Figure 3-4 also demonstrates that a complex organizational structure with a hierarchical arrangement governs most schools. There are multiple levels

of decision making that exert influence on American public schools. The purpose of presenting the political context of the educational organization is to provide a brief look at the interplay among various components that impact education and to recognize the various people and groups that have the power to bring about educational change.

INTERPROFESSIONAL EDUCATION: A COLLABORATIVE APPROACH

Corrigan (1993) suggests interprofessional education as one way to educate all students and repair the leaky roof. *Interprofessional education* provides a way "of reforming education, health, and human services . . . [by] recognizing that colleges of education, schools, and community agencies are interacting components of one system" (p. 6). Corrigan continues by suggesting that the schools are the locus of advocacy for all children:

> the poor and the deprived as well as the rich and the powerful. Because the school is the only community institution that sees every child every day, school leaders must accept the responsibility for helping to mobilize community resources. (p. 6)

These health and human services are needed by all students because family upheaval, family health concerns, poverty, and emotional problems can place children at risk of failing. These conditions affect a child's intellectual and personal growth, and the role of schools and educators becomes one of social service providers who take learning seriously and provide a place in which learning is enjoyable, lively, humane, and an intellectual pursuit (Corrigan, 1990; Corrigan, 1988). This does not mean that the school provides all the health and human services, but rather performs the following functions (Corrigan, 1993):

FIGURE 3-3   The Texas State Board of Education: A View from the Inside

HELP WANTED: State Board of Education district representative. Must be U.S. citizen, qualified voter, minimum of 30 years of age, and a resident of the district for the past year. Responsibilities will include state educational policies, management and oversight for education of 3.5 million Texas public schoolchildren in over 1,000 school districts with over 260,000 educators. Potential for future political advancement a possibility but not likely. Application to be reviewed by over 1,000,000 constituents in two-step partisan process in March primary and November general elections. Salary will be $0. File application with Secretary of State by January 10, 1992.

Early January One Year Later. Austin, Texas

I landed the job, and the day of my first meeting finally arrived! One year after filing for office, today's swearing-in ceremony was the result of months of intense political campaigning with victories in the March primary and the November general election. I was sworn in by the Secretary of State in a rather auspicious ceremony which marked the beginning of my term of office.

My previous experience as a local school board member for eleven years, as a classroom teacher for several years, and as an actively involved parent of school-age children made me anxious to get to this core of educational decision-making, and I was excited and optimistic about the opportunities for really making a difference for students. Shortly after the ceremony, as I considered the various action items on the agenda, it quickly became apparent to me that I had been somewhat idealistic about my ability to accomplish this goal, given that I was not only one of four rookies but a member of the minority party. Welcome to Austin and the world of partisan politics!

Over the next few months, I received numerous phone calls and letters of concern about various matters, but nothing like what was to occur the following fall when we began to consider the adoption of high school health textbooks (translation: sex education). Literally hundreds of phone calls and letters were a daily occurrence throughout the fall months. Each special interest group pleaded that the State Board abide by their particular wishes, which ranged from throwing out all of the textbooks to making revisions to keeping all five of the publishers' versions with no changes. The final decision to adopt all five books with numerous changes was, of course, a compromise, which in the end, made no one happy!

The Second Year of Office.

By now I had a much clearer picture of just how challenging this responsibility was going to be—so much for practicality and common sense! It began to look like these were viewpoints which are generally not advocated by the constituents who took the time to contact their elected representatives. Since decisions in government are obviously influenced by the viewpoints of citizens whose voices are loud and clear, I concluded that it was unfortunate that there was not an advocacy group for ordinary people who are happy and content! The bottom line is that organized pressure groups have figured out how to make themselves heard.

The ongoing challenge of making wise decisions in this environment soon transformed me to the experience level of a veteran politician. Nonetheless, the SBOE and I have survived to work through many important decisions affecting our schoolchildren. And I learned the answers to the following questions I had about the Texas State Board of Education.

Just exactly how did our current arrangement of an elected board of fifteen members with staggered four-year terms come to be?

Since 1898 when the first Texas State Board of Education consisted of the Governor, Secretary of State, and the Comptroller, the State Board of Education has undergone many transfigurations. In 1929, a separate State Board was created as a nine-member body appointed by the Governor, and then in 1949, it was converted to an elected board by the Gilmer-Aiken Act. As a result of House Bill 72 in 1984, the SBOE once again became a gubernatorial appointment. Today's elected version began in 1989 after a referendum was approved by a majority of the people of Texas.

How does this compare to other states?

Texas is unique among the 50 states in its educational governing process. While members of the SBOE are elected, the commissioner or the education chief, is appointed by the governor. There are about four governance models which are used widely. These include those nine states which appoint both the state board and the state chief and the eight states which elect the state board who appoints the state chief. However, most of the states use a model in which the chief state school officer is elected and the board is appointed by the governor. And finally like Texas, several other states use methods which do not conform to any of these models.

What is the internal organizational structure of the SBOE?

The organizational structure of the State Board is fairly simple. The chair of the Board is appointed by the Governor and is limited to two 2-year terms. The other officers, consisting of the Vice-Chair and the Secretary, are elected by fellow Board members. There are five standing SBOE committees: Finance, Personnel, Student, Permanent School Fund, and Long-Range Planning. The Committees are appointed by the Board Chair, and each Committee elects its own chair.

When and where are meetings held?

The State Board holds its regular meetings at 1:00 PM on the second Friday of each month except August and December. Committee meetings are generally held the day before the regular board meetings. All meetings are open, and members of the public may testify before the Board by registering their intent. Agendas are published in advance and available to interested parties.

What does the SBOE do?

The State Board of Education is the educational policy-making body for public education. This includes an array of topics ranging from the essential elements of the curriculum to the adoption of recommended textbooks, to high school graduation requirements, to management of the Texas Permanent School Fund, to educator preparation and certification. Furthermore, the State Board writes guidelines and rules for the implementation of legislative and statutory requirements.

The SBOE also appoints special task forces or ad hoc committees to examine particular issues in depth. Recent examples of these committees are the Middle School (1991), High School (1992), and Early Childhood/Elementary (1993) Task Forces. Usually resulting in major Board policy statements, the membership of these committees is broad and includes members of the public as well as educators.

FIGURE 3-3, *continued*

Who are the people who serve on the State Board?

Typical personal attributes of a Texas State Board could be reviewed by taking a look at the characteristics of the board as of the November 1994 election: eight are members of the Republican party and seven belong to the Democratic party; eight are males and seven are females. The ethnic diversity includes three Hispanics, two African-Americans, and ten Caucasians, who bring their perspectives of varied geographic, educational and vocational backgrounds. Some have previously served as local school board members, and several members are former or current educators, while others come from professional or business orientations.

What is the likely future of the State Board?

Recent legislative actions have gradually decreased the responsibilities of the Texas State Board of Education, and there are indications that this trend will continue. The popular notion of decentralization has been the impetus for this shift of power from the state to the local district level.

Ultimately, reporting results to the public and facilitating the flow of information is part of the ongoing goal of communication that is necessary in the entire process of accountability for education in the state. Finally, as an advocate for children and schools, the State Board of Education works in partnership with the governor, the legislature, and the local school boards to see that an excellent and equitable system of free public education is established and maintained in the state.

In conclusion, I personally believe that it is of crucial importance to the future of this state and this country that boards of education continue to attract citizens who are genuinely interested in bettering the education of all of our youth. My experience at the local and state level has given me enough insight to cause me to become even more concerned about the future of the process of educational decision-making in general.

Source: Contributed by Diane Patrick, District 11 Representative on the Texas State Board of Education (elected November 1992, served through January 1997). Reprinted with permission.

■ educates all children so they can make intelligent decisions

■ connects children and their families with service care providers

■ actively seeks to develop collaborative relationships with other professionals in an effort that will result in creating healthy, humane communities

When one considers all of the social, cultural, economic, and political factors that impact children and their education, it is a wonder that schools are able to accomplish as much as they do. The Kentucky reform initiative provides a new perspective on initiating social change by linking schools and communities through the HANDS (Housing and Neighborhood Development Strategies) program (Murray, 1993). In the final analysis, it is the classroom teacher who seems to make the difference. In studying the success of poor minority youth from one school, sociologists noticed that they all had the same teacher. When the teacher was interviewed and asked what she had done that so many of her students, who statistically had little chance of success, had been so successful in life, she replied, "I

FIGURE 3-4 Hierarchy of a Suburban School District

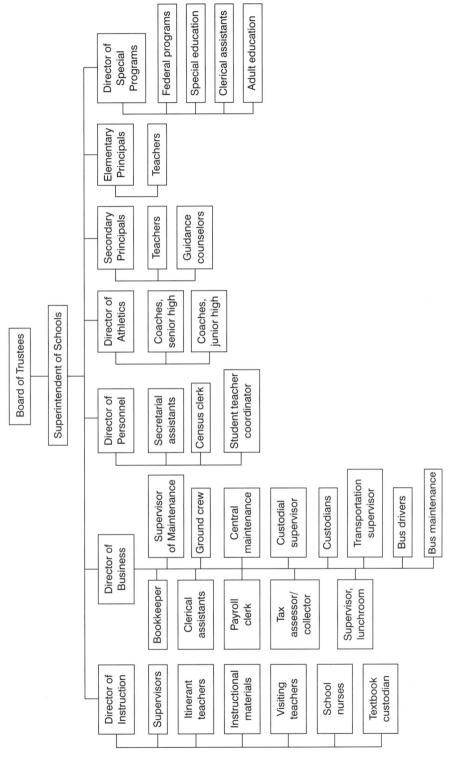

simply loved them" (Butterworth, 1993). Elementary teachers must be willing to work with all children to help them be successful.

SUMMARY

The educational program did not develop in a vacuum, nor does it change in isolation. This chapter has presented a discussion of social forces that impact elementary education. The issues discussed here are not the only ones that influence the organization and operation of schools, but they are some of the common factors shaping the elementary school at this point in time. As society changes, so will the forces that influence the educational practices and programs at the elementary level.

These changes may be most evident in what is occurring in the home and in society at large. Everyone seems to have something to say—or wants to have something to say—about the educational process. Citizens believe they have the answers to many of the pressing problems of the public schools in the United States. As stressed in this chapter, the issues facing educators are very complex, and the school is the microcosm of the larger society in which it functions.

Teachers, more than anyone else, see the changes that are taking place in society because they experience them every day: the changing nature of populations, crime and violence, and the political context within which school operates. The family structure is changing, and teachers become aware of these changes when they find out that a child has an aunt/uncle who is his/her guardian, rather than a birth parent(s). Teachers discover quickly that their new student speaks another language when they are unable to communicate directly with the student or the parents. Teachers have a greater understanding of school crime when they are personally fearful of walking in the halls or to their cars. Finally, teachers feel the precarious position education is in regarding funding, because support for their profession increases or decreases depending on the political climate.

Educators must be aware of changing conditions in society because there is a direct correlation with conditions in the school: the type of relationship teachers have with parents and/or guardians, the type of education that will be provided, the instructional strategy that will be used, and the amount of money spent on education all vary, depending on the social contexts.

Educating students for the twenty-first century will require collective action on the part of many individuals. A window of opportunity seems to be open now; such a window rarely stays open very long. Corrigan and others contend that there is still a chance to make a difference.

■ YOUR TURN

1. Read the conclusions of the Coleman report, written in 1966:

Schools bring little influence to bear on a child's achievement that is independent of his background and general social context; ... this very lack of an independent effect means that the inequalities imposed on children by their home, neighborhood and peer environment are carried along to become the inequalities with which they confront adult life at the end of school. For equality of educational opportunity must imply a strong effect of schools that is independent of the child's immediate social environment, and that strong independent effect is not present in American schools. (Coleman et al., 1966, p. 325)

The Coleman report is 30 years old. Do you think it is still viable, in the light of all the changes that have been and are taking place in society? Why? Why not? Be able to defend your answer.

2. Visit the central office of the local school district. Obtain information about how the district operates, the members of the school board, the name of the superintendent, and so on. How many members are on the board of education? When was the last election? What issues is the board dealing with?

   a. Develop a chart depicting the organizational structure of the district. What is the composition—sex, age, ethnicity—and how does this reflect the student population of the school district? For example, a profile of members of school boards in 1990 showed that "61 percent are males, mean age is between 41-50, and 93 percent are white with a family income of between $40,000-80,000" (Freeman, Underwood, & Fortune, 1991).

   b. If possible, interview the president of the school board; draft a series of questions. Review the chapter for ideas.

   c. Attend a regularly scheduled school board meeting. Obtain a copy of the agenda. What are the issues being discussed? Were decisions made? If none were made, why?

3. For the next five days, read the newspaper carefully for articles that address the conditions presented in this chapter—the family, demographics, violence in the school, and politics. Mount them in a journal: cut out the article and, after reading it, write down your thoughts. How do you feel? Why do you feel this way? Has this issue dominated the news? What implications will these issues have on teaching school?

If you do not find any related articles, which seems unlikely, investigate the following court case:

Ray v. School District of DeSoto County, 1987: "Children with AIDS are no threat to other children in school if certain precautions are followed, and denying them entrance violates their rights."

4. Although only federal and state governments were addressed in this chapter, professional organizations also influence education. How do they influence education? In what ways do they influence it?

Some of these organizations include the National Education Association and the American Federation of Teachers. Locate the local office of each of these organizations, and obtain publications that address important issues in education. Obtain copies, determine each organization's philosophy on various issues, and, in your journal, make a chart for each one, to compare and contrast them. Some topics might include the voucher system, class size, teaming, theme teaching, the political issues they are fighting for and supporting, etc.

5. Educators/teachers have frequently been caught in the crossfire in the battle over local control versus national standards. States and local communities have viewed education as their purview and have rejected the idea of a national curriculum and national standards. At the same time, states and communities want to be sure their students "measure up" to what students are doing in other states and communities.

   a. What is your general reaction to their dilemma? Do you agree with those who want local control? If so, why? If not, do you support national standards? Why? Provide some reasons for your support.

Or do you favor both local control and national standards? In your journal, jot down why you feel that both are essential (if that's how you feel).

b. Why is there a desire for local control of schools and curriculum or site-based management? Why is this so important?

c. What implications would a national yardstick (the use of a national curriculum and national testing, and so on) have on individual school districts and schools?

6. What do the statistics at the beginning of this chapter mean to elementary teachers? What will the home conditions be for a child whose mother was fourteen years old when she discovered she was pregnant? What types of health problems could the child have if the mother's pregnancy did not go full term? What will be the child's potential health and learning problems if the mother did not have prenatal care? What are the chances of the mother completing high school and getting advanced training? Obtain some statistics from the Children's Defense Fund (1989) to better respond to the following questions.

a. What can teachers do to help children be winners in school, knowing that "what is coming toward the educational system is a group of children who will be poorer, more ethnically and linguistically diverse, and who will have more handicaps that will affect their learning" (Hodgkinson, 1991)?

b. How would Corrigan's "interprofessional development schools" help in centering the community's efforts in delivering needed human services? How can these interprofessional development schools provide services to the whole child and families in a community-based system?

■ REFERENCES

American Association of University Women. (1994). *Unmasking religious right extremism.* Washington, DC: American Association of University Women.

Bell, C. (1991). Traumatic stress and children in danger. *Journal of Health Care for the Poor and Underserved, 2*(1), 175–188.

Butterworth, E. (1993). Love: The one creative force. In J. Canfield & M. V. Hansen (Eds.), *Chicken soup for the soul* (pp. 3–4). Deerfield Beach, FL: Health Communications.

Carlsson-Paige, N., & Levin, D. E. (1993, March). A constructivist approach to conflict resolution. *The Education Digest, 58*(7), 10–26.

Children's Defense Fund. (1989). *A vision for America's future.* Washington, DC: Children's Defense Fund.

Coontz, S. (1995, March). The American family and the nostalgia trap. *Phi Delta Kappan, 76*(7), K1–K20.

Coleman, J. S., Campbell, E. Q., Hobson, C. J., McPartland, J., Mood, A. M., Weinfield, F. D., & York, R. L. (1966). *Equality of educational opportunity.* Washington, DC: Government Printing Office.

Corrigan, D. C. (1993, September/October). An idea whose time has come—Again. *ATE Newsletter, 27*(1), 6–7.

Corrigan, D. C. (1990, March). Context for the discussion of the collaborative development of integrated services for children and families: The education sides. Paper presented at the National Symposium on Integrated Services for Children and Families, Alexandria, VA.

Corrigan, D. C. (1988). Creating the American school: Reaction paper #2. In D. C. Corrigan (Ed.), *Purposes of American education today: Conceptions of schooling* (pp. 1–50). College Station, TX: Texas A & M University.

Cortes, C. E. (1990a, March/April). A curricular basic for our multiethnic future. *Doubts & Certainties, 4*(7/8), 1–8.

Cortes, C. E. (1990b, Winter). E pluribus unum: Out of many one. *California perspectives: An anthology from the immigrant students projects*, Monograph Vol. 1, pp. 13–16.

Freeman, J. L., Underwood, K. E., & Fortune, J. C. (1991). What boards value. *American School Board Journal*, *178*(1), 34.

Hodgkinson, H. (1991, September). Reform versus reality. *Phi Delta Kappan*, *73*(1), 9–10.

Imber, M., & Van Geel, T. (1995). *A teacher's guide to education law*. New York: McGraw-Hill.

Kotulak, R. (1990, September 28). Study finds inner-city kids live with violence. *Chicago Tribune*. pp. 1, 16.

A look to the future. In *Annual edition, education 89/90* (16th ed.). Guilford, CT: Dushkin.

Morrison, G. S. (1993). *Contemporary curriculum K-8*. Boston: Allyn and Bacon.

Murray, G. J. (1993). KERA and community linkages. *Equity and excellence in education*, *26*(3), 65–67.

Neill, G. (1980). Education department explains its structure and purposes. *Phi Delta Kappan*, *61*(10), 701–702.

Olson, L. (1990, April 4). Parents as partners. *Education Week*. p. 19.

Pynoos, R., & Eth, S. (1985). Children traumatized by witnessing personal violence: Homicide, rape or suicide behavior. In S. Eth & R. Pynoos (Eds.), *Posttraumatic stress disorder in children* (pp. 19–43). Washington, DC: American Psychiatric Press.

Rand Study. (1995). The cost of performance assessment in science: The Rand perspective. Arlington, VA: National Science Foundation. (ERIC Document Reproduction Service No. ED 383-732)

Ravitch, D. (1993, September 11). When school comes to you. World politics and current affairs. *Economist*, *328*, 43-49.

Ryan, K., & Cooper, J. M. (1993). *Those who can, teach* (6th ed.). Boston: Houghton Mifflin Company.

Ryan, K., & Cooper, J. M. (1995). *Those who can, teach* (7th ed.). Boston: Houghton Mifflin Company.

Salkind, N. J. (1994). *Child development* (7th ed.). New York: Harcourt Brace College Publishers.

Saylor, J. G. (1982). *Who planned the curriculum? A curriculum plans reservoir model with historical examples*. West Lafayette, IN: Kappa Delta Pi.

Simpson, M. D. (1995, February). Immigrant backlash puts kids at risk. *NEA Today*, *13*(6), 17.

Smith, T. E. C. (1990). *Introduction to education* (2nd ed.). St. Paul: West Publishing Company.

Study says 26% of kids under 6 are living in poverty. (1995, January 30). *The Dallas Morning News*. p. 3A.

Terr, L. (1981). Forbidden games: Post-traumatic child's play. *Journal of American Academy of Child Psychiatry*, *20*, 741–760.

Wallach, L. B. (1993). Helping children cope with violence. *Young Children*, *48*(4), 4–11.

Wiley, D. C. (1995, October). Advocating for our profession: The struggle with extremism. *Texas Association HPERD Journal*, *64*(1), 8–13.

Willis, S. (1993, September). Multicultural teaching: Meeting the challenges that arise in practice. In *ASCD Curriculum Update* (pp. 1–7). Reston, VA: Association for Supervision and Curriculum Development.

Zinsmeister, K. (1990, June). Growing up scared. *The Atlantic Monthly*, *265*(6), 49–66.

Zirkel, P. A. (1978, April). A test on Supreme Court decisions affecting education. *Phi Delta Kappan*, *59*(8).

chapter 4

Views of Children: How They Grow and Learn

AFTER READING THIS CHAPTER, YOU WILL BE ABLE TO DO THE FOLLOWING:

■ Describe specific ways that psychology and theories of learning are used by elementary teachers to develop curriculum for children.

■ Identify the general principles of human development and discuss their implications for teachers.

■ Describe the physical and cognitive development of elementary children.

■ Explain the implications of multiple intelligences information for elementary teachers in developing curriculum.

■ Discuss the views of Erikson, Piaget, Vygotsky, Gardner, Kohlberg, and Gilligan with regard to elementary students.

■ Describe and give an example of the various learning challenges that elementary children face.

■ Compare and contrast the views of behaviorism, humanism, and constructivism as they impact the curriculum.

Elementary schools are busy places, full of active children who are involved in learning and who may be as young as five in kindergarten and as old as twelve or thirteen in intermediate grades or middle schools. Watch children on the playground, and you will have a sense of their boundless energy and activity. On any school day, if you visit an elementary school, you will probably find a newly turned six-year-old learning to count or recognize letter sounds in kindergarten, while down the hall a sixth-grade girl who has just entered puberty is coping with the physiological changes of becoming a young lady.

The needs and cognitive abilities of these two students are very different, yet elementary teachers must be prepared not only to work with each child but to develop a curricular program that is appropriate for each one. As teachers plan for teaching, they need to be cognizant of the growth and development of elementary-aged

children so that they can match the curriculum and instructional activities to the developmental characteristics and needs of their students. This match between the curriculum and the developmental characteristics of learners is referred to as a *developmentally appropriate curriculum.*

Educators draw upon psychology and theories of learning and development to provide an understanding of children—how they grow, develop, and learn. By applying a knowledge of learners, derived from developmental psychology to curriculum development, teachers can adopt teaching behaviors that are more appropriate and thereby enhance student learning. In describing the importance of the psychological foundations, Salkind (1994) suggests that teachers need to be aware of the scientific study of how children develop in terms of the physical, psychosocial, and cognitive changes that occur over time. Mathis, Cotton, and Sechrest (1970) believe that knowledge of educational psychology provides the means of changing learner behavior. The curriculum of the elementary school should be founded on the principles of psychology as they relate to human development. For some educators, curriculum planning is predicated on knowledge of the characteristics of learners, for as Popham and Baker (1970) note,

> The learner . . . is the first basic data source. . . . We should have some idea of the abilities of the learner so that we can decide what he/she is likely to know. In addition, we might use the learner's own interests and needs as a basis for . . . curricular decisions. (p. 49)

Children ages six to twelve undergo a variety of physical and physiological, as well as psychosocial, changes as they progress through school. These developmental characteristics affect the quality of the students' interactions in school, their sense of themselves, and ultimately the quality of their learning.

The curriculum is also shaped by the cognitive abilities of the learners and the psychological principles associated with learning. In addition to an understanding of the physical and psychosocial development of their students, teachers need an understanding of how children learn and process information. In studying learners and the learning process, teachers should "seek to identify needed changes in behavior patterns of the students which they . . . should seek to produce" (Tyler, 1949, p. 6).

Another factor that helps shape the behavior of elementary students is their moral development. As children develop beliefs and values, they begin to establish a moral view of their world, and their interactions with adults and others fit predictable patterns. An understanding of this belief or value system also can aid teachers when designing plans for teaching.

Whole textbooks are devoted to the details of child and human development. Our purpose in this chapter is to provide a general overview and set the stage for curriculum planning by helping you better understand this dynamo called the elementary school student by identifying some general principles of human development that apply to all developmental ages. In addition, the chapter describes various characteristics of physical development, including developmental milestones. The chapter includes a discussion of the cognitive abilities of elementary students, as well as various theories of how children learn and how they construct an understanding of the world in which they live. Finally, the chapter concludes with a discussion of the moral development of elementary learners.

GENERAL PRINCIPLES OF HUMAN DEVELOPMENT

To better understand the nature of elementary students, it is helpful to examine both their physiological and their cognitive development. Three general principles of human growth and development appear to apply throughout life:

■ There are identifiable characteristics common to learners within a particular age or period of development.

■ The movement from one age, period, or stage of development to the next is sequential.

■ The rate of movement through each period and from one period to the next depends on the individual (Glickman, 1981).

These principles help explain the growth patterns elementary students experience. For example, all elementary students share similar developmental characteristics (cognitive, psychosocial, moral, physical), and as these students move through the period appropriate for their age, they experience similar developmental events (for example, they loose baby teeth in first grade) before they move to another period. At the same time, because of the individual nature of development, some children move more slowly or more rapidly than others into and out of the period, as well as through the period.

Students at the entry and exit levels are in transition from one stage to another and may exhibit characteristics that overlap other developmental periods. Human development is not a static process. A six-year-old first grader might exhibit many of the characteristics of an early childhood student (ages three to five); a twelve-year-old sixth grader may exhibit many of the characteristics of the pubescent preadolescent. Thus, the grade level they are in does not always match their physical, psychosocial, cognitive, or moral development. In elementary classrooms, teachers will have students in various stages of development; just because children are in the same grade and generally are the same age does not mean they are all alike. In fact, they exhibit a range of abilities and behaviors.

It is just as erroneous to assume that all fourth-grade boys wear the same sized shirt, pants, and shoes as it is to assume that they learn the same amount, in the same way, and retain the same amount of knowledge. Moreover, while there are common characteristics among children of roughly the same age, the range of differences among them widens as children get older, and the differences are considerably greater by the time the children leave the elementary school. These ranges of differences have implications for curriculum development.

The fact that cognitive abilities are more homogeneous when students enter than when they exit elementary school creates one of the difficulties of teaching in the elementary school, especially in the upper grades, where a teacher can encounter a wide range of student abilities. When teachers have to meet the needs of both gifted students and remedial students, the task becomes formidable. Experts suggest that, as a result of these widening abilities, by focusing on several key factors, such as self-concept and educational background of the mother, as well as student achievement, educators can identify at-risk

students as early as fifth or sixth grade (Slavin, 1989).

PHYSICAL AND PSYCHOSOCIAL DEVELOPMENT OF ELEMENTARY STUDENTS

The period of development during which children are in the elementary grades is referred to as *middle childhood*: children are developmentally between early childhood and adolescence. Their growth during these years is characterized as moderate and steady. Unlike toddlerhood and the preschool years, during which children often change clothes sizes every few months, growth during middle childhood is less dramatic. On the average, children grow two-and-a-half inches in height and gain approximately five pounds each year they are in elementary school. During the last year or two, growth is more dramatic, especially for girls, and by age twelve, students will have attained approximately 85–90 percent of their adult height and will weigh about 80–85 pounds (Helms & Turner, 1986).

Perhaps the most notable feature of physical development for students during the early elementary grades is the loss of "baby" contours and features and the emergence of a leaner overall appearance as the preschool fat layers diminish. Contributing to that leaner look are the rapid growth of arms and legs and the active behavior students engage in. Salkind (1994) notes that "as children grow, their trunks tend to become slimmer, their chests broader, and their arms and legs are longer and slimmer" (p. 471). He also points out that, toward the end of middle childhood, the uneven growth of body parts gives an awkward appearance and movement. Slavin (1994) notes that "muscular development is outdistanced by bone and skeletal development [which] may cause the aches commonly known as 'growing pains'" (p. 88). Up to age nine, boys are generally taller and heavier than girls. After age nine, until boys go through their adolescent growth spurt, girls are generally taller and heavier than boys (Helms & Turner, 1986; Slavin, 1994). This growth of the skeleton and muscles also contributes to the elementary child's restless energy. Elementary classrooms are active, busy places, especially in the primary grades.

In the elementary grades, children develop improved neuromuscular coordination and motor skills to the point where they have running, jumping, throwing, and catching abilities and enough balance to learn to ride a bicycle without training wheels. During the primary grades (1–3), the fine and gross motor skills improve and children switch from big pencils to the regular-sized ones. Students also become proficient at cutting out shapes and pictures as they gain greater control with scissors.

A change in facial features is another notable characteristic that is manifested in children in the early elementary grades. The face takes on a new look as the forehead flattens and the nose develops or becomes more prominent. "Baby," or deciduous, teeth are replaced by permanent teeth. Children with front teeth missing are common in the first and second grades. It is not unusual for teachers in these grades to have "teeth charts," to record the number of teeth each child loses during the year. When the new front teeth do come in, they often appear larger—almost too large for the child's mouth. By the time children leave elementary school, they have their full set of permanent teeth, with the exception of some molars, and their faces are longer and leaner. In the fifth and sixth grades, as they get their permanent teeth, some children also receive orthodontic appliances or "braces" to help straighten the teeth.

As children progress through the elementary grades, they begin a journey toward maturity. For some, especially girls, by the time they leave the elementary grades, they will have taken a major step toward becoming young adults. As Slavin

(1994) notes, during the fifth grade, most if not all of the girls have begun their growth spurt, and by sixth grade girls are at the peak of their growth and many either start or have started their menstrual period.

It is important to remember when referring to growth figures and developmental characteristics that these are only averages and that there are wide variations among growth patterns. Developmental specialists caution that average rates are useful for comparative purposes but that each child is unique. Growth and development can be affected by such factors as nutrition, heredity, glandular imbalance, exercise, and health care.

The importance of the overall physical appearance and bodily structure is critical to the development of skills, aptitudes, and even the self-concept and emotions of elementary school children. The elementary child's sense of self is strongly linked to physical appearance (Tanner, 1973).

As children enter elementary school (preschool–kindergarten), their social world expands as they interact with other children and adults. As students progress through elementary school, their sense of self, or self-esteem, becomes more complex in social interactions and classroom experiences. Erikson (1963, 1968, 1980) recognized the impact of the social environment on development and proposed a psychosocial theory of development. Although his theory described social development throughout life, he identified the period of the middle childhood as a time of industry versus inferiority. During the elementary school years, children work hard to maintain a positive self-concept as they learn and make things. Erikson (1980) suggests that the child's psychosocial development is tied to his or her self-concept which, in elementary school becomes "I can learn" or "I am what I learn." Entwistle and Hayduk (1981) note that children enter school with the belief and expectation that they can and will learn: they expect success. However, as they encounter other children and the structure and process of school, they begin to realize that there are many different abilities and levels, and they begin to modify their expectations and views of themselves.

Erikson (1963) suggests that schools should be places where students acquire the tools they need to be successful in society. Teachers must therefore work to equip each child with the necessary skills and knowledge (tools), which in turn promote or help to maintain a positive self-concept, a can-do belief. The developing child's psychosocial development is greatly impacted by the school and by the learning environment established by the teacher.

Figures 4-1 and 4-2 provide descriptions of Seth, a seven-year-old boy, and Sarah, an eleven-year-old girl. These profiles of elementary students illustrate many of the developmental char-

acteristics that are considered "typical" for the age group.

COGNITIVE DEVELOPMENT OF ELEMENTARY STUDENTS

During the middle childhood years, the cognitive abilities of students improve significantly. As preschoolers and kindergartners, children's cognitive abilities are often limited because they focus on single traits or characteristics and are considered perception bound. They also have an egocentric view of the world. Piaget (1967, 1952), Piaget and Inhelder (1973), Bruner (1968, 1960), and Vygotsky (1978) are developmental psychologists frequently associated with the cognitive

FIGURE 4-1   Elementary Student Profile: Seth

Seth is a seven-year-old boy. He has two older sisters and a younger sister who is two. His older sisters are in high school and junior-high school. His parents, married for 18 years, are both employed in hourly jobs, and his father has two jobs. Although his mother has worked since Seth was a toddler, this has not been a problem for him because he has had older family members at home.

Seth's interests involve many outdoor activities. He enjoys all kinds of sports, especially soccer and basketball. Although somewhat small for his age, what he lacks in size is made up for in energy. Seth is constantly in motion exploring, playing, and having fun with other kids. Seth's friends are mainly boys from the neighborhood and range in age from five to about eight or nine. Seth lives in a government-subsidized apartment in a large city and attends an elementary school in another neighborhood. Seth plays mostly in a small area in the apartment or on the sidewalks. When at home, he enjoys watching TV, particularly cartoons in the afternoon and on Saturday. His favorite shows are mainly about action heroes. Although he enjoys reading, he seldom reads at home. Seth likes school, especially PE, where he excels in many of the activities, but he also likes language arts and music, where according to Seth they "do fun things with the music." Recently, Seth lost one of his front teeth and has that "snaggle tooth" appearance.

Seth's grandmother lives nearby in another apartment and from the time he was an infant, he has spent a lot of time with her. In addition to his mother and father, his grandmother is a very important person in his life. Seth says his grandmother cooks special food for him, as well as his favorite cookies.

FIGURE 4-2   Elementary Student Profile: Sarah

Sarah is eleven years old and the youngest of three children in her family. Her brother is a high-school sophomore, and her older sister, now 22, lives and works in another state. Her parents, married for 25 years, are both employed in professional positions, and Sarah enjoys the benefits of an upper-middle-class family. Her mother has worked since Sarah was born, but she adjusted well to day care, and as she has gotten older, she has had older family members at home to care for her after school.

Sarah's interests are varied and involve many outdoor activities. She enjoys walking/jogging, playing basketball, and swimming. Sarah is active in after-school activities such as gymnastics, piano lessons, and youth league basketball through the parks and recreation program in her community. She also enjoys going shopping at the mall for clothes.

When at home, she enjoys listening to the radio, watching TV, and reading magazines such as *American Girl*. She is selective about which television programs she watches, but her current favorites are situation comedies and cartoons after school and on Saturdays. She has started talking for periods of time on the telephone to friends, especially to her best girlfriend and her new boyfriend. Sarah is very interested in athletics and competes in basketball tournaments. Sarah has developed a close friendship with two girls at her school, and she frequently goes to the movies or skating with them. Sarah is beginning to have disagreements with her parents and is developing, as her mother says, "an attitude problem." This independent attitude has begun to cause some conflicts with her family as she establishes her sense of identity. Sarah is caught between the world of childhood and the world of preadolescence. At times she plays with her "Barbies," while at other times she is trying to dress and behave like a young lady. She has become increasingly aware of her physical self; with braces on her teeth she works hard at fixing her hair and looking "just right."

development view of children and their learning. The cognitive view of learning focuses on the developing mental abilities of students.

Bruner

Bruner's (1968,1960) work concentrated on perception, learning, memory, and other aspects of cognition in children. Bruner argued, with his concept of the "spiral curriculum," that any subject could be taught to any child at any stage of development, if it were presented in the developmentally appropriate manner. According to him, all children have a natural curiosity and a desire to become competent at various learning tasks.

When a task presented to them is too difficult, however, they become bored. Therefore, tasks must be presented at an appropriate level, to challenge the student's current developmental stage of cognitive development. The toddler and preschooler learn through the *enactive mode*, which involves doing things. For example, elementary concepts of physics can be presented using a toy such as a spinning top.

The elementary child (ages six through eleven) learns primarily through the *iconic mode*, which involves the use of pictures or visual illustrations. It is not by accident that elementary textbooks are full of pictures and illustrations. Teachers use bulletin boards and learning posters to further create a visual classroom. Even mathematics workbooks include pictures or visual representations with problems.

Older students, and adults, learn primarily through the *symbolic mode*, using numbers, words, and other symbols. These students can read the text or solve the problems without illustrations or actual examples. In studying the perception in children, Woolfolk (1995) defines it as "the meaning we attach to the information received through our senses" (p. 245). Bruner concluded that children's individual values significantly affect their perceptions, further reinforcing the individual nature of learning.

Piaget

Piaget's (1967, 1952) ideas have been used to form one of the most often cited theories about the development of cognitive abilities. He has greatly influenced teaching in elementary classrooms by describing essential cognitive tasks that children master. (These tasks are discussed in greater detail later in this chapter.)

Piaget believed that the core of human development is rationality and that intelligence develops from the interaction of heredity and environmental forces. Although he tended to believe that biological forces play the greater role in development, Piaget was more concerned with the *how* of thinking and not so much with the *what*; therefore, his views of human development have helped to explain how students think rather than what they are thinking.

As children learn, they create a mental filing system, which Piaget called *schema*. As they learn information that can fit into an existing mental file, they *assimilate*. In addition, as they create new mental files, they *accommodate*. All learners seek to achieve equilibrium between assimilation and accommodation. When science teachers present new concepts and use a startling experiment, they create disequilibrium, which causes students to reconsider their cognitive structure and go beyond their senses.

Piaget described the thinking or cognitive process when he established four stages, with specific cognitive characteristics or behaviors unique to each stage. Although a general time frame is often cited, Piaget did not link these stages specifically to chronological ages or benchmarks. For him, each stage was dependent upon individual developmental behaviors instead of specific ages.

Sensorimotor. Piaget's first stage of cognitive development is called *sensorimotor development*, and it occurs generally from birth to about age two. During this two-year period of time, the infant organizes and coordinates his or her sensations and perceptions of personal actions and/or the physical environment. One of the major cognitive tasks that develops during this period is *object permanence*, knowing that an object exists even when not seen. As a result, when children acquire language, they become good describers of objects and events. Children also learn cause-and-effect relationships during this period. If they drop a spoon, someone picks it up and the dropping becomes a game.

Preoperational. Piaget's next stage of cognitive development is called the *preoperational stage*, which generally occurs between the ages of two and six. During this stage, the child is largely egocentric, shows an increase in language and concept (e.g., size, shape, color) development, and toward the end of the stage is able to use symbolic representation (a block becomes a truck or a hand becomes a cup and saucer). The preschool child does not understand the law of conservation (that things are neither created nor destroyed; only their form changes), and in general has thinking that is intuitive and impulsive. Children do become good explorers as a result of their increased mobility in their physical environment. Most preschool and kindergarten students are still at this level of cognitive development, and many first-grade and even some second-grade students may be at this cognitive level because of their age and individual developmental pattern.

Concrete Operations.   The next stage, *concrete operations*, usually occurs between seven and eleven years of age and is a primary view for understanding the thinking of most elementary children. At this time, major cognitive tasks are accomplished as the child develops an ability to perform logical operations such as adding, subtracting, multiplying, dividing, as well as conserving, reversing, and ordering things by number, size, or class. The child's ability to understand and relate to time and space also matures during this period, although there are still vestiges of egocentric thinking. As a result of improved cognitive skills (conservation and reversibility), elementary students become good investigators of their world and the phenomena that surrounds them. The conservation tasks learned during this time frame form the basis for higher level thought processes.

Formal Operations.   Piaget's last stage, *formal operations*, normally occurs from age eleven through adulthood. Depending on individual characteristics and circumstances, some students in fifth and sixth grades may be transitional to this cognitive level; however, not all individuals function at the formal level of thought for all subjects. Students in transition from the upper elementary grades (fifth and sixth) to junior high school or middle school are just beginning to operate at the formal level. During this stage, there is a marked change in cognitive development, due to the students' ability to understand abstractions and perform hypothetical reasoning. Students are able to function on a symbolic, abstract level as they develop greater mental capacities for conceptualizing events, issues, concepts, and thoughts of what might be. Preadolescents and some adolescents are just beginning to develop the ability to perform hypothetical reasoning with inductive and deductive logic. With intellectual skills greatly improved, students become quite adept at manipulating variables and thinking of several possible outcomes when solving problems.

Implications of Piaget's Stages for Elementary Education.   The stages of development that most concern elementary educators are the preoperational for primary grades, the concrete operational level for most elementary grades, and transition to formal operations for upper elementary grades.

According to Piaget, thinking is "doing," which in turn is rooted in taking action that has been internalized (Madaus, Kellaghan, & Schwab, 1989). Figure 4-3 presents a scenario that puts Piaget's view of learning into practice. In what ways is the curricular program at Middlebrook Elementary School using the principles of cognitive development?

Vygotsky

Like Bruner and Piaget, Vygotsky (1978) recognized the importance of biological factors in cognitive development, but he believed that cognitive development occurred as a result of the interaction between maturational factors and social influences. Vygotsky holds that learning and biological development are not the same but interrelated because the sociocultural milieu plays a role in stimulating overall development. He notes that, at certain times in development, the biological components are the primary force, but, at other times, other social factors effect changes in the individual. Vygotsky believed the following:

- Children construct knowledge as they engage in learning activities.
- Learning leads the overall development of individuals.
- Development cannot be separated from its social context.
- Language plays a critical role in cognitive development.

FIGURE 4-3 Scenario: Piaget's View

At Middlebrook Elementary School, the focus of the curriculum is on developing students' decision-making abilities by getting them to develop their critical-thinking skills. The teachers and administrators adhere to the principles of learning and development advocated by Piaget and other developmental psychologists, particularly their view that knowing and perceiving are a critical part of the developing mind.

Teachers have developed a curriculum that actively involves students in the learning and matches the developmental levels of the students. Younger students learn mathematics concepts by using manipulatives, and they experience scientific principles directly through concrete laboratory experiments or demonstrations (such as observing the behavior of gerbils in class or the germination of seeds). When studying about their environment, students are involved in "magical thinking" and by identifying with a person or situation. Older students in the upper elementary grades are presented with hypothetical "if–then" situations, which are designed to encourage students to reason and develop deductive-thinking skills. The students are asked to think through possible responses or courses of action to make decisions when confronted with a situation or character role. For example, how can an employee of a logging company that destroys the habitat of wildlife (a species of owls) be personally concerned about the environment? Trying to understand their world and deciding on responses and actions provide a problem-solving orientation that is important to learning in the overall instructional program at Middlebrook Elementary School.

Children are encouraged to be active in their learning, and regardless of their subject area, teachers use pictures, demonstrations, and many hands-on experiences to provide students with direct experiences with the concepts they are learning. Students are also encouraged to think, rehearse, and store information as they explore and test all possibilities in solving a problem. They are asked to evaluate the data they are given to support or justify the decisions they make with appropriate evidence. Through such experiences, students learn to think logically and deductively as they move from the concrete operational thinking of the younger child to the formal reasoning of the preadolescent. The curriculum is designed to help students learn how to think!

Vygotsky proposed a view of development that suggested that children operate at two levels of abilities. One level represents the tasks or mental operations that children can actually perform independently on their own. The second level represents the potential developmental level and involves the tasks or problem-solving activities children can do with assistance from an adult or a peer.

As children grow, develop, mature, and interact with others, the potential level of performance becomes the actual level. The gap between independent performance and assisted performance is called the *zone of proximal development*. For example, a psychomotor skill that most young children have mastered by the first grade is the ability to tie their shoelaces on their own. They may not be able to wrap a package and tie a bow without adult/peer assistance. The difference between the ability to tie their shoes and the difficulty in tying a bow on a package represents the zone of proximal development. Vygotsky (1978) maintains that an essential feature of learning is that it creates the zone of proximal development, that is, learning awakens a variety of internal developmental processes that are able to operate only when the child is interacting with people in his enviroment and in cooperation with

Teachers must constantl
dents' learning to deter
and develop curriculu
encourages higher level
must plan daily instruct
zone of proximal develop
is not too easy or too comp

Teachers can also appl
ment as they consider w
classes and kinds of learn
times students who have gi
become teachers in a cooper
as they work with class mem
lower level in the zone of pro

Teachers may use scaffolo
& Ross, 1976) as a technique t
prompts at the different lev   zone of
proximal development. *Scaffolding* occurs when teachers provide the support at the early stages of learning a new skill or concept. For example, a teacher may provide a graphic organizer with all parts labeled to prompt students in writing a friendly letter. As students become proficient and master the skill of letter writing, they no longer need the graphic organizer and prompts.

Multiple Intelligences

Howard Gardner (1983) set forth the argument in *Frames of Mind: The Theory of Multiple Intelligences* that the concept of intelligence is too narrow, and he identified seven intelligences for humans. The seven intelligences or sets of capabilities that all people possess include the following:

- Interpersonal: the intelligence of social understanding
- Bodily-kinesthetic: the intelligence of the whole body and the hands

- Intrapersonal: the intelligence of self-knowledge
- Linguistic: the intelligence of words

matical: the intelligence of
soning

igence of pictures and

igence of tone, rhythm,

nding Gardner's theory
pt to apply his theory to
plication of the theory of
"helps students become
es school more engaging
ables more students to
. 1). Having a broader
kes possible an elementhe strengths and abilimstrong (1994) has
intelligences and calls them logic smart, word smart, picture smart, music smart, body smart, people smart, and self smart. These are discussed in greater detail in Chapter 6.

Learning Research

Numerous studies have been conducted on the factors that influence learning, which has resulted in a knowledge base of 11,000 statistical findings (Wang, Haertel, & Walberg, 1990; Reynolds, Wang, & Walberg, 1992). In analyzing the research on learning, Wang, Haertel, and Walberg (1993/1994) found that factors that impact learning appeared to have a direct or indirect influence. They describe *direct influences* as the time teachers spend on a concept or topic and the kinds and quality of interactions that the teachers have with students. *Indirect influences* are the policies enacted by a school board or state agency, as well as organizational components such as site-based decision making (Wang, Haertel, & Walberg, 1993/1994). They identified twenty-eight factors that appear to influence school learning and are classified into six categories:

- Student aptitude
- Classroom instruction and climate
- Context
- Program design
- School organization
- State and district characteristics

In examining the question "What helps students learn?" Wang, Haertel, and Walberg (1993/1994) found that the different kinds of teaching strategies and classroom environments had almost as much impact on student learning as did student aptitude. They define *student aptitude* as "gender, academic history; and a variety of social, behavioral, motivational, cognitive, and affective characteristics" (p. 76).

This research reinforces the notion that the kinds of teaching–learning interactions in the elementary classroom have a significant impact on student learning. At a time when teachers may feel that the many academic and social factors that impact children's lives are beyond their control, the message from this research suggests that their influence is as powerful as the aptitudes that children bring with them to class. Elizabeth Ballard (N.D.) recalls a teacher's encounter with Teddy, a fifth grader she initially disliked but learned to help and appreciate after his Christmas gift to her (his deceased mom's bracelet and perfume). In his three letters to his teacher after leaving her class as a success, Teddy informed her that he graduated second in his high school class, first in his university class, and then completed medical school. He then asked his teacher to be present at his wedding to sit where his deceased parents would have sat. In responding to his request, his fifth-grade teacher tells him she is honored and congratulates him for his successes. In short, teachers, as they plan curricular experiences, still make a difference in the learning of children, as Elizabeth Ballard shares in her story.

In addition to student aptitude and classroom instruction and climate, Leinhardt (1992) has suggested that the type of knowledge and how that knowledge is acquired are fundamental to learning and teaching. Leinhardt (1992) views knowledge as "a complex network of ideas, facts, principles, actions, and scenes" (p. 22). And the different levels of knowledge (simple or complex), the influence of prior learning, and the ways we interact as we acquire knowledge all have implications for curriculum planning and teaching. Being aware of what is taught as well as how it is taught has consequences for structuring learning experiences such as providing for whole-class instruction, cooperative teams, manipulatives, media programs, role playing, and/or independent study.

In recognizing the role that prior knowledge plays in learning, teachers need to be explicit in incorporating it into the teaching–learning process. Leinhardt's (1992) research makes it clear that learning is a social endeavor and that by using private speech (described by Vygotsky, 1978) and talking with others, students have an opportunity to rehearse new terms and ideas and practice recently learned skills.

The implications from research on learning suggest that as elementary teachers plan for teaching and learning they should pay particular attention to the kinds and quality of interactions they have with their students, assess prior knowledge and build this into the presentation of new knowledge, and present new knowledge in ways that allow students to interact, discuss, and verify what they have learned. For example, if students are learning map skills (latitude and longitude), teachers need to provide a variety of interactions: using a flat map, students move a red string for latitude and a blue string for longitude. In assessing prior knowledge of grids, teachers can make the analogy that latitude and longitude are a way to grid a map. Teachers can also provide opportunities to apply this new learning to a globe and have students talk about and discuss what they have learned.

Brain Research

As Cohen (1995) notes, "learning has always been 'brain based,' but the growing body on brain research helps to provide a biological basis of support as to why educational programs and practices work" (p. 1). Brain research provides support for implementing such educational practices as integrated thematic planning, portfolio assessment, and the recognition of individual uniqueness in learning, because individuals learn differently yet have equally valid ways of constructing meaning. Brain research also suggests that teachers abandon such educational practices as drill and practice, reliance on textbooks, and the use of worksheets (Cohen, 1995).

According to Caine and Caine (1991), "brain research establishes and confirms that multiple complex and concrete experiences are essential for meaningful learning and teaching" (p. 5).

The secret to building on brain research is the development of a school curriculum that works with the way the brain functions, by providing an abundance of experiential learning. Whether learning to read or to solve mathematical problems, the key process in the brain is its ability to incorporate emotions, experiences, and learning to make useful connections as well as to prune the unused and inefficient (Sylvester, 1995). Students need many opportunities to test learning by engaging in such activities as role playing, projects, field trips, listening to community speakers, and even designing and planning many of their own learning experiences to include work on products and services for the school and community.

Hart (1983) has reinforced this notion of learners planning their own experiences by suggesting that the brain functions in a way so as to sort out patterns from all the confusion and to make sense of the world. The more raw material, or input, the learner experiences, the better the brain becomes at sorting out relevant data and creating meaning. The more opportunities students have to see, hear, touch, and manipulate, the more patterns and programs they create. Throughout life, the brain has *plasticity*, the ability to "grow and adapt to environmental stimuli" (Cohen, 1995, p. 4), and the architecture of the

brain changes as a result of experiences in life. As students encounter complex events, Caine and Caine (1991) note that each interaction embeds

> information in the brain and links what is being learned to the rest of the learner's current experiences, past knowledge, and future behavior. The primary focus for educators (teachers), therefore, should be on expanding the quantity and quality of ways in which a learner is exposed to content and context. (p. 6)

This process is called *immersion*. According to Cohen (1995), the implications of immersion and other aspects of brain research "cut against the grain of many school practices" (p. 4) and will result in more interdisciplinary instruction with less emphasis on textbooks and worksheets.

Children with Learning Challenges

Children come to elementary school with a wide variety of academic abilities. Most curriculum planning is directed at students who are in the midrange of ability, but teachers also must recognize and plan for students with abilities at each end of the academic ability continuum. Children who are outside the midrange of abilities that you may encounter are academically challenged or mentally retarded students; physically challenged students; students with communication, emotional, or behavioral challenges; and high-functioning or gifted students.

Academically Challenged Students.   Mental retardation has often been viewed as a score below a particular point on an intelligence test, frequently below 70 IQ points. The American Association on Mental Deficiencies (1992) has defined mental retardation this way:

> substantial limitations in present intellectual functioning . . . characterized by . . . subaverage intellectual functioning existing concurrently with related limitations in two or more of the follow-

ing . . . skill areas: communication, self-care, home living, social skills, community use, self-direction, health and safety, functional academics, leisure and work. (p. 5)

Intellectual functioning is usually measured by IQ tests, but IQ alone is not sufficient to diagnose a child as mentally retarded. There should also be indications of problems in adaptive behavior. The ranges of IQ scores used to describe the degree of retardation are 50 to 70–75, mild; 35 to 50–55, moderate; 20 to 30–35, severe; below 20–25, profound.

Most elementary teachers will not have moderate to severely retarded children in their classrooms unless the school district participates in a full-inclusion program. But many elementary teachers work with mildly retarded children in their regular classrooms.

The curriculum planned for students who are at the low end of the academic ability continuum must include an emphasis on concrete and kinesthetic experiences. In addition, the content dimension of the curriculum must be addressed in terms of learning goals and expectations that are achievable for individual students. According to Woolfolk (1995), the learning goals for mildly retarded elementary students include developing competence in reading, writing, and arithmetic; knowledge of the school and local environment; appropriate social behaviors; and personal interests and skills.

In working with students with special learning needs, teachers may find it necessary to plan a modified curriculum. The following six suggestions may prove helpful in meeting the diverse learning needs of students in an elementary classroom.

■ *Establish learning stations or centers*. These stations or centers should contain resources, experiments, activities, games, manipulatives, and computers/technology for students to use individually or in small groups. If instructions for the stations or centers are needed, they should be clearly written to minimize student dependence on the teacher for completing the activities.

■ *Reduce the amount of in-class work and outside-class assignments to be done*. Careful editing of outside assignments, of questions or problems to answer, and of experiments to be performed will help the student identify the major focus of the instructional task. The basics, or essentials, of the lesson content should remain.

■ *Provide material in a format other than reading*. Teachers can audiotape material from the textbook, questions to be answered, problems to be solved, or other material so that students can listen as they read along.

■ *Provide an outline or brief summary*. An outline helps students follow the major points in the lesson by listing content in sequential order. A summary provides an overview of major points and helps students focus on important information.

■ *Use visuals (charts, posters, graphic organizers) to illustrate concepts*. When introducing new concepts or information, teachers can use pictures, posters, charts, or graphic organizers to illustrate important aspects. The visuals can be used in combination with learning stations or learning center activities or any of the other ways to modify the lesson.

■ *Simplify lengthy passages, technical descriptions, or complex problems*. The lesson presentation, activities, examples, and discussions provided by the teacher can make the instructional material more understandable to students. Thus teachers should edit long, written passages from the textbook, focus on technical vocabulary, and/or reduce complex procedures to the simplest steps.

These six ways of modifying a lesson can help you reach students who need the information presented in a different way because of their individual academic abilities. These suggestions are merely a beginning point. Modifying information to accommodate special needs is a challenge and often time consuming, but the results of this effort can be astonishing. For more information about teaching academically challenged students, consult *The School Survival Guide for Kids with Learning Differences* (Cummings & Fisker, 1991).

Physically Challenged Students.   Many teachers encounter students with physical challenges. Physically challenged students range in mobility from those with orthopedic or prosthetic devices to those who are in wheelchairs. Other physical challenges some students face include hearing impairment, vision impairment, seizures (epilepsy), and palsy. Teachers who have these students in their classrooms must modify the curriculum in ways that match or meet each learner's needs. *Lee, the Rabbit with Epilepsy* (Moss, 1989) and *Don't Worry, He Won't Get Far on Foot* (Callahan, 1989) are useful resources for teachers with physically challenged students.

Students with Communication, Emotional, or Behavioral Challenges.   In addition to physically challenged students, you may also encounter students with a variety of disorders in communication, emotion, behavior, or attention and hyperactivity. Communication disorders include speech impairments (stuttering and inarticulateness) and problems with oral language development (nonverbal, qualitatively different, delayed, or interrupted). Emotional/behavioral disorders include behavior that is aggressive, destructive, disobedient, uncooperative, distractible, disruptive, and persistent (Quay & Peterson, 1987). Children with hyperactivity and attention disorders exhibit atypical, excessive restlessness, are often inattentive to tasks, have great difficulty sustaining attention, and behave impulsively. For more information about teaching students with communication, emotional, or behavioral challenges, see Kauffman (1997) and Williams (1992).

Elementary teachers may encounter any or all of these special students in their classrooms, as more and more school districts move to *full inclusion*—the involvement of all students, regardless of their special needs, in regular classes. Hardman (1994) notes that supporters of full inclusion believe that children learn best from other children and that they all have the need to belong and feel wanted within an environment that allows them to have fun, make noise, laugh, cry, take risks, and even get hurt. Children need to experience the real world, not an isolated, unreal classroom environment.

Academically Gifted Students.   Another group of students with special learning needs is the gifted and talented. Many states require modifications in the curriculum to accommodate the needs of gifted students. The main issue in meeting the academic abilities of these students is determining *giftedness*. Gardner (1983) and Armstrong (1994) have identified and discussed seven kinds of intelligences, or potential areas of giftedness. Guilford (1988), in describing the structure of the intellect, suggests that there are 180 kinds of intelligences.

Renzulli (1982) notes that educators should distinguish between academic giftedness and creative giftedness. Generally, students who have a talent that they pursue beyond the classroom, such as working at a computer, remain engaged as they proceed. These students are motivated to stay at the computer for hours until they accomplish the task(s) they have set for themselves. Other students who are considered gifted take principles they have learned and pose questions that propel their learning and force them to delve further into the topic. These students may not be equally motivated in all they learn; their specific interests may guide their level of commitment to any task.

Giftedness is a complex issue but is generally considered to include above-average academic ability, a creative ability, and a high degree of motivation and commitment to learning tasks (Renzulli & Reis, 1991). The identification of truly gifted students is still difficult for most teachers. Walton (1961) posed seven questions in a study of gifted students that still provide valid guidelines for teachers:

- Which students in your class learn easily and rapidly?

- Which students use common sense and practical knowledge as they solve problems?

- Which students easily remember what they have heard or learned?

- Which students seem to have a depth of general knowledge—they know what other students don't?

- Which students have a well-developed vocabulary and accurately use a large number of words?

- Which students are able to see relationships and comprehend concepts and meanings?

- Which students are alert and observant and respond quickly to situations?

Although many states require special certification for teachers of gifted students and special classes for those students, many elementary teachers will have to accommodate these learners in their classrooms or at least participate in the identification of such students. For this reason, teachers should develop lessons that promote conceptual thinking and abstract thinking. As students encounter new and abstract concepts, they should be encouraged to express themselves in creative (nontraditional) ways. Woolfolk (1995) suggests that teachers need to be creative, flexible, and unthreatened by the abilities of gifted and talented students. For more information about teaching academically gifted students, see Pendarvis, Howley, & Howley (1990).

OTHER VIEWS OF DEVELOPMENT

If you ask anyone, "What is the purpose of going to school?" the first response would be, "to learn." This section focuses on learning research

that has influenced educational practice and includes discussion of behaviorism, humanism, and constructivism. Behaviorism is one of the best examples of how experimental studies in learning impacted not only learning in the elementary school but teaching as well (Madaus, Kellaghan, & Schwab, 1989).

Behaviorism

Behaviorism is a view of human development that emphasizes the impact of the environment on the individual and the resulting behavior. Green (1989) states that "the central tenet of behaviorism is that individuals should be studied . . . in terms of observable characteristics" (p. 115). Behaviorism is built on the foundation established by Pavlov's work that distinguished between innate (unconditioned) and learned (conditioned) reflexes. By demonstrating the principle of *classical conditioning* as a procedure by which a neutral stimulus comes to elicit a response by being paired with a stimulus that regularly evokes the response, Pavlov greatly advanced the scientific analysis of behavior (Green, 1989). Through the classical conditioning process, responses can be acquired or eliminated.

Behaviorism has been further developed and systematized by Watson (1924), Thorndike (1931, 1933) and Skinner (1948, 1953, 1968). Green (1989) says that Watson took an extreme position when he said he could train children to become whatever he wished (doctor, lawyer, etc.) regardless of ability, talent, or tendency. Thorndike proposed the *law of effect*, which focused on goal-oriented behavior: the law of effect

> holds that responses increase or decrease in likelihood as a function of the effects they produce. Sometimes the effects make the previous response more likely to occur in the future; sometimes they make the responses less likely. (Green, 1989, p. 117)

The law of effect added to our understanding of learning in that it provided an explanation for how the likelihood of a response is affected by the consequences of the response.

Skinner (1953, 1968) built upon Thorndike's work to help explain the acquisition of new behaviors. Skinner's view of learning is built on the idea of *operant conditioning*, which is very different from classical conditioning. Operant conditioning, often associated with reinforcement, emphasizes the individual's operating or acting on the environment, with behavior controlled by external consequences. In such a view of development, an individual's behavior results from the controlling forces in the environment.

According to Skinner (1953, 1968), as we operate on our environment, the consequences of our actions shape our development (who and what we are) and the consequences can be *rewarding* (reinforcement) or *punishing* (punishment).

Figure 4-4 shows an application of behaviorism in a school situation in the Friendswood School District. It emphasizes the use of rewards in the school environment to shape learning behavior. Think about the different ways, if any, that the teachers are getting the students to prepare for the state achievement test.

FIGURE 4-4   Scenario: Behaviorism View

> With all the rhetoric about declining scores on achievement tests, Friendswood School District now requires elementary students in grades 4–6 to take a basic literacy test—reading, writing, mathematics, with some general knowledge in science and social studies. The elementary teachers are somewhat nervous because they are held responsible for getting the students to pass this basic skills test. The charge to the faculty was to have as many students as possible pass this test. The teachers have decided to use rewards to help produce short-term goals.
>
> The administration has indicated that as many students as possible must pass this test. Confronted with this dilemma, the teachers developed a series of drill and practice exercises for each curriculum area (reading and writing, mathematics, science, and social studies) for each grade level (4–6). These computer-generated exercises became part of the tutorial sessions that were offered at different times (before, after, and during) the school day. As students worked the series of exercises, the computer tracked each student and each class for correct responses. Each student got a token for taking the exercise and the top student for each day received five tokens.
>
> Students, faculty, and parent volunteers were responsible for monitoring these tutorial sessions as well as answering any questions that the students might have. The monitors of the tutorial program were not concerned with the students' in-depth understanding of the answers to the questions, but rather how many they answered correctly and what could they remember over the short term.
>
> The token reward system was devised to help motivate the students to attend the tutorial practice sessions. Students earned tokens that could be "cashed in" for prizes—records, tapes, posters, movie tickets, food coupons (pizza, burgers, and nachos). Many of these items were donated by local businesses. It was hoped that through the drill and practice exercises (responding to a core of questions prepared for each curriculum area), coupled with an incentive/reward system, the students would attend the sessions and a high percentage of them would pass the tests.

Humanism

Another view of learning and development is *humanism*, which places a strong emphasis on the role of self and self-fulfillment in the development of the individual. The humanistic view recognizes the importance of a student's needs, and the degree to which he or she fulfills these needs is a key organizing principle. This developmental theory was described by Maslow (1971, 1968, 1954) and supported by the work of Rogers (1961, 1969).

Maslow (1968) proposed a theory of *need gratification*, which he saw as "the most important single principle underlying all development . . . that binds together the multiplicity of human motives" (p. 55). He believed that individuals are wanting beings and that no sooner is one desire satisfied than another takes its place. Maslow elaborated on this theory by arguing that each person has a hierarchy of needs that must be satisfied. These needs range from basic physiological requirements to love and self-esteem. Biehler (1993), in interpreting Maslow's hierarchy, says,

> when a person has the lower needs (physiological, safety, belongingness and love, esteem) satisfied, he [or she] will feel motivated to satisfy the higher being . . . needs (self-actualization, knowing and understanding, aesthetic)—not because of a deficit but because of a desire to gratify higher needs. Being needs are the basis for self-actualization. (p. 411)

Self-actualization, the highest need of the hierarchy, refers to the full attainment of one's talents, abilities, and potential. It is the relatively rare individuals who have their lower needs sufficiently satisfied so that they can develop the motive or drive for self-actualization. Maslow found that self-actualized people attain a degree of independence from society and are much less conforming. They seem less molded and shaped by the social environment and remain more spontaneous, although rarely behaving in unconventional ways (Crain, 1992). Maslow (1968) distinguishes self-actualized people from most in that they are unusually healthy psychologically, perceiving everyday life realistically and accepting it without defensiveness.

The applications of Maslow's theory of development suggest that educators should make sure that the lower-level needs of students are met. Biehler (1974) notes that

> students will be more likely to be primed to seek satisfaction of the needs to understand and know in [their] classes if they are physically comfortable, feel safe and relaxed, have a sense of belonging, and experience self-esteem. (p. 414)

The greater the extent to which students have their basic needs satisfied, the more likely it is that teachers will be able to foster motivation for higher needs and promote healthy development. Growth, as a part of development, is the result of a never-ending series of situations offering freedom of choice between the attractions and dangers of safety and growth (Biehler, 1993).

Rogers (1961, 1969) has added to the humanistic view of learning and development by applying his principles of psychotherapy to educational settings. He views the child's *perception* of the world as more important in understanding the child's development than his or her actual behavior. In studying the self, Rogers believes in utilizing both direct observations and psychological tests to measure growth. He further suggests that individuals (teachers and students) could gain a greater understanding of themselves through intensive group experiences which he calls *learner-centered* teaching (1969). This approach is essentially an ultimate version of the discovery approach to teaching (Biehler, 1993). Rogers (1961, 1969) contends that learner-centered teaching helps the participants explore their attitudes and interpersonal relationships. Figure 4-5 describes Prest Elementary School as it is now and as it was before a humanistic approach was applied to their school situation. In many respects, the curriculum is student- and

FIGURE 4-5   Scenario: Humanism

Students and faculty at Prest Elementary School are proud of their school and take pride in their contributions for making it a nice place to be. To promote student and faculty harmony, as well as individual development, the faculty and students regularly attend sessions where they discuss needs and problems and share successes. The key ingredient in this school is a sense of well-being because students feel good about themselves, and teachers are eager to affirm each child.

The teachers are dedicated to helping each student achieve his or her maximum potential because they believe each student has special talents to be developed. In this environment, students are anxious to tell about themselves—what they have learned, accomplished, and what they hope to achieve. This caring attitude permeates the entire school.

In creating such a learner-centered approach, the focus of instruction is on the needs and interests of the students—not the instructional results. Teachers are given time during the school day to visit other schools where such programs have been implemented and are provided with ongoing support from the principal and central office staff. Students participate in group activities so that they can explore attitudes and interpersonal relationships as they consider their strengths and shortcomings. Through such opportunities, the students learn to better analyze who they are and where they want to go. As teachers increase their praise vocabulary, go out of their way to let students know when they are correct, and offer suggestions in a positive way when students were not correct, students become more concerned with their learning.

After five years of this kind of approach, Prest Elementary School is what it is today. Ask most students or teachers how they feel about the school, and they will tell you that they are happy to be at school and that they think they are learning what they need to know to be successful in their own way.

---

faculty-centered. Can you identify the concepts of humanism in the scenario? If so, what are they?

Cognitive development (which was discussed in the section on cognitive development of elementary students), behaviorism, and humanism are three major views of learning and development. No single theory adequately explains human learning, development, and behavior, but each one contributes significantly to our understanding of the individual student and provides insights for teachers establishing educational programs for children. Those who are concerned about the total development of the elementary student will be able to draw upon the concepts of all the theories to produce a well-rounded educational program.

Constructivism

In addition to theories of learning, researchers are concerned with how children come to make sense of their world as how they construct knowledge. There has been much written on constructivism. Brooks and Brooks (1993) contend that if educational reform is to take place it must start with "how the students learn and how teachers teach" (pp. 3–4). They go on to say that construction of understanding of the world we live in is key if we are going to make sense of new experiences and relate them to previous learning. If the proposition of learning by constructing new understandings is accepted, then educators need to invite students to experience the opportunities in their world and to empower them to ask questions and to answer them. With such experiences, understanding of the complexities of the world comes forth.

Through experiences, students search for meaning, learn to appreciate uncertainty, and seek answers in a responsible way. Noddings (1990) states that the constructivist premise "recognizes the power of the environment to press for adaptation, the temporality of knowledge, and the existence of multiple selves behaving in consonance with the rules of various subcultures" (p. 12). Often, the curriculum is something to be "covered," rather than something that helps students truly understand their world and be successful. That practice comes from the notion that there is a fixed body of knowledge that students need to learn and that the curriculum is an absolute (Brooks & Brooks, 1993). Teachers tend to be reluctant to tamper with the curriculum, in spite of knowing that not all students are understanding the concepts. Gardner (1991) notes that there is a body of research that documents that even when students are successful in school, they "typically do not display an adequate understanding of the material and concepts with which they have been working" (p. 3).

Constructivism is included in this chapter because students' cognitive abilities are significant in the process of formulating understandings. To be an effective teacher, you need to have an understanding of cognitive theory; then you can interpret and appreciate student responses in the context of cognitive developmental theory (Brooks & Brooks, 1993).

In the following journal entries, it is clear that this first-year teacher has elements of constructivism in her plans as she prepares for the opening of school:

9/2

Here it is, Labor Day, the day before I start my new job. I'm scared to death. Last week, I had a meeting with my team teacher. We talked about what we are going to teach for the first few weeks. It was very sketchy. She also talked about something called "the big picture." I'm not quite sure what she meant. She gave me an example. If only I could remember it now. We're starting the microscope unit. Oh, that's another thing. I always thought that we would just follow the textbook. She tells me to "start thinking in terms of units." If I could only get an opening to start this unit off with I'd be a little more at ease.

9/3

. . . Tomorrow with the kids I have to have a grabber lesson. Tomorrow, I'm THE TEACHER. My team teacher told me to get an idea of what the microscope unit is all about. Nothing has come to me yet. Perhaps, if I could only relax, I could think.

9/4

It happened! This morning around 4 a.m. I got an idea. A microscope "takes a closer look at life." My topic today was "Taking a Closer Look at Life." I paralleled a story about people wanting to take a closer look at what was happening at the scene of a fire to taking a closer look through a microscope lens. Not a very close analogy, but, in a sense, it worked. (Brooks & Brooks, 1993, pp. 11–12)

Although the journal certainly reflects elements of constructivist teaching, this new teacher did limit the students' opportunity when she structured the plan and did not invite the students to explore the topic, "Taking a Closer Look at Life." It is evident from this scenario that being a constructivist teacher is complex and developmental, and requires "continual analysis of both curriculum planning and instructional methodologies during the process of learning to be a teacher" (Brooks & Brooks, 1993, p. 13).

Yager (1991) offers some constructivist strategies that teachers can use to invite students to explore, propose explanations and solutions, and take action:

Invitation to Learn

■ Observing the surroundings for points of interest

■ Asking questions

■ Considering responses to questions

■ Noting discrepant events

■ Identifying situations in which student perceptions vary

Learning to Explore

■ Engaging in play that is focused

■ Brainstorming possible alternatives

■ Looking for information

■ Experimenting with different materials

■ Designing a model and defining parameters

■ Collecting, organizing, and analyzing data

■ Implementing problem-solving strategies

■ Discussing possible solutions with other students

■ Assessing choices and identifying risks

Taking Action

■ Making decisions

■ Applying knowledge and skills

■ Sharing information with others

■ Asking new and different questions

■ Developing products and promoting ideas

■ Using models to elicit discussion

This list indicates that elementary teachers who are interested in implementing constructivist strategies in their classrooms need to do several things:

■ Encourage students to take and accept student initiatives for learning.

■ Involve students with primary sources as well as concrete materials.

■ Frame tasks in cognitive terms (classify, analyze, and predict).

■ Respond favorably when students lead the lesson and suggest ways to alter the strategies as well as the content.

■ Value and encourage discussions that explore contradictions and generate hypotheses with students.

■ Encourage students to ask thoughtful and open-ended questions.

■ Use wait time when questioning and receiving student responses in order to construct relationships and create metaphors (Brooks & Brooks, 1993).

Constructivism not only finds its way into teaching practices, but it also has merit when resolving conflicts between students. Carlsson-Paige and Levin (1992) observe using a constructivist approach teaches elements of conflict resolution that involve "defining the problem, brainstorming solutions, using negotiation skills, and choosing solutions that satisfy both sides" (p. 11). They go on to suggest that there are "many conflict-resolution activities and techniques that can be incorporated into the class curriculum. . . . [And] children need lots of opportunities to experiment with their developing skills" (p. 13).

MORAL DEVELOPMENT: THINKING AND REASONING

In addition to the learning theories discussed previously, it is also appropriate to discuss the development of moral thinking and reasoning in elementary students. Moral development concerns the rules and conventions that individuals use in their interactions with other people. In studying these rules, developmental psychologists typically examine three different domains of moral development: thought, action, and feeling.

Piaget

As a part of his study of the cognitive development of children, Piaget (1965) studied the development of moral reasoning. Piaget recognized and acknowledged that a person's cognitive development is paralleled by the individual's moral development. He saw moral development as involving the acceptance of social rules and concern for equality and justice in relationships. According to Helms and Turner (1986), Piaget considered morality to be a set of rules handed down from adults to children and "through training and practice, children learn to respect these standards of conduct" (p. 381). Piaget (1965) proposed three stages of moral development, which he called the premoral period, the period of moral reciprocity or moral realism, and the moral relativity period.

In the *premoral period* (birth to seven years), the child initially focuses on self and is highly egocentric. In the first two years, the child has little awareness of rules and is not capable of making moral judgments because of limited cognitive development and a high degree of egocentrism. In the later part of the premoral period, there is a shift from self to a focus on authority. Rules that govern the child's behavior come from a parent or other authority figure, and the child believes that any deviation from the rules will result in some form of punishment. Children often focus on the consequences of their actions rather than on their intentions; as a result, it is not uncommon for them to report when others have broken the rules.

In the second period, *moral reciprocity*, or *moral realism* (eight to eleven years), the child moves from an exclusive focus on authority to more prosocial behavior and a concern for interactions with others in specific situations. During this period, the student develops a sense of autonomy and, according to Schiamberg (1988), moral behavior is influenced by the student's recognition of the following:

■ Social rules are not absolute and can be challenged when necessary.

■ It is not always wrong to break the rules.

■ In understanding the behavior of others, feelings and viewpoints should be considered.

■ The nature of the rule that was broken, the intentions of the person, and the type of correction (retribution or restitution) should be taken into account if there is to be any punishment.

One of the dangers of this period is that the student may become inflexible in moral reasoning and develop an eye-for-an-eye level of morality in dealing with others.

The *moral relativism* period (age twelve through adolescence and adulthood) normally begins during the junior high-school years and continues into adulthood. Piaget recognized that not every individual attains this stage of moral development, because moral development is tied to cognitive development and not all individuals attain the formal level of cognitive development. At this stage, individuals view rules as products of mutual consent and respect based on certain principles, and they can make realistic applications of moral values in specific situations, taking all factors into account. Moral decisions, therefore, tend to be based on the specific situation and the circumstances involved and have a social, logical, and cooperative quality.

Kohlberg

Kohlberg (1981, 1968) proposes an expanded theory of moral development. He believes that moral development is based on moral reasoning that unfolds in three different levels with two stages in each level. The first level (birth to nine) he calls *preconventional morality*, in which the child shows no internalization of moral values and little conception of socially acceptable or moral behavior. In the first stage of this level, *obedience and punishment orientation*, children generally obey rules in order to avoid punishment. Children normally conform to rules imposed on them by people in authority. In the second stage, *naively egoistic orientation*, children are motivated to behave correctly because they believe they will earn some concrete or tangible reward. It is not unusual to hear parents and adults telling children that if they behave in a specific way—to sit still and not talk, for example—they will get a treat.

In Kohlberg's second level, *conventional morality* (ages ten through fifteen), students learn the nature of authority in society as well as family. In the third stage, *good boy-nice girl orientation*, students exhibit considerable conforming behavior and learn to recognize that they must abide by the rules in order to receive approval and praise. This conformity in their behavior fosters an internal awareness of rules and, therefore, promotes respect for others, especially those in authority. In this stage, students become enforcers of the rules and tell or tattle on those students who break the rules. In the fourth stage, *law and order orientation*, the focus shifts to organizations and institutions in society that provide rules that guide or govern behavior. The school and the church, as well as many youth organizations (scouts, for example), often codify appropriate behavior for students. Children learn to recite various pledges or oaths as their moral reasoning becomes codified.

Sometimes an intervening stage occurs between stages four and five, as the student begins to question seriously society's definition of what is right and wrong. This questioning of accepted behaviors, while a rejection of conventional morality, does contribute to self-realization. Because this intervening stage corresponds with the preadolescent and adolescent years and the struggle for independence from adult supervision, it is not surprising that students also tend to question and reject some of the values of their parents.

The third and final level of Kohlberg's moral development theory is called *post conventional morality* (age sixteen through adulthood) and represents the highest level of moral reasoning. At this level, morality is completely internalized—not based on the standards of others—and the individual reaches a mature understanding of moral behavior. In the fifth stage, *contractual legalistic orientation*, individuals, especially teenagers

and young adults, select moral principles that guide their personal behavior. Students are also careful not to violate the rights and wills of others. The sixth stage, *universal ethical principle orientation*, marks the onset of a true conscience that prompts individuals to select the most appropriate forms of behavior that affirm their rights as well as the rights of others. Kohlberg believes that relatively few people attain stage six of moral reasoning.

Gilligan

Gilligan (1982) observes that there are differences in the ways boys and girls respond to the moral dilemmas used to identify the level of moral reasoning. According to Gilligan, males are more consistent with Kohlberg's stages, as they base their responses on their understanding of concepts such as justice and individual rights. Females, however, give different responses that tend to rely more on their understanding of and experiences with personal relationships and interpersonal behaviors. Rather than responding to the moral dilemmas, females tend to use, to a greater degree, a "care" perspective.

Gilligan and Attanucci (1988) note that "individuals know and use both a justice and a care orientation" (p. 233) in responding to the moral dilemmas presented, but women tend to use a care focus more often than men. For example, when asked about the decision to smoke or not to smoke, a justice-oriented response would indicate a yes or no based on some standard of what is right or wrong. A care-oriented response would acknowledge the peer pressure to smoke and other motivations some people have for smoking, but at the same time would recognize that in a peer situation, the person's "real friends" would accept the decision made.

Understanding of moral development is important for educators because it helps not only in the development of curriculum but also in the ways we structure learning in the classroom and the ways we interact with students. Research suggests that moral development in elementary students can be enhanced by the way elementary teachers structure the classroom environment. If we want students to be more self-regulated and move away from a classroom atmosphere that is controlling and forces strict adherence to rules because of the threat of punishment, then teachers must be verbal, rational, caring, and create a cooperative climate (Berk, 1996). Likewise, students who work in an environment that emphasizes conformity based on the threat of punishment will obey the rules, but their growth of self-control and regulation are limited (Eggen & Kauchak, 1997).

Teachers can provide opportunities for students to grow in moral development by "creating a moral community in the classroom" (Lickona, 1993, p. 69) and by encouraging them to share and analyze their behaviors and views. Eggen and Kauchak (1994) suggest the following guidelines for teachers to use in conducting discussions with moral dilemmas:

- ■ Use concrete conflicts (i.e. an example of a story the class has been reading where one of the characters stole something) and focus on alternative ways of dealing with the conflict.

- ■ Have students role play various characters or individuals to clarify roles and perspectives of the various people involved.

- ■ Have students discuss what they would have done had they been in the same situation and tell why they made that choice.

- ■ Encourage students to examine different courses of action and discuss the pros and cons of each.

- ■ Do not support one student's response over another's.

By incorporating respect and responsibility in the classroom community, providing opportunities for interaction with peers, exposing students to thinking about moral dilemmas, and involving students in such discussions, teachers present students with the opportunity to apply, learn, and assess their moral development reasoning.

Educators need to be knowledgeable not only of the general principles of human development but also of the basic theories of learning as they plan learning activities for elementary students. Only by understanding the physical and cognitive nature of the learner can we plan a developmentally appropriate curriculum.

SUMMARY

This chapter has presented the role of the psychological foundations in planning and developing curricular programs for elementary students. The content of the chapter revolves around the various ways psychological principles are associated with the learning process and shape the curriculum. In addition, the three general principles of development were discussed as a guiding framework for development. These principles suggest that, as children grow and develop, there are individual differences that emerge, and as children move from stage to stage and mature, the range of abilities among them widens.

A major part of the chapter was devoted to the cognitive theory of learning. This view of how human beings learn was presented in great detail. The purpose of the scenario that accompanied the discussion was to provide the application of the cognitive theory in a real or contextual situation.

The chapter also discussed behaviorism and humanism as theories of development. It ended with a discussion of moral development and how children acquire the rules and behaviors that govern their interaction with others, especially in regard to gender differences in moral development, as described by Gilligan.

The information and descriptions in this chapter make it evident that there is no single, all-encompassing theory for explaining the physical, cognitive, social, and moral development of children. Understanding a variety of theories and perspectives gives you an opportunity to determine how each contributes to understanding the elementary child, a perspective that in turn is applied to the curriculum planning process.

>>>
<<<<<<<<<<<<<<<<<<<<<<<<<<<<<<<<<<<<<<<<<<<<<<<<<<<<<<<<<<<<<<<<<<<<<<<<<<<<<

■ YOUR TURN

1. Read the following quote from Tracy Kidder's book, *Among Schoolchildren*:

   Clarence was a small, light brown-skinned boy with large eyes and deep dimples. Chris watched his journeys to the pencil sharpener. They were frequent. Clarence took the longest possible route around the room, walking heel-to-toe and brushing the back of one leg with the shin of the other at every step—a cheerful little dance across the blue carpet, around the perimeter of desks, and along the back wall, passing under the American flag, which didn't quite brush his head. Reaching the sharpener, Clarence would turn his pencil into a stunt plane, which did several loop-the-loops before plunging in the hole. (p. 7)

   a.   What thoughts come to mind as you read this passage? Do you remember doing this as an elementary student? Why was it so important to get up and take a stroll? Record your thoughts in your journal. Why do you think Clarence takes the longest way to the pencil sharpener? When he reaches the sharpener, he transforms his pencil into an airplane—why do you think he does this?

   b.   Now that you have read the chapter and this passage, how does the information presented in the previous pages help you better understand these boys—and perhaps yourself when you were their age?

   c.   Visit an elementary classroom and confirm that children take the longest way to the trash can, pencil sharpener, and/or just to get materials. Draft a few questions and, if possible, survey the students about what they like best about school, their favorite subject, and what they do best physically and cognitively. See if you can validate the general principles of learning presented at the beginning of Chapter 4.

2. Below is the mission statement of P.S. Elementary School 2061. Read and identify the ways that learning and development are manifested in these short paragraphs.

   Mission of P.S. Elementary School 2061

   We, at P.S. Elementary School 2061 believe that each child is special, with unique physical, intellectual, and psychological needs and abilities. The instructional and curricular program is flexible and designed to meet the physical, emotional, social, cognitive, and moral growth that will take place as each student develops and matures.

   Students will be active learners who will take responsibility for their learning. Such learning will take place in a classroom that is rich in print materials, equipment for exploring, and adults who are available to guide each student's learning. All students will have opportunities to describe, explore, discover, and perform. Through such experiences, the students at P.S. Elementary School 2061 will develop trust in themselves and their teachers, confidence in their abilities, and an independence that is built on an awareness of who they are and where they want to go in the future.

The curriculum is designed collaboratively to better reflect the larger community from which our students come. The hope is to have a closer home-school alliance for the good of each student. The faculty, administration, and staff at P.S. Elementary School 2061 are guided by the belief that all students are capable of learning and they should be given every opportunity to develop their individual talents.

a. Is the mission clear for P.S. Elementary School 2061? Why or why not?

b. As you read this mission statement, does a visual of what this school is like come through? What type of instructional program do they have at P.S. Elementary School 2061? How do they treat their students? What type of interactions take place between teacher and students? Record your comments in your journal.

3. Along with the theories of learning presented in this chapter regarding the development of cognitive abilities, Howard Gardner proposed a somewhat different view, called the "multiple intelligences":

■ Interpersonal intelligence

■ Bodily-kinesthetic intelligence

■ Intrapersonal intelligence

■ Linguistic intelligence

■ Logical-mathematical intelligence

■ Spatial intelligence

■ Musical intelligence

The question of *How do we learn?* has been answered by Gardner. What research has been done to substantiate his conclusions? How do his ideas differ from those of Piaget, Bruner, and Vygotsky? What implications do his ideas have for planning an elementary school curriculum?

4. In investigating the influence of B. F. Skinner on the operation of the elementary school and the kinds of teaching and learning activities used, answer the questions that follow, based on a visit to an elementary school.

a. Can various forms of behaviorism be found in the elementary school? Examine how the curriculum is organized, investigate the type of instructional strategies teachers use, and find out the discipline/management systems that are employed and implemented.

b. What is the basic premise that governs how the elementary classroom is managed? Who is in control? Who makes the decisions? How are children acknowledged for answers and good behavior?

5. What implications does brain research have for curriculum development in the elementary school?

■ REFERENCES

American Association on Mental Deficiencies. (1992). *Mental retardation: Definition, classification, and systems of support* (9th ed.). Washington, DC: American Association on Mental Deficiencies.

Armstrong, T. (1994). Multiple intelligences: Seven ways to approach curriculum. *Educational Leadership*, *52*(3), pp. 26–28.

Ballard, E. (N.D.) *Three Letters from Teddy*. Unpublished manuscript.

Berk, L. (1996). *Child development* (4th ed.). Boston: Allyn & Bacon.

Biehler, R. F. (1974). *Psychology applied to teaching* (2nd ed.). Atlanta: Houghton Mifflin.

Biehler, R. F. (1993). *Psychology applied to teaching* (7th ed.). Boston: Houghton Mifflin.

Brooks, J. G., & Brooks, M. G. (1993). *In search of understanding: The case for constructivist classrooms*. Alexandria, VA: Association for Supervision and Curriculum Development.

Bruner, J. S. (1968). *Toward a theory of instruction.* New York: W. W. Norton & Co.

Bruner, J. S. (1960). *The process of education.* Cambridge, MA: Harvard University Press.

Caine, R. N., & Caine, G. (1991). *Making connections: Teaching and the human brain.* Alexandria, VA: Association for Supervision and Curriculum Development.

Callahan, J. (1989). *Don't worry, he won't get far on foot: The autobiography of a dangerous man.* New York: Morrow.

Carlsson-Paige, N., & Levin, D. E. (1992, November). Making peace in violent times: A constructivist approach to conflict resolution. *Young Children 48*(1), 4–13.

Cohen, P. (1995, September). Understanding the brain: Educators seek to apply brain research. *ASCD Education Update, 37*(7), 1, 4.

Crain, W. C. (1992). *Theories of development concepts and applications* (3rd ed.). Upper Saddle River, NJ: Merrill/Prentice Hall.

Cummings, R. W., & Fisker, G. L. (1991). *The school survival guide for kids with learning differences.* Minneapolis, MN: Free Spirit Publishing.

Eggen, P., & Kauchak, D. (1994). *Educational psychology: Classroom connections* (2nd ed.). Upper Saddle River, NJ: Merrill/Prentice Hall.

Eggen, P., & Kauchak, D. (1997). *Educational psychology: Windows on classrooms* (3rd ed.). Upper Saddle River, NJ: Merrill/Prentice Hall.

Entwistle, D., & Hayduk, L. (1981). Academic expectations and the school achievement of young children. *Sociology of Education, 54*(1), 34–50.

Erikson, E. (1963). *Childhood and society* (2nd ed.). New York: Norton.

Erikson, E. (1968). *Identity, youth, and crisis.* New York: Norton.

Erikson, E. (1980). *Identity and the life cycle* (2nd ed.). New York: Norton.

Gardner, H. (1983). *Frames of mind: The theory of multiple intelligences.* New York: Basic Books.

Gardner, H. (1991). *The unschooled mind: How children think and how schools should teach.* New York: Basic Books.

Gilligan, C. (1982). *In a different voice: Psychological theory and women's development.* Cambridge, MA: Harvard University Press.

Gilligan, C., & Attanucci, J. (1988, July). Two moral orientations: Gender differences and similarities. *Merrill-Palmer Quarterly, 34*(3), 223–237.

Glickman, C. D. (1981). *Developmental supervision: Alternative practices for helping teachers improve instruction.* Alexandria, VA: Association for Supervision and Curriculum Development.

Green, M. (1989). *Theories of human development.* Upper Saddle River, NJ: Merrill/Prentice Hall.

Guilford, J. P. (1988). Some changes in the structure of the intellect model. *Educational and Psychological Measurement, 48*, 1–4.

Hardman, M. L. (1994). *Inclusion: Issues of educating students with disabilities in regular educational settings.* Boston: Allyn & Bacon.

Hart, L. (1983). *Human brain, human learning.* New York: Longman.

Helms, D. B., & Turner, J. S. (1986). *Exploring child behavior.* Monterey, CA: Brooks/Cole.

Kauffman, J. M. (1997). *Characteristics of emotional and behavioral disorders of children and youth* (6th ed.). Upper Saddle River, NJ: Merrill/Prentice Hall.

Kohlberg, L. (1981). *The philosophy of moral development.* New York: Harper & Row.

Kohlberg, L. (1968, September). The child as a moral philosopher. *Psychology Today*, pp. 25–30.

Leinhardt, G. (1992). What research on learning tells us about teaching. *Educational Leadership, 49*(7), 20–25.

Lickona, T. (1993, September). Creating a moral community in the classroom. *Instructor, 103*(2), 69–72.

Madaus, G. F., Kellaghan, T., & Schwab, R. L. (1989). *Teach them well: An introduction to education.* New York: Harper & Row.

Maslow, A. H. (1971). *The farther reaches of human nature*. New York: Viking.

Maslow, A. H. (1968). *Toward a psychology of being* (2nd ed.). Princeton, NJ: Van Nostrand.

Maslow, A. H. (1954). *Motivation and personality*. New York: Harper & Row.

Mathis, B. C., Cotton, J. W., & Sechrest, L. (1970). *Psychological foundations of education*. New York: Academic.

Moss, D. M. (1989). *Lee, the rabbit with epilepsy*. Kensington, MD: Woodbine House.

Noddings, N. (1990). Constructivism in mathematics education. In R. B. Davis, C. A. Maher, & N. Noddings (Eds.), *Constructivist views on the teaching and learning of mathematics*. Reston, VA: National Council of Teachers of Mathematics.

Pendarvis, E., Howley, M., & Howley, C. (1990). *The abilities of gifted children*. Upper Saddle River, NJ: Merrill/Prentice Hall.

Piaget, J. (1967). *Six psychological studies*. New York: Random House.

Piaget, J. (1965). *The moral judgment of the child*. New York: Free Press.

Piaget, J. (1952). *The origins of intelligence*. New York: International Universities Press.

Piaget, J., & Inhelder, B. (1973). *Memory and intelligence*. New York: Basic Books.

Popham, W. J., & Baker, E. L. (1970). *Establishing instructional goals*. Upper Saddle River, NJ: Merrill/Prentice Hall.

Quay, H. C., & Peterson, D. R. (1987). *Manual for the revised behavior problem checklist*. Coral Gables, FL: Author.

Renzulli, J. S. (1982). Dear Mr. and Mrs. Copernicus: We regret to inform you . . . *Gifted Child Quarterly, 26*, 11–14.

Renzulli, J. S., & Reis, S. M. (1991). The schoolwide enrichment model: A comprehensive plan for the development of creative productivity. In N. Colangelo & G. Davis (Eds.), *Handbook of gifted education* (pp. 111–141). Boston: Allyn & Bacon.

Reynolds, M. C., Wang, M. C., & Walberg, H. J. (1992, September/October). The knowledge bases for special and general education. *Remedial and Special Education, 13*(5), 6–10, 33.

Rogers, C. R. (1969). *Freedom to learn*. Upper Saddle River, NJ: Merrill/Prentice Hall.

Rogers, C. R. (1961). *On becoming a person*. Boston: Houghton Mifflin.

Salkind, N. J. (1994). *Child development* (7th ed.). Fort Worth, TX: The Harcourt Press.

Schiamberg, L. B. (1988). *Child and adolescent development*. Upper Saddle River, NJ: Merrill/Prentice Hall.

Skinner, B. F. (1968). *The technology of teaching*. New York: Appleton-Century-Crofts.

Skinner, B. F. (1953). *Science and human behavior*. New York: Free Press.

Skinner, B. F. (1948). *Walden two*. Upper Saddle River, NJ: Merrill/Prentice Hall.

Slavin, R. E. (1994). *Educational psychology*. Boston: Allyn & Bacon.

Slavin, R. E. (1989). Achievement effects of substantial reductions in class size. In R. E. Slavin (Ed.), *School and classroom organization* (pp. 127–152). Hillsdale, NJ: Erlbaum.

Sylvester, R. (1995). *A celebration of neurons: An educator's guide to the human brain*. Alexandria, VA: Association for Supervision and Curriculum Development.

Tanner, H. M. (1973). *Growth at adolescence* (2nd ed.). Oxford: Blackwell Scientific Publications.

Thorndike, E. L. (1933). A proof of the law of effect. *Science, 77*, 173–175.

Thorndike, E. L. (1931). *Human learning*. New York: The Century Company.

Tyler, R. (1949). *Basic principles of curriculum and instruction*. Chicago: University of Chicago Press.

Vygotsky, L. S. (1978). *Mind in society*. Cambridge, MA: Harvard University Press.

Walton, G. (1961). *Identification of the intellectually gifted children in the public school kindergarten*. Unpublished doctoral dissertation. University of California, Los Angeles.

Wang, M. C., Haertel, G. D., & Walberg, H. J. (1990, September/October). What influences

learning? A content analysis of review literature. *Journal of Educational Research*, *84*(1),
30–43.

Wang, M. C., Haertel, G. D., & Walberg, H. J.
(1993/1994). What helps students learn?
Educational Leadership, *51*(4), 74–79.

Watson, J. B. (1924). *Behaviorism*. New York:
Norton.

Williams, D. (1992). *Nobody nowhere: The extraor-
dinary autobiography of an autistic*. New York:
Times Book/Random House.

Willis, S. (1994). The well-rounded classroom:
Apply the theory of multiple intelligences.
ASCD Update, *36*(8), 1, 5–6, 8.

Wood, D. J., Bruner, J. S., & Ross, G. (1976). The
role of tutoring in problem solving. *Journal of
Child Psychology and Psychiatry*, *20*(17), 89–100.

Woolfolk, A. E. (1995). *Educational psychology* (5th
ed.). Boston: Allyn & Bacon.

Yager, R. E. (1991, September). The constructivist learning model: Towards real reform in
science education. *The Science Teacher*, *58*(6),
52–57.

Areas of Study that Impact the Elementary School Curriculum

Having investigated the areas of study that impact curriculum development, history, social contexts, views of children and their learning, and the elementary school organization (see Figure 1-6), we are ready to set in motion the steps that complete the curriculum development process. Chapter 5 elaborates on the role of educational philosophy in shaping teaching and learning. That chapter also discusses five curricular designs and how a teacher's philosophy influences the selection of a particular design. Chapter 6 articulates the importance of reflection in the planning step in the elementary curriculum. As teachers consider various aspects of planning—the goals and objectives within a lesson and unit, characteristics of students, teaching strategies, resources and materials, and content to be taught—they address the complexities of teaching and learning in the elementary school.

The implementation-of-teaching-plans step is the focus of Chapter 7, which provides descriptions of strategies along a continuum that range from group instruction to individual instruction. Chapter 8, focusing on the assessment step in curriculum development, presents strategies for formative and summative assessment, along with suggestions for varying the assessment procedures (including authentic assessment and portfolios). Chapter 9 concludes Part Two with an overview of the use of educational technology in the curriculum of the elementary school.

chapter 5

The Curriculum Development Process: Setting the Stage

AFTER READING THIS CHAPTER, YOU WILL BE ABLE TO DO THE FOLLOWING:

- Identify the major philosophies of education and give the instructional implications of each.

- Describe how a teacher's educational philosophy influences the curriculum development process in the elementary school and classroom.

- Write a personal philosophy of education.

- Discuss the relationship between curriculum and teaching.

- Describe the characteristics of each curriculum design and discuss the strengths and weaknesses of each.

- Identify the sources of the curriculum and explain how these sources influence the curriculum development process.

- Define scope, sequence, and continuity and give an example of each in the elementary curriculum.

Elementary curriculum is built on a framework that includes historical perspectives; the current structure and organization of the elementary school; social, political, and economic contexts; and characteristics of children as they grow and learn. These four areas of study are crucial not only in helping you understand the underlying issues of the curriculum development process but also, more importantly, in structuring teaching and learning so that the results are appropriate and meaningful. Figure 1-6, provided in Chapter 1, is our model for viewing the total curriculum development process. The process begins with an examination of the areas of study that represent the beginning of the curriculum-development process and set the stage for planning, implementing, and assessing the elementary curriculum. These areas of study also illustrate that curriculum development does not occur in a vacuum. Quite the contrary is true: before curriculum development can take place, teachers must consider data and information from these four areas of study as they construct a meaningful curriculum for their students.

Chapters 1 through 4 presented information about the history and development of elementary education, some of the social contexts in which elementary schools operate, and the basics of the learning process of elementary students. You may have encountered the content of those chapters in expanded form as courses in your teacher-preparation program. They are included in this book as a review of the background information vital to the curriculum-development process. Without this background information, the curriculum-development process might seem like a mystery or magic at best, or an accident at worst. It is neither: there are reasons teachers teach what they do, reasons the school year has normally been organized around a nine- to ten-month calendar, and reasons most students go to school until 3:30 P.M. The reasons stem from a combination of factors—partly history (this is the way we have done it), partly the current economic and political circumstances, and partly what we believe to be the way children learn best. An experienced teacher, Andre, describes this process of considering these other areas of study in the curriculum development process.

 Voice of Experience

Andre is a fourth-grade teacher at City Elementary School. As he begins to plan for the year, he must gain some understanding of his pupils—their needs and abilities, their home environment, and their expectations about school. While Andre knows what content and concepts should be taught and mastered by fourth-grade students, as mandated by the district and the state, he also knows that he needs to make learning relevant and fun for them. Before getting copies of the textbooks and other curriculum-planning documents and beginning to plan units and lessons, Andre likes to spend some time thinking about what is really important for his students to learn, as well as talking and listening to students, parents, business people, and other educators in the community. Such an exercise, he says, "Helps me to better understand what my beliefs are, what I value most, and to see these beliefs against the needs of my fourth grade students."

Chapter 5 brings closure to this foundational framework and begins to focus attention more directly on the planning process, by examining several other aspects of curriculum development shown in Figure 1-6. This chapter discusses the impact of our beliefs about educational practices, which can be traced to philosophies of education, on the development of curriculum. The role and origin of a philosophy of education is presented as a beginning point for understanding the roots of a belief system. Four philosophies are presented, along with scenarios that help illustrate the quali-

ties of each. The chapter concludes by explaining the relationship between curriculum and teaching, the various curriculum designs, the sources of the curriculum, and finally, the components of the curriculum (scope, sequence, and continuity).

THE ROLE AND ORIGINS OF A PHILOSOPHY OF EDUCATION

As teachers work with students and gain experience in teaching, they continually modify their belief system, or value system, adding to and subtracting from their original beliefs. This belief system influences the type of teacher they become and the type of instructional program they work to implement in their classrooms and schools. Taking David Berliner's (1996) view that "teaching is a moral craft," developing an idealogy that is compatible with the best in educational practice means addressing value-laden questions such as *What do I teach and how do I teach it?* Berliner goes on to say that a philosophical orientation (the moral aspect of teaching) answers these questions. For him, being able to articulate what is best for students within the context of a curriculum platform and educational preference requires having a position backed up with an ideology.

When educators find themselves in situations that cause them to question decisions or practices, they need to know what they believe in (what is important to them) and have a rich knowledge base about what is good for children, to support their developing philosophy. Berliner (1996) concludes by saying strong professionals recognize that all knowledge is subject to question and debate and that the issue of best practices is ethically grounded in their ideology. Whether the issues are student punishment, retention and grades, after-school programs, or gifted and talented education, there is a moral dimension to teaching because of human variability. Teachers have to recognize the role their beliefs play when developing their voice about these and other issues related to the curriculum.

These views about what one considers to be true are embodied in what are generally referred to as *philosophies of education*. These philosophies represent the theoretical and intellectual underpinnings of educational practices and, ultimately, the curriculum-building process. An examination of major philosophies can help teachers clarify and better understand their own beliefs and views about the learner, the school, the curriculum, and education in general. The challenge for elementary educators, as we approach the twenty-first century, is to think of the curriculum in ways that will meet the needs not only of the current but also of future generations of children and balance these needs against the reform initiatives aimed at increased academic achievement.

An understanding of what elementary teachers do and why they are doing it is key to reflective teaching and the professional development of educators. Knight (1989) stresses that as educators examine the what and the why of teaching, they "develop a clear vision regarding the purpose of education and its relation to the meaning of life" (p. 3). Knight goes on to say that a philosophy of education brings educators face-to-face with the big questions that underlie the meaning and purpose of education.

Having a professional belief system guides the development of a personal vision for teaching (Reinhartz & Beach, 1992). This vision embodies both the means and ends of curriculum development. As teachers think about teaching and learning, they think not only in terms of content, concepts, and skill, but also about ways to teach the curriculum in ways that will make it meaningful for their students, as well as about ways to assess learning. Teachers should be able to articulate their views regarding such issues as the benefits of cooperative group learning, the use of positive reinforcement during instruction, or the appropriateness and inappropriateness of teaching

about sexual behavior, drugs, and AIDS. Reflecting on these and other issues helps educators consider options and make decisions that are consistent with their belief system. Because philosophy is central to the educational decision-making process, it is the foundation upon which educational practices and curricular decisions are built and ultimately rest.

A philosophy shapes teachers responses to questions regarding the elementary curriculum: What should it be? How is it organized or how should it be organized? What subjects should be included and excluded? These are value-laden questions, and the answers establish the boundaries that provide direction for developing a curriculum for the elementary school. An understanding of the curriculum development process would not be complete without some consideration of various philosophies and their impact on teaching and learning. While there are a variety of ways to organize beliefs into a philosophy, we have chosen four philosophies—idealism, realism, pragmatism, and existentialism—as a basis for examining the curriculum, student learning, and teacher behavior.

The roots of the word *philosophy* communicate the essence of the term; *philo* means "love" and *sophos* means "wisdom." For teachers, the study of philosophy as it relates to education provides a vehicle for criticizing and analyzing fundamental beliefs. Plato and Aristotle, in their time, used the tools of questioning and reasoning to scrutinize the accepted practices and beliefs of the day. Ryan and Cooper (1995) note that Socrates described this process of examination as rocking the boat, or unobedient questioning.

In discussing various philosophies and the development of a personal educational philosophy, it is helpful to examine the components of a philosophy:

■ *Metaphysics*, which seeks to answer the question: What is real?

■ *Epistemology*, which attempts to answer the question: What is truth?

- *Axiology,* which looks to finding responses to the question: What is of value?
- *Logic,* which focuses on modes of arguing using deductive and inductive reasoning strategies.

As we examine each philosophy, we will explore the ways in which each attempts to define reality, truth, value, and reasoning, particularly in regard to the elementary curriculum and educational practices.

The elementary curriculum has developed in response to the intellectual demands and beliefs of educators and members of the community in order to articulate the purpose and mission of elementary education. The ideas expressed in a school's mission statement that begin with "we believe" should guide decisions about all facets of the educational program. It is not surprising, then, that the study of philosophy is integral to curriculum development. To help guide their thinking regarding educational issues, teachers have to assess their own beliefs, as they develop their own educational philosophy. Andre, our "Voice of Experience" for this chapter, describes this process.

 Voice of Experience

Although Andre has never really thought about his belief system as a philosophy of education, he admits that it influences his teaching. Translating his views of teaching and learning into a philosophy of education is new for this fourth-grade teacher. He begins by thinking about what he believes in, the values he was taught as a child, his moral and religious beliefs, his attitudes toward how children develop and learn, and why he chose teaching as a career. Andre says he also began to think about why he decided to become an *elementary* teacher. As Andre takes this important step, he ponders that and other questions. Andre says, "Although I never thought about it, my colleagues tell me I am very opinionated. I guess I really do have some strong beliefs about teaching in the elementary school."

ORIGINS AND SOURCES OF A PHILOSOPHY

Where does a personal philosophy of education come from? How does it develop? The sources of an educational philosophy are many and varied, and an individual's belief system is shaped and influenced by several factors:

- the culture into which a person was born and lives, with its myths, traditions, heroes, and heroines
- the experiences a person has while growing up and throughout life
- the religious or moral principles a person has adopted
- what a person has read

These sources of a philosophy affect the curriculum and educational decisions teachers make or fail to make. These sources can be compared to the roots of a tree: the roots are deep but not visible, yet they are extremely important in determining the type of tree that will grow—its size, the quantity and quality of the leaves, and the general health of the tree. The actions taken are represented by the tree aboveground, and the belief system that influences these actions is represented by the root system underground.

When teachers make decisions about the purpose of education, the skills and behaviors they expect from their students, the instructional strategies they use, or the type of assessment they implement, their belief system plays a key role. This belief system is the foundation of what they know to be true and becomes their personal educational philosophy. The decisions that teachers make about teaching and learning reflect their belief systems, which are grounded in one or more identifiable educational philosophies. Saylor and Alexander (1954) suggest that as teachers make instructional decisions, they are acknowledging that education is a moral venture, one that necessitates choosing among a wide spectrum of values and constitutes the starting point for curriculum development.

Fullan (1993), like Berliner (1996), claims that teaching is a moral profession with a moral purpose. It is *moral* in the sense of making decisions in the hope of making a difference and of bringing about change. Fullan goes on to say that this "moral purpose keeps teachers close to the needs of children and youth; [and] causes them to develop better strategies for accomplishing their moral goals" (p. 12). For example, Three Oaks Elementary in Ft. Myers, Florida, has implemented Hirsch's Core Knowledge Curriculum ("Core Knowledge Curriculum Project," 1992). In describing the curriculum, principal Constance Jones says she likes the idea of having specific information to teach in a very sequenced manner. This curriculum is seen as providing consistency in content and continuity in learning. Teachers at Three Oaks Elementary use an integrative approach when teaching literature in their history classes and introducing mathematics concepts in science; in addition, they tie skills to critical content. Such a view of the curriculum, which focuses on essential content, is expressed in the philosophy of realism.

Tanner and Tanner (1987) suggest that the curriculum of a school is determined largely by the educational philosophy of the faculty and staff. Therefore, in the final analysis, an educational philosophy gives "meaning and direction to actions taken by teachers regarding development and implementation of the curriculum" (Beach & Reinhartz, 1989, p. 102).

PHILOSOPHIES OF EDUCATION: FOUR PERSPECTIVES

Before reading this section, turn to item 1 in the Your Turn section at the end of this chapter. As you read this section on philosophies, refer to each statement and see if you can determine which philosophy is being described. These statements serve as an illustration of the philosophy in an educational context.

Idealism

Idealism embraces a belief in unchanging principles or eternal truths. The search for these principles is not gained through the human senses but "found only in the intangible world of the mind" (Armstrong, 1989, p. 10). From the idealist perspective, some disciplines are better suited than others for developing the mind and its rational powers; these subjects include philosophy, theology, literature, and the liberal arts (Armstrong, 1989). These subjects have recurring themes that bring students in contact with the great thinkers such as Plato, Socrates, Adler, and others.

Idealism as it is practiced in schools "should assist students to realize fully [their] potentialities [and] expose students to the wisdom contained in the cultural heritage" (Gutek, 1988, p. 25). Hutchins (1936) writes that a curriculum with an idealist position holds principally to those "permanent studies" that reflect the elements common to human nature. Idealists believe that knowledge is, by nature, constant and timeless, and that education should do the following things (Reinhartz & Beach, 1992; Gutek, 1992):

■ Be an unfolding of the mind in each person.

■ Concentrate on the development of the mind through knowledge and reason and the Socratic method.

■ Be concerned with the pursuit of truth, which is universal.

■ Provide an example or moral and cultural model in the teacher.

Teachers who adopt the idealist view emphasize a curriculum that is constant and is built on what has been identified as truth. Great books and tradition play a major role in determining what is taught. *Aesop's Fables* is an example of literature for children that provides universal moral truths. Stories of heroes and heroines in the Great Books provide another source of moral behavior for the classroom. In studying about democracy in the classroom of an idealist, students read and discuss the great ideas of the past.

Idealism presents some problems as a basis of educational philosophy: foremost among them is the idea that truth is everywhere the same, which leads to the idea that the education process everywhere should be the same (Tanner & Tanner, 1995). Another major problem is the emphasis on the cultivation of the intellect at the exclusion of the student's interests and needs; by refuting these, the idealist embraces the doctrine of mental discipline and a one-sided view of human nature.

Realism

Realism is another philosophy seen in educational practice. The central tenet of realism is a focus on knowledge of objects, the laws that govern the real world of objects, and the relationship of these objects to one another. For the realist, as described by Aristotle (1954), knowledge is gained through the use of methods of observation and the investigation of natural and social phenomena. *Knowing* involves an interaction of the world (objects and matter) with the human mind.

From the perspective of a realist, education prepares students for life and helps them to know, using

- the study of an organized body of knowledge
- the senses to observe and record data
- the study of nature and natural laws
- the study of human events that comprise history

A realist curriculum is subject-centered and concerned with equipping children with intellectual powers so that they can come to master facts and achieve academic excellence. As early as 1907, Bagley wrote that the role of the teacher in such a curriculum is to represent a storehouse of organized knowledge. Within this philosophy, teachers are viewed as subject-matter experts who work with students to master the acquisition of information. In such a classroom, teachers use every opportunity to observe, quantify, catalog, or categorize, as students collect data about an event or phenomenon. Language arts is structural and emphasizes the laws or rules that govern usage. Science and mathematics also focus on laws, theorems, and algorithms. Social studies involves collecting information about a period, in quantitative as well as descriptive ways. For example, in studying democracy, students might analyze numbers of voters, exit polls, and voting trends. If implemented in its purest form, realism emphasizes facts, data, and specific pieces of information without providing a sense of the whole. Students may fail to see any connectedness between and among subjects as well as within subjects.

Idealism and realism are often combined in the public schools in a philosophy of education called *essentialism*. According to Tanner and Tanner (1980), essentialism holds that "the curriculum must be centered on intellective training and that the path to intellective power is to be found only in certain academic studies" (p. 8). The essentialist position calls for studying certain subjects and searching for the academically talented. "Even with the advent of progressive education, the essentialist view of education exerted an enormous influence on education during the first half of the twentieth century" (Tanner & Tanner, 1980, p. 7). The application of idealism and realism to the classroom is presented in Figure 5-1, which provides a profile of the implementation of essentialism in an elementary classroom.

FIGURE 5-1   Idealism and Realism: Essentialism in the Classroom

Our elementary school has developed a curriculum that helps students develop their cognitive abilities and master the essential content taught in school. Students focus on the basic subjects, which means they learn to read, write, and compute mathematically as well as study other subjects as time permits. It is our belief that as students master the "essentials" they become better equipped to learn other content as well. Whether in science, mathematics, social studies, or language arts, there are specific skills and concepts—a body of knowledge—at each grade level that students must learn in order to be eligible for promotion to the next grade. These basic subjects form the core of the curriculum in the elementary school and guide learning by providing students with the knowledge and skills that will help them be productive citizens.

In response to the many news reports and articles that criticize current educational practices and programs as containing "fluff" and including contemporary issues such as rap music, drugs, or movies, our school has returned to what we know works best and helps students score well on achievement tests. The "frills," which were taking up too much time in our curriculum and shortchanging students in their efforts to gain a solid education, have been eliminated. We have revised our schedule to include a minimum of fifty-five minutes each day for language arts and mathematics. We have also encouraged our students to read books that include the great ideas of the past. By focusing on a curriculum that provides students with a basic understanding of their world and culture through language arts, science, math, and social studies, teachers serve as models and gatekeepers, helping students master facts and concepts as they learn to reason and critically analyze their world.

Pragmatism

Pragmatism, a third basic philosophy, is based on the idea that knowledge and truth are tentative and are derived from human experience. It emphasizes experimentation or doing. Pragmatists test the consequences of actions as they experience their world. Dewey (1902, 1906), considered the architect of *progressivism*, the educational version of pragmatism, believed that the interaction of the student with the environment creates experience that encourages the student to learn by doing. This attitude is evident in Dewey's (1906) suggestion that

the whole cycle of self-activity demands an opportunity for investigation and experimentation, for trying out one's ideas upon things, discovering what can be done with materials and appliances. (p. 353)

Pragmatism judges success in terms of the consequences and outcomes, and progressivism stresses results from the development of problem-solving skills. The social sciences become important, in providing the subject area best suited for developing these problem-solving skills. Progressive educators capitalized on the research of psychiatry, medicine, and the social sciences and presented a more integrated view of the nature of *knowledge*. They demolished the notion that the mind was a separate entity (Tanner & Tanner, 1995). From the point of view of the progressive educator, the school's functions were to simplify, purify, and balance the cultural heritage (Dewey, 1906). Educators were to simplify the curriculum by designing units of study concerning the cultural context with opportunities to problem solve.

In a classroom that emphasizes a progressive approach to learning, students are actively involved in learning as they seek answers to problems posed by the teacher. For example, the use of manipulatives in mathematics to help students solve problems leans heavily toward a progressive view of learning. In studying democracy, students learn about this concept by running for office, holding an election, and voting for their candidate. A limitation and often a criticism of the progressive classroom is the lack of the absolute and an inadequate knowledge base that supports

student actions. Students are seen as acting before thinking about their actions.

Figure 5-2 shows how progressivism as a philosophy is implemented in a classroom setting. Such a scenario further illustrates the tenets of pragmatism and progressivism.

Existentialism

The philosophy of *existentialism* emphasizes the conscious awareness of experience and the connection between thought and action; it centers on the individual. Existentialism developed in the early part of the nineteenth century. It focuses on the uniqueness and freedom of each person and is closely related to humanism. One of the early proponents of existentialism was Sören Kierkegaard,

FIGURE 5-2   Progressivism in the Classroom

At City Elementary School, teachers emphasize problem-solving skills throughout the grades. Teachers realize that the students bring to school and the learning process many diverse backgrounds and abilities, but that at school, students can participate in cooperative learning projects as they role play, share information, and solve problems that are typical for their community. For example, recently the students have been concerned with the trash and litter at school. In an effort to deal with this problem, they began to study pollution in their classes. As a project, they collected the trash at school and sorted it into recyclables and nonrecyclables; they weighed and graphed each category, collecting data about the amount and kinds of trash found at school. They also read the letters and monographs of several conservationists/ecologists and started a letter-writing campaign to the mayor and city council. Several of their letters have been published in the local newspaper. By learning about the various people and problems that are associated with pollution, students gain insights that help them not only in solving their local problem but in their understanding as well. They have visited with inspectors from the Environmental Protection Agency, engineers, city water treatment technicians, and supervisors at the city garbage disposal site, and other municipal authorities.

By engaging in this hands-on, collaborative, and problem-centered approach to learning our elementary curriculum helps students develop the skills they will need to solve real world problems that they encounter throughout their lives and to be responsible citizens of their community. Students at our school learn that knowledge is not an abstract fact or theorem, but rather a useful tool that can help them solve problems in their world. Teachers become project directors as we help students identify problems or issues and then develop practical solutions to them.

who believed that human beings have absolute freedom and are totally responsible for the choices they make as they work and live outside of a crowd. From the perspective of an existentialist, there is no way to learn the truth about who you are without experiencing life with all the decisions and choices you make along the way.

One of the premises of existentialism is that human beings seek self-definition, are vital, and have the ability to make decisions and that these decisions, no matter how minute, ultimately help individuals actualize their potential. By centering on the person, existentialism views the state of becoming as central. *Becoming* is defined as the development of an individual's unique potential and abilities. This development unfolds as the individual experiences his/her world. The way an individual values and chooses helps that individual to see himself or herself in relation to the outside world and further defines who the person is.

Other aspects of this philosophy include the nature of individuals, their experiences that are shaped partially by society, and the content of the world at a given moment. Existentialism helps explain how people achieve their individuality. This individuality emerges when people make decisions as they confront the realities (problems of guilt, anxiety, and the environment) of their world. Politics and sociology are important areas of study, as ways to rebuild society and raise social consciousness. For example, in studying democracy, students would be confronted with the decision to run or not run for an office. Ultimately, they would have to decide how they would participate in the election process, as a candidate, a voter, or a nonvoter.

Existentialism seeks to justify in some way the freedom of choice and the importance of the human personality. The root is *existence*, which is used to emphasize the notion that each person is unique and is capable of making decisions and accepting the consequences. From an existentialist perspective, it is the individual who determines his or her own fate and the individual who determines the meaning and purpose of life.

Unlike those who believe that individuals are the product of either heredity or environment, existentialists believe that each person is unique and free to take a stand, to transcend both hereditary and environmental conditions; thus, each individual is ultimately self-determining. In the classroom, the existentialist view shuns any emphasis on or glorification of the group and thus does not typically embrace cooperative learning strategies.

The existentialist also avoids the codification of learning as it is found in behavioral objectives and common educational outcomes that can be measured. As an organization, school is much too structured and group focused, and this threatens or works against an individual's self-definition. The most damaging practice in schools, according to existentialists, comes from the "tyranny of the average," which tends to neglect, or even destroy, individual capabilities in favor of some perceived norm or average. Existentialists also avoid describing a "typical" existentialist education, because from the existentialist point of view, nothing is "typical" if we are all unique. An existentialist curriculum gives students the widest array of possible choices, with many opportunities and activities to help each student define who he or she is. Critics of the existentialist view point out that because of the emphasis on the individual there are few if any standards. Students are free to pursue virtually anything they are interested in, with little accountability. Figure 5-3 describes a classroom constructed with an existential orientation.

A Multidimensional Philosophical Model

Each philosophy presented in this chapter is summarized in Figure 5-4. As these philosophical orientations sit side-by-side, it is easy to compare the overall purposes, the basic nature of the school curriculum, the nature of the learner, and the teaching process reflected in the various philosophies in the elementary classroom.

As you review Figure 5-4, you may begin to think that you hold beliefs from more than one

FIGURE 5-3   Existentialism in the Classroom

As teachers at Oakhill School, we follow the belief that each student is a "lamp to be lighted, not a vessel to be filled." Regardless of the child's background or experience, we view each student as a unique individual, and we tailor our curriculum to meet the unique abilities that each student has that must be cultivated. We allow students to pursue topics of interest to them and build various content themes around their ideas. For example, if a student is interested in skiing, then social studies, literature, science, and even mathematics may be integrated into learning projects and activities for that student that are related to skiing. We tend to work more on a one-on-one basis with the students or in small groups. We reject group norms and group expectations. We want students to have numerous opportunities to make significant decisions about their learning, so they learn more about themselves—their strengths and weaknesses. As students make decisions about their learning, they also learn to live with the consequences of their decisions.

Finally, we try to construct a learning environment where children are willing to take risks as they engage in reflection and learn more about themselves as they explore new topics and ways of thinking. As each child grows and learns, we want him or her to feel that he or she is competent, capable, and special. This focus on the uniqueness of each individual is designed to help all the students reach their potential.

As a teacher in such a school, I spend less time writing curriculum and developing lesson plans for the class and more time looking for resources and materials that will match the wide range of needs and interests of the students in my class. We discourage competition between and among students and promote cooperation and individual achievement, as each child gains a sense of self-worth and competence and seeks to attain his or her own potential.

of these philosophies. This eclectic attitude is common. Most teachers, while they may have one dominant philosophy, also embrace components of others. By having beliefs that overlap with more than one philosophy, most educators have developed a multidimensional model (see Figure 5-5).

Teachers may view the curriculum from a content perspective and tend to see learning as mastering basic facts and skills (realism), while at the same time they want students to be able to use this information in practical ways to solve personal as well as societal problems (progressivism). They may also recognize the uniqueness of each student and try to individualize instruction to accommodate the differences among their students by providing choices and options (exis-

tentialism). Beliefs influence the philosophy of education a teacher holds dear. The lines between the four philosophies in Figure 5-5 are not straight and illustrate that rarely is an educator clearly an idealist, a realist, a progressive, or an existentialist. For most teachers, it is more accurate to describe oneself as having a multidimensional or eclectic philosophy.

Figure 5-6 describes a view of educational philosophy developed by a novice educator. In his discussion are attributes of the various philosophies, and as he expresses his own philosophy, the multidimensional nature of a personal philosophy is evident. His statement that "there are almost as many educational philosophies as there are educators" illustrates how, as teachers incorporate various beliefs within their own per-

FIGURE 5-4 Educational Philosophies

Philosophy	Purpose(s) of education	Nature of the Curriculum	Nature of the Learner	The Teaching Process
Idealism	Development of the mind (reason); fostering of intellect	Timeless; pursuit of truth through study of great ideas	Achieve academic excellence by cultivating mental powers; Socratic method	Teachers model and analyze the text, then pose questions
Realism (Essentialism)	Development of knowledge of the world and laws that govern relation of objects to each other	Study of organized, well-defined body of knowledge—nature and natural laws, and human experience	Intellectual power to master facts	Teachers function as subject-matter specialists; knowledge and skills gained through process skills and observation of the world
Progressivism	Development of problem-solving skills through application of knowledge and skills	Tentative and unfolds with experience; emphasis on social sciences and real world problems and situations	Learn by doing and experimentation; activity; cooperative learning teams/groups	Teachers promote application of knowledge to solve social problems; team building as the way to promote discussions and problem-solving skills
Existentialism	Development of each individual through conscious awareness of choice	Opportunities for making choices and to experience consequences; person centered	Learners free to make choices and experience life along with consequences of choices; self-definition	Teachers provide opportunities for introspection and self-analysis and choice through individualized learning activities

FIGURE 5-5 A Multidimensional Model of Educational Philosophies

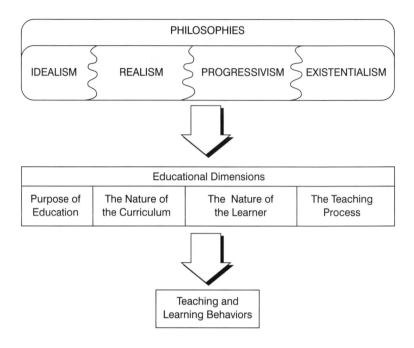

sonal philosophy, they are creating something unique that works for them, and may change over time as their beliefs are tested in the fire of experience.

Sometimes an essentialist perspective is used when a teacher supports the basics in the curriculum, but in the classroom this same teacher may also be supportive of cooperative learning groups to develop problem-solving skills. To complicate matters, this teacher may feel strongly about developing individual skills and promoting each student's self-esteem, which means working with each student on a one-on-one basis rather than in groups. Being an elementary teacher is complex, and all decisions that are made about the curriculum and learning process can seldom be traced consistently to one philosophy; there is often crossover or blending of beliefs depending on a given issue and/or the situation.

Return to Figure 5-5 and find the one arrow that leads from the group of philosophies to the educational dimensions. The dimensions related to education include the purpose of education, the nature of the curriculum, the nature of the learner, and the teaching process, and these are influenced by the philosophies of education. The philosophy in the stated purpose of an elementary school will shape not only what is taught but also the kinds of teaching and learning activities for that school. Similarly, the purpose of education translates into a mission statement for the school that describes how the teachers perceive the learners and what they think students are capable of accomplishing. The purpose, the curriculum, and the attitudes toward the learners affect the teaching process and help determine how teachers view their role and the type of teaching strategies they use. The last item in Figure 5-5, teaching and learning behaviors, leads to the ultimate question educators must ask about their curriculum: were the students successful in accordance with the purposes identified, the curriculum planned, the nature of elementary learners, and the principles of effective teaching?

FIGURE 5-6   Robert Smith's Philosophy of Education

Ever wind up at Grand Central Station on a busy Friday afternoon? No? Believe me, it's just a bit chaotic and confusing. It seems to be the same for beginning educators as they try to make sense of the vast amount of teaching philosophies. Tell you what, since I'm on vacation from my job as social director of the Shady Pines Mobile Home Ranch and R.V. Park, I'll be your personal guide as we ride the rails across that wide and varied terrain known as Educational Philosophy. We'll be making several stops along the way, so just sit back and soak up some of the scenery. Where we'll end up is rather difficult to predict, but we'll be making stops at Progressivism and Essentialism, and we may even end up at my place. Where you go after that is up to you, but trust me, it'll be worth the ride.

If you look out of your window to the left of the center, you'll see the camp known as progressivism. This group views a child's play as their form of learning. They stress natural development, expression of ideas, creativity, and respect of differences. Progressives see a teacher as coordinator who must be ready to change with the times as environments change and as new knowledge is made available (Shermis, 1967). A progressive teacher might employ hands-on construction, games, field trips, and play as methods of instruction. Personally the biggest strength I see in this philosophy is the emphasis on problem solving. The only hitch is with this idea of natural development. The ability to judge between essential and non-essential knowledge is not inborn. It is a product of mental discipline and maturity, and children are not likely to cultivate this themselves (Kneller, 1964).

As we pull into the next station, you'll see a large, hard-nosed group to the right, the conservative Essentialists. These folks came together from two older groups called idealists and realists (Ryan & Cooper, 1988). They believe learning always comes through hard work and application, and that initiative should rest upon the instructor rather than student. I once heard that they "teach the young the best their group has to offer, but lead them to look beyond their own culture to the total experience through the centuries" (Hocking in Munk, 1965, p. 58). The essentialists believe real freedom comes through real discipline, and they have a deep respect for intellectual discipline and scholarly excellence. An essentialist educator is likely to use lecture and texts as their primary or only mode of instruction. I agree with the essentialists that the

> environment carries in itself the stamp of the past and the seeds of the future, the curriculum must inevitably include that knowledge and information which will acquaint the pupil with the social heritage, introduce him to the world about him, and prepare him for the future (Kandel in Kneller, 1964, p. 117).

But this seems to be a bit too rigid for our changing culture. It also, sadly enough, discourages independent thinking and intellectual initiative.

FIGURE 5-6, *continued*

Now for our last scheduled stop. It doesn't have a name and it's not well known, but it's mine and that's all that matters. I personally believe education should be related to the interests of the students and that education is always in a process of development. Our methods must change with the times and I stress problem solving as one of the most important tools a person can possess. Hard work and discipline are invaluable to any knowledge base, and I believe social forces and issues must shape the way we teach. Education can be fun and rewarding to the student and educator if the lessons are relevant, topical, and on the appropriate level. Testing is necessary, but there are alternative ways to test than the standardized form. Each and every child is special. Each is unique and can add something special to everything they touch. It is our job as educators to bring out the potential in them whatever it takes!

Well, that about sums it up. Clear as mud, right? Just remember, there are almost as many educational philosophies as there are educators and the only person who can find the best philosophy is the person using it. My advice is to be yourself and learn as you progress.

References

Kneller, G. (1964). *Introduction to the philosophy of education.* New York: John Wiley & Sons.

Munk, A.W. (1965). *Synoptic philosophy of education.* New York: Abingdon Press.

Ryan, K. & Cooper, J. (1988). *Those who can, teach.* Boston: Houghton Mifflin Company.

Shermis, S. (1967). *Philosophic foundations of education.* New York: American Book Company.

Source: Robert Smith, classroom teacher. Reprinted with permission.

THE RELATIONSHIP BETWEEN CURRICULUM AND TEACHING

This section discusses commonly used terms associated with curriculum development. These terms often have ambiguous or multiple meanings, depending on their use. When educators hear the word *curriculum*, they are often unsure of its meaning. What is meant by *curriculum*? Too often the term has been used interchangeably with other terms such as *teaching* and *instruction*.

Zais (1976) suggests that this ambiguity continues to plague curriculum specialists and writes of Johnson's (1967) view of curriculum as "a structured series of intended outcomes, [and] all other planning (e.g., of content, learning activities, and evaluation procedures) is viewed as instructional, not curriculum" (p. 9). In an actual classroom with children engaged in learning, this would be considered *teaching*, not *curriculum*. Johnson's (1967) point is that the curriculum embodies outcomes (the ends) and teaching the means to these ends; this seems logical, but often in practice such a view is difficult to separate and comprehend. Popham and Baker (1970) refer to curriculum as the desired "consequences" of teaching.

We, like Johnson and Popham and Baker, believe that there is a relationship between curriculum and teaching, but where we disagree is when they create a dualism—making the two things mutually exclusive. The curriculum includes the outcomes to be achieved, and the teaching provides the means for accomplishing them. We do not want to reduce a curriculum to just ends, isolated from teaching or means; together they create a whole that is greater than the sum of their parts. We find it helpful to view curriculum and teaching as a sandwich. The curriculum is the concepts and skills you plan to deliver, and the outcomes are the results. These are sandwiched around teaching, which comes in the middle to make sure what is planned is learned.

Establishing a relationship and making this distinction between ends and means have implications for teaching and learning as well. Macdonald (1965) proposes that schooling involves the interaction of various systems. One system, teaching, is defined as the

> professionally oriented behavior of individual . . . teachers . . . . [learning includes] actions that students perform which teachers perceive to be task related [and instruction is] the action context within which formal teaching and learning behaviors take place . . . (p. 3)

For Macdonald, a curriculum is the written plan that guides teaching and the actions of both teachers and students. We concur and view curriculum as not only the planning, but the outcomes, the content and the learning experiences as well. Beauchamp (1968) defines *curriculum* similarly: "a curriculum is a written document which may contain many ingredients, but basically it is a plan for the education of pupils during their enrollment in a given school" (p. 6).

What makes a curriculum workable is what Zais (1976) calls the acid test of "how well it functions in live situations" (p. 11). As the curriculum is implemented or taught, it becomes more and more invisible because it is "filtered" through the teaching-learning situations (the nature of the learners, the nature of the school and classroom environment, and the teacher). Thus, the action or implementation of the curriculum is the definition of *teaching*. The curriculum is a mental construct or written plan that operates in the classroom. In addition, the curriculum guides and governs the teaching and learning experiences that take place in an elementary school. The implementation step of the curriculum development process will be addressed in Chapter 7.

Our purpose in emphasizing the relationship, as well as making the distinction, between a curriculum and teaching is to help clarify when and how these terms are used. A curriculum can be compared to a travel itinerary: it maps out specific destinations as well as the route that will be taken, always leaving opportunities to make side trips if time and interests warrant. The actual trip is comparable to teaching: it puts the travel itinerary (curriculum) into operation. In the final analysis, curriculum and teaching are interdependent, and it is our belief that one does not exist without the other.

CURRICULUM DESIGNS

Curriculum design is the way the curriculum is organized; a curriculum can be organized around subjects, students, correlated/broad fields, problem-solving situations, and/or integrative themes. The curriculum is the focus of the teaching plan.

If the curriculum is based on discrete subjects (such as science or mathematics), with little or no integration of information, skills, or concepts, the design of this curriculum is described as *subject centered*, or discipline centered. The subject-centered curriculum design is the most traditional. In this design, the content of the subject is the focus of the curriculum, and students learn different subjects at different times during the day without regard for overlap and repetition of content and skills. Implicit in this design is the view of the student as passive—a container to be filled. This design is most compatible with the essentialist belief that the subject matter is "fixed and ready-made in itself, outside of the child's experience as something hard and fast" (Dewey, 1902, p. 11).

If the curriculum design is *student centered*, or learner centered, the educational outcomes focus on the characteristics and needs of the students. This design takes into consideration how elementary students grow and develop cognitively, socially, and physically, and it incorporates this knowledge when developing the curriculum. Rather than viewing children as having adult needs, it recognizes the needs and abilities of children. It was the progressives who first advocated that "virtually all school learning activities be centered around the felt needs and interests of the child" (Tanner & Tanner, 1980, p. 14). The existentialist would carry this a step further by designing a curricular program that would be unique for each student.

The *broad field*, or correlated, design takes disciplines that are closely related—such as reading, writing, listening, speaking, and literature—and treats them as a combined field of study—such as language arts. In an elementary schedule, language arts would be listed; *language arts* as the collective term reflects a variety of subjects that are taught. For example, in a language arts class, before reading *The Great Kapok Tree*, the children might predict orally or in writing what they think will happen in the story; next, as a whole, the class might construct a concept map about the tropical rain forest in preparation for reading the book; and finally, after reading the story, the students would share their reactions. The broad field curricular design groups and integrates subjects that are related. Another example of a broad field design is found in social studies, which includes history, geography, economics, sociology, anthropology, and civics. For example, a social studies lesson dealing with societal issues such as environmental pollution might focus on the 1989 Exxon *Valdéz* oil spill, studying this historical event and its sociological impact along with the legal, geographical, and economic implications. It would be impossible to isolate this piece of history without considering these other fields of study. The fine arts (art, music, and theater) and the sci-

ences (life, earth, and physical) are other examples of broad field curriculum designs. This curriculum design lends itself to the progressive problem-solving approach to teaching and learning.

When the curriculum is organized to address a specific issue or concern and promote critical-thinking skills, a *problem-solving-centered* design is used. In such a curriculum design, individual and group activities and projects are used to engage the students in situations that require identification of the problem, generation of options, and a decision on the strategy for solving the problem. For example, as students study about people of the world and learn about the concept of prejudice, they may participate in role-playing situations where they act out stereotypical behaviors and then discuss how they might overcome such thinking to reduce prejudice. The common element in this design is the use of problems or dilemmas to cause students to collect data or information to apply to the concepts and skills they encounter in real-life situations. They learn by applying concepts from mathematics, science, language, and history to solve the problem before them. This design also is easily adopted and used within the progressive view of teaching and learning.

Another design that has gained prominence in recent years is the *integrated* thematic-centered design. Such a curriculum design is organized around a theme or topic that connects skills and content in several fields of study. For example, fourth-grade teachers may decide to use an ocean theme, "Our Vacation at the Beach," to get students to apply skills and information from mathematics, reading, science, and geography. Using an integrated curriculum, students learn a variety of skills—in mathematics they might learn about mileage and scales, as they convert inches to miles to calculate how far it is to the beach. In science, they might learn about above and below sea level and the sea life that lives in the ocean—air breathers and non air breathers. When developing listening skills in language arts, students might hear a tape of whales communicating with each other and learn about the use of sonar to locate obstacles in the water. Finally, they might read books about going to the beach and write about whales (for example, writing poems or a story from the whale's point of view) or develop a position paper on a specific environmental issue related to the ocean ecosystem. This design is very compatible with a progressive view of education and could also be adopted by the essentialist view.

Rarely does a school adhere exclusively to one of these curriculum designs. More often than not, a curriculum will embody two or more designs, and teachers may use a variety of designs throughout the year. The designs that teachers use to plan for teaching should reflect the mission and educational philosophy of the school, which makes them multidimensional in nature.

SOURCES OF THE CURRICULUM

Where do the content, concepts, and skills of the curriculum come from? How do elementary teachers know what they are to teach? Many curriculum sources have been proposed during the past ninety years by Dewey (1902), Bode (1927), Montessori (1967), Tyler (1949), and Doll (1995). For Dewey and Montessori, the child was the major source for the curriculum and what was taught should be directly related to his or her needs. Dewey did not see the child separate from the society. In his laboratory school at the University of Chicago, he conceived and structured the classroom as a miniature society, where the child's needs were considered within the social dynamics of this environment.

As a philosopher, Dewey "searched for unities in ideas and experiences . . . [and] argued against compartmentalizing knowledge and experience" (Farnham-Diggory, 1990, p. 14). At the Dewey laboratory school, three principles guided the development of the curriculum:

1. . . . focus on the development of the student's mind, not on blocks of subject matter;

2. [education designed to] . . . be integrated and project-oriented, not divided into small units (for example, forty minutes of English, forty minutes of social studies); and

3. . . . the progression [is] . . . from practical experiences (such as planting a garden) to formal subjects (such as botany) to integrated studies (such as the place of botany in the natural sciences). (Farnham-Diggory, 1990, p. 15)

Bode (1927), like Dewey, saw the child as a primary source of the curriculum, and Doll (1995) suggested additional sources, which include science, society, and eternal truth.

Tyler (1949) took a somewhat different approach to identifying sources for the curriculum. He proposed a model for developing the curriculum that has become known as the *Tyler Rationale*. This rationale for selecting content, concepts, and skills for the curriculum includes, in addition to the needs of the student, the subject matter and the values of society. The needs of the students were considered along with the expertise of the subject-matter specialists and the values of society. After identifying these three sources, Tyler posed a series of questions that provided focus for the curriculum planning process:

1. What educational purposes should the school seek to attain?

2. What educational experiences can be provided to help attain the purposes?

3. How can these educational experiences be effectively organized?

4. How can we determine whether the purposes have been attained? (Tyler, 1949, p. 1)

 Voice of Experience

Recently when working with a student teacher, Andre was asked, "Where does curriculum come from? What are the sources?" Andre responded honestly by saying, "I'm not sure; that is a question that has often haunted me as well. I receive a curriculum guide developed by subject specialists and master teachers in the district, which has been approved by the school board. I also have been told that my curriculum should be developmentally appropriate to meet the needs of my students. What complicates things is that not all my students have the same abilities. I hardly know where to begin. As I plan, I feel tremendous pressure to meet the individual as well as the collective needs of my students, while at the same time present concepts and skills that have been determined for fourth graders. In addition, many of the parents might question the need for students to know about AIDS, etc. It is no easy task for teachers to address each of these sources."

___

Regardless of the sources that teachers use in organizing the elementary curriculum, if these sources get out of balance and one becomes more important, it may lead to the exclusion of the others. When there is such imbalance (a misalignment), then the danger is that the other sources may be ignored and the curriculum will take on features that make it liked by some and disliked by others (Reinhartz & Beach, 1992).

For example, when the source of the curriculum is the student or learner, Dewey would recommend focusing on occupations such as carpentry, manufacturing, or whatever interests the students. Exploring occupations involves making observations, conducting investigations, and making predictions (Farnham-Diggory, 1990). For some classes, studying various occupations would mean that the students would not get the basics such as reading, writing, and mathematics. Such a concern raises the issue of one approach to the exclusion of others.

The challenge for educators as they build the curriculum is to keep the concept of sources in mind as they formulate the mission and goals of the educational program to avoid the trap of

exclusion. Without considering the various designs and multiple sources of curriculum, the educational program at the elementary level must be coherent so that all its parts work in harmony to contribute to the overall cohesiveness (Ornstein & Hunkins, 1993).

According to Komoski (1990), a curriculum lacking a clear focus becomes fragmented. For example, in an attempt to improve its performance on state-mandated achievement tests, an elementary school focused almost exclusively on content and organized the curriculum around discrete subjects. As a result, students learned content, concepts, and skills in isolation, and concern for the overall development of the student was neglected. While students knew discrete, isolated bits of information, they were unable to apply this information in a meaningful way to their own lives. This lack of connectedness contributes to a curriculum that may not match the overall mission of the school.

OTHER ASPECTS OF THE CURRICULUM: SCOPE, SEQUENCE, AND CONTINUITY

Teachers do not tend to think of their philosophy in terms of idealism or progressivism, and they do tend to have an eclectic view of classroom teaching and learning, a combination of two or more philosophies. This kind of belief system guides the way they organize the curriculum and structure learning experiences in their classrooms. In the "Your Turn" section at the end of this chapter, there is an inventory that will help you to identify your own educational belief system. After you have done this exercise, you may have a better understanding as to why you prefer a subject-centered approach to curriculum (essentialism) rather than a problem-solving focus (progressivism), or vice versa. With this knowledge about your own orientation to the curriculum development process, you are ready to engage in a more detailed part of curriculum development.

Important components of the curriculum that teachers must consider are scope, sequence, and continuity. The *scope* of the curriculum refers to the *content* (what will be taught and learned), along with the experiences that will be included during instruction. The *concepts* are the general ideas in each subject area for which the teacher can provide definitions, descriptions, and/or examples and nonexamples. Concepts are not normally taught in isolation, and the teacher must consider the context for the teaching of this content. Many decisions are made regarding the depth to which a concept is presented and the approaches used to achieve understanding. When teachers make decisions about the scope of the curriculum, they are faced with difficult choices. These choices are relative to many factors including the prior knowledge and experience of both teachers and students, and the decisions are guided by the stated mission and goals of the school as they accommodate the nature of the students and their developmental readiness. According to Reinhartz and Beach (1992), "the scope of the curriculum provides answers to the age old question, 'what should the school teach?' and gives form to the curriculum" (p. 141).

The *sequence* of the curriculum refers to the order in which concepts and skills are taught, or the *when* of curriculum (Saylor & Alexander, 1954, 1981). Sequencing can occur before or as decisions are made regarding the what, or the scope. In addition to identifying what will be taught, the structure and sources of the curriculum should be considered along with the psychological principles presented in Chapter 4 to ensure that elementary students are developmentally ready.

Sometimes school districts or textbook publishers provide a scope-and-sequence chart for all elementary grades by subject so that teachers can see which concepts and skills are taught in preceding and following grade levels. In math, for example, kindergarten children learn that fractions represent (equal) parts of a whole; some aspect of fractions continues to be included in math study each year, until in fifth and sixth grade the students learn to multiply and divide fractions.

Following this paragraph is an outline of a scope and sequence of elementary physical science topics. It includes eight topics with several subareas. The sequence was determined by asking the questions *What do students need to know about these topics?* and *What did the students need to know in order to move on to the next topic?*

    I. Force
       A. What is force?
       B. Sensing force
       C. Origins of force
       D. Effects of force

    II. Motion
       A. Kinds of motion
       B. Laws of motion
       C. Applications

    III. Work and Energy
       A. What is work?
       B. Units of work
       C. What is energy?
       D. Kinds of energy
       E. Power

    IV. Machines
       A. Simple machines
       B. Machines that transform energy from one kind to another
       C. Efficiency
       D. Conserving energy

    V. Electricity
       A. Static electricity
       B. Circuits, DC, and AC
       C. Electric power and energy

    VI. Magnetism
       A. Permanent magnets
       B. Magnetic fields
       C. Current and magnetism
       D. Transformers and generators
       E. Electric power production and transmission

VII. Gravity
   A. Mass and weight
   B. Newton's gravity
   C. Weight and free fall
   D. Mass, volume, and density

VIII. Matter
   A. Solids, liquids, and gases
   B. Physical and chemical changes
       (reactions)
   C. Mixtures and solutions
   D. Periodic Table: Elements and compounds

Reinhartz and Beach (1992) offer several suggestions for determining the sequence of content for elementary students. (These suggestions were used in developing the physical science scope and sequence just outlined.) As teachers decide on the what and when in planning, these suggestions may prove helpful. It is important to keep in mind the following:

■ Learning proceeds from simple to complex, from the concrete to the abstract level.

■ Prerequisite skills and knowledge should be identified.

■ Deductive learning (general to particular) provides a generalization, principle, or definition first; the specifics, with examples and nonexamples and parts, are introduced later, with experience.

■ Inductive learning begins with specifics based on experience, moves to a discussion of examples and nonexamples, and concludes with a generalization, principle, or definition.

■ A chronological approach provides a learning organizer for content and skills.

One final aspect of the curriculum to consider is *continuity*. Continuity is the presentation of concepts at different times and at different levels of difficulty throughout the elementary school. It was Bruner (1960) who introduced the concept of the "spiral curriculum," which is in the spirit of continuity. According to Tanner and Tanner (1980), concepts are

> developed and redeveloped in a spiral fashion, becoming deeper and wider, as the child progresses through the higher grades . . . [and therefore] the concept of the spiral curriculum relates not only to the vertical integration or deepening of knowledge [but also to the horizontal integration]. (p. 541)

Once the sources have been identified, the decisions regarding the scope, sequence, and continuity of the curriculum are made to ensure that the educational program is planned and is appropriate for a specific group of students.

SUMMARY

The four fields of study, as identified in Figure 1-6, that form the foundation for the curriculum development process include historical perspectives; the current nature of the elementary school; the social, political, and economic contexts that shape elementary education; and an understanding of how children grow and develop. Andre, the "Voice of Experience" for this chapter, helps you better understand why these fields of study are so important when developing a curriculum for elementary students.

In addition to these fields of study, teachers must come to understand their own professional belief system and how it affects their educational practices. Such an analysis involves a review of the four educational philosophies. Being aware of some of the possible frames of reference for a professional belief system makes it possible for you to understand why an educator teaches the way he or she does and has certain attitudes toward students and learning.

This chapter presented four philosophies: idealism, realism, progressivism, and existentialism, along with profiles of each philosophy in practice in an actual classroom setting. It explored the role and origins of a philosophy to help you recognize the importance of where a philosophy comes from and become aware that a belief system starts early in a teacher's career and shapes a teacher's outlook. Most educators do not adhere to one philosophy exclusively. Depending on the situation, a teacher may cross over from one philosophy to another. The lines between philosophies are fluid, and, in the last analysis, many teachers have an eclectic approach. This does not mean that a teacher is not operating from one dominant philosophy; it does mean that a teacher is flexible in reviewing all the facts before taking a final position.

Another topic discussed in this chapter was the relationship and distinction between curriculum and teaching. All too often, the dualism between process/product or means/ends forces educators to choose curriculum over teaching or vice versa. In reality, as described in the chapter, curriculum and teaching complement each other, and curriculum sets the stage for and leads to teaching. You cannot have ends without means or products without processes. Curriculum and teaching are two sides of the same coin.

The chapter continued with a discussion of the various designs for organizing a curriculum. Five specific curriculum designs—subject centered, student centered, broad field, problem-solving centered, and integrated—were discussed briefly. These teaching-and-learning designs organize a curriculum from a specific perspective, and they provide the beginning point for developing an elementary-education curriculum. One design is not inherently better than the other: they all serve as models from which educators can choose when creating an overall school curriculum, grade-specific units, and individual lessons.

The section on sources explored the key question, *Where does the curriculum come from?* Depending on the curriculum theorist, whether it be Dewey, Bode, Tyler, or Doll, the sources of the curriculum revolve around a few common themes: the students and their needs, society and its needs, and subject-matter experts. In the end, these sources serve as the catalyst for the curriculum-planning process.

After the design(s) and sources have been decided, the teacher is ready to address the scope, sequence, and continuity issues of the curriculum, which prepares teachers for the planning process described in Chapter 6. Chapter 5 provided the infrastructure for the next steps of curriculum development—planning, implementing, and assessing.

>>>
<<<<<<<<<<<<<<<<<<<<<<<<<<<<<<<<<<<<<<<<<<<<<<<<<<<<<<<<<<<<<<<<<<<<<<<<<<<<<<<<<<<

■ YOUR TURN

1. Read each of the following statements and determine which philosophy of education it best exemplifies: (1) idealism, (2) realism, (3) progressivism, (4) existentialism. Use the numbers 1–4 to code each statement. To check your response, refer to the key at the end of the Your Turn section.

a. Effective elementary teachers ask a variety of higher-order questions to develop reasoning skills.

b. The purpose of education is to help society improve.

c. Elementary teachers use inquiry strategies.

d. Students develop critical-thinking skills using classical literature.

e. Elementary teachers use demonstration and class participation to ensure that students understand the topic.

f. Elementary students should become aware of the rules that affect the physical world.

g. The elementary curriculum should include those topics and issues that foster self-reflection and choice making.

h. Applied learning is the core of the curriculum program because societal problems can be addressed.

i. The role of the elementary teacher is to facilitate learning.

j. Searching for meaning through reason is important if students are to discover the truth.

k. Having subject-matter specialists as teachers ensures that students receive an education that is content-oriented.

l. The most effective teaching method is telling and fact finding.

m. The curriculum should include a variety of subjects for self-exploration, including the arts.

n. One of the best ways for students to learn is to be involved in their own learning by experiencing it.

o. Fostering intellectual competence is the purpose of elementary education.

p. To become successful adults, elementary students must learn a common body of knowledge and common core of skills.

q. Teachers model a problem-solving technique.

r. By working in groups, students learn to share ideas and to come to consensus regarding ways to solve the problem.

s. Students learn about their environment through their senses.

t. Truth is absolute and can be determined by exploring the ideas contained in great literature.

2. Now that you have challenged yourself by labeling the statements above with a specific educational philosophy, take some time and respond to the following questions:

a. What is the ultimate purpose of elementary education? To prepare students to fit into society? To change society? To meet individual needs or society's needs? Decide how you feel and write a response. Then analyze why you feel this way. What educational philosophies do your statements reflect?

b. What do you think education is? Why do you think so? Is it different from training or schooling? Support your answer with examples to illustrate your points.

c. How do students learn? learn best? Why do you believe this? What influences their learning? How? In what ways? What implications does this have for elementary teachers?

d. What role does environment play in determining success in school? What role does heredity play in determining success in school? Do they play a role at all? Why? Why not?

3. If an educator asked what shaped your belief system, what would you say? Make a list of what and who influenced your belief system, and place them in a time line. Using these items, write your philosophy of education.

4. Review your philosophy and decide what category of educational philosophy it best represents. Did you think you were a progressive, based on your original ideas regarding your philosophy of education, but now do you find that you are more traditional in your orientation? Why? What from your background is having the greatest impact on this decision? Explore these influences a little

more, but this time in relation to a controversial issue. Challenge yourself to find out what influences you by reflecting on the beliefs that you hold dear.

Answers for Your Turn (# 1)

a.	4	h.	3	o.	1
b.	3	i.	3	p.	2
c.	3	j.	4	q.	3
d.	1	k.	2	r.	3
e.	2	l.	2	s.	2
f.	4	m.	4	t.	1
g.	2	n.	3		

■ REFERENCES

Aristotle. (1954). *Ethics Book I and Politics Book II* (W. D. Ross, Trans.). Chicago: Henry Regnery Company. (Original work published about 340 B.C.)

Armstrong, D. G. (1989). *Developing and documenting the curriculum.* Boston: Allyn & Bacon.

Bagley, W. C. (1907). *Classroom management.* Upper Saddle River, NJ: Merrill/Prentice Hall.

Beach, D. M., & Reinhartz, J. (1989). *Supervision: Focus on instruction.* New York: Harper & Row.

Beauchamp, G. A. (1968). *Curriculum theory* (2nd ed.). Wilmette, IL: The Kagg Press.

Berliner, D. (1996, February 27). *Research and social justice.* Paper presented at the Seventy-Sixth Annual Meeting of the Association of Teacher Educators, St. Louis, MO.

Bode, B. H. (1927). *Modern educational theories.* Upper Saddle River, NJ: Merrill/Prentice Hall.

Bruner, J. S. (1960). *The process of education.* Cambridge, MA: Harvard University Press.

Cherry, L. (1990). *The great kapok tree.* San Diego, CA: Gulliver Books, Harcourt Brace Jovanovich.

Core knowledge curriculum project. (1992, February). [Profiles in excellence: innovative instruction.] *Executive Educator, 14*(2), A2–27.

Dewey, J. (1902). *The child and the curriculum.* Chicago: University of Chicago Press.

Dewey, J. (1906). *Democracy and education.* Upper Saddle River, NJ: Merrill/Prentice Hall.

Doll, R. C. (1995). *Curriculum improvement* (9th ed.). Boston, MA: Allyn & Bacon.

Farnham-Diggory, S. (1990). *Schooling: The developing child.* Cambridge, MA: Harvard University Press.

Fullan, M. G. (1993). Why teachers must become change agents. *Educational Leadership. 50*(6), 12–17.

Gutek, G. L. (1992). *Education and schooling in America* (2nd ed.). Boston, MA: Allyn & Bacon.

Gutek, G. L. (1988). *Education and schooling in America.* Upper Saddle River, NJ: Merrill/Prentice Hall.

Hutchins, R. M. (1936). *The higher learning in America.* New Haven, CT: Yale University Press.

Johnson, M. (1967, April). Definitions and models in curriculum theory. *Educational Theory, 17,* 127–140.

Knight, G. R. (1989). *Issues and alternatives in educational philosophy.* Berrien Springs, MI: Andrews University Press.

Komoski, P. K. (1990, February). Needed: A whole-curriculum approach. *Educational Leadership, 47*(5), 72–77.

Macdonald, J. B. (1965). Educational models for instruction—Introduction. In J. B. Macdonald and R. R. Leeper (Eds.), *Theories of instruction* (p. vi). Washington, DC: The Association for Supervision and Curriculum Development.

Montessori, M. (1967). *The child.* Wheaton, IL: The Theosophical Publishing House.

Ornstein, A. C., & Hunkins, F. P. (1993). *Curriculum: Foundations, principles, and issues* (2nd ed.). Boston, MA: Allyn & Bacon.

Popham, W. J., & Baker, E. I. (1970). *Systematic instruction*. Upper Saddle River, NJ: Merrill/Prentice Hall.

Reinhartz, J., & Beach, D. M. (1992). *Secondary education: Focus on curriculum*. New York: HarperCollins.

Ryan, K., & Cooper, J. M. (1995). *Those who can, teach* (7th ed.). Boston: Houghton Mifflin Company.

Saylor, J. G., & Alexander, W. M. (1981). *Curriculum planning for better teaching and learning*. New York: Holt, Rinehart & Winston.

Saylor, J. G., & Alexander, W. M. (1954). *Curriculum planning for better teaching and learning*. New York: Holt, Rinehart & Winston.

Tanner, D., & Tanner, L. N. (1995). *Curriculum development theory into practice* (3rd ed.). Upper Saddle River, NJ: Merrill/Prentice Hall.

Tanner, D., & Tanner, L. N. (1980). *Curriculum development theory into practice* (2nd ed.). Upper Saddle River, NJ: Merrill/Prentice Hall.

Tanner, D., & Tanner, L. N. (1987). *Supervision in education: Problems and practices* (2nd ed). Upper Saddle River, NJ: Merrill/Prentice Hall.

Tyler, R. W. (1949). *Basic principles of curriculum and instruction*. Chicago: University of Chicago Press.

Zais, R. S. (1976). *Curriculum principles and foundations*. New York: Harper & Row.

chapter 6

Curriculum Planning:
The Reflection Step

AFTER READING THE CHAPTER, YOU WILL BE ABLE TO DO THE FOLLOWING:

- Describe the importance of curriculum planning in the curriculum development process.

- Define the term *planning* and describe the components of the planning step.

- Discuss the importance of reflection as teachers engage in planning for teaching and learning.

- Explain how constructivism influences a teacher's plans for teaching and learning.

- Identify and describe the functions of curriculum planning.

- Compare the two common unit designs and discuss the benefits of each.

- Identify and give examples of the items teachers need to consider when planning.

- Distinguish between goals and objectives in planning documents, and explain the importance of the domains of learning in writing objectives.

- Discuss the implications of the concept of multiple intelligences to curriculum planning.

In a climate in which immediate solutions and the ability to "think on your feet" are often valued over deliberation and reflection, some people think teaching is simple. Those people feel that all anyone has to do is go into a classroom and start teaching. It may be that a few teachers, drawing on their years of experience, can do that. However, most teachers—particularly those just starting out—must think through their lessons and plan in some form for teaching and learning, if they are to increase their effectiveness in the classroom.

Why would teaching a lesson or series of lessons be any different from other important aspects of life? Consider giving a party: seldom does this event just "happen." For a social event to be a success, the host or hostess writes out the guest list, plans for refreshments and decorations, develops a budget and list of materials, and antic-

ipates the number of guests. The success of the event ultimately depends on the kinds of plans and decisions that are made beforehand. Teaching works very much the same way. Planning is a prerequisite to effective teaching (Manatt, 1981). Just as in planning for a party, the excitement and anticipation of the lesson(s) builds when planning for teaching.

Many new teachers are nervous when they think about their first week of school. They wonder, *What do I do?* This reaction is natural and normal. Even veteran teachers admit to getting butterflies as they anticipate the first week of school and the special unit or theme they choose to begin the school year. The second thing that happens after these teachers sit down and catch their breath is ask some questions that help them focus and reflect on what they will teach. Frequently, their biggest concern is, *What will I do when I stand before a group of elementary students?* Other questions that come to mind include these: *What content do I teach, and when? What resources do I have or can I use to design lesson plans for my class? Will the lessons be appropriate for my students?* and *What is the best way to teach this topic, concept, or skill?*

Teachers frequently seek answers to these questions in some form as they develop lesson plans. These questions, along with their answers, form the core of the planning step. Chapter 6 offers suggestions for addressing these questions related to curriculum planning. It begins with a description of the aspects of planning and continues by describing issues for teachers to consider when planning for teaching and learning. *Reflection* (thinking about prior experiences with both students and the content) plays a significant role in planning because it encourages teachers to think about what, when, and how to teach a concept in the elementary curriculum. The chapter also provides insights about the planning step which come from master teachers and the professional literature. By the end of this chapter, you will have a series of snapshots of the planning step to provide a greater sense of what a teacher does to plan for teaching effectively.

ASPECTS OF PLANNING

Although the research base on teacher planning cannot provide solid, empirical evidence as to a single best way to plan, it does provide insights that can be used to understand the complexities of the role of the teacher in the planning step. Posner (1995) suggests that the planning process looks different because of the "format of the curriculum and the emphasis given to each of the format categories" (p. 41), such as objectives, activities, materials, or content (Woolfolk (1995) and other researchers (Clark & Yinger, 1987; Shavelson, 1987) have asked teachers how they

plan and found that teachers do the following things:

- View planning as an important step in teaching and curriculum development.

- Engage in several levels of planning (i.e., district, building, grade as well as yearly, unit, daily).

- Use plans to reduce but not totally eliminate uncertainty and ambiguity.

- Recognize there is no single model for effective planning.

The research also verifies that teachers who plan are more effective overall in the classroom (Manatt, 1981). Teachers also consider planning to play a central role in linking curriculum to teaching and learning (Clark & Yinger, 1987). Planning gives credence to the image of the teacher as a reflective practitioner; it provides teachers an opportunity to think about and rehearse mentally and on paper what will take place when they teach. As teachers think about the planning process, Frieberg and Driscoll (1996) describe it as visualizing possibilities or thinking in terms of what can be. They further suggest that, as teachers engage in planning, they need to "listen to the voices of opportunity" (p. 23) that come from internal and external sources and include the teacher's "voice, a colleague's voice, and students' voices" (p. 24). As we listen to our own voices, we begin to transform concepts and content into meaningful learning behaviors for our students. As we listen to colleagues' voices, we begin to expand and enrich not only our understanding of the concepts and skills to be taught but our capacity to include a greater variety of strategies as we add to our teaching repertoire. As we listen to our students' voices, we become more aware of their lives and the things that motivate them, and as we engage them in the planning process, we increase their stake in its success.

Planning is a multidimensional process involving many factors to consider that are not necessarily sequential. Eggen and Kauchak (1997) have described *planning* as organizing content, selecting and sequencing learning activities, grouping students for instruction, determining assignments, establishing assessment procedures and grading practices, and establishing classroom management strategies. They further suggest that planning serves three functions:

- It builds emotional and professional security by reducing teacher anxiety.

- It provides organization for teaching and learning.

- It provides an opportunity for reflection.

As teachers plan, they engage in continuous self-assessment and monitoring of not only their teaching behavior but also student success. When teachers begin the planning step, they must take time to consider their prior knowledge and experiences in teaching concepts and skills associated with the unit to be taught.

Planning as Reflection

It is during the initial part of the planning step that teachers have the most time to engage in reflection. Osterman (1990) describes reflection as the "mindful consideration of one's action, specifically, one's professional actions" (p. 134). He goes on to say that

> reflective practice is a challenging, focused and critical assessment of one's own behavior as a means towards developing one's own craftsmanship. [It] is a dialectic process in which thought is integrally linked with action. (p. 134)

Reflection, according to Schon (1987), is a "dialogue of thinking and doing through which [one] become[s] more skillful" (p. 31):

Schon (1987, 1990) has popularized the term *reflective practice*. Reflective practice is historically rooted in the work of Dewey and theories of learning, because with reflection comes learning and with learning comes changes in teacher behavior. A series of reflective experiences helps

teachers to see the flow of events as continuous and not as isolated instances. Christine, our "Voice of Experience" in this chapter, engages in reflective practices as she looks for answers. Reflection begins as she sits down and thinks about previous years of teaching and all the children she has taught. She takes the time to examine her actions and the circumstances from the inside out. In Christine's case, reflection guides her decisions regarding what she teaches, in what order, how, and what resources to use and when. Christine uses these decisions to develop alternate plans and strategies.

 Voice of Experience

Christine recently told a colleague that "reflection helps me grow professionally because it causes me to think about my teaching and it encourages me to examine my belief system, values, and assumptions about teaching and how children learn." Christine says, "When I spend time reflecting on my teaching, I begin to teach myself. It also helps me to be more confident by getting me to appreciate not only what I know, but also why I know it. In effect, my knowledge base about teaching has grown as my confidence has grown." [The goal of reflection for Christine has been to move from a teacher who delivers services to one who constructs a personal knowledge base about classroom life and teaching in a way that relates to students.] As Christine puts it, "This new information helps me have greater control of my professional life, which is so important when planning lessons." As Christine reflects on the past, she begins to plan for the new year.

Planning as a Process

Many beginning teachers have the impression that the planning step in the curriculum development process is linear and sequential, involving one instructional decision at a time. This view of planning is grounded in a model advocated by Tyler (1949) in *Basic Principles of Curriculum and Instruction*. Over the years, this linear model has been presented in textbooks as a strategy for planning (Arends, 1994; Jacobsen, Eggen, & Kauchak, 1993). The linear model has four sequential steps:

1. statement of learner objectives
2. selection of learning activities
3. organization of learning activities
4. establishment of assessment procedures

Teachers also use task analysis as a planning tool to help break a concept or skill into component parts and identify prerequisite learner behaviors. A variation of the linear model begins with one of the other steps.

Within the multiple steps of planning, a teacher may not necessarily begin with the same step each time. Lesson planning generally includes objectives, concepts and/or content, procedures and/or activities, resources and/or materials, and assessment. Posner (1995) also adds rationale, learner characteristics, sequencing, schedule, teacher abilities and attitudes, and administrative structure as parts to planning. In a truly linear model, teachers begin by writing objectives based on content, then they select and organize procedures/activities, and finally they establish assessment procedures. However, teachers may modify this process by beginning the planning step at any point, such as by focusing first on activities, matching them with objectives and then establishing assessment procedure(s).

In reality, teachers may consider a number of these steps simultaneously. As they think about a specific concept, they also think about ways to teach that concept at the same time. Making a *semantic map* as a beginning point may be helpful. To do this, the teacher places the concept or theme in the center of a sheet of paper; then, as thoughts related to the topic come to mind, these

are added to the map by drawing lines from the center where the topic or theme is written. The design that develops looks very much like the spokes of a wheel that radiate out from the hub. Figure 6-6, item C, provides an example of a semantic map.

Planning as Constructivism

According to some researchers (Yinger, 1977), planning looks to the future and provides a framework for guiding action by causing teachers to think about what is to come and reflect on their actions. Such a view of planning draws heavily from cognitive psychology and a constructivist view of learning. Teachers may plan for instruction by recognizing a growing body of research that suggests that students do not necessarily learn discrete, isolated skills or concepts before moving to more complex learning. In such a view, learning is constructed by each student based on his or her prior knowledge and experiences, the context in which the learning occurs, and the real-world application.

The constructivist view of planning puts the student in the center of the process. Figure 6-1 presents this learner-centered view and begins by considering the sequence that learners use to construct new learning as they process new information. This view also shows respect for the knowledge and experience learners bring to the classroom.

From a constructivist view, planning not only involves setting goals and objectives, but also recognizes that the process of learning and the depth of understanding are as important as the outcomes (Eggen & Kauchak, 1997). Activities involve students in actual or authentic problem-solving situations, as a way of providing an appropriate context for learning—instead of the presentation of a series of abstract, isolated facts or pieces of information.

Another description of the planning process examines *what* teachers do when they plan. In combining views, Clark and Yinger (1987) see

FIGURE 6-1 Constructivist
View of Planning

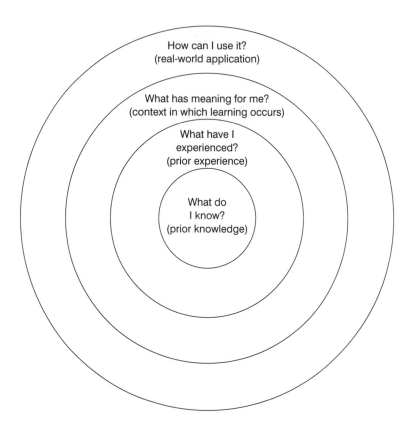

planning as "both a psychological process and a practical activity" (p. 345).

We see the planning step as engaging teachers in reflecting and thinking about the teaching-learning process, but we also view the planning step as going beyond thinking and actually recording in some written form plans that teachers can follow. These written records provide a blueprint for guiding teachers as they work with students in the reality of the classroom setting. To do this requires teachers to make a number of decisions (Sardo Brown, 1988).

Planning: Where to Begin

The key question that initiates the curriculum planning step is *Where do I begin?* Christine, the "Voice of Experience" for this chapter, provides some insights to help answer that question.

 Voice of Experience

Christine begins to plan a unit on geometry. For her to make planning manageable, she identifies the major goals, objectives, and concepts of the unit. Christine thinks, "This should be easy because I have taught this unit a few times before," but she confesses that she is still not sure of where and how to get started.

As Christine begins to plan this unit, she jots down the kinds of planning questions she must answer, such as

1. What theme or focus should the geometry unit have?

2. What learning outcomes (goals and objectives) do I want my students to achieve?

3. What concepts/content and skills do I need to teach?

4. What questions can I ask so that I have some idea about what students already know as well as what they want to learn about geometry, how geometry impacts their daily lives, and what projects can be done to capitalize on their abilities?

5. What strategies/delivery systems will I employ to achieve unit goals and objectives, meet student needs and interests, and provide meaningful experiences for students?

6. How do I get students involved, and what degree of interaction is needed?

7. What instructional materials and resources—games, visuals, media, software, magazines, and newspaper articles—will I need? Are they available?

8. How much time will it take to teach the unit?

9. How will I know if students have learned the concepts/content and skills?

Christine realizes that these questions are fundamental to the planning step, and each teacher, as he or she plans, must consider many of these same questions.

One advantage Christine has over the beginning teacher across the hall is experience. Christine tells the teacher that "planning should be easier for me because I have taught the material previously." She continues, "I have previous experience and knowledge to draw upon as I think about the geometry unit." Christine is empathic with her new colleague because she remembers when she was starting out how difficult planning was for her as a beginning teacher.

UNIT PLANNING: TWO PERSPECTIVES

What the curriculum looks like and how it is delivered depends on the decisions that teachers make in the planning step—the goals and objectives, ways of accommodating the needs and abilities of students, strategies for teaching the content and skills, instructional resources and materials, and ways to measure what the students have learned.

As teachers begin planning for the year, they often divide the year into blocks of time that help them to manage the process, such as semesters, and then, within each semester, consider the number of reporting periods (e.g., 3 six-week periods or 2 nine-week periods). Each of these reporting periods can then be divided into units of instruction, from which daily lesson plans are developed.

In some school districts, curriculum-planning forms are provided to teachers and ask for essential information about teaching. The school district may require teachers to complete these forms because they provide some degree of structure, uniformity, and/or accountability for the planning step. The forms and formats for recording planning information vary greatly and are limited only by the imagination and/or preferences of the local district and the teacher. Teachers can also use computer technology to generate unit and lesson plan forms.

Topical Unit Planning

For most teachers, the unit is the basic planning format for teaching and normally includes goals, objectives, content/concepts, materials/resources, and assessment procedures that form the basis for the series of lessons linked to the unit topic. When planning a unit, teachers can conceptualize the process from two perspectives: the unit perspective and the lesson perspective.

■ They can begin by thinking about the total unit topic—which may include brainstorming the concepts to be taught, the learner objectives, and the resources needed. This perspective of planning is often accomplished using a semantic map to encourage random thinking about the unit topic.

▪ They can begin by addressing the individual components, called *lessons*. The lesson perspective includes not only the objectives for the day, but also the activities to accomplish the objectives. These activities include engaging the learners, exploring prior knowledge, explaining new content/concepts, modeling or elaborating on new learning, assessing student understanding, and closing the lesson.

Figure 6-2 presents these two perspectives of unit planning.

Unit planning provides a holistic view of what is to be accomplished over several days or several weeks. Using a unit format, the focus of the planning process is long-term (to facilitate curriculum spiraling) yet comprehensive (to provide an understanding and appreciation of the topic under study). Figure 6-3 provides a sample unit-planning form, and Figure 6-4 provides a

sample lesson-planning form. These figures illustrate the kind of information normally included in developing unit and lesson plans.

A third-grade social studies unit on Antarctica is presented as an example using these unit- and lesson-planning forms. Figures 6-5 and 6-6 are based on the unit and lesson plans completed by a third-grade teacher resident, Susan Gruber.

Integrated Thematic Unit Planning

Teachers have recently engaged in a variation of the unit-planning format previously discussed. Instead of focusing on a concept in a single subject (e.g., Antarctica in social studies), the integrated thematic curriculum design, discussed in Chapter 5, is multidisciplinary and based on the belief that learning is integrative and establishes connections among various subject areas (Fredericks, Meinbach, & Rothlein, 1993).

FIGURE 6-2   Perspectives of Unit Planning

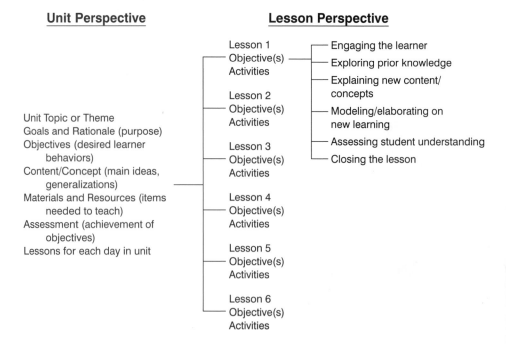

FIGURE 6-3 Perspective One: The Unit Plan Form

Teacher's Name: _____   Grade: _____

Number of Days: _____   Theme/Topic: _____

Unit Goals and Rationale

_____

Unit Objectives

_____

Content/Concept (main ideas, generalizations)

_____

Materials and Resources (items needed to teach)

_____

Assessment (achievement of objectives)

_____

Unit Closure

_____

FIGURE 6-4   Perspective Two: The Lesson Plan Form

Theme/Topic: _____   Grade Level: _____

For Day: _____

Lesson Objective(s): _____

_____

_____

Activities

    A. Engaging the Learner:_____

_____

    B. Exploring Prior Knowledge: _____

_____

    C. Explaining New Content/Concepts: _____

_____

    D. Modeling/Elaborating on New Learning: _____

_____

    E. Assessing Student Understanding:_____

_____

    F. Closing the Lesson: _____

Materials: _____

_____

To many elementary students, the traditional topical, subject-centered curriculum "presents an endless array of facts and skills that are unconnected, fragmented, and disjointed" (Beane, 1991, p. 9), and the students must take the word of an adult that the pieces really make sense and fit together. There are many advantages of integrated thematic units. Most not only emphasize the relationships that exist between and among the content areas of language arts, social studies, science, mathematics, and the fine arts, but also recognize the need to see relationships between and among ideas. Frazee and Rudnitski (1995) note that "an integrated curriculum addresses a diversity of learners more naturally" (p. 14). By deliberately modeling and including the connections, teachers ensure that students have opportunities to transfer knowledge from one subject area to others, and they witness firsthand the interdependence of all subject areas in the elementary curriculum. Teachers break down the boundaries between and among subject areas by

FIGURE 6-5 Perspective One: Sample Unit Plan

Teacher's Name: Susan G.	Grade: 3
Number of Days: 5	Theme/Topic: Antarctica

Unit Goals and Rationale: Students will be able to (1) locate Antarctica and the South Pole on a map and globe and describe the type of environment, (2) identify and decribe three different types of animals that live in or near Antarctica, (3) identify the largest type of penguin and describe its relationship to other penguins, (4) demonstrate listening skills by listening, (5) explain how glaciers and icebergs form, (6) describe what happens to water as it freezes, and explain why expansion occurs, and (7) discuss why ice weighs less than water and why icebergs float.

Content/Concept (main ideas, generalizations): (1) Where Antarctica is and what is the coldest it can get there? (2) Does water and ice weigh the same? (3) Why do icebergs float? (4) Are seals smart? (5) Do seals and walruses live in Antarctica? (6) Is there a snow monster? (7) Do polar bears live in Antarctica? (8) Are there people in Antarctica? (9) How many kinds of penguins are there and do they have feathers? (10) Do sea leopards eat penguins? (11) Why is there so much ice in Antarctica?

Materials and Resources (items needed to teach): (1) *Mr. Popper's Penguins* (Atwater, R. & Atwater, F. Boston: Little, Brown & Co., 1938), (2) Video: "Penguins of the Antarctic", (3) graduated cylinders (one with frozen blue water), (4) paper cup, (5) disposable pipette, (6) paper towel, (7) balance and gram weights, (8) water, blue food coloring, (9) CD-ROM map of Antarctica (*Groliers Encyclopedia* on CD-ROM), (10) lab/discovery sheets: (a) Detective Notes, (b) Cool Colonies, (c) Sizing Up Penguins, (d) Why Do Icebergs Float? (e) Amazing Antarctica—Antarctic foodchain.

Assessment (achievement of objectives): Each student will have an Antarctica folder that they will decorate. Each notebook will contain the lab/discovery sheets listed above. Each sheet will be assessed based on written responses and the degree to which they clarify or explain key concepts (vocabulary, spelling, phrases, elaboration, critical attributes). At the conclusion of the unit, each lab group will have a series of questions from the "What I Want to Know about Antarctica" chart to respond to. The teacher will meet with individual students and pose probing questions to determine the level of understanding related to the objectives and suggest additional activities as needed. These anectdotal notes wil be shared with the student and his/her parents or guradian at the end of the grading period.

Unit Closure: Write the questions from the "What I Want to Know" chart on the board and have students in pairs write interview questions to ask of an Antarctic scientist (possibly using the computer with Internet capabilities). Then have students interview each other using the same questions and responses they generated.

choosing a theme or topic and then planning learning experiences that help students make connections as they read, write, discuss, conduct science investigations, engage in mathematical problem solving, and utilize music and art (Eby & Kujawa, 1994, 1997).

An integrated thematic approach to curriculum design in the elementary school capitalizes on the curious nature of elementary students, who interact with the learning environment in such a way that they integrate that experience into their thinking and learning. Beane (1991) notes that integration is what students do when they start with a whole picture of a problem and then seek to solve it. An integrated thematic curriculum

FIGURE 6-6   Perspective Two: Sample Lesson Plan

Title/Topic/Theme: Antarctica   **Grade Level:**   3rd

Lesson Objective(s): The student will able to (1) describe what happens to water as it freezes, (2) explain why expansion occurs in freezing water, and (3) discuss why ice weighs less than water.

For Day: 3

Activities

A.   **Engaging the Learner:** Read selected pages form *Mr. Popper's Penguins*; have equipment of graduated cylinder with ice and without ice and ask students to make observations and predictions.

B.   **Exploring Prior Knowledge:** Ask a series of questions related to the measurements and predictions the students made about the (blue) water from the previous day.

C.   **Explaining New Content/Concepts:** Describe after students respond to questions and make their observations and predictions that frozen water expands which may/may not validate their responses. Uses other examples to explain the principles of expansion.

What I want to Know About Antarctica Chart

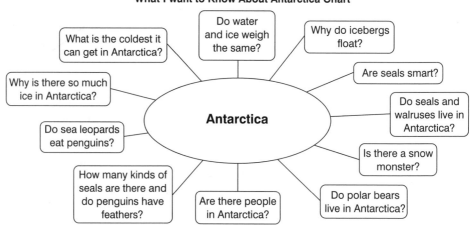

D.   **Modeling/Elaborating on New Learning:** Compares new cylinder of blue water with a cylinder of water that has been put in the freezer. Asks which cylinder of water (liquid) or water (solid) has more volume or weighs more. This demonstration is a way of linking the formation of icebergs and why they float.

E.   **Assessing Student Understanding:** Listens and takes brief notes while students offer comments (predictions, weighs materials, and checks their lab sheets).

F.   **Closing the Lesson:** Asks questions and asks students to share their answers with their neighbor of how and what they just learned, and explain why icebergs float.

Materials: Graduated cylinder with frozen blue water from previous day, empty graduated cylinder (same size as frozen one), blue food coloring, disposable pippette, water, balance, gram weights, paper towels, and a paper dixie cup.

implies wholeness and unity rather than separation and fragmentation . . . and real curriculum integration occurs when young people confront personally meaningful questions and engage in experiences related to those questions. (Beane, 1991, p. 9)

A curriculum that is integrated helps students construct connections and meanings that are within their personal scaffold of learning; consequently, it has wide appeal from early childhood programs through the middle school. As students are confronted by problems within an integrated thematic unit, they use prior knowledge and skills to seek answers and possible solutions that have meaning for them at their level of development.

The two perspectives of planning shown in Figure 6-2 remain unchanged for the integrated thematic unit. However, there is an additional consideration for the teacher when planning individual lessons that are a part of an integrated thematic unit. In the unit perspective, when planning an integrated unit, teachers need to ensure not only that the goals, objectives, and content relate to the topic but also that each area of study (e.g., science, math, language arts) is included in this planning. In the unit perspective, the question the teacher addresses is *How does each content area relate to the theme?* The question must also be asked in the second perspective. Not only must objectives and activities relate to the topic or theme, but also, different concepts from language arts, social studies, fine arts, science, and mathematics must be incorporated.

Elizabeth Lawley, a sixth-grade teacher, planned an integrated thematic unit for the first week of school, called "Exploring the Unknown" to acquaint students with their new building. Over the past few years, all the teachers on her team had spent several days covering the same theme, which involves helping the students feel comfortable in their new surroundings. The sixth-grade team used a semantic map to identify each of the subjects (see Figure 6-7). This unit is not only functional, but it also models how the

subjects of mathematics, language arts, science, social studies, and art are connected in a meaningful way by relating content to an issue that students can identify with as they encounter a new building—a new unknown. In this thematic unit, "Exploring the Unknown" (Figure 6-7), each subject area relates to the theme while incorporating concepts from each subject area. As teachers design lessons for this unit, they make sure that the content from each subject area relates not only to the theme, but also to the other subjects in the curriculum.

ITEMS TO CONSIDER WHEN PLANNING

Regardless of the written form unit planning takes, teachers may want to use a semantic map as a way to begin to reflect on the planning step. At first glance, the semantic map provided in Figure 6-8 may look intimidating, but it's not that hard to interpret. Begin at the center of the map: there's the theme of the unit. Each item radiating from this unit theme addresses some item of the planning step.

Figure 6-8 shows six items associated with the planning step:

■ goals and objectives

■ students

■ teaching strategies

■ resources and materials (including technology)

■ content

■ assessment

As teachers go through the various items, they are often required to complete some kind of unit-planning form. Figure 6-9 shows a completed unit-planning form, a sample unit on "All About Me" that addresses the six planning items.

FIGURE 6-7   Integrated Thematic Unit: Exploring the Unknown

Mathematics
- Mapping the building by taking the schedule, touring, and coloring in the rooms.
- Measuring distances: How far is the office, cafeteria? What is the locker capacity (estimate how many items will fit)?
- Visit from secretary (absence policy, use of phone, lost and found, need lunch money); from custodian (his/her duties and how they can help); bake muffins for secretary and custodian

Language Arts
- Reading about other schools-one-room schoolhouse, private schools; compare and contrast with their school
- Visit from librarian (describing what he/she does)
- Preparing a class book for the librarian to include art work, list of their favorite books/types of books
- Writing thank-you notes to the nurse, cafeteria workers, custodian, and the secretary

THEMATIC UNIT: EXPLORING THE UNKNOWN

Science
- Touring lab and reviewing rules
- Visiting the lunchroom and talking about importance of breakfast, how junk food affects people; discussing the food groups in sample menus and calculating the calories for one lunch
- Visit from the school nurse (what do you do if you get sick; talk about ways to keep healthy and the need for exercise)

Social Studies
- Drawing a map of the school campus (parking lots, bus pick-up area, playground, etc.)
- Discussing why it is important to be organized (offer suggestions: use binders, keep a calendar)
- Discussing ways to be a good school citizen in the library, cafeteria, lab, and in the halls
- Talking with the counselor to share what his/her role is at the school in helping students
- Writing pledge cards for being a good citizen (I pledge to . . .)
- Writing the job descriptions of all these workers
- Keeping a journal of assignments and to record feelings and thoughts
- Reading student handbook together and discussing it
- Getting students to respond to "What I heard about 6th grade . . ."

Art
- Making artwork for the school—wall murals with theme or topic
- Designing stationery and envelopes for thank-you notes and letters
- Decorating binders and developing symbols to use on their calendar to remind them of important events

FIGURE 6-8 Items to Consider When Planning

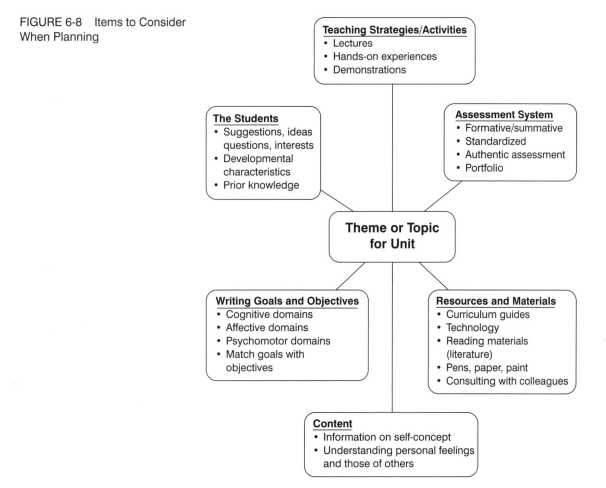

The questions Christine poses in the "Voice of Experience" scenario show the items in Figure 6-8 in operation. There is no particular sequence in which the items must be addressed. Some teachers may begin by asking students about what they know, what they want to know, and how they can find out; others may begin by consulting resources, materials, or technology, or by visiting with colleagues. Most teachers seek some degree of balance as they examine each of the items and get information for teaching the unit.

In reality, a teacher may decide on a unit theme while he or she addresses several of these items: the student audience, the goals and objec-

tives of the unit, what information to teach, the strategies, resources to use, or ways to assess student results. The theme of the example unit in Figure 6-9 is "All About Me"; it is a unit for first graders. Any of the items in Figure 6-8 can be considered first, but we prefer to start the planning step by focusing first on the goals and objectives.

Unit Goals and Objectives

Once the teacher has established a clear theme (in this case, "All About Me"), the goals are generated, and the teacher is ready to convert goals

FIGURE 6-9   Completed Sample Unit Planning Form: All About Me

Unit Theme: All About Me.   *Level:* First Grade   *Time:* One Week (5 days)

Unit Goals:
- The child will learn that he/she is an unique individual.
- The child will appreciate the uniqueness of his/her classmates.

Unit Objectives:

1. When asked, the child will be able to say his/her name. (cognitive)
2. When names are written on a birthday calendar, the child will be able to point to the names of at least 4 of his/her classmates. (cognitive)
3. During a class discussion, the child will be able to identify at least 3 of his/her classmates (i.e. gender, language, physical characteristics, ages, etc.). (cognitive)
4. When a classmate is talking, each child will listen politely—not talk or bother his/her neighbor. (affective)
5. During center activities, the child will be able to write the first letter of his/her name in chocolate pudding spread on a clean desk. (psychomotor)

Ideas from Children:

1. The children would like to have a play-like birthday party. (body smart)
2. The children want to listen to stories. (word smart)
3. They asked if they could draw on large pieces of butcher paper using paints and markers. (picture smart)
4. From talking with children, it is evident that they would enjoy just expressing their feelings and ideas. (self smart)
5. They would like to try all the centers, and work with their friends. (people smart)

Resources and Materials:

1. Use "me" dolls to promote attention to each child.
2. Need flip cards and butcher paper for large graphs when polling children about their likes and dislikes (food, television cartoons, etc.).
3. Paints, aprons, brushes, and markers for self-portraits.
4. Ingredients for making the cookies and things to decorate them and the chocolate pudding for writing their names.
5. Music and songs for performing large moves in space.
6. Obtain the book *All About Me*.

Content: Social Studies

1. Self as a part of other entities
2. Uniqueness of people in a community
3. Celebrate holidays (birthdays)
4. Knowing others and treating them with respect

Teaching Strategies:

1. Activities/learning centers where small groups of children can work and perform tasks
2. Discussion about their favorite foods and cartoons on television
3. Direct instruction when asking students to follow directions
4. Activities when making their own body silhouettes

Assessment System:

1. Group/center activities will be assessed by teacher looking for evidence of cooperation, working together, and listening to each other.
2. Oral participation by all children during center work and class discussions.
3. Submission of samples of the child's work—entire body silhouettes.
4. As the children share, there is evidence that they recognize that they are unique and special.

Teacher Reflection (Thinking about what took place)

into more concrete and measurable learning results. Gronlund (1991) suggests starting with the general and moving to the specific. Writing objectives from general goals is the approach that is frequently advocated (Woolfolk, 1995). Figure 6-10 provides an example of a set of goals for the "All About Me" unit and the corresponding learner objectives for the unit; generating this information is referred to as the goal reduction process (GRP).

As seen in Figure 6-10, the goals are general statements of learning for the unit and the objectives are descriptions of specific learning behaviors. For example, to address the goal of "recognition of individuals," the teacher selects the behavior for the student, "to say his/her name."

At this point in planning a unit, the teacher establishes the student behaviors that will demonstrate that learning has occurred, normally referred to as instructional objectives. *Instructional objectives* are clear and unambiguous descriptions of student performance that are observable and/or measurable. An objective gives focus to learning because it describes what the student will do to demonstrate proficiency. Objectives should therefore be stated with the greatest clarity possible to avoid ambiguous meanings. By focusing on learner behavior as one of the first items in planning, the teacher also clarifies his or her understanding of the learning process.

In writing instructional objectives, teachers should consider three criteria:

■ the behavior to be performed

■ the conditions under which the behavior will occur (i.e., outside or in the lab)

■ the acceptable level of behavior/performance (Mager, 1975)

General behaviors such as *know* or *understand* are not considered appropriate behavior verbs for instructional objectives because they lack specificity; these verbs are more appropriate for goal statements.

FIGURE 6-10   Goal Reduction Process: Converting Goals to Objectives

Unit Content:	Social Studies
Unit Theme:	All About Me
Unit Goals:	The child will learn that he/she is a unique individual.
	The child will appreciate the uniqueness of his/her classmates.
Learner Objectives:	• When asked, the child will be able to say his/her name. (cognitive: recall)
	• When names are written on a birthday calendar, the child will be able to point to the names of at least 4 of his/her classmates. (cognitive: comprehension)
	• During a class discussion, the child will be able to identify at least 3 of his/her classmates (i.e., gender, language, physical characteristics, ages, etc.). (cognitive: analysis)
	• When a classmate is talking , each child will listen politely—not talk or bother his/her neighbor. (affective)
	• During a center activity, the child will be able to write the first letter of his/her name in chocolate pudding spread on a clean desk. (psychomotor)

In describing behaviors that teachers can look for as evidence of learning, Gagné (1985) has identified five possible outcomes:

■ *Verbal information*: knowing facts, names, dates, and characteristics

■ *Intellectual skills*: knowing how to use symbols to communicate and interact with the environment and solve problems

■ *Cognitive strategies*: thinking about thinking (metacognition) or processing information

■ *Attitudes*

■ *Motor skills*

Gagné (1985) has taken a different approach to identifying learning results from Bloom, Engelhart, Furst, Hill, and Krathohl (1956), who established the domains of learning. Gagné has refined the cognitive domain by identifying verbal and intellectual outcomes and adding cognitive strategies as a way to acquire information and skills. Bloom and his colleagues (1956), however, view learning as occurring within three domains: cognitive, affective, and psychomotor. Figure 6-11 provides a comparison of Bloom's and Gagné's views of learning.

Traditionally, teachers have used Bloom's domains of learning to describe student behaviors. Because of the popularity of Bloom's taxonomy in writing instructional objectives, we will also use that classification system and briefly elaborate on each domain.

The *cognitive domain* (Bloom et al., 1956) is divided into six levels, commonly referred to as Bloom's Taxonomy. The first two levels, knowledge and comprehension, are considered lower-level cognitive skills because they involve recalling facts and information and translating that information or restating it. The next four levels—application, analysis, synthesis, and evaluation—are considered higher-level cognitive behaviors because they involve using information in new ways, breaking down ideas or concepts into component parts, creating new entities, and making judgments. Teachers have tended to emphasize lower-level cognitive skill objectives, but research suggests that teachers need to focus on higher-level cognitive outcomes or higher-order thinking skills (HOTS) (Redfield & Rousseau, 1981; Gall, 1984; Berliner, 1987). Figure 6-12 identifies Bloom's cognitive levels and provides a sample list of action verbs and question starters that can be used when writing cognitive objectives.

Curricular goals and objectives are also linked to the developmental levels and needs of the students. Elementary students function primarily at the concrete level and have limited abstract thinking abilities (see Chapter 4). Teachers must write learner objectives and match them with experiences that move students from concrete, low-level thinking to more complex, higher-order, abstract thinking skills.

The *affective domain* (Krathwohl, Bloom, & Masia, 1964) emphasizes values, feelings, atti-

FIGURE 6-11   Comparison of Bloom's Domains of Learning and Gagné's Outcomes of Learning

Bloom's Domains of Learning	Gagné's Outcomes of Learning
• Cognitive	• Verbal information Intellectual skills Cognitive abilities
• Affective	• Attitudes
• Psychomotor	• Motor skills

FIGURE 6-12 Bloom's Taxonomy: Levels of Cognitive Domain, Sample Action Verbs, and Question Starters

Knowledge	Comprehension	Application	Analysis	Synthesis	Evaluation
Picture of a child who is painting something	Picture of a child with a bar graph on the floor leaning over and pointing to one column of plant growth	Picture of a child classifying/sorting buttons	Picture of a child who is using a cut apple to show fractional parts	Child drawing a picture/writing a poem	Two children standing on a balance beam—one higher than the other (labeled A & B)
Verbs	Verbs	Verbs	Verbs	Verbs	Verbs
• Label • Recall • Read • Listen • Watch • Direct	• Report • Explain • Translate • Restate • Give examples • Describe	• Use ideas • Solve • Interpret • Demonstrate • Illustrate • Show	• Take apart • Break down • Dissect • Debate • Differentiate • Experiment	• Design • Create • Assemble • Arrange • Prepare • Set up	• Judge • Assess • Measure • Compare results (best/worst; least/most) • Appraise
Typical Qs	Typical Qs	Typical Qs	Typical Qs	Typical Qs	Typical Qs
• Who . . . . • What . . . . • Where . . . . • When	• Asking to compare, contrast examples	• How can you apply . . . . • How can you use	• What does this mean? • Why does the experiment work?	• What if . . . . • What plan can you develop for . . . . • What model would typify	• What is the most meaningful interpretation . . . . • What conclusion can be made about . . . .

Low Level Thinking Skills ⟶   ⟶ Higher Level Thinking Skills tudes, and emotions, and is divided into five levels. The first two levels—receiving and responding—involve being sensitive to or aware of the stimuli in the environment ("paying attention and being respectful") and actively involved in the lesson by contributing to class discussion or working on an assigned task. These first two levels often parallel class rules and expectations. The next level—valuing—involves the student in telling why something is important to him or her. The fourth and fifth levels include organization and characterization by a value system. In these two higher levels, students behave in ways that are consistent with the values they have and are able to control behavior according to these values. For example, students learn to value that cheating is not appropriate, and they control their own behavior by doing their own work and not cheating on an assignment or test. Teachers include affective objectives in their plans because they impact student motivation and behavior; they are not necessarily measured on an individual basis. To determine success, teachers may provide questionnaires or informal attitude assessment.

The *psychomotor domain* (Harrow, 1972) involves physical skills and neuromuscular coordination. The domain is divided into six levels. The first two—reflex behaviors and basic fundamental movements—occur early in life and are composed of involuntary movements and locomotion (sitting, crawling, walking) and prehension (holding and grasping), and they form the basis for more specialized movements. At the next two levels—perceptual abilities and physical and mental components—students can make split-second physical responses (i.e., hitting a ball when thrown) and demonstrate the qualities of endurance, strength, flexibility, and agility. The last two levels—skilled movement and nondiscursive communication—involve the acquisition of physical skills with high levels of efficiency and performance, to the degree that movement is used to communicate. Both manuscript and cursive writing involve fine motor skilled movements. Behaviors at the highest levels range from the use

of nonverbal facial expressions (frowning), to including other movements (tumbling and dancing), to mime as a way of communicating.

As teachers plan units, they write instructional objectives in one or more of these three domains of learning (cognitive, affective, or psychomotor). The kinds of objectives teachers select are often related to their beliefs about the learning process. The values are a part of the teacher's educational philosophy and as such affect instructional objectives related to what and how children learn. Figure 6-9 presents sample objectives for each domain as a part of the unit "All About Me."

Objectives written by teachers have the greatest impact in the classroom because the teachers have ownership of them. With this ownership, meaningful teaching and learning take place. Teachers often conceptualize objectives mentally and jot down the key behaviors as they plan for instruction. This practice, especially with novice teachers, tends to lead to greater emphasis on activities than on objectives. These teachers frequently jump right into the "activities" because they want to involve students in the lesson. The danger in this choice is that students may fail to recognize the objective of the lesson. The failure to state objectives allows the teacher to favor the lower end of Bloom's Taxonomy because the tasks are easier to measure and assign a grade to at the conclusion of a grading period. In the end, these teachers may not have an opportunity to think through what they want their students to do and learn, which often results in a mismatch between the learning activity and the learning results.

To prevent a mismatch between the planned learning activity and what the student learns, a task analysis should be conducted for each instructional objective. A *task analysis* involves examining the prescribed student behavior indicated in the objective and any prior knowledge or prerequisite skills. This procedure helps teachers in the planning process by suggesting appropriate learning activities and their sequence, teaching behaviors, and assessment procedures. For example, in Figure 6-10, the objective "during a class discussion, the child will be able to identify at least three classmates by gender, language, and physical characteristics" assumes that the child has the prerequisite knowledge regarding the concept of gender as it relates to personal identity.

The Students

After teachers have had an opportunity to identify goals and objectives based on their own knowledge of the topic and on their professional judgment of what they think is important and essential to know, they are ready to review them in the light of what the students suggest (see item "The Students" in Figure 6-8). At this point in the unit planning step, teachers need to check their perceptions of what to teach against the ideas, suggestions, needs, and interests of their students.

One way to check these perceptions is to formulate four to six questions to initiate a discussion either with the whole class or in small groups. Taking time to determine prior knowledge and interests is time well spent. During this class "town meeting," teachers have a unique opportunity to gather information about the unit content—what projects might be included; what students particularly like about the topic as well as what they dislike and why; what examples, demonstrations, videos, and activities to use; and what materials might be especially helpful to the students (Smith & Neale, 1989).

 Voice of Experience

As Christine reflects on the planning process, not only does she have to answer the central questions related to what content she must teach, but she must also be aware of the developmental characteristics of the students in her class. Christine voices her concern about one of her students, Sean, who she says "learns best when he has an opportunity to look and touch materials/objects." With Sean in mind, Christine must decide if all her students are capable of handling this information (geometric concepts including shapes, perimeter, and area). Are her students developmentally ready to learn about this information? If the answer to this question is yes, it is with one caveat. The caveat is that they can handle this information if they experience the concepts visually and kinesthetically, as well as orally. Christine shares with her colleagues that "elementary students, especially students like Sean, need concrete experiences; otherwise, they will become frustrated and disengage from the geometry lesson."

In addition, teachers need to consider the students' learning styles, to discover various ways to motivate them (Campbell & Burton, 1994). When teachers acknowledge the students' developmental levels and cognitive styles, the students "learn more effectively and retain what they learn longer" (Dunn, 1990, p. 18). Students have typically been viewed as either right-brain (creative) or left-brain (logical) and either visual (seeing), auditory (hearing), or bodily-kinesthetic. Teachers have also come to recognize the concept of multiple intelligences and the seven avenues of learning described by Gardner (1983) and extended by Armstrong (1994) in ways that relate directly to classroom practices. The following examples demonstrate how the various ways of learning can be incorporated in the unit "All About Me" (Figure 6-9).

Word smart: Tell in your own words about the people in the book *All About Me*.

Logic smart: In the book *All About Me*, how many ways did he/she find out about himself/herself?

Picture smart: Draw a picture of the person in the book and show what he/she enjoys doing.

Body smart: Role play how you would act at a birthday party for a friend.

Music smart: Using the book *All About Me*, compose a song about yourself.

People smart: Describe how you are like or not like one of your brothers or sisters, or mother or dad.

Self smart: Describe what you like about yourself; what do you do best?

If students have input into what they learn, they are more likely to be eager to participate and be more responsive to the instructional experiences. In addition, teachers will gain insights into what individual students consider meaningful and relevant in their lives. These are powerful messages that teachers receive when they take time to talk with their students.

Teaching Strategies

There are many terms used to describe how teachers present the unit or lesson(s). We have decided to use the term *strategy*, rather than teaching method or approach. Determining the strategy or strategies to use is another important issue to resolve when planning a unit. Deciding whether a demonstration or a hands-on experience is better takes time, and individual teachers will need to analyze what they are going to teach and review the goals and objectives and the resources they have available.

According to Leinhardt (1987), the use of particular teaching strategies will enable students to learn and develop the conceptual understanding central to the content of the unit. Chapter 7 describes in more detail a variety of teaching strategies that teachers can select.

Resources and Materials

As part of the unit-planning step, teachers review resources and materials related to the theme. From experience, we know that teachers need to have background information to successfully use any resource or material. Resources and materials are tools that teachers use to implement a particular learning task. They are not more important than the teacher; they aid the teacher in delivering instruction. Resources and materials can enrich the instructional strategy that is used, and they help meet individual student learning styles and needs.

The chalkboard, chalk, and textbooks have served as the basic tools of teaching for decades, even centuries, but the classrooms of the 1990s demand more variety and diversity in presentation of content. The resources and materials a teacher will use compete with the television, computers, and magazines in students' homes. With this in mind, varying the instructional resources to include technology is extremely important. There are many resources and different types of materials to consider—curriculum guides, technology and software, professional and children's literature, as well as recommendations from colleagues. Figure 6-9 lists some of the resources used for the unit "All About Me."

Historically, the curriculum guide has been the key resource teachers used as a way to extend the material and information in the textbook. Curriculum guides are rich resources that include learning goals, objectives, and background information; they are organized around topics or themes with student activities. Originally these guides were written by curriculum specialists, but in recent years they have been written by groups of teachers and targeted to specific grade levels. When organized in this way and written by practitioners, they are a valuable resource for both beginning and experienced teachers.

Educational technology is also included in the resources and materials item. Because technology has become increasingly more important in the educational experiences of children in the elementary school, this topic will be discussed in greater detail in Chapter 9. As Kristine Lynes of Oyster River Elementary School (Durham, New Hampshire) says, "I've been in the classroom for

20 years and technology has made teaching a lot more exciting" ("There's Never Been a Better Time," 1993, p. 34). She summarizes the benefits of using technology as a resource in the classroom by saying, "Now the whole world comes into my room every day, bringing with it new opportunities for my students and [me] to explore things we wouldn't have access to without computers" (p. 34).

Technology comes in all forms and provides students with a variety of learning experiences that can introduce, explain, reinforce, and/or review concepts presented. In addition, technology (computers, laser discs, videos, and so on) plays to the students' learning styles by presenting not only images, but also opportunities to interact with text. Such opportunities vary the way students learn and more closely replicate experiences at home and outside school. Chapter 9 expands on the use of educational technology, which is growing in importance with each school year.

Content and Assessment

The last items identified in Figure 6-8, content and assessment, are crucial. For our "All About Me" unit, the social studies content area was selected. Social studies is the content area responsible for helping primary students understand themselves and their relationship to others in a family, classroom, community, and beyond. The "All About Me" unit focuses on the concepts of self and others and the uniqueness of people. (An examination of the content in each major subject area is provided in Part 3 (chapters 9–13) of this text.) Teachers may consult curriculum guides, textbooks, and other reference material to determine what content, concepts, and skills should be taught, in what order, and at what grade level. The sample unit assesses learner behaviors in a group format, by oral participation in learning activities, and submission of individual work (pictures drawn). Assessing student progress plays a role in the planning step, and Chapter 8

provides a broader view and presents not only a common definition, but also many ways to assess.

SUMMARY

Figure 6-8 presents many of the key items that need to be considered during the planning step. We have emphasized that the order for responding to each is based on the teacher's frame of reference and preference—once again reinforcing the idea that planning does not proceed linearly. There are always opportunities for branching and revisiting items already considered. The degree to which teachers write out their plans and the forms they use is personal and based largely on district policies. It is important, however, to remember these points:

- Planning is central to effective teaching (Eby & Kujawa, 1997; Clark & Yinger, 1987; Manatt, 1981).

- Experienced teachers note that unit planning is critical to teaching (Clark & Peterson, 1986; Clark & Yinger, 1988).

- Plans should be viewed as flexible guides for action (Frazee & Rudnitski, 1995).

- The focus of the planning process should be the student (Eggen & Kauchak, 1997).

Even though a teacher has planned and addressed each of the questions presented and tried to anticipate all the variables that will be encountered with students, there is always the potential for the unexpected and the resulting moment that causes teachers to change their plans.

Historically, curriculum development courses have suggested that teachers first begin with goals and objectives, but in reality teachers may begin at any point because, as veteran teachers note, "planning is personal and we each develop a format over time that works for us."

The planning step gets its true test when it is used in a classroom. That is when the plan is modified to respond to the existing and changing contexts that are a part of a dynamic, interactive elementary classroom environment. Context is an important part of classroom learning and is influenced by such factors as place, feeling, people, as well as information being presented (Woolfolk, 1995).

As you reflect on what you know about elementary students, the content to be taught, and its relationship or relevancy to your students, you are making a continuous stream of decisions that are all part of the curriculum-planning step. As you reflect, you may begin to consider planning as reflection or constructivism. You will also have to decide on a topical or integrated thematic unit approach. These and other questions are part of the decision-making process undertaken in the planning step.

After decisions have been made regarding content and sequence, and consideration has been given to how the topics or themes will be taught, the planning step is underway. As you begin to answer the nine questions posed by Christine, along with the items of the planning step presented in Figure 6-8, you begin to answer the question *Where do I begin?* and put the planning process in context. When you know what the items involved in planning are, the planning step becomes less mysterious.

Effective teachers do not wing it; they are prepared to teach lessons as part of a larger entity, a unit. They have worked through the items of topic or theme, goals and objectives, the students, the resources and materials, teaching strategies, content, and assessment. In addition, with successful implementation of these plans, planning becomes an important prerequisite to good teaching.

The purpose of this chapter was to allay some of the fears you might have had about preparing to teach elementary children. Another important part of being prepared is to think about the multidimensional nature of teaching that contributes to becoming a reflective practitioner. Good teaching does not just happen: it takes time and effort. This time and effort is called planning.

■ YOUR TURN

1. You are ready to begin teaching a thematic unit on different biomes such as the desert, tundra, or the ocean. Think through the planning step. Where would you begin? Review Figure 6-8 and decide which item you will begin with. Then make a list of other items that would follow. Look over the list and try to determine why you listed the items in this particular order. Remember, there is no right or wrong answer; this is an opportunity to decide what is important to you and why.

2. Visit several school districts and collect samples of the various unit/lesson planning forms. Compare the forms, noting similarities and differences with specific reference to the items discussed in this chapter. Would you make any changes in any of the forms? If yes, develop one of your own.

3. Analyze the plans provided in Figure 6-9, "All About Me." Make a T chart, with the left column labeled "What I have learned from this unit" and the right column "How can I apply it?" Would you change anything? How would you make these plans more compatible with your thinking or meet the developmental needs of another grade level?

4. What does the statement, "There is no single best way to plan," mean to you? Find a com-

fortable location and reflect on this statement in your journal. (Hint: It might be helpful to think about your philosophy of education. Why do you want to become a teacher? What is important to you? What do you bring to the elementary classroom?)

5. A sixth-grade teacher is planning a unit on chemistry, specifically chemical reactions. In particular, she would like to develop a series of tasks parallel with Howard Gardner's intelligences. Following are a few developed by Jan Harmon, Science Supervisor for Mansfield Independent School District, Texas. See if you can develop a few.

   a. [Visual/Spatial] Design a sculpture of iron or steel using discarded items you might have at home or might find in a field or vacant lot. Then tell how you might protect it from corrosion.

   b. [Musical] Create a poem/song/rap about chemical reactions.

   c. [Intrapersonal] Your work site is near the sea. What factors in the environment might you need to consider to design a maintenance program that will protect your yard-care equipment from rust?

   d. [Bodily/Kinesthetic] Devise and carry out an experiment to measure the amount of heat given off in respiration.

   e. [Verbal/Linguistic] Assess the implications for your home of using leaded gasoline in older cars.

■ REFERENCES

Arends, R. (1994). *Learning to teach* (1st ed.). New York: Random House.

Armstrong, T. (1994). *Multiple intelligences in the classroom*. Alexandria, VA: Association for Supervision and Curriculum Development.

Beane, J. (1991). Middle school: The natural home of the integrated curriculum. *Educational Leadership, 49*(2), 9–13.

Berliner, D. (1987). But do they understand? In V. Richardson-Koehler (Ed.), *Educator's handbook: A research perspective* (pp. 257–293). New York: Longman.

Bloom, B. S., Engelhart, M. D., Furst, E. J., Hill, W. H., & Krathwohl, D. R. (1956). *Taxonomy of educational objectives, Handbook I: Cognitive domain*. New York: David McKay Co.

Campbell, M., & Burton, V. (1994, April). Learning in their own style. *Science and Children, 31*(7), 22–24, 39.

Clark, C. M., & Peterson, P. L. (1986). Teachers' thought processes. In M. Wittrock (Ed.), *Handbook of research on teaching* (3rd ed.) (pp. 255–296). Upper Saddle River, NJ: Merrill/Prentice Hall.

Clark, C. M., & Yinger, R. J. (1987). Teaching planning. In D. Berliner & B. Rosenshine (Eds.), *Talks to teachers* (pp. 342–365). New York: Random House.

Clark, C. M., & Yinger, R. J. (1988). *Talks to teachers*. New York: Random House.

Dunn, R. (1990, October). Rita Dunn answers questions on learning styles. *Educational Leadership, 48*(2), 15–19.

Eby, J. W., & Kujawa, E. (1997). *Reflective planning, teaching, and evaluation: K–12* (2nd ed.). Upper Saddle River, NJ: Merrill/Prentice Hall.

Eby, J. W., & Kujawa, E. (1994). *Reflective planning, teaching, and evaluation: K–12*. Upper Saddle River, NJ: Merrill/Prentice Hall.

Eggen, P., & Kauchak, D. (1997). *Educational psychology: Windows on classrooms* (3rd ed.). Upper Saddle River, NJ: Merrill/Prentice Hall.

Frazee, B., & Rudnitski, R. A. (1995). *Integrating teaching methods*. Albany, NY: Delmar Publishers.

Fredericks, A. D., Meinbach, A. M., & Rothlein, L. (1993). *Thematic units: An integrated approach to teaching science and social studies*. New York: HarperCollins College.

Frieberg, H. J., & Driscoll, A. (1996). *Universal teaching strategies* (2nd ed.). Boston: Allyn & Bacon.

Gagné, R. M. (1985). *The conditions of learning and theory of instruction* (4th ed.). New York: Holt, Rinehart & Winston.

Gall, M. D. (1984). Synthesis of research on teachers' questioning. *Educational Leadership, 41,* 40–47.

Gardner, H. (1983). *Frames of mind: The theory of multiple intelligences.* New York: Basic Books.

Gronlund, N. (1991). *How to write and use instructional objectives* (4th ed.). Upper Saddle River, NJ: Merrill/Prentice Hall.

Harrow, A. J. (1972). *A taxonomy of the psychomotor domain.* New York: David McKay Co.

Jacobsen, D., Eggen, P., & Kauchak, D. (1993). *Methods for teachers: A skills approach* (4th ed.). Upper Saddle River, NJ: Merrill/Prentice Hall.

Krathwohl, D. R., Bloom, B. S., & Masia, B. B. (1964). *Taxonomy of educational objectives, Handbook II: Affective domain.* New York: David McKay.

Leinhardt, G. (1987, July). *Situated knowledge: An example from teaching.* Paper presented at the Teachers' Professional Learning Conference, University of Lancaster, England.

Mager, R. F. (1975). *Preparing instructional objectives.* Belmont, CA: Fearon.

Manatt, R. P. (1981). *Evaluating teacher performance* [Videotape]. Alexander, VA: Association for Supervision and Curriculum Development.

Osterman, K. J. (1990, February). Introduction. *Education and Urban Society, 22*(2), 131–132.

Posner, G. J. (1995). *Analyzing the curriculum* (2nd ed.). New York: McGraw-Hill.

Redfield, D. L., & Rousseau, E. W. (1981). A meta-analysis of experimental research on teacher questioning behavior. *Review of Educational Research, 51,* 181–193.

Sardo Brown, D. (1988). Twelve middle-school teachers' planning. *The Elementary School Journal, 89*(1), 69–87.

Schon, D. A. (1990). *Educating the reflective practitioner* (2nd ed.). San Francisco: Jossey-Bass.

Schon, D. A. (1987). *Educating the reflective practitioner.* San Francisco: Jossey-Bass.

Shavelson, R. J. (1987). Planning. In M. Dunkin (Ed.), *The International Encyclopedia of Teaching and Teacher Education* (pp. 483–485). New York: Pergamon Press.

Smith, D. C., & Neale, D. C. (1989). The construction of subject-matter knowledge in primary science teaching. *Teaching and Teacher Education, 5*(1), 1–20.

There's never been a better time to use technology! (1993, October). *Instructor, 103*(3), 34–35.

Tyler, R. (1949). *Basic principles of curriculum and instruction.* Chicago: University of Chicago Press.

Woolfolk, A. (1995). *Educational psychology* (6th ed.). Boston: Allyn & Bacon.

Yinger, R. J. (1977). *A study of teacher planning: Description and theory development using ethnographic and information processing methods.* Doctoral dissertation, Michigan State University.

chapter 7

Curriculum Implementation:
Teaching as an Interactive Step

AFTER READING THIS CHAPTER, YOU WILL BE ABLE TO DO THE FOLLOWING:

- Define teaching and discuss its role in the curriculum implementation and curriculum development processes.

- Explain what is meant by "teacher as technician" and "teacher as orchestrator."

- Discuss the role of teaching strategies and delivery systems in the curriculum implementation process.

- Identify various strategies from the range of possibilities teachers have available, and describe the kind of teaching and learning implied with each strategy.

- Identify and discuss the implications of the various teaching behaviors for the curriculum implementation step.

- Describe how curriculum planning and curriculum implementation are separate but integral steps in the curriculum development process.

As described in Chapter 6, the curriculum development process is rooted in planning, the step in which the teacher makes a series of decisions regarding instruction prior to teaching. The implementation of those plans—teachers and students interacting in the elementary classroom—is the next step in developing the curriculum. Shulman (1987) describes *planning* as passing on the "wisdom of practice." *Implementation* or *teaching* means acting on that wisdom. Over the decades, planning practices have taken hold as they have been passed from one generation of teachers to the next. This accumulation of practices provides insight into not only how important the planning step is but also how central it is to teaching (implementation of curriculum). As Frieberg and Driscoll (1996) describe the relationship, planning provides the framework for teaching: "the execution of the plan may require several adjustments along the way. . . . The changing dynamics of the classroom reduce the certainties of the lesson plan" (p. 41).

Taking the party analogy presented in Chapter 6 one step further, planning means sending invitations, anticipating the number of guests, purchasing refreshments, and then acting as host or hostess for the party. As the plans are implemented and the party progresses, adjustments may need to be made for accommodating guests who arrive late, for having more guests than anticipated, and for running out of refreshments. Throughout the party, the hostess or host will have to monitor and adjust to the changing dynamics that occur.

A similar relationship between the planning and implementation steps exists for teaching. When teachers plan for instruction, they must consider possible strategies and/or delivery systems to use in teaching a concept. As the plans teachers have made are carried out, teachers engage in microdecisions, answering questions like these:

- What order should be followed to teach concepts after asking some general questions to determine what the students already know?

- What adjustments in the plans will need to be made after students provide feedback?

150

- What happens if more or less time is spent on a concept than planned for?

- What adjustments will need to be made for individual interests in topics that hadn't been planned for?

These decisions involve the application of effective teaching practices moment by moment, as teachers link curriculum plans with curriculum implementation. The itinerary for the teaching-learning journey comes to life as students become involved with the curriculum.

Curriculum implementation is also affected by the dynamics of the classroom environment. For example, in a discovery, or inductive, classroom, the teacher provides a lesson that presents topics for students to investigate. In such an environment, the students have the primary responsibility for investigating the topic and learning. In an expository, or deductive, classroom, the teacher provides the structure or conceptual framework for learning. In such an environment, the teacher is responsible for the procedures to be followed in completing a task and learning the material. The curriculum-implementation step (teaching the plans) is influenced by microdecisions made by the teacher within the context of the classroom environment and the kinds or types of teaching and learning behaviors.

Chapter 7 describes the implementation step in the curriculum development process, which we refer to as *teaching*. In many teacher-education programs, entire courses and textbooks are devoted to effective teaching practices or to teaching strategies. This chapter provides an overview of teaching that promotes learning. It presents different views of teaching, various teaching strategies or delivery systems, and behaviors that have been identified with effective teaching. In discussing the implementation step, the links between making plans and teaching them are reinforced by providing descriptions of teaching episodes based on identified teaching behaviors and practices as found in the literature. The "Voice of Experience" sections in the chapter provide teaching examples to illustrate various views of teaching, and these examples demonstrate the changes the teacher makes regarding the strategies to use, ways of involving the students, and the movement away from being an expository teacher.

VIEWS OF TEACHING

The implementation of the curriculum, as teachers interact with students in the classroom, is more commonly referred to as *teaching*. In this book, the terms *curriculum implementation* and *teaching* are used interchangeably. Views of teaching have an impact on the teaching strategies teachers select and on the teaching behaviors that are considered effective. Before examining specific, discrete behaviors associated with effective teaching, it is helpful to look at the "big picture," to see implementation in a broader context beyond individual teaching behaviors.

In defining *teaching*, Eby and Kujawa (1994) see it as "a common and natural occurrence" (p. 168) and Lefrançois (1994) provides a more detailed view when he says that teaching is the arrangement of events in a specific situation to facilitate learning, retention, and transfer. Beach and Reinhartz (1989) view teaching as "a complex, complicated, and multidimensional enterprise that takes many forms. . . . [It] may be: telling, explaining, defining, providing examples and nonexamples, stressing critical attributes, modeling, and demonstrating" (p. 124), and puts into action the collective information generated in the planning step. Shulman (1992) sees teaching as involving "a fundamental tension between ideas [concepts/content] as they are understood by . . . scholars of a discipline and as they might be grasped by school children" (p. 27). Teachers provide the link between what is known about the world and students who find out about their world. As Shulman (1992) states, in the act of teaching, teachers explain complex ideas to children by offering examples, analogies, or metaphors, by telling stories or providing demonstrations, by building bridges between the mind of the child and the . . . understanding in the mind of the teacher. (p. 27)

Hunter (1984) further describes the curriculum implementation step as a "constant stream of professional decisions that affects the probability of learning: decisions that are made and implemented before, during, and after interaction with the students" (p. 169). Good teaching involves detailed planning, and the planning step (Chapter 6) relies on the science of teaching, as teachers use their knowledge to establish objectives, decide on activities to help students learn, and design developmentally appropriate lessons.

During the implementation step, the art and science of teaching merge. Rubin (1983) sees teaching as an art that makes use of proven methods but is pliable and inventive and fosters spontaneity and individuality. Eisner (1983) believes that scientific inquiry provides teachers with guidelines for their interpretation and judgment when interacting with students. Such inquiry also provides a frame of reference that enhances the teachers' perceptions about the teaching-learning process without mechanistically controlling the interaction. Eisner (1983) continues by suggesting that when applying their art and craft "teachers are more like orchestra conductors than technicians. They need rules of thumb and educational imagination not scientific prescriptions . . . [and] teachers orchestrate the dialogue moving from one side of the room to the other" (p. 10). Salomon (1992) agrees with Eisner and suggests that the foremost role of the teacher in implementing the curriculum is that of orchestrator. He further suggests that teachers must also assume responsibility for the teaching-learning process and resultant outcomes, as well as giving serious attention to "consideration, selection, and design of instructional means, activities, materials, [and] tasks" (p. 45).

Teachers use their knowledge of human learning and development and their experiences observing and working with children to establish objectives and construct lessons that are developmentally appropriate for their students. For example, if a teacher decides in the planning step that a particular unit needs performance-based activities designed to engage students in a series of investigations, then the teacher must ensure that the material is at the appropriate level of development and that there are sufficient management strategies in place for students to be successful. Brent, a classroom teacher, provides insights from his experience, and describes how he views teaching.

Voice of Experience

Brent has refined his teaching skills over the years; he readily admits that he is not the teacher today that he was the first few years. As a beginning teacher, Brent often used a trial-and-error approach to teaching and experimented with a variety of styles and strategies. In this process, he developed his own personal style, as he discovered what worked best for him, given the nature of the students and the content he was teaching. But Brent says, "I often wonder about the children I had the first couple of years. I hope they learned, because in the beginning I was learning right along with them as I tried different strategies in my classroom."

As Brent describes his situation, he says, "The emphasis in my education classes was on direct or expository teaching, where the teacher was clearly in charge of the lesson. I found myself using this strategy most of time during my early years of teaching because it helped me to survive."

Brent notes that he found this strategy particularly helpful when teaching subjects that had basic or fundamental concepts and that were the building blocks for higher-level thinking skills, or when he was unfamiliar with the content. He says, "As I gained confidence in my ability to teach and interact with elementary students, I began to see the intricacies and the relationship between the art and science of teaching. I began to be more creative—more of an artist— not only in planning activities for the classroom, but in executing those plans as well. I began to explore and use other strategies such as coop- erative learning and learning/interest centers as a way of structuring learning for my students."

As teachers like Brent reflect on their teach- ing, new knowledge emerges about their role in the implementation step. This reflection leads to a more refined view of the realities of classroom life, and they begin to see teaching as a personal experience. Decisions that teachers make about teaching, coupled with reflection, produce con- tinued personal and professional growth. As teachers engage in this reflective process, this movement from roles of mechanical to reflective practitioners is predictable. In the "Voice of Expe- rience" section, as Brent grew personally and professionally, he began to view teaching as com- plex.

As teachers gain experience and reflect on their teaching, they are able to orchestrate the parts of the lesson and interact with their stu- dents more effectively within the nuances of the classroom environment. Eisner (1983) suggests that as teachers become more artistic, they are able to "give the piccolos a chance—indeed to encourage them to sing more confidently but also . . . to provide space for the brass" (p. 11).

For example, a teacher may begin teaching a unit in language arts, "The World of Poetry," with *expository instruction*, or direct instruction. Such a strategy includes defining and giving examples of the various forms of poetry, providing students with key words or terms to define, and having them construct a poetry notebook following spe- cific guidelines provided. A reflective practitioner

takes time to review the unit that has been taught and begins to make some changes before teaching the unit again. Slowly, changes are implemented and different strategies—such as providing groups of students with different kinds of poems, using brainstorming, and then recording the information on a graphic organizer to identify the different poetry forms—are used. Students can be given flexibility in structuring their poetry notebooks as well as writing original poems. Using these strategies, students begin to con- struct their own knowledge base related to poetry. In the reality of the classroom, the teacher recog- nizes that making significant changes in teaching strategies takes time.

As teachers think about what they have taught (engage in reflection), they become expert teachers who can "demonstrate their expertise in myriad ways" (Henderson, 1992, p. 1). They can, as Jackson (1986) notes, "spot an inattentive stu- dent a mile off [and] detect signs of incipient dif- ficulty. Their senses are fully tuned to what is going on around them. They are not easily rat- tled" (p. 87). As teachers implement their plans and meet with success, they develop confidence in their ability to teach. As they become more confident in their teaching, they expand their repertoire of teaching strategies/skills.

STRATEGIES AND DELIVERY SYSTEMS

As teachers implement their curriculum plans, they select from a range of strategies or delivery systems, and they pick from a cafeteria of alterna- tives. A delivery system involves a series of strate- gies with varying levels or steps that work in con- cert with each other. Strategies are specific activities or procedures that occur within a lesson in the classroom. A *strategy* is a deliberate teaching act that teachers select after analyzing the material to be taught and considering student characteris- tics. The strategy selected determines how a concept is taught. Strategies involve the "how" of teaching. Within a delivery system, there may be many strategies from which to choose.

Teachers have a variety of strategies to choose from. These range from direct instruction, where the teacher has the greatest control and is in charge of the learning process, to independent study, where students have greater control over their learning. Direct instruction has a group focus, and independent study has an individual focus. Figure 7-1 represents this range or continuum of teaching strategies.

In the following section, each of these strategies on the continuum will be discussed. The characteristics of each strategy, along with teacher and desired student behaviors will be presented. Figure 7-2 provides a description of the characteristics of each strategy along with the tasks that the teacher performs and the anticipated student behaviors.

Direct Instruction

Mastery of basic skills and improved student learning are emphasized in this particular strategy which is sometimes called *expository teaching*. As described in the "Voice of Experience" example earlier, Brent used direct instruction as a beginning teacher when teaching his language arts unit. Rosenshine (1986, 1979) has called direct instruction *explicit teaching*, Good (1983) refers to this strategy as *active teaching*, and Hunter (1982,

1991) calls it *mastery teaching*. Goodlad (1984) referred to it as *frontal instruction*. And for Rosenshine (1979), "direct instruction refers to academically focused, teacher-directed [lessons] using sequenced and structured materials" (p. 38).

The basic steps in the directed teaching strategy include the following:

1. Getting students ready to learn by setting the stage for learning and creating an anticipatory set and focus. This is accomplished by having students review and check the previous day's assignment or work, posing higher-order questions related to the content, using advance organizers, or instructional objectives to focus on the learning that is to occur, and/or using a demonstration or other visual to capture students' attention.

2. Communicating learning goals and instructional objectives by describing the purpose of the lesson and the expected student learning outcomes.

3. Presenting information in a clear and effective way by providing examples and nonexamples, descriptions, definitions, and modeling by using the chalkboard or overhead projector.

4. Providing opportunities for practicing new skills and checking for understanding by giving practice problems or asking questions, doing work at the board, soliciting group or

FIGURE 7-1   Continuum of Teaching Strategies

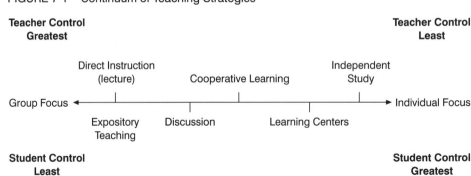

FIGURE 7-2 Summary of Teaching Strategies

Teaching Strategies	Characteristics	Teacher Behaviors	Student Behaviors
Direct Instruction	Academically focused, teacher-directed, sequenced and structured	In charge of lesson and responsible for presenting information	Receive information, take notes, respond when prompted by teacher, master basic skills
Guided Discussion/ Reciprocal Questioning	Discussion and higher-level thinking about concept/topic	Models formulation of questions, prompts students by asking questions, and encourages students to "think aloud" and elaborate	Respond to questions individually and in groups, generate additional questions, and demonstrate understanding by elaborating and "thinking aloud"
Cooperative Learning	Students in groups or teams that respond to a question, resolve a dilemma situation, or conduct an experiment	Serves as a facilitator by setting the stage with materials, resources, questions, and/or situations; monitors group progress and responsibilities	Perform assigned roles and responsibilities within the group as the group/team problem solve, role play, or complete task
Learning Centers	Place where students work individually or in small groups to accomplish objectives; provides for individual differences and multiple tasks	Construct area(s)in room for center(s) with multisensory items for students to use; breaks learning into steps	Work individually or in groups to complete a task using a variety of materials and resources
Independent Study	Students work independently at own rate and level; delivery of information provided in a variety of formats (i.e. tutoring, computer assisted instruction).	Designs instruction at the level of individual student and provides for delivery of information	Work independently using one or more formats to accomplish objectives

choral responses, and/or listening (or observing) for misunderstandings.

5. Monitoring, adjusting, and providing corrective feedback to students during the lesson and reviewing the lesson with the students to ensure their understanding of the concept/content presented.

6. Giving independent practice by having students work problems, design projects, and/or answer questions on their own either during class or at home.

7. Checking for mastery and providing for closure by asking questions, having students summarize key concepts, and/or observing

student behavior during individual and group work.

Variations on this strategy include not only these steps but others as well. The steps of direct instruction are incorporated into an illustration that is often referred to as the *teaching cycle* or the *lesson cycle*. Figure 7-3 provides an example of the steps in the direct instruction teaching cycle. The steps in the cycle are sequenced and provide a guide for teachers to follow when teaching.

While these steps may vary according to the instructional programs and the topics to be taught, they are basically similar in their intent: student mastery of basic skills and content.

FIGURE 7-3   Direct Instruction Cycle

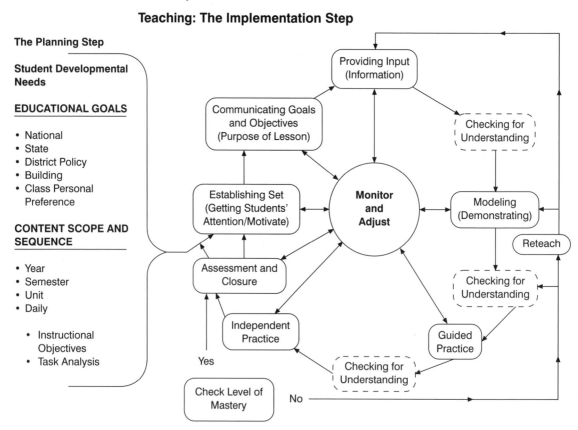

Teaching: The Implementation Step

Source: From *Supervision: Focus on Instruction* by D. M. Beach & J. Reinhartz, 1989. New York: HarperCollins, p. 134. Used by permission.

FIGURE 7-4   Direct Instruction Strategy

Name	
Unit Addition: one and two digit numbers	Lesson No.

Procedure	*Content*
State learner objective.	The student will be able to demonstrate understanding of place value by regrouping ones and tens.

Review prerequisites.	Put on board the following problem:
	
	    17
	  + 9
	  ———
	    26
	
	Ask how many tens in 17? how many ones? How many tens in 9? How many ones?

Demonstrate learning activity.	Hand out straws in bundles of ten and have students work the problem using bundles of straws and "rebundling" or regrouping to find the answer.
Present new problems.	Using the overhead projector have the students work the following problems using the bundles of straws: 12 15 11 18 19 + 8 + 7 + 9 + 3 + 6 ——— ——— ——— ——— ———
Provide independent practice.	Assign worksheets for students to complete on their own to check tomorrow.

Figure 7-4 illustrates a sample lesson using the direct instruction strategy. Direct instruction is considered one of the most efficient ways of teaching, which involves telling students what they will learn prior to instruction, telling them what they are learning during instruction, and then telling them one final time what they have just learned as the lesson ends.

Guided Discussion/ Reciprocal Questioning

In the guided discussion strategy, the teacher, after the initial presentation of the concept or topic, prompts the students with questions about specific elements of content. King (1990) advocates that questions be used to prompt students to engage in discussion and get them to elaborate on the concept(s) being studied. These prompts can include such questions as these:

1. What is a different or another example of _____ ?

2. How are _____ and _____ similar? Are they different?

3. What might happen if _____ ?

4. How could you use _____ to _____?

5. Can you explain why _____?

6. Which material is the best/worst in _____?

The use of questions to foster discussion within the group tends to encourage higher-level thinking skills (Welty, 1989; Johnson & Johnson, 1979; Johnson & Johnson, 1989; Johnson, Johnson, & Holubec, 1994a). To initiate the questioning strategy, teachers model ways of asking, along with ways of answering the questions. This "think aloud" strategy helps students learn not only how to answer questions but also to formulate questions that prompt further thinking.

Questioning is a powerful teaching strategy. Teachers should become experts in the number and types of questions they ask, involving all students in the class in providing prompts, waiting between asking a question and soliciting a response (wait time) (Rowe, 1974, 1986), and increasing the cognitive level of questions.

If teachers do not use whole-class reporting techniques after asking questions, they can have students work in small groups or pairs to submit not only the questions but also the answers generated by members of the group or pair. Using such a strategy, teachers assess the students' level of understanding by monitoring not only responses, but also the types of questions asked. Figure 7-5 is an abbreviated lesson plan that incorporates discussion and reciprocal questioning as a teaching and learning strategy.

Cooperative Learning

The cooperative learning strategy has students working in groups or teams to learn concepts/content. Cooperative learning is built around student teams (Slavin, 1994), group projects (Sharan & Schachar, 1988), and discussion

FIGURE 7-5 Guided Discussion/Reciprocal Questioning

Name	
Unit Animals	Lesson No.
Procedure	*Content*
Begin lesson by reviewing content of previous lesson.	Have students list characteristics of carnivores (meat eaters) on board.
Develop concept.	Have students work in groups to answer the following questions: • How are carnivores different from herbivores (plant eaters)? • How are carnivores different from omnivores? Give students a deck of cards with different foods listed on each one, and have students sort the cards according to the kind of animal that would most likely eat that food.
Closing.	Have each group report their answers to the total group and check for any discrepancies.
Independent practice.	Have students complete worksheet on herbivores, carnivores, and omnivores for homework.

(Johnson & Johnson, 1979; Johnson, Johnson, & Holubec, 1994b). This strategy has been effective in increasing student learning over more traditional strategies.

Slavin (1991) highlights the results of research on cooperative learning. The most successful strategies used to enhance student achievement have two elements: group goals and individual accountability. The groups are rewarded on performance but only if all the individual members of the group learn and are successful. The effects of cooperative learning on achievement have been "about the same degree at all grade levels (2–12), on all major subjects, and in urban, rural, and suburban schools" (Slavin, 1991, p. 71). The effects of achievement are "equally positive for high, average, and low achievers" (p. 71). Slavin continues by saying that cooperative learning consistently has had positive effects on "self-esteem, intergroup relations, acceptance of academically handicapped students, attitudes toward school, and ability to work cooperatively" (p. 71).

According to Johnson and Johnson (1989), six hundred experimental studies and at least one hundred correlational studies have been conducted focusing on competitive, cooperative, and individualistic strategies for teaching and learning. These studies of cooperation compared to competition and individualism revealed the following:

■ There were greater efforts to achieve by all students, regardless of their cognitive level, long-term memory, intrinsic motivation, time on task, and higher-order thinking.

■ There were more positive relationships among the students, which translated into a commitment to learning and an increase in esprit de corps.

■ There was a greater feeling of competency and social development, which led to improved self-esteem and an increased ability to deal with adversity (Johnson,

Johnson, & Holubec, 1994b; Johnson & Johnson, 1989).

For Johnson, Johnson, and Holubec (1994b), cooperative learning has many important outcomes that separate it from "other instructional methods and make [it] one of the most important tools for ensuring student success" (p. 12). In their book, *The New Circles of Learning*, Johnson, Johnson, and Holubec (1994b) present cooperative learning as part of a broader paradigm of teaching that is based on three principal activities:

■ Students construct, discover, transform, and extend their own knowledge [so that] learning is something a learner does, not something that is done to . . . [him or her].

■ Teachers' efforts are aimed at developing students' competencies and talents.

■ Teachers and students work together, making education a personal transaction. (p. 103)

These activities are made possible and fostered within a cooperative learning context.

Although there are many forms of cooperative learning, it generally involves mixed-ability groups of four or five students, with group membership initially determined by the teacher. Usually, the groups stay together for several weeks, perhaps for an entire reporting period. Each member of the group is given a specific responsibility, such as getting materials or recording the results of an experiment and writing up the procedure.

When Brent, the "Voice of Experience" for this chapter, teaches a science unit on simple machines, he uses a cooperative learning strategy and puts students in teams or groups; in addition, he assigns each group member a specific responsibility (e.g., principal investigator, materials manager, recorder/reporter, and maintenance director) as well as tasks such as examining the various types of simple machines and experimenting with class I and II levers. Figure 7-6 shows how teachers can use a cooperative learning strategy in the classroom.

FIGURE 7-6   Cooperative Learning Strategy

Teacher Name:_____

Unit Title: *Constructing Stories*   **Lesson Number 2**

Objective: Following the cooperative learning activity, the student will be able to identify the
following parts of a story using semantic maps: characters, setting, major events or
incidents. Students will also be able to create a story of their own using these three
components.

Procedures   **Content**

1. After checking roll, have   1.
    students get in their preassigned
    cooperative learning groups.

2. Distribute packets "Understanding   2. Each packet contains a story that the
    a Story" to each cooperative   group is to read and a semantic map
    learning group.   for the group to complete.

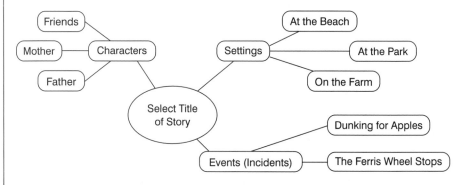

3. The designated leader in each group will read   3. Members of each group jot down notes
    the story in the packet. As the leader reads,   about
    the group members will individually record   • characters
    examples of characters, setting(s), and events   • settings
    or incidents.   • events/incidents

4. When the group leader has completed reading   4. Using their notes, group members
    the story, the members of the group compare   compile a list of items for each category.
    their notes.

5. The designated recorder/reporter completes   5. Group members contribute to the
    the semantic map using the list made by the   completion of the map.
    group.

6. The report/recorder makes a report to the   6. Using the semantic map, the reporter/
    whole class when called upon.   recorder makes a presentation to the
                                                         class.

7. The leader will facilitate the development of a   7. As a group, members create one story
    story by reviewing the items generated under   utilizing items on their map.
    each category on the semantic map.

Learning Centers

A *learning center* is "a physical area where children engage in a variety of learning activities and experiences" (Forte & Mackenzie, 1972, p. 9). Generally, it is a place where students work independently or in small groups to accomplish various lesson objectives at multiple levels of difficulty (Beach, 1977; Joyce, 1994; Isbell, 1995). The purpose of using learning centers as a teaching strategy is to involve students directly in taking responsibility for their learning. Learning centers can be used in the following ways:

■ to teach a specific skill, such as alphabetizing words

■ to develop critical or higher-order thinking skills by having students analyze and classify objects, stories, and events

■ to utilize techniques and various technology (computers, calculators, laser discs) to capture the students' interest and enthusiasm (Beach, 1977; Isbell, 1995)

Hopkins (1985/86) describes a learning center classroom as a place where students work in small, interactive groups using hands-on activities and independent activities as well. Learning center classrooms also provide an excellent way for students to use computers. Kourilsky and Quaranta (1987) suggest three essential components of learning centers: they must be independent of the teacher, intrinsically motivating, and provide continuous feedback.

Lemlech (1994) suggests that learning centers can be used to "differentiate instruction to meet individual ability levels and learning style needs" (p. 97) by luring, coaxing, and appealing to students' natural inquisitiveness. In designing centers, teachers should focus on the purpose and objective(s) of the lesson, plan a task to accomplish the objective(s), present the content/concepts, give clear and precise instructions, identify materials and resources needed, and write a description of how the students will be assessed. Figure 7-7 provides an example of a lesson designed to use a learning-center strategy.

Independent Study

An independent-study strategy provides the greatest opportunity for each student to work at his or her own level and rate. Normally, some form of an information delivery system is used. The delivery of information can be provided in a variety of ways, including an adult, a peer, instructional media and technology (e.g., sound-on-page or computer), and/or written material. Bloom (1984) and Wasik and Slavin (1993) have found that tutoring, within the individualized instruction delivery system, can produce powerful results in student achievement, because instruction can be customized to meet the needs of individual students.

Teachers can provide a variety of formats for the delivery of information within the independent-study strategy. One format involves the completion of a contract where a student researches a question such as "What is an ozone alert?" In carrying out the research, the student would have to address the following questions:

■ What sources would/did you consult?

■ How would you present your findings?

■ Why is this topic important to study?

Programmed instruction and computer-assisted instruction are variations of the independent-study strategy. In *programmed instruction*, students work with structured lessons using instructional materials (visual, written, commercial, etc.) designed for their academic level and geared to their learning rate (Fletcher, 1992). These materials give students a step-by-step explanation of the concepts as they move from simple to more complex skills.

As teachers engage in teaching, they must consider a variety of strategies for delivering instruction. Joyce and Weil (1996) refer to these options as *models of teaching* and suggest that teachers need a basic repertoire of teaching strategies as they help students acquire and develop ideas and skills and assist them in developing ways to express themselves as they learn.

FIGURE 7-7   Learning Center Strategy

Thunder Cake was written and illustrated by Patricia Polacco and published by Scholastic in 1990. The author retells a childhood memory of the way her Russian immigrant grandmother, her "Babushka," helped her to overcome the fear of thunderstorms. Together they count the seconds between flashes of lightning and claps of thunder to calculate the distance of an approaching storm. They go to the barn and the dry shed to gather baking ingredients, including the ripe tomatoes that are Babushka's secret ingredient. This well-written, touching story can be used to introduce a study on weather and to reassure young children who may be frightened of storms.

Learning Center #1
Counting the Distance of a Thunderstorm

By counting the time that occurs between seeing lightning and hearing thunder, the approximate distance of an approaching thunderstorm can be calculated. One second equals approximately one mile. Students can use a stopwatch or a slow verbal count with the one-one-thousand or one-Mississippi method. Lacking a real thunderstorm, simulate one in the room to practice the counting and calculating.

Process skills used in this center activity include creating models, generalizing, interpreting data, manipulating material, measuring, observing, and using numbers.

Directions for making an indoor storm:

1.   Darken the classroom.

2.   Flip the overhead lights on and off to simulate lightning.

3.   Begin counting: one-one-thousand, two-one-thousand, etc.

4.   Wait several seconds. Vary the wait time with each repetition to simulate the movement of a storm.

5.   Shake sheets of poster board to simulate thunder.

6.   Spray the room lightly with water using a spray bottle or plant mister to simulate rain.

7.   Repeat.

Students should take turns controlling the lightning, thunder, and counting actions.

Learning Center #2
Creating Your Own "Weather Food"

In a group, brainstorm to create lists or semantic maps of weather words and food words. Each student will create a new "weather food" and write a recipe or description with a "secret" ingredient.

Process skills used in this center include creating models, making decisions, and replicating.

Directions for making a "weather food" recipe card (materials you will need: one large index card, crayons or markers, and a pencil):

1.   Choose a weather word and a food word to create the name of your new taste treat.

2. Use your imagination and choose a "secret" ingredient to include in your "weather food."

3. On the lined side of the index card, write the name of your "weather food." Make a list of ingredients and a description or recipe for your creation. EXTRA: Include serving instructions.

4. On the blank side of the index card, draw a picture of your "weather food."

Learning Center #3

Bake and Eat Thunder Cake

The book includes a recipe for Babushka's "Thunder Cake." The recipe has been adapted to use a cake mix for convenience and reliable results when cooking with children. (The secret tomato ingredient adds moistness and texture but does not add a tomato taste.)

Have capable fifth- and sixth- grade students make two cakes. A comparison could be made between the adapted recipe and the one from scratch recipe in the book or between the adapted recipe and a regular box mix made according to the directions on the box.

Process skills used in this center include manipulating materials, measuring, and observing.

Thunder Cake (Adapted)
1 box of Pillsbury Plus Butter Recipe Chocolate Cake Mix
3 eggs
1¼ cups milk (substituted for water)
¼ cup (decreased from ½ cup) softened margarine or butter
½ cup canned tomato puree

Using an electric hand mixer, mix all ingredients on low until moistened. Beat 2 minutes at high speed. Pour into greased and floured pan or cupcake tin. Makes one 9- inch by 13- inch sheet cake or approximately 36 small cupcakes. Bake approximately 20 minutes for cupcakes or 35 minutes for sheet cake. Cake is done when toothpick inserted in center comes out clean or cake springs back when lightly touched in center.

Source: From work by Marilyn Mutchler, 1993, classroom teacher. Used with permission.

EFFECTIVE TEACHING BEHAVIORS

Research on teaching has had a long history, but linking teacher behaviors to student achievement is a more recent development (Eggen & Kauchak, 1994). Historically, teacher effectiveness focused on teacher traits that proved less than satisfactory in defining teaching quality. With the publication of the *Coleman Report* in 1966, which initially implied that teachers had little impact on student learning, a reexamination of the report revealed a different conclusion. Researchers (Gage, 1985; Gage & Giaconia, 1981; Good & Brophy, 1986; Good & Brophy, 1991) found, after viewing many hours of teaching, that teachers taught differently in higher-achieving classes (Eggen & Kauchak, 1994).

In addition to this research, Wang, Haertel, and Walberg (1993/1994) identified six categories that seem to influence learning (these were identified in Chapter 4). These include student aptitude, classroom instruction and climate, context, program design, school organization, and state and district characteristics. The *student aptitude* category includes such characteristics as metacognitive processes, cognitive processes, social and behavioral attributes, motivational and affective attributes, psychomotor skills, and student demographics. The *classroom instruction and climate* includes such factors as classroom management, student and teacher social interactions, quantity of instruction, classroom climate, classroom instruction, academic interactions, classroom assessment, and classroom implementation and support. *Context* includes factors such as home environment/parental support, peer group, community influences, and out-of-class time. *Program design* includes teaching and learning factors of curriculum design, curriculum and instruction, and program demographics. *School organization* includes such characteristics as school culture, teacher/administrator decision making, parental involvement policy, school demographics, and school policies. Finally, *state and district characteristics* include factors such as state-level policies, district demographics, teacher licensure requirements, and school district size. Wang, Haertel, and Walberg (1993/94) concluded that the kinds of teaching strategies and the type of classroom environment that is established have almost as much influence on student learning as does the student's academic ability.

Leinhardt (1992) identified three constructs from research that are key to learning and teaching: "(1) multiple forms for knowledge, (2) the role of prior knowledge, and (3) the social nature of knowledge and its acquisition" (p. 20). According to Leinhardt (1992), these types of knowledge have consequences for teaching and learning that include being aware that knowledge

needs to be presented in a variety of ways to accommodate all learners. Strategies become the vehicle for linking concepts and content to learners, under the guidance of the teacher. By recognizing that prior knowledge can motivate and draw students into the lesson, teachers need to ensure that students' past experiences become part of the lesson as they make connections in the curriculum for teaching and learning.

Teaching is impacted by not only school environment and climate but by other variables as well. Yet some people often try to simplify teaching, as if it can be reduced to a recipe with a few basic ingredients to be used by all people at all times. Effective teaching occurs when alignment exists among the strategies, content, objectives, and teaching behaviors, so that students learn. For effective teaching to occur, teachers must not only draw upon what is known about the teaching-learning process from research, but also orchestrate all the dimensions within the classroom to produce maximum learning for all students.

Teachers must be aware of the range of behaviors associated with effective teaching. A growing body of research on teaching effectiveness links teacher variables to student academic achievement. That body of knowledge, referred to as *teacher effectiveness literature*, defines *teacher effectiveness* as the teacher behaviors associated with high student achievement (Eggen & Kauchak, 1997). This research is related to teacher characteristics or behaviors that correlate positively with student achievement or learning gains (Ryan, 1960; Rosenshine & Furst, 1971; Medley, 1979; Walberg, Schiller, & Haertel, 1979; Manatt, 1981a, 1981b, 1987; Rosenshine, 1983; Greenblatt, Cooper, & Muth, 1984; Weinert, Helmke, & Schrader, 1992). These teaching behaviors include the following:

1. *Instructional clarity* (is clear about the purpose of the lesson, objectives, tasks, and content/presentation): having a lesson focus ensures that students will be engaged throughout the lesson.

2. *Knowledgeable of content* (knows the content, knows how to structure and present it, and integrates concepts with other areas of the curriculum): effective teachers self-monitor their teaching to be sure the information is clear, that it is logically presented, and that the teacher understands that content.

3. *Variation in teaching* (uses learning opportunities other than listening): teacher plans a variety of strategies in class that involve students in learning in ways other than passive learning.

4. *Establishment of learning expectations* (communicates anticipated learning results to students based on the purpose of the lesson): teachers present learning objectives to students prior to teaching the lesson.

5. *Utilization of resources* (uses a variety of instructional materials): teachers use many different materials (math manipulatives, models) to illustrate and reinforce concepts.

6. *Knowledge of principles of learning and development* (modifies content and strategies to meet the needs of their students): teachers are aware of the research on helping students construct their own knowledge or multiple levels of intelligences.

7. *Communication with students on multiple levels* (asks lots of questions, including ones that promote higher-order thinking; keeps students engaged; monitors student performance; and provides immediate written and/or oral feedback that is specific and positive in tone): clear communication is essential and it influences teaching effectiveness. Such communication means using precise terms, connecting points in a lesson, having signals when making transitions, and emphasizing points (Eggen & Kauchak, 1997).

8. *Enthusiasm* (presents lesson in a positive and energetic way): teachers show excitement about their students and what they are teaching.

As teachers implement instruction in their classrooms, they must consider not only the delivery system that gives focus and direction to the lesson and the strategies that provide the vehicle for learning, they must also consider their individual teaching behaviors that can impact the overall quality of the lesson.

There is no single, best strategy or list of effective teaching behaviors. Teachers can select strategies from a continuum, and there are numerous discrete lists that range from a few behaviors to numerous behaviors. What we have presented in this chapter is a representative sample of teaching behaviors that appear throughout the literature with respect to promoting student academic learning gains. Depending on your style and your school's expectations, you may want to modify these behaviors as you plan and implement the curriculum in your elementary classroom.

SUMMARY

This chapter presented a description of teaching and the various ways in which the written curriculum can be implemented in classrooms. Curriculum implementation is teaching, and it is a complex, multidimensional process that involves a variety of teaching behaviors that include telling, explaining, defining, modeling, and demonstrating.

In carrying out their written plans, teachers have the option to select a variety of instructional strategies that will facilitate student learning of the content or skills to be taught. These strategies include but are not limited to: direct instruction, guided discussion/reciprocal questioning, cooperative learning, learning activity centers, and independent study.

In addition to these instructional strategies, teachers have available to them specific, discrete teaching behaviors that help to increase the probability that learning will occur. The lists of these behaviors vary, depending on the source of the list. This chapter noted eight teaching behaviors that are important for effective teaching and learning: instructional clarity, knowledge of content, variation in teaching procedures, establishment of learning expectations, utilization of a variety of resources, utilization of principles of learning and development, interaction with students on multiple levels, and enthusiasm.

No single instructional strategy or teaching behavior can ensure success in implementing the written curriculum. The teacher must consider the nature of the material to be taught, the nature of the learners themselves, and the teacher's own personal and professional characteristics while engaging in teaching in the elementary classroom.

■ YOUR TURN

1. Your second-grade team is considering ways to modify the curriculum in social studies. Members of the team would like to vary their instructional strategies rather than relying on direct instruction all the time. Pick one of the instructional strategies described in this chapter and create a list of possible social studies concepts that could be taught using the strategy you have chosen. Look at this list of concepts and identify the advantages and disadvantages of using this strategy you selected.

2. You are preparing for an interview for a position in the fourth grade at a nearby school. On the application, there are several questions that require you to reflect on key issues about teaching and learning. One of these questions is *What is effective teaching?* What would you include in your response?

3. Look at the list of specific teaching behaviors described in the chapter. Envision yourself teaching in an elementary classroom. List each of these teaching behaviors, and beside each one describe ways in which you would demonstrate these behaviors if you were teaching.

4. Look back at your philosophy of teaching statement and the teacher characteristics/strategies associated with that philosophy. Are there some characteristics/strategies associated with your philosophy? Is there a close match? Somewhat of a match? If so, which characteristics/strategies?

5. Examine the direct instruction cycle (Fig. 7-3). Using this figure as a model, develop a plan for teaching a concept in language arts using cooperative learning. Review the plan with a friend in the class. Could you use this lesson plan with a group of elementary students? (If you have an opportunity to teach this lesson to elementary students, it will help you determine whether your plan is thorough enough and where you may need to make changes. Ask a classroom teacher for feedback.)

6. Over the next several weeks, informally observe a variety of people in teaching situations, from tutoring to coaching to classroom teaching, etc. As you observe, record your reactions to the teaching-learning situations. List the strategies that were implemented. What concepts were taught? Would you have taught the lesson differently? What would you change? Why would you make these changes.

■ REFERENCES

Beach, D. M. (1977). *Reaching teenagers: Learning centers for the secondary classroom*. Santa Monica, CA: Goodyear Publishing.

Beach, D. M., & Reinhartz, J. (1989). *Supervision: Focus on instruction*. New York: Harper & Row.

Bloom, B. (1984, June/July). The 2 sigma problem: The search for methods of instruction as effective as one-to-one tutoring. *Educational Researcher, 13*(6), 4–16.

Coleman, J. S., Campbell, E. Q., Hobson, C. J., McPartland, J., Mood, A. M., Weinfield, F. D., & York, R. L. (1966). *Equality of educational opportunity*. Washington, DC: U.S. Department of Health, Education, and Welfare.

Eby, J. W., & Kujawa, E. (1994). *Reflecting, planning, and evaluation*. Upper Saddle River, NJ: Merrill/Prentice Hall.

Eggen, P., & Kauchak, D. (1997). *Educational psychology: Windows on classrooms* (3rd ed.). Upper Saddle River, NJ: Merrill/Prentice Hall.

Eggen, P., & Kauchak, D. (1994). *Educational psychology: Classroom connections* (2nd ed.). Upper Saddle River, NJ: Merrill/Prentice Hall.

Eisner, E. W. (1983). The art and craft of teaching. *Educational Leadership, 40*(4), 4–13.

Fletcher, J. D. (1992). Individualized systems of instruction. In M. C. Alkin (Ed.), *Encyclopedia of educational research* (6th ed.) (pp. 613–618). Upper Saddle River, NJ: Merrill/Prentice Hall.

Forte, I., & Mackenzie, J. (1972). *Nooks, crannies and corners: Learning centers for creative classrooms*. Nashville, TN: Incentive Publications.

Frieberg, J., & Driscoll, A. (1996). *Universal teaching strategies* (2nd ed). Boston: Allyn & Bacon.

Gage, N. (1985). *Hard gains in the soft sciences: The case of pedagogy*. Bloomington, IN: Phi Delta Kappa.

Gage, N., & Giaconia, R. (1981). Teaching practices and student achievement: Causal connections. *New York University Education Quarterly, 12*, 2–9.

Good, T., & Brophy, J. (1991). *Looking into classrooms* (5th ed.). New York: Harper & Row.

Good, T., & Brophy J. (1986). School effects. In M. Wittrock (Ed.), *Handbook of research on teaching* (3rd ed.) (pp. 570–604). New York: Harper & Row.

Good, T. L. (1983). Classroom research: A decade of progress. *Educational Psychologist, 18*, 127–144.

Goodlad, J. (1984). *A place called school*. New York: McGraw-Hill.

Greenblatt, R. B., Cooper, B. S., & Muth, R. (1984). Managing for effective teaching. *Educational Leadership, 41*, 5, 57–59.

Henderson, J. G. (1992). *Reflective teaching: Becoming an inquiring educator*. Upper Saddle River, NJ: Merrill/Prentice Hall.

Hopkins, J. (1985/86, December/January). The learning center classroom. *The Computing Teacher, 13*(4), 8–11.

Hunter, M. (1991). Hunter design helps achieve the goals of science instruction. *Educational Leadership, 48*(4), 79–81.

Hunter, M. (1984). Knowing, teaching, and supervising. In P.L. Hasford (Ed.), *Using what we know about teaching* (pp. 169–203). Alexandria, VA: Association for Supervision and Curriculum Development.

Hunter, M. (1982). *Mastery teaching*. El Segundo, CA: TIP Publications.

Isbell, R. T. (1995) *The complete learning center book*. Beltsville, MD: Gryphon House.

Jackson, P. W. (1986). *The practice of teaching*. New York: Teachers College Press.

Johnson, D. W., & Johnson, R. T. (1979). Conflict in the classroom: Controversy and learning. *Review of Educational Research, 49*(1), 51–70.

Johnson, D. W., & Johnson, R. T. (1989). *Cooperation and competition: Theory and research*. Edina, MN: Interaction Book Company.

Johnson, D. W., Johnson, R. T., & Holubec, E. J. (1994a). *Cooperative learning in the classroom*. Alexandria, VA: Association for Supervision and Curriculum Development.

Johnson, D. W., Johnson, R. T., & Holubec, E. J. (1994b). *The new circles of learning: Cooperation in the school*. Alexandria, VA: Association for Supervision and Curriculum Development.

Joyce, A. (1994, December). Combining learning styles and learning centers in a fourth grade language arts classroom. Partial fulfillment of the requirements, Master of Arts in Educational Processes.

Joyce, B., & Weil, M. (1996). *Models of teaching* (5th ed.). Boston: Allyn & Bacon.

King, A. (1990). Enhancing peer interaction and learning in the classroom through reciprocal questioning. *American Educational Research Journal, 27*, 664–687.

Kourilsky, M., & Quaranta, L. (1987). *Effective teaching: Principles and practice*. Glenview, IL: Scott, Foresman.

Lefrançois, G. R. (1994). *Psychology for teaching* (8th ed.). Belmont, CA: Wadsworth.

Leinhardt, G. (1992). What research on learning tells us about teaching. *Educational Leadership. 49*(7), 20–25.

Lemlech, J. (1994). *Curriculum and instructional methods for the elementary and middle school* (3rd ed.). Upper Saddle River, NJ: Merrill/Prentice Hall.

Manatt, R. P. (1981a). *Evaluating teacher performance* [Videotape]. Alexandria, VA: Association for Supervision and Curriculum Development.

Manatt, R. P. (1981b, November). *Manatt's exercise in selecting teacher performance evaluation criteria based on effective teaching research* [Mimeograph]. Albuquerque, NM: National Symposium for Professionals in Evaluation and Research.

Manatt, R. P. (1987). Lessons from a comprehensive performance appraisal project. *Educational Leadership, 44*(7), 8–14.

Medley, D. M. (1979). The effectiveness of teachers. In P. Peterson & H. Walberg (Eds.), *Research on teaching: Concepts, findings and implications* (pp. 11–27). Berkeley, CA: McCutchan.

Rosenshine, B. (1986). Synthesis of research on explicit teaching. *Educational Leadership, 43*, 60–69.

Rosenshine, B. (1983). Teaching functions in instructional programs. *Elementary School Journal, 83*(4), 335–352.

Rosenshine, B. (1979). Content, time, and direct instruction. In P. Peterson & H. Walberg (Eds.), *Research on teaching: Concepts, findings, and implications*. Berkeley, CA: McCutchan.

Rosenshine, B. & Furst, N. (1971). Research in teacher performance criteria. In B. O. Smith (Ed.), *Research in teacher education: A symposium* (pp. 37–72). Upper Saddle River, NJ: Merrill/Prentice Hall.

Rowe, M. (1986). Wait time: Slowing down may be a way of speeding up. *Journal of Teacher Education, 37*(1), 43–50.

Rowe, M. (1974). Relation of wait-time and rewards to the development of language, logic, and fate control: Part one—wait time. *Journal of Research in Science Teaching, 11*, 81–94.

Rubin, L. (1983). Artistry in teaching. *Educational Leadership. 40*(4), 44–49.

Ryan, D. G. (1960). *Characteristics of teachers*. Upper Saddle River, NJ: Merrill/Prentice Hall.

Salomon, G. (1992). The changing role of the teacher: From information transmitter to orchestrator of learning. In F. K. Oser, A. Dick, & J. L. Patry (Eds.), *Effective and responsible teaching: The new synthesis* (pp. 35–49). San Francisco: Jossey-Bass.

Sharan, S., & Schachar, C. (1988). *Language and learning in the cooperative classroom*. New York: Springer.

Shulman, L. S. (1992). Research on teaching: A historical and personal perspective. In F. K. Oser, A. Dick, & J. L. Patry (Eds.), *Effective and responsible teaching: The new synthesis* (pp. 14–30). San Francisco: Jossey-Bass.

Shulman, L. S. (1987). Knowledge and teaching: Foundations of the new reform. *Harvard Educational Review, 57,* 1–22.

Slavin, R. E. (1991, February). Synthesis of research on cooperative learning. *Educational Leadership, 48*(5), 71–82.

Slavin, R. E. (1994). *Using student team learning* (4th ed.). Baltimore, MD: The Johns Hopkins University Center for Research on Elementary and Middle Schools.

Walberg, H. J., Schiller, D., & Haertel, G. D. (1979). The quiet revolution in educational research. *Phi Delta Kappan, 61*(3), 179–183.

Wang, M. C., Haertel, G. D., & Walberg, H. J. (1993/1994). What helps students learn? *Educational Leadership, 51*(4), 74–79.

Wasik, B. A., & Slavin, R. E. (1993). Preventing early reading failure with one-to-one tutoring: A review of five programs. *Reading Research Quarterly, 28*(2), 178–200.

Weinert, F. E., Helmke, A., & Schrader, F. W. (1992). Research on the model teacher and the teaching model. In F. K. Oser, A. Dick, & J. L. Patry (Eds.), *Effective and responsible teaching: The new synthesis* (pp. 249–260). San Francisco: Jossey-Bass.

Welty, W. W. (1989). Discussion method teaching. *Change, 21*(4), 40–49.

chapter 8

Curriculum Assessment

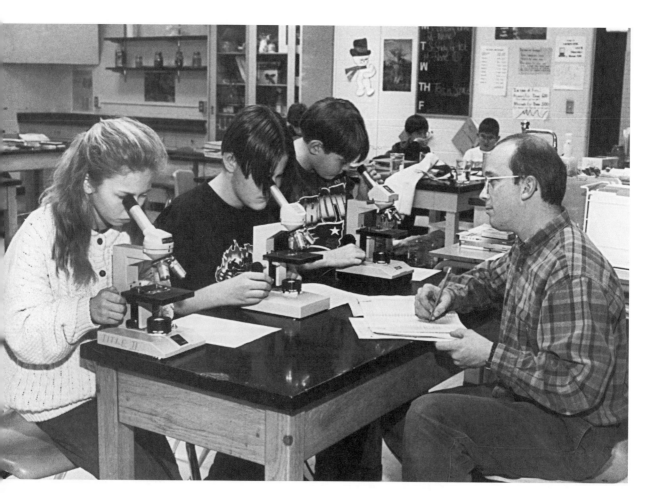

AFTER READING THIS CHAPTER, YOU WILL BE ABLE TO DO THE FOLLOWING:

- Describe the relationship of the assessment step to the other steps in the curriculum development process.

- Define and give examples of the terms *assessment, measurement,* and *evaluation*.

- Identify and describe the domains of curriculum assessment.

- Identify the levels of curriculum assessment, and discuss the kinds of assessment procedures used and data collected at each level.

- Discuss the relationship of formative and summative procedures to curriculum planning and implementation.

- Describe how teachers conduct formative and summative assessment in the classroom.

- Identify and describe the various kinds of classroom assessment procedures and strategies teachers can utilize.

- Discuss the unique qualities of authentic assessment and portfolios.

The previous chapters described the steps of planning and implementing the curriculum, which are the first two steps in the curriculum development process. This chapter describes ways of assessing the overall effectiveness of planning, teaching, and learning. The importance of the assessment step can be seen in the belief that many have that the fastest way to affect teaching and learning is to change the assessment system (Elton & Laurillard, 1979). Assessment serves a variety of functions and occurs at multiple levels in the school organization. However, this chapter emphasizes assessing student performance in the elementary classroom. As Frieberg and Driscoll (1996) point out, "The ultimate purpose [of assessment] is to measure student learning. The additional purposes are improvement of teaching, curriculum, and conditions for student learning" (p. 382).

Historically, the term *curriculum evaluation* has been used to describe this third step of the curriculum development process (see Figure 1-6).

The term *evaluation* connotes judgments and/or decisions based on values (Woolfolk, 1995). *Assessment* is a term used to describe the process of obtaining data or information about materials, programs, and students, on which teachers then make judgments about teaching and learning. For us, *assessment* connotes a broader scope and suggests that there are many ways to determine curriculum and teacher effectiveness and to measure student learning.

Assessment may be the most difficult part of the curriculum development process, for in this step teachers design ways to collect information about their overall effectiveness in planning and implementing the curriculum and the degree to which students have learned. The data collected are then used to make decisions about the curricular program and about student achievement or performance.

Teachers tend to teach those things for which they are held accountable (Shavelson, Baxter, & Pine, 1992; Smith, 1991). Yet in spite of the importance of the assessment step, teachers often feel inadequate in dealing with the complexities of the process (Linn, Grave, & Sanders, 1990). Even experienced teachers express their concerns about test construction, test validity, and grading (Crooks, 1988). The complexities of the process are illustrated by Rose, our experienced teacher.

 Voice of Experience

Rose has just completed a unit and wants to find out whether the students mastered the objectives for that unit, so she sets out to assess student learning. Rose says, "I realize that there are a variety of ways to determine if students have mastered the objectives. In fact, one of the most common forms of assessment I use is a unit test that measures, to some degree, the content (facts, names, etc.) from the unit that the students have mastered. But I want to think about other ways to measure student learning. I could have the students submit a project or product that would demonstrate their level of understanding of the material. I could also use daily work activities to assess learning along the way. Finally, I could have the students use the information in an actual or role-playing situation so they could show what they have learned by applying it in an authentic way." Rose is also aware that the material covered in this unit will be tested on both district-wide and state achievement tests, and this also influences her decisions about the kind of assessment procedures she will use.

Curriculum assessment applies not only to the type of instructional program or areas of study, but also to how each program is doing in promoting student learning. The *curriculum assessment* step is the process of gathering information from a variety of sources, including student achievement data as benchmarks, to determine

the effectiveness of educational programs. *Assessment* is a naturalistic process used to gather a variety of data and information about both program and teacher effectiveness and about student performance. As Simmons and Resnick (1993) suggest, the emphasis recently has been on using assessment to improve teaching and learning. Throughout this chapter, we discuss the ways teachers measure the effectiveness of their instructional program as well as the ways they determine the success of individual students in their classrooms. As teachers obtain assessment data, they should use this information from previous experience to plan future units and lessons; the activities that did not produce desired results may be eliminated and others added for the next day or the next year.

This chapter describes the various dimensions of curriculum assessment. Topics to be addressed include views and definitions of key terms, domains of curriculum assessment, levels of curriculum assessment, formative and summative assessment, and assessment strategies, including testing, authentic assessment and portfolios, and reporting techniques. The chapter concludes with suggestions for using assessment results to modify the curriculum.

VIEWS AND DEFINITIONS OF ASSESSMENT TERMS

The assessment process follows planning and implementation and provides the means for collecting the necessary data or evidence to demonstrate that the objectives have been accomplished and learning has occurred. Two questions are often asked:

■ Did the students learn the concept(s) and/or skills that were planned and taught?

■ Were the plans and materials effective in promoting student learning?

Using the data/evidence gathered in the assessment step, the teacher examines the results of the total teaching-learning process to answer this question. For many, the ultimate test of curriculum planning, and in turn classroom teaching, is to determine whether and what students have learned. To accomplish this, teachers might use one or more of the following procedures or strategies to collect data about the curricular program:

■ Products or observations from daily learning activities (daily work) that students engage in while in the classroom (investigations, writing assignments, skill and drill worksheets, or cooperative learning tasks)

■ Documents from independent learning assignments such as reports; papers researching an issue, dilemma, or concern; laboratory experiments to test hypotheses; or creative pieces such as poems, essays, songs, short stories, sketches, and photographs

■ Projects such as dioramas, salt maps, art work, long term science investigations, or notebooks and journals

■ Cooperative group projects or oral reports

■ Teacher-made or school/departmental tests

■ Process and literacy skills of observing, predicting, inferring, hypothesizing, reading, writing, speaking, listening, investigating, and creating models

Assessment, Measurement, and Evaluation

Assessment is the process whereby data are collected about the teaching-learning process. *Measurement* is defined in quantitative terms, the numeric description of an event, behavior, or characteristic (Woolfolk, 1995). Measurement provides the numeric scores that establish qualitative differences, or levels of proficiency. For example, a score of 75 percent on a test has no inherent meaning until the standard for "passing"

is established. The score of 75 percent could be failing if the degree of qualitative performance (passing) is established as 80 percent. Educators give meaning to data by making value judgments. Making judgments about scores based on a set of values is *evaluation* (Woolfolk, 1995).

Lemlech (1993) defines *evaluation* as the process of using information or some type of evidence and making a judgment after considering all the data. Evaluation seeks to answer these questions:

■ How many students demonstrated mastery of the content at this level if a specific score is established as passing?

■ How effective was the curricular program in preparing students for this level of achievement? For example, if 80 percent has been established as the passing or mastery level and only ten out of twenty-four students achieve that score, then how effective was the curricular program?

For many, the ultimate criterion for assessing the effectiveness of the curriculum is based on the academic success of the students (Caswell, 1978). Assessment is a reciprocal part of the total curriculum development process: teachers plan on the basis of feedback from assessment and then conduct assessment on the basis of planning. Assessing without planning or planning without assessing is incomplete and hence unwise (Saylor, Alexander, & Lewis, 1954).

Curriculum Assessment

Although *curriculum assessment* is presented as the third step of curriculum development (Figure 1-6), it really occurs simultaneously as teachers plan and implement instruction. Trump and Miller (1968) describe the complexity of the assessment process:

> Knowing whether a school is a good school, . . . whether students are learning what they should be learning, and whether a curriculum change is

better than what it replaced are . . . fundamental factors in good curriculum development. . . . Yet, finding imaginative and comprehensive answers to these questions has plagued curriculum planners for generations. (p. 339)

Ornstein and Hunkins (1993) describe the assessment process as what educators do as they "gather data that will enable them to decide whether to accept, change, or eliminate something regarding the curriculum in general or . . . [a] textbook in particular" (p. 250). Assessment then, should lead teachers to making better decisions, as they select, plan, and implement the curriculum (Stake, 1967).

DOMAINS OF CURRICULUM ASSESSMENT

Think of the assessment process as being composed of three interrelated domains:

■ the learner(s)

■ the school environment

■ the instructional staff

Each domain presented in Figure 8-1 contributes to the teaching-learning process and the curricular program. Each is vital to assessment of instructional effectiveness. These domains also illustrate the complexities of the assessment process. Assessment of learners is influenced by the school environment as well as the instructional staff and their beliefs. As indicated in Chapter 5, the philosophy or belief system teachers hold influences the kinds of assessment procedures and strategies they adopt. For example, teachers who have a philosophy of realism tend to be more concerned with the mastery of facts and data, whereas progressives tend to emphasize problem solving and the authentic assessment procedures discussed later in this chapter.

Rose, the "Voice of Experience" for this chapter, reflects on the relationships between and among the domains of assessment.

FIGURE 8-1   Domains of Curriculum Assessment

LEARNERS
- Individuals/groups
- Needs/interests
- Abilities/capabilities
- Overall development

SCHOOL ENVIRONMENT
- Curricular program
- Delivery system
- Materials/resources
- Classroom arrangement

INSTRUCTIONAL STAFF
- Teacher's background, knowledge, and experience
- Teacher's belief system
- Administrators' characteristics
- Instructional support personnel characteristics

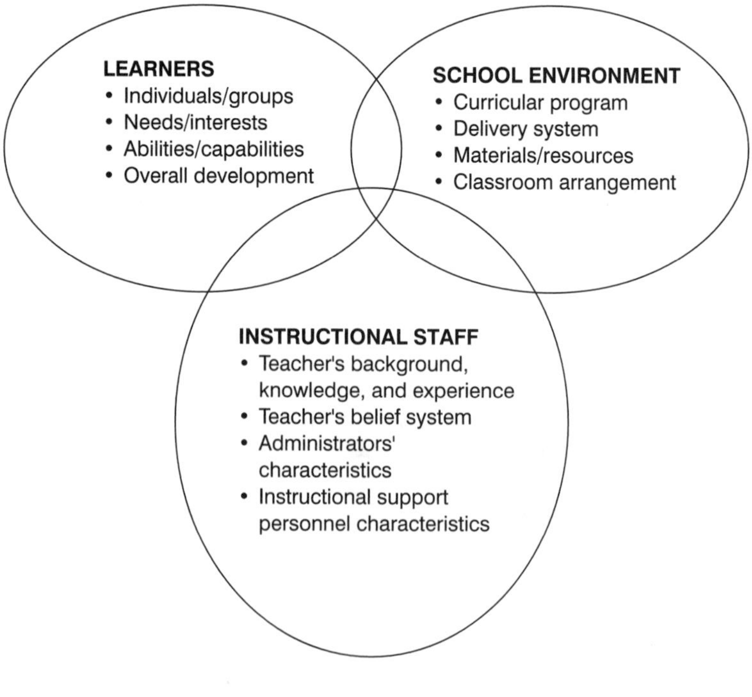

Voice of Experience

As Rose assesses the learners in her class-room, she looks at both individual and group characteristics in order to assess abilities and capabilities. In assessing the curricular program and school environment, Rose examines text-books, curriculum guides, and other resources that impact the delivery system. Rose asks her-self, "Did the materials selected match the objectives and the needs of the learners?" Finally, Rose is concerned about her own over-all teaching effectiveness and considers the results by reflecting on these questions:

- Did students learn?
- What experiences, knowledge, and skills were critical to the success of teaching this unit?
- Were my objectives appropriate for this group of students?
- Could I have established a more appropri-ate sequence?
- Were the learning activities meaningful?
- Was my knowledge and understanding of the subject sufficient to help learners?

Rose examines the total process of curriculum planning and implementation in answering these questions that will also help her evaluate the overall effectiveness of the curriculum.

The domains of assessment provide a mechanism for setting up a checklist and helping teachers make decisions about teaching and learning in regard to each component (students, school environment, and instructional staff). When focusing on the students, the teacher looks at individual learning as well as group learning. In addition, the needs, abilities, and capabilities of individual students are addressed along with the

developmental characteristics. When examining the school environment, not only the instructional materials and resources are assessed, but also the curricular program and the way teachers deliver that program. The third domain, instructional staff, centers on the teacher—his or her background, experience, and knowledge base—along with the support system, which includes administrators, librarians, counselors, and clerical staff.

These domains of curriculum assessment divide the process into manageable components and guide assessment decisions, which are designed to determine the degree of success in teaching and learning. As teachers gain confidence in using the domains of curriculum assessment, they begin to achieve greater specificity and objectivity as they collect and analyze the data.

LEVELS OF CURRICULUM ASSESSMENT

The assessment process involves many different individuals, occurs at multiple levels within and outside the educational system, and ranges from teacher assessment in the classroom to assessment nationwide. Figure 8-2 provides a view of the various levels of curriculum assessment, along with some brief descriptors for each.

Classroom Level

First and foremost, assessment occurs at the classroom level, where teachers seek to gather information about how well their students are performing, and gives teachers a sense of their own teaching effectiveness. Such assessment procedures as student conferences, daily work/tasks, projects, observation checklists, tests, and portfolios are used by teachers for this purpose. The teacher's greatest involvement in curriculum assessment occurs at this level. Because the level

FIGURE 8-2   Levels of Curriculum
Assessment

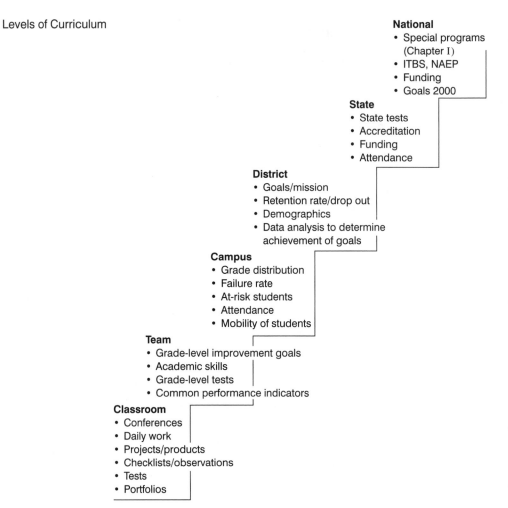

of assessment is extremely important, much of the remainder of the chapter addresses specific classroom assessment strategies and procedures. With each level beyond that of the classroom, the teacher's involvement in decisions related to the assessment process is diminished.

Team Level (or Grade Level)

The second level of curriculum assessment occurs within a team of teachers who teach at the same grade level. At this level, teachers are trying to determine, through tests and observation instruments, whether the improvement goals and academic skills have been mastered for that grade level, using common performance indicators. In the elementary school, there is often a team or grade-level leader who helps to promote collaboration among his or her colleagues within a given grade level. There is horizontal (within grade level) and vertical (across grade levels) coordination to ensure that the scope and sequence of the elementary curriculum is aligned. Curriculum assessment provides needed feedback that can be used to refine this alignment. The team leaders work together in determining the degree of mastery of content and skills that elementary students have achieved. At the team level, the individual teacher's involvement is still felt within the assessment process, but the teacher's direct involvement is lessened because of the input from other team members.

Campus Level (or Building Level)

The next level of curriculum assessment occurs at the campus level or building level. Here, educators seek to determine the effectiveness of the curriculum by looking at grade distribution within and among grade levels, and failure, mobility, and attendance rates as indirect measures. They also develop a school profile based on a variety of achievement test scores by grade level to identify trends within the student achievement data. It is from these data that decisions are made regarding the need to reteach specific concepts, special programs, and the general sense of how well the faculty is doing in achieving the school goals. With the move toward site-based or campus-based management, teachers are taking on more and more responsibilities in deciding the day-to-day operations of the school. In these schools, the role of the teacher in curriculum assessment remains strong.

District Level

At the district level, administrators from the central office become more directly involved in the curriculum-assessment process by establishing goals and missions and retention and dropout rates. They work with building principals and team leaders in analyzing data to determine whether the goals set by the faculty and parents were met, and to what degree. In some districts, if some schools consistently perform below expectations, site visits are conducted and more information regarding the curriculum, teaching, and evaluation is requested. In extreme cases, individual schools are put on probation and a plan must be created to meet the identified deficiencies within a given time period. On the flip side, campuses doing well are often rewarded for a job well done and serve as models within the district.

State Level

State educational agencies become involved in the assessment process as they develop state tests for determining the quality of education, establish or select standards for accreditation, and provide funding for educational programs. Not only are achievement test scores or state-developed test scores reviewed, but in assessing the quality of education the state agencies may also examine such related factors as retention rate, number of remedial courses offered (and for whom), dropout rate, attendance record, mobility rate, and number of children eligible for free or subsidized lunch within each district in the state. This information is used to develop district profiles that, when placed side-by-side, provide the big picture of the quality of education in the state as a whole. State legislators often look at test scores when deciding on levels of funding for public schools. As money is appropriated, there is often a call for greater accountability, which is translated into raising test scores, giving a new test, changing the data for giving the test, and/or holding teachers in some way responsible for below-normal test scores.

National Level

At the national level, special programs and funding issues emerge as Congress examines funding themes related to fostering academic achievement and providing for remediation, at-risk students, grants and special programs (like Chapter I programs and Head Start). America 2000 (developed under the Bush administration) and Goals 2000 (initiated under the Clinton administration) have attempted to galvanize the future direction of elementary and secondary education in the United

States. The Goals 2000 program provides the long view of education and establishes a model for states to review as they begin to set their agendas for the twenty-first century. Efforts have been made to standardize the elementary and secondary curriculum across the United States, but some say the textbooks used already do this. In addition, organizations such as the National Science Teachers Association have established criteria to certify teachers in content fields at the national level; this recognition of content standards within disciplines is highly regarded and encouraged. The National Council of Teachers of Mathematics has established national standards for curriculum.

By examining the criteria and data for each level, the total curriculum assessment step is easier to comprehend. The pieces of information at each level provide a basis for making decisions about the curriculum.

FORMATIVE AND SUMMATIVE ASSESSMENT

The discussion so far has focused on assessment of the curriculum by looking at the big picture and the various levels. There are two general types of assessment that teachers use to guide decisions relative to the elementary curriculum.

■ *Formative assessment* occurs before or during teaching and provides data that help to form or shape curriculum planning and implementation. It helps to identify and diagnose potential problem areas in teaching and learning. The use of diagnostic tests, pretests, or skills checklists (which are not graded) identifies areas of weakness in achievement and the need to modify the planning and/or teaching steps. According to Eggen and Kauchak (1997), a variation of formative assessment is continuous progress or ongoing measurement called *curriculum-based*

assessment (CBA). The use of frequent tests, probes, or questions from the curriculum give an ongoing picture of the student's performance.

■ *Summative assessment* occurs at the end of teaching or several periods of instruction. Its function is to determine the level of performance, and it "provides a summary of accomplishment" (Eggen & Kauchak, 1994, p. 551). Summative procedures are often considered "fit for a grade" because they are used to ascertain students' levels of accomplishment.

To better grasp the meaning of formative and summative evaluation, consider the analogy of a railroad track. One rail of the track represents formative assessment and the other rail summative. The tracks are parallel and do not touch; they complement each other. The railroad ties are the assessment data that connect the two rails. As the data are collected, more ties are added, and these data contribute to the total curriculum-assessment step. From a distance, the tracks may appear to come together, but in reality they never intersect because each type of assessment has its own function and so each rail (formative and summative) maintains its own identify. The data (railroad ties) can be either formative or summative, depending on how they are used by the teacher. Figure 8-3 illustrates the relationship between the two types of assessment procedures.

The ties that connect the rails of the formative-summative tracks include student performance data such as tasks from group work, individual work assignments, projects and products, documents developed, specific skills mastered, and scores on tests.

Formative Assessment and Data Collection Procedures

Formative assessment procedures collect data related to the current educational curricular programs. Formative assessment is used to examine

FIGURE 8-3 Formative and Summative Assessment

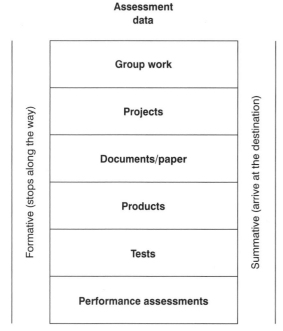

Assessment
data

Formative (stops along the way)

Summative (arrive at the destination)

| Group work |
| Projects |
| Documents/paper |
| Products |
| Tests |
| Performance assessments |

the effectiveness of teaching and learning as well as programs or treatments, and special groups and classes. Formative assessment examines progress along the way and provides an opportunity for all concerned to reflect on what has been done. Formative assessment is sometimes referred to as "continuous," "ongoing," or "developmental" and answers the question, "Is the curriculum producing the kinds of learning outcomes desired?" For Zais (1976), formative assessment

> is conducted during the curriculum development process for the additional purpose of providing data that can be used to "form" a better finished product ... [and] takes place at a number of intermediate points during the development of curriculum. (p. 381)

Educators take this "en route" data and begin to build a profile of what and who is being evalu-

ated. For Farr (1993), the "portfolio in progress" is an example of formative assessment; in such a portfolio, many different items are added without regard to being finished or polished products. By providing information to the students and parents at various points along the journey, the final decisions made regarding proficiency are stronger because of the variety of information that has been collected about instruction, student performance, materials, and programs. Using such a data collection procedure, the students as well as the programs and materials are assessed in a multidimensional way, thereby taking into account the strengths and weaknesses, successes and failures.

Consider the uses of formative assessment suggested by Cronbach (1963):

- obtaining data regarding changes produced in students by completing a grade level

- identifying multiple outcomes and separating the effects of teaching according to the dimensions

- looking for aspects of a course in which revisions are needed

- collecting information while a course is being developed and/or taught

- identifying aspects of the curriculum which produce an effect and looking for what produces the effectiveness

- conducting systematic observations to identify desired pupil behaviors

- identifying outcomes beyond the content of the curriculum such as attitudes, aptitude for future learning, or general understanding

The intent of using formative data collection procedures is to encourage educators to continually monitor and make adjustments that lead to modifications in the instructional and curricular program. This type of assessment allows teachers to fine-tune units and lessons in the curriculum as it is being implemented. It also encourages teachers to remain sensitive to student needs and levels of interest; if something is not working, the lesson should be modified. Judgments about the overall effectiveness, the need to continue a curricular program, and similar decisions are made at this point.

 Voice of Experience

Rose comments on the process of formative assessment by saying, "It never really occurred to me that I used formative assessment in my classroom as I developed and taught my lessons. I have always had my students do a variety of things such as projects, labs, group work or reports, daily work, and tests. As students worked on each activity, I would assess their abilities. Some activities were to help provide insights about the success of my teaching and the particular material I used to present the lesson. It was from those experiences that I would begin to get a composite picture of how effective I was and the worthwhileness of the curricular program. As I teach, I look for ways to adjust not only my own instructional behavior, but also that of the curricular components. I just never had a name for the daily, ongoing, decision—formative assessment."

Summative Assessment and Data Collection Procedures

Unlike formative assessment, summative assessment requires the use of comparative data or information in order to make a judgment or a decision. Summative assessment does three things:

■ It makes comparisons between and among programs and materials so as to determine which one is better or best.

■ It examines the effectiveness of special groups to determine whether the arrangement should be continued.

■ At the individual level, it compares performance data to determine qualitatively what grade a student should receive, or if he or she "passes" a course or is retained at a specific grade level.

According to Zais (1976), summative assessment is conducted "in order to obtain a comprehensive [look at] the quality of a completed curriculum . . . [which] takes place at the completion of the curriculum development process and provides a . . . judgment on the completed product" (p. 381). Summative assessment helps educators arrive at decisions regarding both teaching and curricular effectiveness. Educators then determine which curricular programs should be selected over others, based on the student performance results that are produced.

Student performance data are important aspects of the summative assessment. In summative assessment, the question asked is, "Did the curriculum produce the kinds of results desired?" One thing educators can do is examine student achievement data as they make summative decisions. For example, at the classroom level, the teacher might monitor six-week grades or scores on publisher-made tests to determine the level of student learning. If students are failing or getting poor grades, some decisions will need to be made. One of these decisions relates to instructional objectives and strategies used and the teacher's instructional performance; the other relates to the effectiveness of the curricular materials used.

Summative assessment has been called "outcomes-based," "terminal," or "product" assessment. Horst, Tallmadge, and Wood (1975) identified hazards in making summative decisions and warned against using inappropriate data because, in using these data, it is difficult to determine whether students performed better in a particular curricular program than they would have without them. Among the hazards are the following:

■ Using raw gain scores (posttest minus pretest scores) for comparison purposes

- Using norm-group comparisons with wide variances in test dates

- Using noncomparable treatment and comparison groups

- Using pretest scores (especially low scores) to select program participants

- Using results from tests that have been administered carelessly

- Assuming that achievement gain is solely due to treatment and not recognizing other variables or plausible explanations for the gains

Using inappropriate data to make decisions regarding the curriculum is a mistake, and Zais (1976) cautions that summative assessment should not be thought of as a one-time only procedure that occurs exclusively "at the end." In fact, summative assessment can and should occur at specific or strategic points during teaching and learning and the curriculum development process. Just as the ties on the railroad help teachers make "en route" decisions about the curriculum, the ties connected to the side of the summative rail can be data that help teachers make summative decisions about the students as well as the curriculum.

As educators use summative data to guide the assessment process, one way to develop a continuous system would be to monitor six-week grades and semester grades using not only grade level and subject achievement tests but also work done on projects individually and in group contexts. For example, if a teacher is assessing the effectiveness of the language arts curriculum, he or she would track the number of failures in the class for each six-week reporting period and for each semester. The teacher would also chart achievement test results of students in his or her class on nationally normed tests such as the Iowa Test of Basic Skills (ITBS). The kind of database the teacher would build is a *continuous summative profile*. This profile includes information collected at various points in time and from a variety of sources that would reflect the strengths and

weaknesses of the language arts curriculum in developing a reading, writing, listening, and speaking knowledge base.

CLASSROOM ASSESSMENT STRATEGIES AND PROCEDURES

In collecting data for both formative and summative purposes concerning student achievement and curricular programs, teachers may use a variety of assessment strategies and procedures. Stiggins (1994) advises that assessment procedures should match achievement targets. The targets include assessing knowledge, reasoning, skills, products, and affect. The strategies and procedures used should be consistent with the target behavior.

In addition to matching achievement targets, teachers should remain cognizant of various learning styles as well as Gardner's (1983) seven levels of intelligence. If students learn in a variety of ways, it seems appropriate to identify ways for assessing what is learned linguistically, logically, musically, kinesthetically, spatially, interpersonally, and intrapersonally. For example, if a child's strength in learning is musical, then assessment could be in the form of composing a song and/or singing the song composed. Without this link between how a student learns and measuring this learning in a way that is compatible, there is a mismatch. To avoid this mismatch dilemma, many assessment strategies need to be implemented, thereby ensuring that learning has taken place for individual students.

Mitchell (1992) describes the term *performance assessment* as "a collection of ways to provide accurate information about what students know and are able to do or about the quality of educational programs" (p. 20). She continues by saying that

If students should be able to analyze, synthesize, interpret, and evaluate facts and ideas, then their progress should be charted by direct performances. If students should write well, they should be tested by reading their writing. If they should be able to solve problems using mathematical knowledge, the assessment must ask them to do it. (p. 21)

Using the analogy of railroad tracks and ties, the task before teachers is to select those ties along the evaluation track that will yield critical information and help them in assessing student performance in the classroom. To do this, the teacher may choose to collect formative data procedures, examining processes and "en route" skills, or collect summative data such as projects or products. As teachers gather the data about student performance or achievement, they begin to fit the pieces together to form a picture of each student's accomplishment and ability. Figure 8-4 represents the components of the assessment puzzle and illustrates how they fit together.

There is no single assessment strategy that works universally in all subjects for all students. Teachers will need to collect data from several

FIGURE 8-4   Fitting the Assessment Puzzle Pieces Together

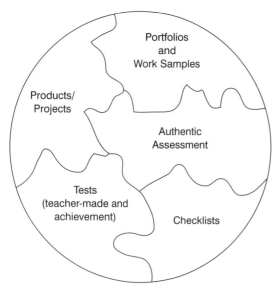

sources before making judgments about student performance. The following section presents briefly several ways that elementary teachers can collect data about student performance in the classroom.

Products, Projects, and Checklists

Teachers have the opportunity to assess student performance by having them construct a product or complete a project related to the topic of study. Teachers have students do salt maps of geographical regions discussed in social studies, illustrate books that they have read about dinosaurs, construct posters using geometrical shapes studied, construct historical dioramas, write or collect examples of poetry for a language-arts journal, or compose an original song. These projects and products demonstrate student understanding of the content and concepts studied in a nontesting situation.

Science teachers frequently have students conduct laboratory experiments, illustrate what they "discovered," plot their data on a graph, and write up and submit their results. Mathematics teachers sometimes have students construct a model house to scale, and students have to apply their knowledge of mathematics to complete the project. The more teachers ask students to demonstrate what they have learned in ways other than using paper-and-pencil worksheets, the more comprehensively they will be assessing student performance. To show this multifaceted approach to student assessment in the elementary school, Rose, the "Voice of Experience" for this chapter, reflects on and describes what she has students do in her classroom.

 Voice of Experience

In Rose's classroom, students are studying about birds. Rose describes the process: "As I begin to think about what the students need to learn and do in this unit, I focus on the instructional objectives and think about the ways that the objectives could be assessed." Rose is thinking in terms of both formative and summative assessment. She begins to consider the instructional activities and curricular materials that will help the students be successful. She says, "For example, I can have the students read one of several books about birds, *Urban Roosts, A Visit to the Country, Feathers for Lunch*, and/or *Peeping in the Shell: A Whooping Crane Is Hatched*, to get them started. The key question for me is: What should students know about birds? I want them to observe the variety of feathers, bills, or beak structures, and the various forms of feet that birds have."

As Rose plans for and conducts the lessons she says, "Students may be able to bring in a variety of pictures of bird nests or even make some out of recycled and natural materials." As she thinks about instruction and the materials that will be used to accomplish the objectives, she begins to formulate questions that will assess student knowledge of birds. First, students can draw different kinds of birds. "As I give the students descriptions of the habitat of specific birds, I can have them match these descriptions to beak and feet structures. Students also will build bird nests or do reports on a specific role of birds in the ecosystem (name of species or order of birds), what a bird eats, what eats it." Rose begins to see that there are many ways teachers can assess student learning and performance, and she decides to develop a rubric for the unit that will help assess student performance. Figure 8-5 is the first draft of the assessment rubric for the bird unit.

FIGURE 8-5 Rubric for Bird Study

Rubric for Bird Study

I.   Read at least one book about birds and discuss five things you learned about birds.

Book title:_____

Things learned:

1._____

2._____

3._____

4._____

5._____

II. Draw at least three different kinds of birds with different beaks and feet. Tell where each bird most likely lives.

Criteria: 1. At least three
          2. Creativity
          3. Location or habitat of each bird

III. Select three habitat cards from the deck and three bird cards. Describe the beaks and feet structures most likely found on birds in each habitat and why.

Grading Scale: Excellent = accomplished all three tasks
                   Good   = accomplished two of three tasks
                   Poor   = accomplished one task only

Along with products and projects, the teacher may use checklists and observe students using manipulatives such as counters or base ten blocks to illustrate a mathematics algorithm such as the operation of addition on single-digit numbers. In reading, the teacher can use a checklist to record observations concerning reading miscues or the students' ability to predict the story outcome(s) from the book jacket, identify the main theme or characters in a story, and/or distinguish fact from opinion using specific examples. Lemlech (1993) suggests that by using checklists throughout reporting periods, teachers can chart student progress. These observation checklists can be stapled to the inside of each student's folder and, using the grading criteria established, the teacher can formally assess the level of comprehension by watching what the student does or does not do. Such a checklist or running record can be beneficial in jotting down anecdotal notes of student-to-student conversations during cooperative group work.

Tests

Although many teachers have concerns about overemphasis on the use of tests and the role of testing in general, tests also serve as an assessment strategy. Tests are only *one* source of assessment data. Keep in mind that students often respond adversely to taking tests, for a variety of reasons—reading ability, dyslexia, anxiety, and negative attitude, for example.

The classroom test for the chapter, unit, or reporting period is the most common form of testing. Such tests should be carefully constructed. As Lemlech (1993) points out, "the vast majority of tests given in classrooms are pencil-and-paper examinations designed by teachers" (p. 214). As teachers construct tests and use testing as an assessment strategy, it is important for them to examine their own philosophy about its purpose, which once again emphasizes the role of a belief system and its impact on teaching and learning as well as on curricular decisions (see

Chapter 5). Consider these questions to determine your philosophy of testing:

■   Does testing compare one student's performance to that of another?

■   Does testing serve to provide data with which to judge a student's performance according to established criteria?

■   Does testing provide data with which to judge a student's performance in relation to his/her own capabilities?

The teacher who answers the first question "yes" has a *norm-referenced* perspective of testing. This teacher would view testing as a way to "ascertain an individual's performance in relationship to the performance of other individuals on the same measuring device [test]" (Popham, 1973, p. 25). In such a view, the test is generally constructed to spread scores along some form of the normal distribution curve.

The teacher who answers the second question "yes" has a *criterion-referenced* perspective of testing and views it as a way to measure an individual's performance against established criteria or standards. With this view, the goal is to help all students attain at least the minimum level of mastery.

The teacher who answers the third question "yes" has a *self-referenced* perspective of testing and views student appraisal as a way to compare the student's individual cognitive growth based on pretest and posttest performance. Teachers with this view recognize the wide range of individual abilities in each class and modify testing to the individual. The self-referenced approach helps to individualize the testing process.

The teacher who answers "yes" to all three questions has an eclectic view and at times holds to comparative norms, at other times uses criteria that have been established against which a student is judged, and at times compares the student to his or her own abilities.

Many elementary teachers have adopted a criterion-referenced view of testing, in which students know the criteria or standard they must achieve. There are advantages and disadvantages to each system. Typically, the criterion-referenced approach provides the following advantages:

- Everyone knows in advance what is expected both in terms of performance and level of performance.

- Students know what they must do to be successful on assignments and tests.

- Students perceive this method of testing as fair because they are being tested against learning objectives that have been taught and not against other students.

- The teacher's subjective judgment is limited.

- The teacher does not create a competitive environment by pitting one student against another.

Because tests may be used by teachers as assessment tools, in the assessment process, it is helpful to examine some testing procedures that can make the process more reliable and valid. Popham and Baker (1970) note that "tests should enable a teacher to gather observations about the students' ability with respect to the instructional objectives" (p. 131) but, they point out, tests provide only a representative sample of a student's behavior and do not exhaustively measure the student's achievement. As teachers seek to construct valid tests that measure the abilities of their students, they need to keep in mind the following guidelines:

- Testing is not a perfect strategy and falls short of assessing students' understanding completely.

- Tests are constructed using a variety of subjective decisions such as the format of the test, the number of items or questions, and the point value of each item.

- Testing reflects the bias of the teacher, in terms of which concepts are considered important and therefore how many items for

each concept or skill are included on each test.

- Students should be given a variety of test formats (short answer, fill in the blanks, matching, multiple choice, open-ended questions based on what has been taught) so that they have the opportunity to demonstrate their strengths as well as their weaknesses.

Collette (1973) says that, "taking a test can be an exciting experience . . . [but] unfortunately teachers . . . use tests for a single function—the determination of grades" (p. 591). In order for testing to be exciting and a positive learning experience, teachers must work hard at developing tests that are appropriate for their students and for the objectives of the unit. Teachers should guard against the exclusive use of publisher-made tests, because these tests may not reflect the teacher's emphasis during teaching and many such tests are designed for low-level cognitive responses. Collette (1973) has identified twenty types of formats of tests that teachers can use in evaluating student performance:

- *Performance tests*: Students are given specific skills to perform, such as successfully loading a program on the computer by following a series of steps or developing a flow chart for arriving at a solution to a problem.

- *Identification tests*: Students use a key or set of criteria to identify objects, such as sorting a group of items according to a scheme of animal, plant, or mineral or a collection of stories and classifying them as fiction and nonfiction.

- *Recognition tests*: Students recognize and categorize objects or events, such as identifying which animals from a list would be herbivores (plant eaters) or carnivores (meat eaters).

- *Name association tests*: Students supply a name when given a description or shown a picture, such as naming five presidents when shown their pictures or playing the Who am I? game.

■ *Modified recognition tests*: Students explain the significance or describe the function and explain how and what something measures, such as using a map key to locate major cities, mountain ranges, or airports.

■ *Picture tests*: When shown a picture, students tell the importance of something, such as being able to identify a picture of a volcano and describe the eruption process.

■ *Diagram and model tests*: Students name the parts of a diagram or label the function of a part, such as labeling the parts of speech in a sentence.

■ *Drawing tests*: Students draw and label parts, such as drawing and labeling the major rivers on a map of the United States or parts to a circle (center, diameter, cord, radius).

■ *Completion drawing tests*: Students complete a drawing when given a prompt, such as a partially formed letter of the alphabet.

■ *Essay question test*: Students explain, compare, and describe in their own words the significance or importance of an object, event, or situation such as explaining the pros and cons of recycling.

■ *Short answer/explanation tests*: Students respond in limited length to a question or term such as "What are two ways birds spread seeds?"

■ *Completion statement tests*: Students fill in the blanks with the word or words that complete the statement such as filling in a blank using the proper form of a pronoun.

■ *Multiple choice tests*: Students are provided with a sentence and a variety of responses that answer the question or complete the sentence, as in the following:

Of the following sentences which one has at least one error in it?

a.   The house is red.

b.   The dog barking loud.★

c.   The girls are smiling now.

■ *Correction tests*: Students must correct statements so that they make sense; for example, students would correct the following sentence: "Tom went to the airport to catch a bus."

■ *Matching tests*: Students match the words in one column with phrases or other descriptors in another column.

■ *Grouping tests*: Students are given a series of terms, objects, events, patterns, or numbers and they must determine which ones do not belong in the group, such as deciding which numbers do not belong in the following group: 5, 10, 15, 20, 23, 25, 30, 35, 37.

■ *Arrangement exercise tests*: Students are given a set of items (terms, objects, situations) that they arrange in some order, such as putting panels of dialogue in a comic strip in the correct sequence.

■ *True/false tests*: Students indicate whether statements are true or false.

■ *Modified true/false tests*: Students correct those statements they believe to be false.

■ *Sometimes/always/never tests*: Students are given a range of qualifying responses as to the nature of a statement, such as "Water exists as a liquid" (sometimes); this is similar to a true/false test.

This list of types of tests is provided to encourage teachers to modify their test format and to incorporate a variety of types within a given test. Of the twenty types suggested, most testing experts agree that the true/false test is the least attractive in measuring student knowledge. In constructing a test, the teacher should complete a test matrix so that the number and kinds of test items accurately reflect the material covered in class with the appropriate emphasis. For example, if the teacher spends only part of one class period discussing carnivores, herbivores, and omnivores, and half of the test is about those terms, the test does not reflect an appropriate emphasis.

With the current pressure to use tests and to measure academic excellence with test indices, it is no wonder that elementary teachers are in a quandary about the purpose of tests. Worthen and Spandel (1991) say that "on their own, tests are incapable of harming students. It is the way in which their results can be misused that is potentially harmful" (p. 67). In the final analysis, the question posed by Linn, Grave, and Sanders (1990) and Shepard (1989) is this: When test scores improve, does it mean that there is an improvement in learning? Teachers have to be able to answer this question for themselves based on their goals and the characteristics of students they are teaching.

Authentic Assessment

Critics of testing point out that many tests take knowledge out of context and focus on isolated facts or bits and pieces of information. Wiggins (1993) says that "The simplest way to sum up the potential harm of our current tests is to say that we are not preparing students for real, 'messy' uses of knowledge in context—the 'doing' of a subject . . . because our testing is based on a simplistic stimulus/response view of learning" (p. 202). Therefore, in order to make assessment more authentic or realistic, we must provide opportunities for students to demonstrate what they know within a context or situation in which that knowledge would be essential or useful, rather than with paper and pencil.

Wiggins (1989) has described the characteristics of authentic tests, but in looking at the appraisal of pupil performance from a broader perspective that includes opportunities other than testing, we have modified these test characteristics to reflect authentic assessment. The characteristics of authentic assessment then include the following:

1. Structure and logistics of assessment
    - is more public and involves an audience or panel
    - does not rely on arbitrary or unrealistic time constraints
    - offers known, not secret, questions or tasks
    - involves multiple opportunities for demonstration such as portfolios or a season of games (not one-shot)
    - is not isolated but requires some collaboration with others
    - recurs and is therefore worth practicing for, rehearsing, and retaking
    - makes assessment and feedback to students so central that school schedules, structures, and policies are modified to support it

2. Intellectual design features of assessment
    - is essential and not needlessly intrusive, arbitrary, or contrived to "shake out" a grade
    - is enabling and constructed so that students are pointed toward more sophisticated use of knowledge and skills
    - is contextualized so that the tasks are not disjointed and isolated from the outcomes
    - involves the student's own research or use of knowledge which incorporates the content
    - assesses student habits and repertoires, not just recall and plug-in skills
    - presents a representative challenge which emphasizes depth more than breadth of knowledge and understanding
    - is stimulating and educational— students learn from the assessment process as well

■ may involve somewhat ambiguous tasks
   or problems to solve

3. Grading and scoring standards for assessment

   ■ involves criteria that assess essentials, and not easily counted and relatively unimportant errors

   ■ does not grade on the "curve" but in reference to clearly articulated performance standards

   ■ demystifies the criteria for success by presenting to students performance indicators that are inherent to success

   ■ makes self-assessment a part of the total assessment process

   ■ uses a multifaceted scoring system instead of one aggregate grade

   ■ outcomes match schoolwide goals and standards

4. Fairness and equity in assessment

   ■ ferrets out and identifies hidden strengths

   ■ constantly seeks to maintain a balance between recognizing achievement and native skill or prior learning and experience

   ■ minimizes needless, unfair, and demoralizing comparisons

   ■ allows appropriate room for student learning styles, abilities, and interests

   ■ can be done with all students

In designing authentic assessment procedures, elementary teachers can use these characteristics to guide their deliberations and their efforts. Newman and Wehlage (1993) suggest that as teachers develop authentic assessment procedures they should keep in mind these three criteria:

(1) students construct meaning and produce knowledge, (2) students use disciplined inquiry to construct meaning, and (3) students aim their work toward production of discourse, products, and performances that have value or meaning beyond success in school. (p. 8)

Recognizing that instruction is complex and that the quantification of learning can be misleading, Newman and Wehlage (1993) have proposed five standards that teachers can use in authentic assessment:

■ *higher-order thinking*: the degree to which students manipulate data and information and combine facts and ideas in order to synthesize, generalize, explain, hypothesize, or draw conclusions

■ *depth of knowledge*: the degree to which students can make clear distinctions, develop arguments, explain circumstances, events or data, and make connections with other topics or concepts

■ *connectedness to the world*: the degree to which students demonstrate that knowledge has value and meaning beyond the classroom and addresses real-world problems, contemporary issues, or personal needs

■ *substantive conversation*: the degree to which students talk to learn and understand the nature of a concept or subject such as exchanging ideas with others, sharing information, and establishing a dialogue which promotes collective understanding

■ *social support for student achievement*: the degree to which students have high expectations for learning, are willing to take risks and accept challenging work, and establish a climate of respect among members of the class or group which contributes to achievement by all

Portfolios and Work Samples

An assessment procedure of recent interest to many elementary teachers is the use of portfolios and work samples. The use of portfolios provides teachers with "a process of looking closely at students' work and . . . a concrete starting place for thinking about [teaching] and learning" (Valencia & Place, 1994, p. 668). The *portfolio* is a collection of student work that has been gathered over a period of time—some would say over an extended period of time.

The work sample, "instead of providing a general snapshot of narrow academic skills at a single point in time, . . . [provides] an ongoing process that reflects the goals and objectives . . . while keeping track of children's progress" (Meisels, 1993, p. 6). The work sample approach is more comprehensive than the portfolio alone because it involves not only the portfolio but also developmental checklists and summary reports.

Ideally, the student selects what he or she wishes to put in the portfolio. The student should reflect on what the item says about his or her performance. Items could be selected to show growth from one reporting period to another. Items could also be selected to show the student's "best" work or "most creative" work. Items that students might consider include tests, reports, laboratory experiments, creative writing samples (with various drafts of the work), journals, and art work or illustrations.

Maeroff (1991) provides a series of questions that can guide teachers in determining the nature and structure of the student's portfolio. He asks three key questions that should help teachers as they plan and implement the use of portfolios: "(1) What should be put in a portfolio?, (2) What should students be asking about the contents of their portfolio?, (3) How can some element of standardization be lent to the process?" (pp. 275–276).

Students should give careful thought not only to what they place in the portfolio but also to how they arrange it. The portfolio should contain a table of contents and a self-assessment by the student, explaining why these items were included and what these items tell about the individual's progress and learning.

In assessing portfolios, teachers should look for the following things:

1. evidence of critical and creative thinking
2. appropriateness of selected display items, variety of items
3. organization of display data
4. patterns in process and the way assignments were completed
5. evidence of understanding
6. use of intellectual tools (inquiry) and subject skills
7. use of technology (computers, calculators, video, audio)
8. research skills
9. logical developmental processes as in writing process and research
10. integrative self-assessment. (Lemlech, 1993, p. 228)

Paulson and Paulson (1991) say that "portfolios tell a story" and that students should include those items that tell their stories. As elementary teachers work with students to build their portfolios, the students should be involved in deciding what should be included and students should be informed of the criteria that will be used to evaluate their work.

UTILIZING ASSESSMENT RESULTS FOR MODIFYING THE CURRICULUM

The third and final step of the curriculum development process is assessing student learning. This step in Figure 1-6 brings to a close the curriculum development process and serves as a check on the entire system. In Step 1, the teacher begins planning for instruction by establishing instructional objectives. In Step 2, the teacher makes decisions regarding the most appropriate ways to teach the objectives. In Step 3, the teacher determines the degree to which the students have mastered the objectives.

The assessment data generated in this third step provide the teacher with the necessary feedback to not only assess student performance but also to modify curriculum and instruction. For example, if students do not do well on a project or test, the objectives may need to be revised in terms of domains and levels before the lesson is taught again. The teacher might decide that the objectives were appropriate but that new methods or strategies are needed to make the content more relevant or concrete. In doing an item analysis of the test or constructing a test matrix, the teacher may discover that the test did not accurately reflect what was planned and taught, and that modifications are needed in the test itself.

English's (1993) model of curriculum alignment suggests that curriculum is composed of three elements: the planned curriculum, the taught curriculum, and the tested curriculum. It is virtually impossible to have all three perfectly aligned because teachers are seldom able to teach all that they have planned, nor do they test or assess everything they teach. In fact, such agreement might not be desirable. However, the degree to which these three elements are congruent or overlap contributes to the quality of the curriculum. In Figure 8-6, the overlap or degree of agreement among the planned, taught, and tested curriculum is graphically presented by the shaded area.

Each of the three elements of the curriculum development process can serve as a focus for curriculum development. Often, activities or strategies drive the curriculum, with teachers focused on doing or teaching. When planning drives the curriculum development process, English (1993) says it is a front-end-loaded curriculum. When testing drives the curriculum development process, English calls it back-end-loaded.

Curriculum assessment serves as a way of not only verifying learning but also assisting teachers in making decisions about future curriculum and instruction. Ignoring the results of

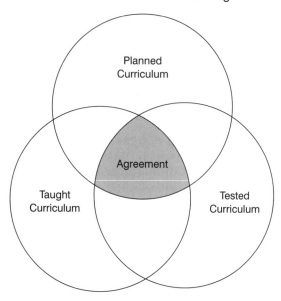

FIGURE 8-6   Elements of Curriculum Alignment

Planned Curriculum

Agreement

Taught Curriculum

Tested Curriculum

this process sets the stage for teachers to repeat mistakes. Worthen (1993) notes that the recent emphasis on assessment, especially alternatives to standardized testing, is the result of several forces that have affected the assessment process. These forces include

- demands for greater accountability with regard to desired student outcomes, and increased use of high-stakes testing in the form of minimum competency tests and standardized achievement tests

- increased negative consequences of testing such as teaching to tests and increased failures

- increased concern and criticism of the standardized test emphasis as a result of inadequacies and misuses of the tests

With these forces at work, the call for alternative assessment procedures, and certainly more comprehensive approaches, grows stronger. Therefore, to be informed decision makers, teachers need to be aware not only of the various assessment strategies and procedures but also of how alignment works and its role in the curriculum-assessment process.

SUMMARY

This chapter has completed discussion of the curriculum development process by presenting various aspects of curriculum assessment. On the surface it appears that curriculum assessment is a process of "looking back" only; upon closer examination, looking back is an important part, but assessment of the curriculum begins when planning starts. As elementary teachers look ahead and put in writing their desired objectives, curriculum assessment attempts to determine to what extent these outcomes are achieved. In effect, curriculum assessment asks the question, "Did the instructional and curricular programs produce the kinds of results desired?" This question is tied inextricably to the beginning of the process when the teachers ask, "What are the kinds of learning we want to produce in children?"

The chapter began with a discussion of assessment terms and then discussed the domains of curriculum assessment and the levels of assessment. The assessment process is multifaceted, involving both formative and summative strategies and procedures, and occurs at multiple levels within education. Formative assessment collects information during the implementation of curricular programs (instruction) so that fine tuning can occur. Summative assessment collects information, especially student achievement and teacher effectiveness data, that is used to make comparisons and ultimately judgments regarding the instructional effectiveness of a curricular program or treatment.

Classroom assessment procedures and strategies were described in great detail in this chapter. When the test strategy was presented, norm-referenced, criterion-referenced, and self-referenced views were defined in some detail. In the remaining part of the chapter, authentic assessment and portfolios were included along with a discussion about their implications for the teacher. The chapter concluded with a section on ways to utilize results from the assessment process in order to modify the curriculum.

To be effective, elementary teachers need an understanding of curriculum assessment and specifically those procedures and strategies they can adopt for their classrooms that will help them make informed decisions about the curriculum and the success of the teaching and learning process.

■ YOUR TURN

1. The professional literature is replete with articles about empowering teachers. Now that you have read this chapter, how do you feel about the teacher's role in assessing the curriculum and the students?

   a. In your journal, respond to the following prompt, "As a teacher, I would rather assess students using . . ." Why?

   b. As a member of a grade-level team, what role would you like to play regarding the curriculum-assessment process? What responsibility should you have? Why do you think so?

2. How are school programs assessed? Who makes the recommendations and who makes the final decisions?

   a. To find answers to these questions, make an appointment to talk with two principals and teachers. Before the interviews, find out whether the school curriculum has a new program (whole language, teaming across disciplines, global education, or interactive computer software, for example) and develop a series of questions to ask.

b. After the interviews, analyze the responses. Do any trends surface? If yes, what are they? Are methods in place to assess these programs? By whom? At what points? When?

3. After reviewing several curriculum guides in at least two different subject areas, jot down the various ways that are listed to assess student achievement. Are there test questions (multiple choice, fill in the blanks, etc., or review questions) to measure whether the objectives were met? For example, an objective might be to use manipulatives in solving mathematics computations. The assessment requires students to demonstrate ways to solve $3 + 2 = \square$ using Cuisenaire rods.

4. Obtain different types of curriculum documents used by teachers and recommended by school districts. Review several documents in at least two curriculum areas (science, social studies, language arts, health), particularly those that may be new or innovative.

    After selecting these documents, turn to the section on assessment that has been suggested. Focus on one of the assessment strategies presented and review the others. Label each strategy as either formative or summative assessment. If there are no evaluation strategies presented, try to identify the examples that follow. After each of the following statements, write an *F* for formative or an *S* for summative.

a. Asking questions to gain information about the student's prior knowledge or point of view.

b. Having students present results of their findings regarding bird beaks—which types are most efficient in gathering food.

c. Having students write down on a 3×5 index card three things they remembered from yesterday's lesson.

d. At the end of a three-week period, having each group of four students turn in their strategy for establishing a bird refuge on the school grounds.

e. Having each student write a poem or essay about an animal—the only criterion is that the information be accurate.

5. What if you as a teacher were asked to use only tests to assess student performance and you did not agree that only tests should be used? What would your response be if you believe in a broader approach to assessment? How could you develop an assessment process based on tests, as well as using projects, artwork, essays, letters, and other non-test performance measures?

6. Turn to Part III of this book, where the curriculum areas are presented. Select a specific curriculum area chapter that interests you. If you were given the responsibility to assess this area for your school, where would you begin? Consider the following:

a. What are the proposed trends?

b. How do these trends affect student learning?

c. What assessment strategies and procedures would you use to determine whether the trends will help students learn?

■ REFERENCES

Caswell, H. (1978, November). Persistent curriculum problems. *The Educational Forum, 43*(1), 103–106.

Collette, A. T. (1973). *Science teaching in the secondary school*. Boston: Allyn & Bacon.

Cronbach, L. J. (1963, May). Course improvement through evaluation. *Teachers College Record, 64*(3), 672–683.

Crooks, T. J. (1988). The impact of classroom evaluation practices on students. *Review of Educational Research. 58*(4), 438–481.

Eggen, P., & Kauchak, D. (1994). *Educational psychology: Classroom connections* (2nd ed.). Upper Saddle River, NJ: Merrill/Prentice Hall.

Eggen, P., & Kauchak, D. (1997). *Educational psychology: Classroom connections* (3rd ed.). Upper Saddle River, NJ: Merrill/Prentice Hall.

Elton, L., & Laurillard, D. (1979). Trends in research on student learning. *Studies in Higher Education, 4*, 87–102.

English, F. (1993). *Deciding what to teach and test*. Newbury Park, CA: Corwin Press.

Farr, R. G. (1993, January). *Portfolio assessment*. Presentation at Duncanville Independent School District Inservice, Duncanville, Texas.

Frieberg, H. J., & Driscoll, A. (1996). *Universal teaching strategies* (2nd ed.). Boston: Allyn & Bacon.

Gardner, H. (1983). *Frames of mind: The theory of multiple intelligences*. New York: Basic Books.

Horst, D., Tallmadge, G. K., & Wood, T. C. (1975). *A practical guide to measuring project impact on student achievement*. Monograph Series on Education, No. 1. Washington, DC: U.S. Office of Education.

Lemlech, J. (1993). *Curriculum and instructional methods for the elementary and middle school* (3rd ed.). Upper Saddle River, NJ: Merrill/Prentice Hall.

Linn, R. L., Grave, M. E., & Sanders, N. M. (1990). *Comparing state and district test results to national norms: Interpretations of scoring—'Above the national average.'* (CSE Tech. Prep No. 308). Los Angeles: University of California, Center for the Study of Evaluation.

Maeroff, G. I. (1991, December). Assessing alternative assessment. *Phi Delta Kappan, 73*(4), 272–281.

Meisels, S. J. (1993). The work sampling system: An authentic performance assessment. *Principal, 72*(5), 5–7.

Mitchell, R. (1992). *Testing for learning: How new approaches to evaluation can improve American schools*. New York: The Free Press.

Newman, F. M., & Wehlage, G. (1993). Five standards of authentic instruction. *Educational Leadership, 50*(7), 8–12.

Ornstein, A. C., & Hunkins, F. P. (1993). *Curriculum foundations, principles and issues* (2nd ed.). Upper Saddle River, NJ: Merrill/Prentice Hall.

Paulson, P. R., & Paulson, F. L. (1991). Portfolios: Stories of knowing. *Yearbook, Claremont Reading Conference* (pp. 294–303).

Popham, W. (1973). *Evaluating instruction*. Upper Saddle River, NJ: Merrill/Prentice Hall.

Popham, W., & Baker, E. (1970). *Systematic instruction*. Upper Saddle River, NJ: Merrill/Prentice Hall.

Saylor, J. G., Alexander, W. M., & Lewis, A. J. (1981). *Cur-riculum planning for better teaching and learning* (4th ed.). New York: Holt, Rinehart and Winston.

Shavelson, R. J., Baxter, G. P., & Pine, J. (1992). Performance assessments: Political rhetoric and measurement reality. *Educational Research, 21*(4), 22–27.

Shepard, L. A. (1989, April). Why we need better assessments. *Educational Leadership, 46*(7), 4–9.

Simmons, W., & Resnick, L. (1993). Assessment as the catalyst of school reform. *Educational Leadership, 50*(5), 11–15.

Smith, M. L. (1991). Meanings of test preparation. *American Educational Research Journal, 28*(3), 521–542.

Stake, R. E. (1967, April). The countenance of educational evaluation. *Teachers College Record, 68*(2), 523–540.

Stiggins, R. J. (1994). *Student-centered classroom assessment*. Upper Saddle River, NJ: Merrill/Prentice Hall.

Trump, J. L. & Miller, D. F. (1968). *Secondary school curriculum improvement* (2nd ed.). Boston: Allyn & Bacon.

Valencia, S., & Place, N. (1994). Portfolio: A process for enhancing teaching and learning. *The Reading Teacher*, 47, 666–671.

Wiggins, G. (1989). Teaching the (authentic) test. *Educational Leadership*, 46(7), 41–47.

Wiggins, G. (1993). Assessment: Authenticity, context, and validity. *Phi Delta Kappan*, 75(3), 200–214.

Woolfolk, A. (1995). *Educational psychology* (6th ed.). Boston: Allyn & Bacon.

Worthen, B. R. (1993). Critical issues that will determine the future of alternative assessment. *Phi Delta Kappan*, 74(5), 444–448.

Worthen, B. R., & Spandel, V. (1991). Putting the standardized test debate in perspective. *Educational Leadership*, 48, 65–69.

Zais, R. S. (1976). *Curriculum principles and foundations*. New York: Thomas Y. Crewel.

chapter 9

Using Technology in the Classroom

AFTER READING THIS CHAPTER, YOU WILL BE ABLE TO DO THE FOLLOWING:

- Discuss the role of technology in the curriculum development process.

- Define interactive and noninteractive technology and cite the characteristics of each.

- Give examples and explain curriculum uses of various kinds of interactive technology.

- Identify and describe some of the challenges and barriers to the use of technology in schools and classrooms.

- Describe the role of the teacher in implementing educational technology in the elementary classroom.

- Provide examples of how technology can be helpful in teaching each subject area in the elementary school curriculum.

- Identify and describe at least one technology resource for each subject area in the elementary curriculum.

As we move into the twenty-first century, technology, which increasingly plays a role in our lives, will continue to affect society and education. Technology helps teachers and students manage the ever increasing volume of information generated each year. Teaching with technology in the elementary classroom requires that teachers be familiar with the potential uses in their classrooms. *Technology* refers not only to computers, which have become the focus in classrooms in recent years, but also to other kinds of interactive as well as noninteractive equipment (i.e., distance learning via satellite hookups, large screen, or multiple screen projection systems, videos, etc.). Nevertheless, computers still generate much excitement in schools.

Use of computers in the classroom grew dramatically between 1983 and 1993, from 9,379 (57%) districts having microcomputers to 15,611 (92%) and from 30,859 (37%) public schools having computers to 82,226 (98%), to change the ratio of students to computers from 125:1 to 16:1 ("There's Never Been," 1993). What a difference ten years can make! Teachers are reporting that using computers in their classrooms has changed their teaching style. They spend more time working with individual students, feel better about students working independently, and have higher expectations with regard to creating original pieces of writing and correcting them ("There's Never Been," 1993).

According to the Office of Technology Assessment (OTA) (1995), the most commonly used technology in the elementary school includes videos for presenting information, computers for basic skills practice, and word processing for developing computer-specific skills. The OTA also states that other technologies that are used include desktop publishing, computer simulations for developing mathematical and scientific reasoning, the gathering of information from CD-ROM or network databases, and electronic mail for communicating. Green (1995) notes that "many schools have networked computer labs, multimedia personal computers (PCs) and CD-ROMs," but she also cautions that, in spite of the technology, schools "still have joyless programs of organized instruction and countless students who fail" (p. 1). Too often, Green says, instructional technology assumes three very unproductive roles of babysitter, entertainer, and drill sergeant.

This chapter provides definitions for interactive and noninteractive educational technology, describes the challenges teachers encounter when teaching with technology, and discusses the role of the teacher in implementing technology. The chapter concludes with a section on teaching with technology and provides lists of resources for each of the elementary content areas.

DEFINING EDUCATIONAL TECHNOLOGY

The term *technology* means different things to different people. Fitzgerald (1992) has captured the essence of the meaning of *technology*:

> a complex, integrated process involving people, procedures, ideas, devices, and organization for analyzing problems and devising, implementing, evaluating, and managing solutions to those problems, involved in all aspects of learning. (p. 7)

Such a broad definition of educational technology conjures up a multitude of images, from word processing, taking a trip, solving real-world problems, to correctly answering an electronic worksheet. One way to better understand the gamut of definitions of educational technology is to begin by differentiating between interactive and noninteractive hardware/technology.

Noninteractive Technology

The noninteractive technology familiar to teachers over the past twenty years includes tape recorders, sixteen-millimeter film projectors, opaque projectors, filmstrip projectors, videocassette recorders (VCRs), and television. Information presented on noninteractive technology can-

not be changed by the viewer; it can be turned on or off, and stopped at appropriate points, but the viewer cannot respond to the media interactively. More often than not the learner is an observer, not a participant. Noninteractive technology is frequently used by the teacher to do the following:

- Introduce a topic or skill.
- Open a lesson and/or unit.
- Motivate students.
- Practice a concept or skill.
- Stimulate discussion.
- Provide background information.
- Close a lesson with a review.

Interactive Technology

On the flip side, using interactive technology such as computers, laser discs, compact disc players, modems, and videodiscs allows the viewer to manipulate the technology for specific learning goals (Frazee & Rudnitski, 1995). Interactive technology is often used by the teacher to provide students with opportunities to do the following:

- Answer questions.
- Record information.
- Add possible outcomes to a situation, experiment, or a story.
- Solve problems.
- Plan and implement a strategy.
- Design models.

This level of interaction places the student in an active learning mode rather than a passive one. Such engagement encourages the learner to function at a higher level of thinking (analysis, synthesis, and evaluation).

A comparison between noninteractive and interactive technology is presented to highlight each and to point out how each has a distinct role to play in teaching. If viewing, practicing, and recalling are the objectives of a lesson, then non-interactive technology is the tool to use. If, on the other hand, higher-order tasks are the objective, interactive technology should be considered.

Because most teachers are familiar with the equipment in the noninteractive category, they tend to need more assistance in working with interactive technology. To help teachers feel more comfortable and acquaint them with technology, an introduction to key terms seems like an appropriate first step. Having a common language will be helpful in pinpointing areas of need. Just as you can drive a car without being a mechanic, teachers can learn to use technology without being computer programmers or technicians. It is useful, however, to have some idea of what is happening under the hood.

After several lessons in ways to use the technology (driving a car), learning about what is under the hood commences. Only then do teachers become stakeholders in using this new teaching tool. Here are some terms you will encounter in working with educational technology:

Hardware refers to the machines that process, transfer, and store information. Examples include computers, modems, scanners, keyboards, printers, diskette drives, hard drives, CD-ROM drives, and other equipment.

Computers contain electronic processing units that with proper programming can function much like the human brain. They may contain *hard drives* where programs and data are stored, and *ports* where cables for printers, modems, and other devices connect.

Modems enable computers to transmit data across telephone lines.

Scanners convert images from something visible on paper into electronic data that can be stored on the computer. These images can be put on a diskette or stored on the hard drive on a computer and can be modified or printed out, using appropriate software. Scanners can scan, or read, legible text, line drawings, and photographs.

Software refers to the programs that give directions to the machines (hardware) to operate and allows computer users to store or process information, play games, or construct designs. Examples include word processing, games, spreadsheets, databases, and computer design packages. (Software can be stored on a number of different kinds of *media*, such as 3½-inch or 5¼-inch diskettes, hard drives, and CD-ROMs).

Multimedia uses various components of technology in combination (audio, video, computer, overhead projector) to achieve the lesson/unit goals and objectives. An example of multimedia software is a CD-ROM that contains sound, text, and moving illustrations.

LCD (liquid crystal display) panel, when placed on an overhead projector and connected to a computer, allows the user to project what is in the computer onto a screen.

Distance learning links students and instructors with others by way of satellite or fiberoptic communications. In rural areas, where elective courses and staff-development programs are hard to provide, distance learning has proven helpful.

Network refers to a computer system used to link hardware within a classroom, within a school, among schools across a district or region, and even across the nation so that data can be shared. Information is transmitted via cables, modems, and telephone lines. The goal of the National Science Foundation is to network universities with public schools by the beginning of the twenty-first century (Lewis, 1991).

Online services can provide information, including reference materials and interactive discussion on specific topics, that students can access using a computer, modem, and telephone line. A few online service providers are America Online, CompuServe, GTE Education Services, National Geographic Kids Network, AT&T Learning Network, Global Lab, and New Access.

The *Internet* is a complex international computer network that links schools, universities, government agencies, companies, and individual computer users around the world. It allows millions of people to correspond, buy and sell products and services, conduct research, copy software, read news updates, and post and read public messages.

Technology provides for instruction through computer simulation and computer-assisted instruction. *Computer simulation* provides real-life experiences or situations that engage students in making decisions and problem solving, which in turn impact the results of the given experience. *Computer-assisted instruction* (CAI) is a kind of computer software that provides students the opportunity to practice basic skills (such as solving math problems or matching terms and meanings) and normally provides immediate feedback on accuracy of performance.

Having a general understanding of the terminology is the first step toward becoming familiar with educational technology. A second significant step is to understand what is meant by *computer literacy*. The goal of having students achieve computer literacy was conceived to help students acquire the necessary skills for entering the workplace. Encouragement from business and industry has helped educators focus on the value of using computers as a form of technology for teaching in the elementary classroom. It seems clear that the workplace of the future will require that employees have computer skills and be able to function in a computer-oriented environment.

On December 9, 1991, President Bush signed into law the High Performance Computing Act, which has the potential to affect the future by changing the way in which all Americans will work, learn, and communicate in the future. A part of this act was a provision for federal funding of a computer network for K–12 teachers, university professors, and administrators as part of the National Research and Education Network (NREN). NREN will supersede the Internet in terms of speed. President Clinton has urged Congress to finance this "superhighway" telecommunication network (Kinnaman, 1993).

It is clear that "doing more of the same will only produce more of the same. Automating current educational practices will not [necessarily] affect the quality of learning" (Campoy, 1992). Being able to click *Y* for yes or *N* for no is not being technologically literate; that experience is merely the beginning. Students from preschool through college find computer technology a challenge but also a rewarding experience. In addition, the various mediums of technology seem to hold students' attention regardless of their age.

CHALLENGES TO TEACHING WITH COMPUTERS

Although the rhetoric about computer technology is very positive and teachers are often enthusiastic, major challenges or barriers exist to incorporating it in greater frequency in elementary classrooms. The initial cost of hardware and software is a key concern for many schools and districts; a second major barrier is that technology changes at a dramatic pace. Finally, the need to prepare teachers and other professional staff members for the use of this new tool presents a challenge for many schools and districts.

For some school districts, the expense of providing adequate technology at the campus level is extremely high, and cost-prohibitive. The purchase of individual computers with CD-ROMs for the purpose of networking within a building or district presents economic as well as logistical demands. Depending on the type and level of sophistication of the computer with printing capabilities, the cost per unit can average $2,500. When that is multiplied by thirty or more classrooms, the cost can run as high as $75,000 to $100,000 per campus. Many schools simply do not have that kind of money. One district, with two primary campuses, one intermediate campus, one junior-high school, and one high school of nine hundred students estimates that it will cost the district more than six million dollars to put a computer in every classroom, outfit the central office, and network the entire system.

Without supplemental funding—such as issuing a bond to support the purchase of technology or receiving help from private industry through gifts and grants—some districts simply cannot afford the price of technology. Some schools have had success in finding funding for technology. Schnitzer (1995) recommends writing grant proposals to finance and meet the educational technology needs of a district. According to her, a well-designed proposal should include a clear description of the hardware and software requested and how it will be used. For example, one school requested two computers and a laser printer in order to establish a publishing center that would help students start their own business. Such a justification is linked to students in a way that helps them gain lifelong skills (Schnitzer, 1995).

In many cases, the reason for resisting widespread adoption of computers within schools is the frequency with which both hardware and software become outdated, which results in a continuous financial obligation for schools. Alvin Toffler (1970), in *Future Shock*, predicted that changes in society would occur at an increasingly fast pace, and the ever-changing world of technology follows his projection in that way. One school district adopted a software system to install on all computers within the district so they could use the same program for creating documents such as tests. No sooner had they installed the hardware and software than a newer version of the program became available. Although the cost of the new program was minimal, it required additional memory for each computer. With new memory and a new version of the software program, some old programs began to develop glitches. The need for constant upgrading and the difficulties that the upgrading process can engender tend to deter the widespread adoption and use of technology.

In school districts where computers and software are available, the training of entire faculties on the use, operational as well as instructional, presents a challenge to staff development. At one school, where the average age of the faculty is thirty-seven and the average length of service is fourteen years, the faculty are resistant to trying computers in their teaching, even though some of them have computers at home. The kinds of hardware and operating systems are often based on personal preference, and teachers say it takes too long to learn a new system because they need lots of "hands-on" opportunities to master the system. Getting faculty to change their attitudes and accept a new perspective is an important key to getting them to use technology as part of their teaching and learning repertoire.

In describing the changes that have occurred in her classroom, Vanessa, the "Voice of Experience" for this chapter, notes that the movement from a traditional classroom to one that integrates technology did not happen all at once, but gradually over four or five years.

 ## Voice of Experience

Vanessa, an experienced elementary teacher, says, "My change to a classroom that incorporates technology occurred slowly, over a period of several years. The first change I noticed was a break in the daily class schedule. I had to divide the class into two groups—one for the computer lab and one to work on projects in class—then I began to make other changes in the schedule. For example, in mathematics, the class was divided into five groups, and one group each day of the week worked at the single computer station in the classroom. As I divided the students into groups, I began to use cooperative learning strategies and more manipulative activities. In fact, I began to structure mathematics so that each week there was a different activity to do each day for each group. This change was the result of trying to get each group at the computer at least once a week.

"As students gained confidence in using the computer, and as I gained more confidence in my own ability to use the computer, I began to have the students word-process many of their language arts assignments. For example, when they wrote poems about themselves concerning the 'don't' in their lives, each sentence began with 'don't,' and the students experimented with font types, sizes, and styles. Many used an outlined *D* which they colored or illustrated to represent the thought in the sentence. Students became more creative in their writing as they experimented with the best way to print their ideas.

"As I was able to obtain more computers (4) for my classroom, I set up learning stations for each subject area and eventually moved to an interdisciplinary (multisubject) format. The computers with CD-ROM capabilities became research tools as students sought information and then became presentation/communication tools as students put their research or problem-solving products in a media format that could be shared with the class."

IMPLEMENTING USE OF TECHNOLOGY IN THE CLASSROOM: THE ROLE OF THE TEACHER

As the push for change in the elementary school becomes stronger, technology is at the heart of this change process (Bruder, 1990; Collins,

1991; Scheingold, 1991). In order for teachers to take advantage of what is currently available in technology, they must seriously assess their own strengths and weaknesses in this area. Key questions for teachers to ask as they reflect on their own knowledge and skill include the following:

■ What do I know about the basics of the hardware and software systems? What do I need to know?

■ What technology has the maximum teaching and learning application for my class?

■ When I review software, what should I look for? What are the indicators: goals, pace, quality, ease of use, directions, format (individual, self-paced, drill, game, problem solving), skill level, sequence, degree of assistance needed, sound, movement, or graphics?

The bottom line in the classroom, and throughout this book, is that teachers are responsible for asking key curricular questions, which may include these: What is to be learned, by whom, and under what circumstances? Why should it be? How should it be presented? Such questions are the mainstays of the curriculum, which prevents technology from wagging the tail of the pedagogical dog (Callister, 1992). The use of educational technology will only be beneficial if teachers understand its use and unique role in the curriculum, feel comfortable using it, and have some degree of skill in implementing its use in the classroom.

For educational technology to take hold, the role of the teacher takes on increased significance. For teachers to be successful in implementing the use of technology in the classroom, they need a stronger knowledge base, more staff-development time, and more practice and involvement with the equipment. Technology cannot, and should not, replace good teachers, nor can it be used without sufficient training and an ongoing support system for teachers from colleagues and administrators. Computer technology is a tool for delivering information; experiencing real-world situations via simulations; linking people, places, and information; and practicing problem-solving skills. Teacher training with periodic followup sessions, along with someone to troubleshoot, is crucial for teachers to be able to effectively use technology as part of the teaching and learning process (Reif & Morse, 1992).

Teachers might find it helpful to ask themselves the following questions as they make decisions about using technology in their classrooms:

- Is the technology appropriate for the developmental level of the students?

- Are the goals of the lesson being met? If not, why? If so, in what way?

- Does the technology involve several senses and skills (such as watching, listening, and thinking)?

- Does the technology provide opportunities for pausing and making comments or elaborating?

- Can the technology be managed in a way that presents several different forms of learning?

Teachers can use technology in the classroom with specific students who have special learning, linguistic, and/or physical needs. For example, ESL (English as a Second Language) students would find ESL Writer (from Scholastic Software) helpful because it has a tool for checking grammar and spelling for students with varied linguistic backgrounds. CD-ROM storybooks, another kind of program, switch from English to a second, and possibly a third, language easily.

Various kinds of hardware can help extend the number of "teachers" in the room, by providing students with interaction that gives them immediate feedback. Interactive equipment and software tend to motivate and stimulate or heighten student enthusiasm. Students like using computers and other technological equipment because they feel they are doing something worthwhile and meaningful.

TEACHING WITH TECHNOLOGY

Technology, especially computer software, has been integrated into the elementary school across many subject areas. This section identifies a variety of software resources for each area. The order of presentation parallels the sequence of chapters in Part III.

Language Arts

Denis Allen (1995) describes using a CD-ROM program called A to Zap to help kindergartners and first graders master the alphabet. The program has students interact with alphabet blocks and characters in 26 activities that match the letters of the alphabet. Each of the letter activities is different, and students learn skills about letters and the corresponding sounds they make. Teachers can supplement this self-paced instructional program by reading *Los ninos alfabeticos* (Ayala & Rodrihuez, 1995), *Z Was Zapped* (Van Allsburg, 1987), or *Chicka Chicka Boom Boom* (Martin & Archambault, 1995).

Students in the fourth grade at Flood Brook School in Londonberry, Vermont, type their stories on the computer using a word-processing program. When a student who wrote an eight-page single-spaced story was asked if he would write that much by hand, he responded "No way!" (Buckley, 1995). Oehring (1990) describes the use of Stone Soup (from the Explore-A-Classic Series). She says that it is perfectly suited to the Thanksgiving season because of its "Gift-from-the-Heart" theme. Students in primary grades can view the story complete with animation; the animation is motivational because the characters can be controlled. With upper-grade students, a friendship salad can be made, and the activities disk allows students to type the invitation. Finally, students can make a class story and publish it as part of the thank-you gifts (Oehring, 1990).

Figure 9-1 identifies A to Zap along with samples of other software programs that elementary teachers can use in teaching language arts.

Mathematics

Allen (1994) describes a software program that teachers can use in teaching mathematics skills of estimation and graphing. DinoPark Tycoon helps students to analyze cause-and-effect relationships as they create a dinosaur theme park. Students must problem-solve and make numerous decisions as they use their "working capital" to purchase land, erect fences, hire staff, obtain dinosaurs, and price and sell tickets.

Bixler (1995) uses calculators to help students with mathematical computations in the third grade. Using a calculator on the overhead projector, she works several problems and demonstrates the function keys of addition and subtraction. She then has students go through sample addition and subtraction problems and checks for understanding and accuracy in the use of this technology.

Allen (1994) suggests the use of Math Blaster: In Search of Spot as a way to help students with basic math facts, problem-solving, and mental math. As students are successful with problems, they move closer to accomplishing their rescue mission in this educational game. Mathematics concepts covered include number patterns, addition, subtraction, multiplication, division, fractions, and percentages. For more ideas for teaching mathematics with technology software resources, review Figure 9-2.

Social Studies

The potential of networking to teach social studies is described by Bradsher (1995) in using "The National Geographic Kids Network." This software (along with the appropriate hardware) allows students to interact with schools in forty-four countries. As students interact with Nelly Rechkalova in Moscow School #222, they ask questions about the world outside the United States and increase their global awareness.

Dockterman (1995), describes an interactive software program called Geography Search, which involves students in setting sail for the New World. Students work in teams of four, taking on various roles as crew members. The program provides them with data concerning the sun, stars, wind direction, and ocean depth. This information helps them determine where they are and plan for what they must do. The information appears for only a few seconds and then disappears. No one student can remember it all, so to succeed they must work together. The program is designed to get the crew members to talk to each other rather than taking action or pushing buttons. With each new data reading, the interaction among the crew members increases dramatically, as they share their readings and plan their strategy.

To travel to far-away places in "The National Geographic Kids Network," students can use Geography Search, to visit Ancient Lands and to explore the artifacts, monuments, and written documents from the ancient societies of Egypt, Rome, and Greece. To follow up on Egypt, elementary students can take a ride up the Nile and tour the ancient Temple of Ramses II. These and other software resources for social studies are featured in Figure 9-3.

Science

In Louden County, Virginia, teachers use technology to enhance their science curriculum. Etchison (1995) describes a second-grade unit on dinosaurs. As a project for the unit, the students used Kid Pix, a computer program with graphics capability, to create dinosaur-related illustrations to accompany their written captions, which described what they had learned. The students wanted to go beyond pictures, with captions assembled as a book, so they used Kid Pix Companion to link their drawings together to

FIGURE 9-1 Software Resources for the Language Arts

Name of Software	Manufacturer	Grades	Description of Software
A to Zap	Sunburst	PK–1	Provides students with 26 activities to learn the alphabet. Macintosh (4 MB, System 7.0 or later, 13" color monitor and CD-ROM drive) and Windows versions available.
Bailey's Bookhouse	Edmark	1–3	Combines interactive technology with proven learning techniques to help students learn letters, words, stories, and rhyming. Five creative activities allow students to write stories, print their own booklets, and design greeting cards and invitations.
English Express	Davidson & Associates	5+	Using videodisc or CD-ROM, students hear a variety of language models and view digitized photos in 67 thematic units.
Exito	Open World Interactive	1+	A Spanish-language, total immersion training program that moves students with no knowledge of the language to high novice proficiency. Can be used as a supplement or review.
Explore-A-Classic	William K. Bradford Publishing Co.	PK–3	Consists of a storyteller, a story maker, and follow-up activities to practice counting, and labeling and classifying. Children read an animated story while moving characters and objects around. The story maker enables children to view the stories without text and rewrite the text or create an entirely new story.
Perfect Copy	Logicus Inc.	4+	Using a set of real-life exercises, students learn grammar, punctuation, and word usage in 11 skill areas and learn 200 grammar rules, while analyzing 500 articles. Includes student tracking capabilities.

Name of Software	Manufacturer	Grades	Description of Software
Read & Rhyme	Unicorn Software	K–2	Includes four activities that develop spelling, comprehension, rhyming, phonetics, and more.
Scrabble	MacPlay	1–6	Provides an electronic way to expand vocabulary and spelling skills.
Stickybear Reading	Optimum Resource	K–3	Exceptional animation and sound will maintain children's attention while building their vocabulary and reading comprehension skills.
Stories and More	EduQuest/IBM	1+	Colorful graphics provide an excellent introduction to children's literature.
Talking Alpha Chimp	Orange Cherry Software	PK–2	Features a digitized voice and high-resolution graphics. Children learn the letters of the alphabet by clicking on a square that contains a letter. The sound of the letter is pronounced and the square changes into a picture of a corresponding word or animal. This program is well suited for prereaders.
WordSmart	Smartek Software	4+	Sold in ten individual volumes ranging in difficulty from grades 4 to adult. Focuses on synonym recall for each word, using visual flash cards, sentence completion, arcade-style multiple-choice, etc., and provides valuable feedback by explaining both correct and incorrect responses.
Writing to Write	IBM	2+	A year-long writing curriculum that gives students a context and structure in which to practice their writing with off-line "learning stations" that include problem solving and reading activities.
Vocabulary Development	Optimum Resource	3–6	Students practice recognizing synonyms, antonyms, homophones, multiple meanings, prefixes, suffixes, and context clues. As they master one level, they automatically advance. The exercises can be printed out and a report card screen allows for viewing up to 40 students.

FIGURE 9-2 Software Resources for Mathematics

Name of Software	Manufacturer	Grades	Description of Software
Fraction Action	Unicorn Software	4+	Allows students to add, subtract, multiply, or divide fractions in an arcade format. Full-screen explanations help students learn from their mistakes. Includes difficulty levels and a timer option for developing speed.
Graphs, Statistics, and Probability	Macmillan/McGraw-Hill	2+	Helps students to learn how to manage data in ways that can be displayed and analyzed.
The Great Brain Robbery	Davidson	4+	By solving word problems, comparing fractions and percentages, and filling in missing pieces of equations, students attempt to recover the brain that evil Dr. Dabble has stolen.
Math Football	Gamco	5+	Combines the excitement of football action with the challenge of math drill. All five Math Football programs (including Fractions, Whole Numbers, Decimals, Rounding, and Percent) offer four levels of play. On each play, students may choose a running play (an easy problem), short pass (medium problem), etc. Correct answers result in yardage gained, first downs, etc.
Math Rabbit	The Learning Company	K–2	Provides colorful graphics, fun animation, and music to explore basic number concepts and develop skills in counting, adding, subtracting, and more.
Math Sleuths	Videodiscovery	5+	An interactive videodisc that provides students with real-life situations for applying math concepts to develop problem-solving strategies to unravel mysteries. They analyze and record information and apply concepts of graphing, geometry, percentages, ratios, and measurement.
Math Workshop	Broderbund Software	K–6	Narration, animation, music, and sound effects are used to teach important math concepts of addition, subtraction, multiplication, division, equivalencies, and estimation.
Mathkeys: Unlocking Probability	MECC	3–6	Simulates a coin toss, marbles, spinner, and dice for learning concepts of probability, and students manipulate the number of trials and then analyze the results.
Money Matters	MCE	2–6	Designed to improve students' ability to understand, identify, and use bills and coins.
Number Munchers	MECC	1–6	Contains five games for practicing multiples, factors, and primes with equalities and inequalities in the choices of addition, subtraction, multiplication, or division. Students move markers around a grid "munching" the correct numbers.
Talking Clock	Orange Cherry	K–3	Features a human voice to learn time-telling skills. There are several activities with various clock faces, including Roman numerals and a digital clock.
Treasure Galaxy	The Learning Company	K–3	Combines critical thinking with visual math concepts such as measurement, fractions, the calendar, and geometric shapes. Players develop their basic skills such as observing, comparing, measuring, analyzing, and sequencing.

FIGURE 9-3   Software Resources for Social Studies

Name of Software	Manufacturer	Grades	Description of Software
Ancient Lands	Microsoft, Inc.	1+	Allows students to explore the historical societies of ancient Egypt, Rome, and Greece by examining artifacts, monuments, and written records of these past civilizations.
Black American History	Queue, Inc.	3+	Documents the struggles and accomplishments of blacks in America. It captures the essence of the African-American experience with more than 75 narrative presentations by famous African-Americans.
Discovering America	Lawrence Productions	2–6	Students visit 16th-century America to learn about extinct Native American tribes, hidden Aztec treasures, and gold. With digitized sound, graphics, and a satellite view map, students work their way toward the Mississippi Delta.
500 Nations	Microsoft, Inc.	3+	Students can learn about North America's first inhabitants while taking video tours of villages and dwellings. They examine artwork and hear stories that have been passed down through tribes.
Hometown, U.S.A.	Publishing International	4+	Enables students to create the buildings, residences, banks, bakeries, gas stations, that have doors, windows, etc., such as those found in a small town. Once printed out and colored with water colors or crayons, the models are cut out, folded, and glued.
Navigating the Nile	Discovery Multimedia	2+	Users ride on an ancient boat to travel up the Nile, while stopping at sites along the way, like a 3-D animated tour of the Temple of Ramses II.
North American Indians	Quanta	4+	An in-depth compendium of the leadership, tribal heritage, religion, family life, customs, wars, art, and resettlement of indigenous Native Americans.
Simcity Town	Maxis	2–6	In a computerized urban environment, students are allowed to design, build, and manage their own neighborhood, which includes people, pets, various kinds of houses, streets, parks, stores, etc. Students learn about city planning, economics, and ecology.
3-D Atlas	Electronic Arts	4+	Comprehensive tool enables students to see the world and gather important data about it from many different perspectives. A game is also included, "Around the World," which is a great motivator for children to learn more geography.
Transportation	January Productions	1–4	Introduces students to the development and importance of transportation in a two-disk program.
ZIPZAPMAP!	National Geographic Software	1+	A game series that tests students' knowledge of states, provinces, or nations, their capitals, major cities, and other significant physical features on the map as they earn points by correctly placing geographic pieces on the map.

create a slide show with a narration about dinosaurs.

In Danville, California, students investigate earth science concepts by networking with other children and using an online service. Novelli (1995) describes how students interact in an open chat area with students from other places by asking questions like: What is the temperature where you live? Is it morning? Afternoon? What types of rocks do you find where you live? How would you describe the topography around your school? As students interact via the online network, they get involved in science and want to learn more.

Weld (1996) reports that there is a World-Wide Web site on the Internet for science teachers called Access Excellence. Access Excellence, developed in 1994 by the Genentech Corporation in San Francisco, links science teachers with scientists at Genentech, which provides a wonderful supply of information and support for teachers. By accessing the WorldWide Web (at http://www.gene.com/al), students have the opportunity, for example, to monitor fall foliage throughout the country.

Students can learn about how balls with different properties bounce in Woolly Bounce and learn about animals when they watch and use the software series called Interactive Nova. Finally, a favorite of sixth graders is Where in Space is Carmen San Diego? As they work through this program, they discover facts about space science.

Figure 9-4 includes additional educational software resources that teachers can use in their elementary science classrooms.

The Fine Arts

When using the software program With Open Eyes, students are introduced to over 200 works of art from the Art Institute of Chicago. Not only does this software enable students to view the works of art, but it lets them listen to specific music clips and narrated background information. Also included in this electronic library is a series of games, activities, maps, and time lines ("Arts and Assessment," 1993).

Students at Ashley River Creative Arts Elementary School in Charleston, South Carolina, experience art using several art software programs. One is Microsoft Art Gallery, which includes several activities: one activity takes students on an electronic field trip to London's National Gallery, which has more than 2,000 paintings, but they become familiar with only a third of these paintings ("Schools Making Art," 1995). Another software program, Frank Lloyd Wright, helps students learn that architectural design is both a technical skill and an art form. Through a series of pictures, video clips, and text with narration, students design their own Wright-style structure.

The Music Ace is an interactive program that introduces students to the fundamentals of music. It includes twenty-four self-paced tutorials designed with increasingly challenging music segments that foster the development of musical skills. Music Ace is an ideal supplement for an elementary music program (Buckleitner, 1995). Figure 9-5 provides additional art and music software resources that could be helpful to elementary teachers.

RESOURCES FOR EDUCATIONAL TECHNOLOGY

After reading about the many ways technology can be integrated into the curriculum, you also need to know that these resources are available in both quantity and quality. CD-ROMs put thousands of images, topics, and experiences at students' fingertips (Peck & Dorricott, 1994). In addition, technology makes networking possible through the telecommunication highway. Figure 9-6 provides a list of suppliers of technology that may prove helpful to teachers. Helping students experience technology by using it in their daily studies does much toward achieving the goal of

FIGURE 9-4   Software Resources for Science

Name of Software	Manufacturer	Grades	Description of Software
AnnaTommy	IVI Publishing	3–6	Allows students to pilot a miniature spaceship through the human body, exploring 10 different body systems.
Bodyscope	MECC	3+	Assists students in an independent study of the body's organs and nine systems to gain a clearer understanding of human anatomy.
Destination Rain Forest	Edmark	1–6	Students will interact with exotic animals and plants as they create lush electronic books with rich illustrations and printed stories.
Endangered Environments	National Geographic Society	4+	Presents a series of images, sounds, and text information about the rain forests and wetlands.
Expert Astronomer	Expert Software	4+	A great reference for students, with information on stars, planets, galaxies, and celestial events. Includes a fast word and phrase search.
Forces & Motion	Science for Kids	3–6	Helps students understand the different types of force and ways to measure it using spring scales and magnets. Other topics include gravity and the laws of motion.
Interactive Nova	Scholastic Software	3+	Based on the WGBH-TV series, this three-program videodisc/software series includes *Animal Pathfinders* (animal studies), *The Miracle of Life* (human reproduction), and *Race to Save the Planet* (environmental studies).
Learning about Our Environment	Queue	4+	Introduces students to environmental problems using an image and text information and asks them to respond to relevant questions.
My Own Stories	MECC	3+	Allows students to create books that contain text and illustrations that can help them prepare science stories, science reports, or science projects.

FIGURE 9-4, *continued*

Name of Software	Manufacturer	Grades	Description of Software
Operation Frog	Scholastic	4+	Turns the computer into a full-color laboratory, so students can dissect frogs onscreen.
Out and About	Optical Data	K–1	One of four units of Kinderventures that cover the four main science disciplines.
Prehistoria	Grolier Electronic Publishing	4+	A guide to more than 500 prehistoric creatures divided into seven animal types, including fish, amphibians, reptiles, and mammals.
Science II Plus	Wicat Systems	5+	Students learn about earth, life, and physical sciences using an interactive, integrated software which combines science-related reading, math, and writing activities.
Simple Machines	Science for Kids	3–6	Explores the world of simple machines in a historic context: the inclined plane's importance in Egypt, the pulley in Sicily, and more.
Super Solvers: Gizmos & Gadgets	The Learning Company	3–5	Contains more than 200 puzzles and simulations to challenge students' physical science skills and concepts through observation and experimentation.
Weather Wizards	Entrex	4+	Students create weather while exploring a cartoon countryside. They create lightning and hail storms.
Where in Space is Carmen Sandiego?	Broderbund	6+	Students chase Carmen through the heavens, discovering facts about astronomy, e.g. constellations, stars, etc.
Wild Science Arcade	Binary Zoo	2+	Students learn about how gravity, friction, power, electricity, and magnetism work using a computer simulation in a game format.
Woolly Bounce	MECC	K–2	Allows young children to explore how balls of different physical properties bounce.

FIGURE 9-5 Software Resources for the Fine Arts

Name of Software	Manufacturer	Grades	Description of Software
Art Gallery	Microsoft	1+	Students take an interactive tour of London's famous National Gallery and examine 2,000 paintings by more than 700 artists.
Composer Quest	Dr. T's Music Software	6+	CD-ROM allows students to explore various musical eras by learning about their composers, history, art, and culture. Spanning the years from 1600 to the present, this database provides a historical approach to the study of music.
Dabbler	Fractal Design Corp.	3+	Unique draw and paint program combines sophisticated applications with a simple, yet detailed interface.
Fine Artist	Microsoft	3+	Students can paint pictures, comic strips, buttons, posters, and stickers. Using brushes, 3-D drawing tools, and special effects tools, students learn about art through interactive lessons on basic drawing techniques and perspectives.
Flying Colors	Davidson & Associates	3+	Contains unambiguous icons, clear tutorials, and can be set at three levels of difficulty. Enables students to concentrate on using their imagination.
Kid Pix	Broderbund	K+	Presents the use of color and abstract shapes in the artworks of Miro, Klee, and Chagall and students have opportunities to demonstrate their own creative talents.
Midisoft Music Mentor	Midisoft Corp.	5+	Turns a computer into a recording studio using MIDI technology, thus allowing students to create original music.
Music Theory	MECC	5+	Students can practice their musical skills by playing a simple instrument and receive feedback.
With Open Eyes	Voyager Company	PK–6	Students can examine more than 200 works from the Art Institute of Chicago, hear audio clips of music, sound effects, poetry, and narrated information.

FIGURE 9-6 Suppliers of Technology

Supplier	Description of Product Line(s)	Technology	Grade Levels
Addison-Wesley Publishing Co. "Innovative Learning Publications" Route 128 Reading, MA 01867 (800)552-2259	This series includes modules which include a VHS video, a teacher's guide with blackline masters, student activity cards, and activity materials.	VHS	3–6
Cambridge Development Laboratory 86 West St. Waltham, MA 02154 (800)637-0047	A great resource for numerous science educational software packages selected from the best of 100 publishers on areas such as general science, health and life science, earth science, and physical science.	Software(for MAC, Apple, and Windows) CD-ROM	Varies 1+
Fas-Track Computer Products, Dept. R-1 7030C Huntley Rd. Columbus, OH 43229 (800)927-3936	This company offers a myriad of different software packages including games, anatomy, meteorology, and locating rare plants and animals in the rain forest.	Software (for MAC, and Windows)	Varies 2+
Films for the Humanities and Sciences, Inc. P.O. Box 2053 Princeton, NJ 08543 (800)257-5126	In the "Children's Collection," there are many videos about specific earth and life science topics; some focus on specific areas of physical science and astronomy (with a complete series of videos comes a teacher's guide and other resources).	VHS	2–6
Insights Visual Productions P.O. Box 644 Encinitas, CA 92024 (619)942-0528	This company supplies a video series entitled "What Earth Science Is All About" which covers such areas as astronomy, geology, oceanography, and meteorology. The videos are broken into different levels of development (i.e., grades K-3 and 4-6).	VHS	K–6
Educational Resources 1550 Executive Drive Elgin, IL 60121-1900 (800) 624-2926	Offers educational software and technology for all subject areas (math, language arts, the arts).	Software, audio visual, and equipment	Pre K+

Supplier	Description of Product Line(s)	Technology	Grade Levels
Microsoft Corp. Redmond, WA (800) 426-9400	The company offers an array of software for elementary students in various subjects.	Software, graphics, video	1–6
National Geographic Society 1145 17th St. NW Washington, DC 20036 (800)368-2728	Available are units on the NGS Kids Network, a telecommunications-based world-wide network of interactive learning. Videodiscs of Newton's Apple, social studies, and much more.	Software (for MAC and Windows), CD-ROM, videodisc, and telecommunications via modem	Varies 1+
SVE, Inc. 1345 Diversey Pkwy. Chicago, IL 60614-1299 (800)829-1900	This supplier specializes in the most recent media technologies for the science classroom. Interactive applications are available. The Frontiers in Science video collection covers such areas as human progress, the environment, technology, and nature.	VHS, videodisc, CD-ROM	Varies PK+
Scholastic Inc. 2931 E. McCarty St. Jefferson City, MO 65101 (800)541-5513	"Interactive Nova" products utilize videodisc technology with an option of software (MAC only) that allows for interactive abilities (level III). The software provides student-centered inquiry experiences.	Software (for MAC, Apple IIGS,and MSDOS), videodisc, and VHS	K–6
Scott Resources P.O. Box 2121 V Fort Collins, CO 80522 (800)289-9299	Products include videos and videodiscs about earth and life science subjects. "Videolabs" which are complete with materials and equipment.	VHS, videodisc	6+
Sunburst 101 Castleton St. P.O. Box 100 Pleasantville, NY 10579 (800)321-7511	This company specializes in computer applications for teaching. For Apple and Macintosh users, there is the "Learn About" collection. Most of the selections are available on CD-ROM.	Software (for MAC, Apple, and Windows/DOS), CD-ROM	Varies PK+
Troll Associates 100 Corporate Dr. Mahwah, NJ 07430 (800)526-5289 x1118	A video collection on the recycling of various materials including a collection on the different kinds of natural and man-made ecosystems.	VHS	3–6
The Wright Group 19201 120th Av. NE Bothell, WA 98011-9512 (800)523-2371	Videos are included in many of the "First Nature Watch" series which cover topics of cycles for various animals, plants, and seasons.	VHS	PK–1

213

technological literacy. Elementary teachers who plan for and use technology as a part of their teaching curriculum inch ever closer to linking the school with the real world.

SUMMARY

This chapter began by illustrating how use of computer technology in classrooms has increased greatly from 1983 to 1993. The section that defined noninteractive and interactive technology provided definitions of some basic technological terms. The purpose of this basic information was to provide a beginning point for discussing teaching with technology.

Making educational technology an integral part of the elementary curriculum is not without its challenges. This chapter provided a brief discussion of the current challenges, terminology, and the role of teachers in using technology. These challenges include the cost of hardware and software, the changing nature of the technology as it continues to be refined and improved, and the need for teacher staff development. These challenges are not insurmountable, and suggestions are provided to address them.

The capstone of the chapter involved the application of the information about educational technology to specific curriculum areas: language arts, mathematics, social studies, science, and the arts. Identifying specific software and other electronic resources in the context of real elementary classrooms is one way to validate that educational technology can be successfully integrated into the curriculum. Educational technology was not designed to replace teachers but to serve the teacher and the students in expanding the walls of the classroom. The figures presented in the chapter provide valuable resources for teachers to increase mastery of using technology in the classroom.

>>
<<<<<<<<<<<<<<<<<<<<<<<<<<<<<<<<<<<<<<<<<<<<<<<<<<<<<<<<<<<<<<<<<<<<<<<<<<<<<<<<<<

■ YOUR TURN

1. Getting started with a self-check: How computer-literate are you?

   a. When you hear the word *technology*, what comes to mind? List all your ideas.

   b. Can you word process?

   c. Have you used technology to present information?

   d. Have you used a software program to learn about a specific topic?

   e. If you had the time and the financial support, what do you feel you would need (or would like) to learn before you are ready to use technology in an elementary classroom?

   Before proceeding, jot down responses to these questions and anything else about technology and your level of proficiency in your curriculum journal.

2. Obtain a copy of a software program recommended in the text or used in a local school district, in each of the subject areas.

   a. Language arts

   b. Mathematics

   c. Social studies

   d. Science

   e. Fine arts

   Take time to "experience" each program. Do you see ways you could use it in teaching? If so, in what ways?

3. Using the checklist in Figure 9-7, rate a software program and its suitability for the age/grade level that the program recommends.

FIGURE 9-7   Software Rating Sheet

1. **Computer**
   ❏ Apple   ❏ IBM   ❏ Macintosh   ❏ Other

2. **Needs/Requirements**
   ❏ Printer   ❏ Mouse   ❏ Color monitor   ❏ Videodisc

3. **Memory Requirements**
   ❏ 1M   ❏ 2M   ❏ 3M   ❏ 4M   ❏ Other

4. **Cost**
   Single package: $_____   Network: $_____

   Total cost : $_____   Cost per student: $_____

5. **Purpose** ❏ Yes   ❏ No   **Instructional objectives**   ❏ Yes   ❏ No

6. **Instructional Strategy** (Check box if present)
   a. Educational adventure   ❏
   b. Problem solving   ❏
   c. Simulations   ❏
   d. Tool-based (word processors, spreadsheets, etc.)   ❏
   e. Educational games   ❏
   f. Tutorials   ❏
   g. Drill-and-practice   ❏

7. **Type of Software**
   a. Interactive
   b. Noninteractive

8. **Examining the Software** (Circle the correct response.)
   a. Does the software match the objectives?   Yes   No
   b. Is the content information correct?   Yes   No
   c. Is the content relevant and current?   Yes   No
   d. Does the program provide feedback to the student?   Yes   No
   e. Are the questions randomly generated?   Yes   No
   f. Can the students determine their own pace?   Yes   No
   g. Are there several loops for students to try?   Yes   No
   h. Are prerequisite skills needed?   Yes   No
   i. Is the readability level appropriate?   Yes   No
   j. Can the teacher customize the program to
      meet student needs?   Yes   No
   k. Are supplementary materials needed?   Yes   No
   l. Are there suggestions for integrating it into the
      curriculum?   Yes   No
   m. Are the graphics and/or animation appropriate?   Yes   No
   n. Is the student able to review previous frames?   Yes   No
   o. Are there opportunities to skip frames if the student
      knows the information?   Yes   No

■ REFERENCES

Allen, D. (1994, January). Byte into math. *Teaching Pre K–8, 24*(4), 22–27.

Allen, D. (1995, September). Word-play for computers, *Teaching Pre-K–8, 26*(1), 22–24.

Arts and assessment software. (1993, September). *Instructor, 103*(2), 46.

Ayala, L., & Rodrihuez, M. I. (1995). *Los ninos alfabeticos* (Shoemaker, K. E., illus.). Watertown, MA: Charlesbridge.

Bixler, K. (1995). Using calculations in third grade math. [Mimeograph].

Bradsher, M. (1995, October). Networking with kids around the world. *Educational Leadership, 53*(2), 42.

Bruder, I. (1990). Restructuring: The Central Kitsap example. *Electronic Learning, 10*(2), 16–19.

Buckleitner, W. (1995). Quick Picks. *Technology & Learning, 15*(2), 18.

Buckley, R. B. (1995). What happens when funding is not an issue? *Educational Leadership, 53*(3), 64–66.

Bush, G. W. (1991, December 9). High performance computing act. Washington, DC: The White House.

Callister, T. (1992). The computer as a doorstep: Technology as disempowerment. *Phi Delta Kappan, 74*(4), 324–327.

Campoy, R. (1992). The role of technology in the school reform movement. *Educational Technology, 32*(8), 17–22.

Collins, A. (1991). The role of computer technology in restructuring schools. *Phi Delta Kappan, 73*(1), 27–49, 78–82.

Dockterman, D. A. (1995, October). Interactive learning: It's pushing the right buttons. *Educational Leadership, 53*(2), 58–59.

Etchison, C. (1995). Tales from a technology teacher. *Science and Children, 32*(7), 19–21.

Fitzgerald, B. E. (1992). Changing the industrial technology curriculum to meet today's needs. *Technological Horizons in Education Journal, 19*(8), 57–59.

Frazee, B., & Rudnitski, R. A. (1995). *Integrating teaching methods*. Albany, NY: Delmar Publishers.

Green, L. C. (1995, November/December). Teachers and instructional technology: Wise or foolish choices. *IDRA Newsletter, 22*(10), 1, 4–5.

There's never been a better time to use technology! (1993, October). *Instructor, 103*(3), 34–35.

Kinnaman, D. E. (1993). Push for data superhighway moves into fast lane. *Technology and Learning, 11*(1), 43–49.

Lewis, P. H. (1991). The technology of tomorrow. *Principal, 71*(2), 6–7.

Martin, B., & Archambault, J. (1995). *Chicka Chicka Boom Boom* (Ehlert, L., illus.). Boston: Houghton Mifflin.

Novelli, J. (1995, March). Turned on to science. *Instructor, 104*(6), 60–62.

Oehring, S. (1990, October). Software workshop: Teaching tips. *Instructor, 100*(3), 52–54.

Office of Technology Assessment (OTA). (1995). Teachers and technology: Making the connections. Washington, DC: Congress of the United States.

Peck, K. L., & Dorricott, D. (1994, April). Why use technology? *Educational Leadership, 51*(7), 11–14.

Reif, R. J., & Morse, G. M. (1992). Restructuring the science classroom. *Technological Horizons in Education, 19*(9), 69–72.

Scheingold, K. (1991). Restructuring for learning with technology: The potential for synergy. *Phi Delta Kappan, 73*(1), 17–27.

Schnitzer, D. K. (1995, October). How to fund technology projects. *Educational Leadership, 53*(2), 71–72.

Schools making art work (1995, May/June). *Electronic Learning, 14*(8), 40–42.

Toffler, A. (1970). *Future Shock*. New York: Random House.

Van Allsburg, C. (1987). *Z Was Zapped*. Boston: Houghton Mifflin.

Weld, J. (1996). Science online. *Educational Leadership. 53*(6), 86–87.

Subject Areas in the Elementary School Curriculum

Each chapter in Part Three represents a major subject area in the elementary school curriculum (language arts, Chapter 10; mathematics, Chapter 11; social studies, Chapter 12; science, Chapter 13; and physical education and the fine arts, Chapter 14). All chapters share several common components: a discussion of the issues, goals and objectives, topics within the subject area when appropriate, management techniques, and ways to assess content learning. In addition, each chapter includes a list of teaching resources and tools, ranging from books to computer software.

Although each subject area is presented in a separate chapter, after reading Part Three, you will be able to see how these subject areas relate to one another. Any of them can be taught across the elementary school curriculum. Each chapter provides examples in sections called "Making Connections," and in other appropriate places, illustrates how each subject area can be integrated across the curriculum. Reference also is made to other chapters in the book for additional illustrations or elaboration.

chapter 10

Curriculum for the Language Arts

AFTER READING THIS CHAPTER, YOU WILL BE ABLE TO DO THE FOLLOWING:

- Define literacy and explain the relationship between literacy and the language arts curriculum.

- Describe the characteristics of an effective language arts curriculum.

- Discuss aspects of integrated language arts and whole language teaching and learning.

- Identify the main curriculum areas of the language arts, and describe curricular outcomes of each.

- Describe the unique aspects of managing and assessing language arts learning.

- Elaborate on ways of making connections between the language arts curriculum and other curriculum areas.

The term *language arts* is used to describe a variety of content areas of the elementary curriculum; these often include reading, writing, and the communication skills of speaking and listening, as well as spelling, grammar, and handwriting. The importance of this curriculum area can be seen in the amount of public and media interest in reading and writing programs and the emphasis given these areas on achievement tests.

Because language is a tool that children and adults use to express themselves, the language arts involve the communication of ideas and information, as well as feelings. Although we often think of the language arts as a specific subject in the elementary curriculum, Lemlech (1994) says that the language arts can be defined as "those activities that occur throughout the school day in which communication happens through reception (listening and reading) and expression (speaking and writing)" (p. 232). The language arts curriculum, then, involves the skills of communication and is incorporated into other subjects throughout the school day.

The process of communication illustrates the interrelatedness of the language arts: as people speak, they must also listen for responses; and as people write, they must also read what they have written or what someone writes in reply. Reading and writing, and speaking and listening are interdependent elements of the language arts curriculum and are essential to learning in general. Finn (1993) suggests that as children learn to communicate, they "learn how to mean" (p. 20). Yonemura (1969) notes that "without an adequate grasp of language, it is impossible to cope with abstract ideas. For this reason, children must be encouraged to develop their language. It enables them to think" (p. 6). Language gives meaning to everything around us.

As Cambourne (1984) suggests, when teachers think of language learning, they often think in terms of learning to talk, but in reality language learning also includes reading and writing. Cambourne (1984) further suggests that for language learning to be successful, seven conditions should be present:

■ Immersion: Language washes over and surrounds children as they hear people using language all around them.

■ Demonstration: Children learn to model what they have heard through the many examples of language they encounter.

■ Expectation: Children develop language because of the expectations of parents, teachers, and others, but they also attach values to the expectations, such as language learning (i.e., grammar) is hard.

■ Responsibility: Children take responsibility for the set of language conventions they develop and master at different ages.

■ Approximation: Children are acknowledged and even rewarded for being approximately right; as their language develops parents and teachers reinforce attempts at language learning and validate efforts that are close to being right.

■ Employment: Children are given many opportunities to use language—to talk, listen, and interact.

■ Feedback: Parents and other adults who teach children give them feedback that is nonthreatening and actually expands language learning.

When teachers approach the teaching of language arts from an integrated perspective, they facilitate learning and discourse because

■ Through reading, students become better speakers, listeners, and writers.

■ Through writing, students become better speakers, listeners, and readers.

■ Through speaking, students become better listeners, readers, and writers.

■ Through listening, students become better speakers, readers, and writers (Finn, 1993).

Teachers should therefore focus on all areas when teaching the language arts in the elementary school and recognize the interrelatedness. As Norton (1993) confirms,

> Language is the most important form of human communication . . . and as such, it is . . . the most exciting part of the elementary curriculum. Its importance is reflected in estimates that the average person listens to the equivalent of a book each day, talks the equivalent of a book each week, and writes the equivalent of a book each year. (p. 2)

This chapter then, provides educators with an overview of the language arts curriculum. It does not provide a comprehensive description of the various approaches or methods advocated for the teaching of reading, writing, speaking, and listening. There are entire textbooks that deal with the methods of teaching reading, writing and other language arts areas. Rather, the chapter presents some general aspects related to teaching the language arts curriculum and includes such topics as: literacy and language learning, effective language arts instruction, integrated language arts and whole language instruction, traditional areas of the language arts curriculum (reading, writing and handwriting, spelling), and managing and assessing language arts learning.

LITERACY AND LANGUAGE LEARNING

Any discussion of the language arts curriculum in the elementary school must also include a discussion of literacy. This concept is changing as our understanding of how children learn and process language information changes. Historically, literacy and language learning have been taught within isolated subjects in the elementary curriculum, such as reading, writing, spelling, and grammar. More recently, literacy and language learning have been seen as a process that integrates all of these areas in a holistic approach.

Only a few years ago, the term *literacy* typically applied only to reading and writing. Such a view of literacy development emphasized the role of the teacher and the language arts curriculum in determining "when and what students should learn to read and write" (Lemlech, 1994, p. 241). This view of language instruction assumes that language learning is sequential and linear and that students lack any understanding of literacy skills until they come to school and receive instruction.

Within this literacy framework, language arts behaviors are often not presented until the child is perceived as "ready." Many kindergarten and primary students engage in literacy readiness activities such as visual discrimination (recognizing symbols and shapes), learning sight words, and/or doing scribble writing to accompany pictures they have drawn. Reutzel and Cooter (1992) note that "research has shown that training children to discriminate between letters and words produces greater transfer effects to the act of reading than does training with geometric forms and pictures" (p. 302). Durkin (1989) recommends teaching sight words to children as a part of reading-readiness instruction because the ability to recognize sight words gives students the feel of real reading.

Jesse, the "Voice of Experience" for this chapter, reflects on the linear view of literacy and language learning and how, as a child, he learned spelling, reading, and writing as isolated, fragmented subjects in the elementary school he attended.

>>>>>> <<<<<< **Voice of Experience** >>>>>> <<<<<<

As Jesse begins to plan his language arts curriculum for the year, he reflects on how things have changed since he was a student in elementary school. Jesse remembers the weekly spelling tests that were put together in a spelling test booklet with a seasonal cover. In September, it was shaped like a leaf; in October, a jack-o'-lantern; in February, a heart. He says, "I remember taking the brown construction paper and cutting a leaf from a pattern, then cutting

notebook paper to fit the leaf to make this booklet. Each Monday, the teacher would give us a list of twenty-five spelling words on the board. We memorized the list during the week and often had a practice test on Thursday, before the final test on Friday. Throughout my elementary school years, spelling was taught this same way—separate from reading and writing."

This has prompted Jesse to think about how he learned to *read*. He says, "I remember being assigned to a reading group of six to eight students where in round-robin style, we would take turns reading from our reader, while the teacher listened, prompted, and gave cues to students who had difficulty in pronouncing the words. Typically, the teacher would introduce new vocabulary words before beginning the lesson, and she might even pose some questions for us to answer when we had finished with the story to check our comprehension. I remember one of my favorite teachers sitting in the reading circle, with the teacher's guide on her lap, following the procedures in a step-by-step method. I loved this teacher because she made me feel comfortable when reading and gently supplied help as needed, but other students were scared to read, even when they were helped by the teacher."

Grammar was something else. All Jesse could remember was worksheets. As Jesse tells a colleague, "Each week the teacher would introduce a new grammar skill—like plural endings, past-tense verbs, noun–pronoun agreement, noun–verb agreement, proper nouns and capitalization, and punctuation. The teacher would illustrate the skill on the board and then give out drill and practice worksheets where we were supposed to demonstrate what we had learned."

As he thought about it, Jesse could not remember much about creative *writing*. He says, "I remember copying a lot of poems and stories from the blackboard. Sometimes the class would make a poetry notebook, but most if not all of the poems were from published sources and chosen by the teacher. Seldom did we get to create our own poems or write our own stories. At best, we would write an alternative ending to a story we had read."

Although he never really had stopped and reflected on it before, Jesse realized how much he taught the language arts in the same way when he first began teaching. Each of the areas, spelling, reading, grammar, and writing, was taught separately and seldom, if ever, did they interrelate. Jesse concludes by saying, "How fragmented such an approach now seems compared to my understanding of literacy today and what students do in my class now."

Where does Literacy Begin?

A more recent view of literacy encompasses more than just reading and writing. In the language learning context, *literacy* is creating and deciphering symbolic texts as we give meaning to our experience ("Literacy," 1994). In the broadest sense, it means being knowledgeable and well informed (Morrison, 1993). Vacca, Vacca, and Gove (1995) suggest four aspects of literacy development in young children:

- Literacy has its beginnings in the parent–child interaction, with parents reading to children so that they come to school with various knowledge and experiences.

- As children (preschool and school age) interact with each other, they continue to acquire literacy skills.

- As children engage in instructional activities, they continue literacy learning.

- Finally, literacy development is fostered through the interrelated activities of speaking, writing, and reading.

How early?

Literacy, which begins early in life and is strengthened in the elementary school, is a continuously evolving process. It is seen as *emergent* because it develops throughout life, rather than just through the years of formal schooling

(Reutzel & Cooter, 1996; Morrison, 1993). Moreover, Strickland (1990) reminds us that "literacy is no longer regarded as simply a cognitive skill but as a complex activity with social, linguistic, and psychological aspects" (p. 19).

Morrison (1993) contends that the skills of reading and writing are part of emergent literacy and are shaped by the contexts as well as the social interactions with adults, peers, and others. Literacy learning is multidimensional and is tied to the child's natural surroundings, which means it is learned at home as well as in the school environment (Strickland, 1990). Children who grow up in homes where language skills are valued are more likely to use language and value it more than those who come from homes where literacy is less important. As Helms and Turner (1986) note, "environmental stimulation is viewed as a critical factor in . . . overall language development" (p. 177). For example, children who are read to and talked to by parents and other adults develop a greater need and appreciation for language and demonstrate literacy skills (Vacca, Vacca, & Gove, 1995).

culturally?

Emergent literacy is also affected by the culture in which children grow up. Language skills are influenced along cultural guidelines and contexts that influence how literate a person becomes. In homes where there are few books and magazines and little conversation and discussion, children often come to view language skills as unimportant. In homes where dialogue and discussion are important, correct grammatical sentences are not only expected but nurtured with corrective feedback, and language ability is encouraged and valued. For McIntyre (1993), "the role of the teacher is to become more informed about literacy development, carefully observe children and to take time to meet with individual learners who need more nudging" (p. 134).

This more comprehensive view of language learning is guided by a series of assumptions that help explain the impact of emergent literacy on the curriculum. The assumptions of emergent literacy (Teale & Sulzby, 1986; Finn, 1993) that influence and guide the language arts curriculum include these:

■ Children demonstrate language behaviors of reading and writing in informal settings such as at home before they experience formal instruction at school.

■ Children learn and use literacy skills in real-life settings to function and accomplish tasks.

■ As children interact socially with adults in reading and writing situations, they learn language behaviors by becoming actively involved in their world and by being presented with adult language models initially and then with models from their peers.

■ As children develop literacy skills, one skill does not precede another—the language arts skills (reading, writing, speaking, and listening) develop concurrently and are interdependent/interrelated, rather than isolated and sequential.

■ Although children progress through general stages of literacy, they move through the stages in various ways and at different times based on their own language-development time clock.

Literacy development is also influenced by drama activities (Wagner, 1988). As children play, they enact their thoughts, become someone else, and speak as that person. Children who engage in dramatic symbolic play have significantly higher literacy development (word and story comprehension and understanding syntactic structures). By engaging in the kinesthetic element of gestures and assuming a posture, students "access not only oral but also written persuasive competence" (Wagner, 1988, p. 50).

As these assumptions suggest, the foundations for language instruction begin long before a student starts going to school. As children hear people speaking and as they listen to conversations or to radio and television, the beginnings of literacy develop. As children learn to speak themselves and as they scribble on tablets or walls, they are starting on their voyage of literacy learning. All of these experiences help children develop language skills and bring them "a growing awareness of . . . [and] ability to create meaning from . . . language" (Graves, Watts, & Graves, 1994, p. 54). The following sections of this chapter focus specifically on helping teachers become more effective in teaching the language arts. Building on the assumptions of emergent literacy, the chapter then discusses various aspects of integrated language arts and whole language teaching.

EFFECTIVE LANGUAGE ARTS TEACHING

The language arts curriculum is designed to help students develop literacy skills and communicate effectively. As teachers plan and organize their curriculum for language arts instruction, they need to be cognizant of the following characteristics of effective language arts instruction (Lemlech, 1994; Finn, 1993; Norton, 1996; Daly, 1991):

■ Teachers recognize the importance of combining oral language instruction and listening skills within the context of being an audience and provide numerous opportunities for students to both speak and listen.

■ Teachers continuously monitor student progress by engaging in "kidwatching" so they can assess the degree to which students demonstrate auditory awareness, oral-language development, reading proficiency, and writing skills and then develop new and exciting learning activities based on this assessment.

▪ Teachers recognize that language learning must take place in a risk-free environment and create a nonthreatening classroom.

▪ Teachers recognize and include the mechanical aspects of writing and speaking by addressing such areas as manuscript and cursive writing, grammar and sentence structure, and spelling, which become important as students communicate with various audiences for a variety of purposes.

▪ Teachers recognize the influence and use of media and technology to motivate students and reinforce language learning by discussing events from the news, programs on television, and/or videos made of stories from books. In the primary grades, teachers use read-aloud books with cassette tapes that match the book; in the upper grades, teachers use computer programs to engage students in language experiences.

▪ Teachers constantly use literature as a part of their language arts instruction and have library areas within their classrooms with many books. They also encourage students to bring books to school, have students give written and oral book reports, have them respond to literature through discussion and/or journals, and regularly read and tell stories to their classes. By using children's books in the language arts curriculum, language learning becomes authentic and children tend to remember it. There are many types of children's books; Figure 10-1 provides a short list.

Language learning is a complex process that starts at birth and continues through adult years, as we acquire many of the skills needed to communicate effectively. Literacy becomes the "set of reading, writing, and other related skills necessary to function in an increasingly sophisticated and technological global environment" ("Literacy," 1994, p. 4). The elementary language arts curriculum is charged with facilitating and reinforcing that process of literacy and language learning.

INTEGRATED LANGUAGE ARTS AND WHOLE-LANGUAGE TEACHING

By applying knowledge of an emergent literacy, elementary teachers can set up an integrated language arts classroom or a whole-language classroom. An *integrated language arts curriculum* is one that, according to Finn (1993), can be described as

▪ viewing language learning as intentional, with the role of the teacher being to facilitate language development

▪ encouraging proximal development where students can do things with language with help from a teacher that they could not do on their own

▪ involving the teacher in collaboration with the student in learning

▪ helping the student internalize language so that external support is not needed

▪ continuously working to facilitate language learning in all areas of the language arts

Such a language arts curriculum uses graphic organizers as a way of helping students see patterns and connections with concepts and examples. Figure 10-2 provides an example of a graphic organizer teachers can use to help students identify information they already know about different types of rocks. In addition, it shows the students how to structure the information and see the relationships between the concepts of sedimentary, igneous, and metamorphic rocks included in the cyclical graphic organizer.

The adoption of this approach is often difficult for teachers who have taught the language arts curriculum areas separately. Reutzel and Cooter (1996) advocate a transition to a balanced approach to literacy instruction. For them, traditional approaches "rely heavily on teacher directed instruction usually in conjunction with basal reader textbooks" (p. 4) and employ a skills-

FIGURE 10-1   Children's Books

I. There are many ways to use literature in a classroom—for example, to begin or end a lesson/unit. Here are some ideas.

A.   To emphasize and practice a repetitive pattern of phrases or sentences
1. *Brown Bear, Brown Bear* (Martin)
2. *The Important Book* (Brown)
3. *If All the Seas Were One Sea* (Domanska)
4. *Drummer Hoff* (Emberley)
5. *Everybody Needs a Rock* (Baylor)

B.   To practice sequencing
1. *Good Night Owl* (Hutchins)
2. *A Letter to Amy* (Keats)
3. *The Very Hungry Caterpillar* (Carle)
4. *If You Give a Mouse a Cookie* (Numeroff)

C.   To illustrate point of view
1. *Two Bad Ants* (Van Allsburg)
2. *Little Red Riding Hood As Told by A. Wolf* (Scieszka)
3. *The True Story of the Three Little Pigs* (Scieszka)

D.   To practice compare and contrast
1. *The Desert is Theirs* (Baylor)
2. *When I was Young in the Mountains* (Rylant)
3. *Town Mouse, Country Mouse* (Brett)

E.   To read poetry
1. *The New Kid on the Block* (Prebitsky)
2. *The Giving Tree* (Silverstein)
3. *Where the Sidewalk Ends* (Silverstein)

F.   To get a feel for history
1. *Samuel Eatons' Day: A Day in the Life of a Pilgrim Boy* (Waters)
2. *An Ellis Island Christmas* (Leighton)
3. *Aunt Harriet's Underground Railroad* (Ringgold)

first emphasis, whereas whole language is a philosophical stance that integrates the four language modes in all areas of the curriculum. Heilman, Blair, and Rupley (1994) further elaborate on this approach:

> Whole language is not a method or program of . . . instruction, it is an orientation toward development of literacy. Whole-language advocates believe that language acquisition (including reading and writing) is an essential part of an individual functioning within the environment. (pp. 64–65)

As teachers plan for language learning in their classrooms, they must be aware of factors such as physical, perceptual, and language characteristics that influence emergent literacy. For example, children who come to school malnourished and experience difficulty in seeing and hearing are limited in their language development by those physical characteristics. Teachers must therefore be aware of physical limitations that the student may bring to the language-learning process and be willing to make appropriate accommodations.

FIGURE 10-1, *continued*

II. Literature used to promote different letter sounds
  A.   "Short A" sound
      1. Book: *Annie and the Wild Animals* (Brett)
      2. Poetry: *Polly Anna Ate a Banana* (Dowell)
  B.   "D" sound
      1. Books
          a. *Danny and the Dinosaur* (Hoff)
          b. *My "D" Sound Box* (Moncure)
      2. Poetry: *The Dirtiest Man in the World* (Silverstein)
  C.   "P" sound
      1. Books: The *Paddington Bear* books (Bond)
      2. Poetry: *Peter Piper Picked a Peck of Pickled Peppers* (Jones)
  D.   "S" sound
      1. Books
          a. *Sammy the Seal* (Hoff)
          b. *My "S" Sound Box* (Moncure)
      2. Poetry: *Sarah Cynthia Sylvia Stout* (Silverstein)

In addition, children with physical limitations may also have difficulty distinguishing or discerning various symbols or words. They may be unable to hear specific sounds in the English language. These visual and auditory perception abilities may also hinder language development. Children who enter school may also have discrepancies in their print awareness (their ability to understand that graphic symbols of printed words have corresponding meanings in oral communication). Students may also lack an understanding of syntax or the effect of word order on meaning and grammar, or the knowledge of the structure of sentences.

Children also have discrepancies in their kinds of language experiences. Some have been read to since infancy, while others have had very little read to them. Literacy programs are more effective when they can provide children with a wide variety of language experiences. Children may also have to adjust to the language used in the classroom because the language spoken at school may not be the same as that spoken at home. As Graves, Watts, and Graves (1994) describe the school context, they note that

> In order to understand [school language], students must distinguish between *front* and *back;* know the meaning of the word *next,* distinguish among *before, during,* and *after,* and distinguish the top of the page from some other part of the page. (p. 59)

Children who come to school with an interest in language learning are at an advantage over those students for whom language development has not been cultivated at home. "Interest and motivation are strongly related to success in anything we do" (Graves, Watts, & Graves, 1994, p. 59), and teachers must create an environment for elementary children that will heighten their interest and stimulate their curiosity. The approach of incorporating an awareness of developing language with an inclusive focus on reading, writing, speaking, and listening skills is known as a *holistic* approach, which is used in many language arts classrooms.

FIGURE 10-2 Rocks and the Rock Cycle

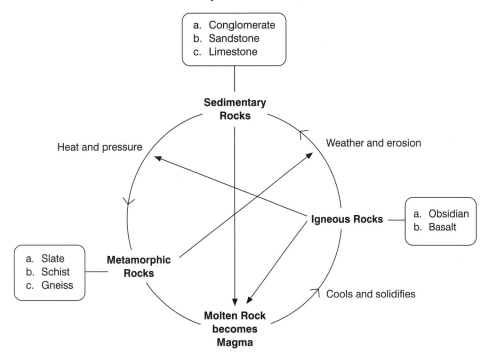

Success in whole-language teaching and learning (Cambourne, 1988; Goodman, 1986; Holdaway, 1979) involves creating a language arts classroom environment that conveys the idea "that language development, reading, writing, speaking, and listening are integrated and related processes" (Morrison, 1993, p. 215). Such a classroom environment fosters the development of literacy skills through a variety of experiences that are built upon the following understandings about language learning:

1. Literacy acquisition is a natural process.

2. The conditions for becoming oral language users are the same as for becoming readers and writers.

3. Young children enter school with much knowledge about literacy.

4. Becoming a reader and becoming a writer are closely related.

5. Optimal literacy environments promote risk taking and trust.

6. Becoming literate is a social act and a search for meaning.

7. Literacy development is continuous.

8. Genuine literacy acts are authentic and meaningful. (Routman, 1991, p. 9)

In addition to these understandings, the whole-language classroom is also marked by the teacher's awareness of the developmental level of each learner, the readiness of each child to learn, and the student's background, experiences, and interests. With this awareness of developmental and interest levels as the foundation, the teacher then establishes the expectation that language learning occurs at different levels for different students. The teacher begins by focusing on the strengths of each student and what the student likes to foster language achievement. In a whole-language classroom, the teacher emphasizes what the child can do and then works by demonstrating and encouraging risk taking to develop new skills.

The whole-language classroom has a process orientation to literacy development rather than a product focus. Teachers examine and reinforce what students do in the process of learning reading, writing, speaking, and listening. In examining the process part, the teacher engages in ongoing evaluation of the students' language learning. Such a classroom environment also enhances independent actions, as students begin to take more responsibility for their learning to read, write, speak, and listen.

Also within the whole-language classroom, the teacher begins to look at the curriculum in a very different way and sees possibilities for language learning across the curriculum. Teachers also begin to allow students choices in their selection of reading materials, content themes, and writing topics. In such an environment, the instructional role of the teacher also changes from that of giver of information to that of demonstrator, facilitator, and co-learner. The teacher models reading, writing, speaking, and listening skills and spends less time controlling the activities.

Finally, whole-language classrooms establish a climate where students share in what they have studied or read about. There is social interaction as students talk about and discuss their experiences and ideas. Teachers may establish an author's corner where students present to their classmates samples of their own composition or reviews of materials they have read. Group sharing is critical in building literacy skills and reinforces the importance of the social dimension of language learning.

Jesse, the "Voice of Experience" for this chapter, describes his transition from a traditional language arts teacher in his first years of teaching to a more holistic, integrated language arts teacher today. This transformation has not occurred overnight. It has taken a number of years for Jesse to determine what he wants his

students to accomplish in the language arts curriculum.

>>>>>> <<<<<< Voice of Experience >>>>>> <<<<<<

As Jesse talks with a visiting teacher, he says, "Now, instead of a lot of large group activities with drill and practice sheets, I do a lot of small group and cooperative learning activities. I have learned that as my students function in group settings they practice listening skills as they interact with each other, and they also practice speaking skills as they discuss the problem or issue before the group. The group members prepare for their writing by engaging in prewriting activities which provide the motivation to write, get them to generate vocabulary, and get them to share their ideas. The group members then practice their writing skills as they draft, either individually or collectively, a response to the question or problem and then edit their work. The groups also practice reading skills as they read the problem and related information concerning the issue and then as they read, again either individually or collectively, their written response. The conversations that occur in the group settings are very helpful in language development, and as the groups develop their responses they may extend the activity into a panel discussion or debate, which further strengthens language learning."

When asked by the visiting teacher how he handled reading, Jesse responds, "Initially, I liked to use the basal reader and had several reading groups that participated in round-robin reading. More recently, however, I have been experimenting with a variety of strategies and workshops that allow the readers to select material that is of interest to them and check out school or class library books or bring materials from home to read. Some students enjoy reading books that have been bound or 'published' by members of previous classes or their classmates.

"As they complete their reading, I allow them to choose from several approaches to demonstrate their reading skill and their understanding of the material. They may choose to give the report of the book orally, becoming a famous critic and doing a book review for the local TV station. They can also do a written critique of the book and write a column for the local paper. Some like to become the author of the book and discuss the story from the author's point of view, sitting in the author's chair in the classroom. Still others may write a letter to a friend or to me describing the book and story. I try to provide a variety of opportunities for students to respond to what they have read and may use literature circles where students talk about their reading or use reading journals where they write about what they have read. Regularly, I have brief conferences with individual students to discuss their progress. At times throughout the year, the class will pick a theme or topic and all of the different reading materials have to fit that theme or topic. In that way, students then explain why they selected the material and how it fits them when they review the reading material.

"As I listen to their reports and as I conference with them, I am able to identify any language-development problems. This provides an opportunity for me to teach or correct any areas where the students are having difficulty. Recently several members of the class were mispronouncing words because they were putting the emphasis on the wrong syllable. This provided me with an opportunity to provide instruction to them on dictionary skills and syllable intonation or inflection. This skill was not needed by all members of the class, so I turned it into a small group session rather than involving the whole class.

"In addition to the reading materials of interest, I try to reinforce reading skills in the other curriculum areas such as social studies and science, and use every opportunity to build vocabulary and concept understanding through the reading of content materials."

The visiting teacher was amazed that Jesse could integrate so many different strategies into the teaching of reading and she also wanted to know about the teaching of writing. Jesse responded by saying, "I work with the children to help them identify a topic of interest to them and then describe or collect information about that topic. I also encourage them to think about their audience—who else might enjoy their topic and what they would need to know. I suggest that as they plan for writing, they jot down pieces of information that will help them as they construct their writing, and this might include list-making and clustering ideas. Once they have completed their prewriting strategies, I encourage them to develop a rough draft. After this document has been created, the students are given numerous opportunities to read, edit, revise, and proofread what they have written before they submit a final copy. Finally, I ask the students to share what they have written. This takes a variety of forms. We have developed a class newspaper, and some pieces are appropriate for that. We are in the process of developing a monthly class magazine, and some material is suitable for that. Other written materials are displayed on bulletin boards for all to see and read, while other pieces are bound and become a 'published book' for the classroom. Other times, the students will do an Author's Corner and will read and interpret their writing for the rest of the class."

One other area that often gives teachers concern is spelling, and Jesse indicates that he has replaced words from the spelling book with words from reading and other curriculum areas. These words become a part of the students' word bank (students write these words on index cards and store them in a shoebox in alphabetical order). "Sometimes," he says, "I give a spelling demons quiz of difficult spelling words from the spelling textbook, but mostly we develop the spelling list together from words previously encountered in class in some way."

Jesse admits that he still hasn't found a way to totally replace the weekly spelling test, but he is working on that and has placed less emphasis on it this year.

When the visiting teacher asks Jesse if he is an integrated, holistic, whole-language teacher, Jesse responds by saying, "At this point, I would have to say that I am more like Regie Routman (1988) in that I am fairly comfortable in integrating listening, speaking, reading, and writing, but I am still struggling hard to integrate more areas of the curriculum with the language arts, which is difficult to attain. I also frequently teach from part to whole and emphasize data and facts over concepts and processes. Being a holistic, integrated, whole-language teacher will continue to evolve and is something that I will have to work on for quite some time. But one thing I can say is that the students and their own language development are foremost in my mind, not just the skills."

Not every elementary school may embrace and/or subscribe to the concept of integrated language arts or whole-language instruction. Some schools still teach the language arts areas separately. It is important that in an overview of the language arts curriculum teachers have a sense of what is taught in such areas as reading, writing, handwriting, and spelling. Therefore, the next section examines each of these areas briefly and describes the kind of curricular expectations in each.

THE LANGUAGE ARTS CONTENT AREAS

Reading

Perhaps no other area in the school curriculum has received as much attention as the reading curriculum. Not since the great debate prompted by Chall's emphasis on a phonetic approach to the teaching of reading has so much controversy surrounded a curricular component. The debate continues with renewed opposition from the advocates of the whole-language classroom who view literacy development as a process that integrates the areas of listening, speaking, reading, and writing and uses a variety of approaches to help students become literate. So the discussion continues. Should teachers use a phonetic, skills-based or code-breaking approach, or should a more integrated approach be utilized in the teaching of reading? There is no clear answer and, according to Lemlech (1994), "research has failed to demonstrate which approach to the teaching of reading is superior or more efficient" (p. 251). She continues by saying that teachers seldom use one pure form of reading instruction. However, depending on the school and community, one approach may be emphasized over the other. Recent efforts have centered on a more comprehensive, integrated approach.

Approaches to reading instruction over the years have included basal readers, a linguistic emphasis, and creating language experiences. Strategies that are frequently employed include silent reading, oral reading, skills and drills, and recreational reading. Each approach utilizes a different focus to involve students in the reading process. Carbo (1995) suggests a continuum of reading strategies that include sustained silent reading, paired reading, choral reading, neurological impress, repeated reading, recorded books, and shared reading. The basal reader approach provides for ability levels and the sequential acquisition and development of vocabulary and reading skills. Silent sustained reading (SSR) is normally designed to allow students an opportunity to focus on comprehension to practice reading skills individually while emphasizing the development of new vocabulary words as students read for pleasure. Oral reading emphasizes the ability of the student to model intonation, expression, and other speaking skills and to verify that the student understands the information.

Skill-and-drill approaches normally emphasize word attack skills and vocabulary building.

Recreational reading utilizes the students' interest in a subject to link language learning with that interest. In addition to these common approaches, reading is also taught using the "Great Books," emphasizing the other subjects of the curriculum in teaching reading skills, and focusing on reading about things that children experience as part of growing up. They may read about pets if they have a pet at home and then write about that pet.

The objectives of the reading program over the years have included the following:

■ Developing the fundamental reading skills of recognizing words, securing word meanings, comprehending and interpreting what has been read, reading silently, reading orally, and using books efficiently.

■ Providing opportunities for students to select from a rich and varied choice of reading materials and promoting the enjoyment of reading.

■ Developing a wide and varied vocabulary not only for reading but for other forms of expression as well.

■ Using reading in resourceful ways to secure information to meet particular needs and interests.

Some reading programs focus on three distinct components of the reading process and identify skills to be accomplished during pre-reading, active reading, and postreading. For *prereading*, students engage in such activities as making predictions about the reading selection, applying prior knowledge to the selection, discussing a particular reading strategy, or engaging in brainstorming activities about the author, characters, setting, or events. In *active reading*, students read and then discuss or answer questions, either individually or in pairs or trios, about what they have read. They may also outline or diagram the content of the selection, read to one another, or read silently and then prepare for a postreading activity. In *postreading activities*, students might enter their response to their selection in a log,

extend the story beyond its boundaries, produce a written analysis of the text, conduct an oral discussion or report of the text, or construct a creative dramatic piece to represent the text.

Writing

The writing process involves such activities as correspondence (letter writing), note taking, journal keeping, making responses to assignments (record keeping), as well as creative writing and composition. Teale and Sulzby (1986) say one of the biggest challenges now is how to implement writing into the language arts in a way that makes it an integral, vibrant, lively part. Part of the philosophy of the writing-as-a-process movement involves moving away from an emphasis on mechanics over content; time is not spent on grammar (Lucas, 1993). The most common process advocated for the teaching of writing (Graves, 1983) involves prewriting, drafting, revising, editing, sharing, and publishing. For a student or group members who "don't know what to write about," Maimon (1988) offers the following ideas: adventures, wishes, announcements I want to make, favorite places, as well as predicting future events in stories. By using books as a stimulus for writing, teachers link the reading and writing process. For example, after reading *Peanut Butter and Jelly* (Nelson, 1989), second-grade students could write out the directions for first graders on how to make a peanut-butter-and-jelly sandwich.

In *prewriting*, topics are considered and developed, and students engage in brainstorming activities, concept mapping or webbings, and/or in research through visits to the library or computer laboratory. In *drafting*, the student composes his or her thoughts on paper by constructing a narrative, descriptive, or persuasive composition. In *revising*, the writer revises, rethinks, rearranges, or refines the composition working either individually or in a team or pair. In *editing*, the writer examines the details of composition by checking spelling, syntax, grammar, or accuracy of information and may ask a partner, the teacher, or other member of the class to check the composition. Finally, in *sharing*, the writer presents what he or she has written through a variety of activities, either to the teacher in a formal paper, to peers in groups, to the class as a whole, or to some publication.

The elementary classroom should be a place where teachers model good writing skills and encourage students to write as much as possible. Writing is an important ingredient in the learning process as children learn what they write. The ability to transcribe information into a written document enhances the learning process.

Handwriting

The actual handwriting process or the act of making letters and words on a page is an important component of elementary language arts instruction. It is considered essential for the developing writer, for handwriting provides a tool for expression. Because of the development of eye, arm, and hand coordination, initially this process may involve scribble writing in preschool children. Young children have difficulty controlling the pencil and have to learn directionality and the left-to-right movement important in writing. They also have difficulty with sizes and shapes. By kindergarten, students are beginning to learn the manuscript writing they will use in the primary grades; they should be encouraged to develop legible and fluent writing and to use appropriate form. At the end of the second grade or beginning of third grade, most students have developed sufficient neuromuscular coordination or psychomotor skills so that they can begin to learn cursive writing.

Spelling

Spelling is another curriculum area of the language arts. Preschool children begin writing by using their own version of invented spelling. What begins as a game of converting speech and letters back and forth becomes the foundation for literacy (Moffett & Wagner, 1993). It helps students express themselves, particularly in written form.

Some schools still have spelling textbooks that have a list of spelling words for each week. These words are designed not only to help students understand the relationship between sounds and letters, vowels and consonants, and pronunciation, but also to provide opportunities for vocabulary development through word meanings and dictionary skills.

Other schools derive spelling words from the interests and needs of the students. Some words may come from reading selections, and others may come from other subject areas. Many words come from the children's own writing, for these words are the ones they need to spell. The teacher holds the students responsible for knowing not only how to spell the words but also for knowing their meanings.

According to McClaran (1996), teachers need three things to teach spelling: "(1) a list of words, (2) a few rules, and (3) a good strategy" (p. 7). When teaching spelling, McClaran (1996) identifies four principles that should be a part of spelling instruction:

- It is important for children to learn to spell correctly because misspelling words slows the reading process and hinders communication.

- Only a few rules of spelling (approximately twelve) have enough consistency to be valuable in learning how to spell; if the three hundred or so spelling rules in English were always followed, students would correctly spell words only 50 percent of the time.

- Spelling word lists are important to help children focus their attention on correct spelling, and these word lists can come from reading words, other subject areas, or words that students commonly misspell in their daily writing.

- The few rules and lists of words can be taught using simple daily strategies.

The language arts curriculum in the elementary school is one of the most important components of instruction. Not only are the skills learned in this area applied to other subjects, but also language learning helps students learn to think and then express those thoughts to others. As Reutzel and Cooter (1996) suggest, children need to be immersed in daily opportunities for literacy development. Through the development of language arts skills students can find success in other areas of the curriculum. Figure 10-3 lists children's literature and other resources for teachers to consult. The lists include software programs and associations that can be of assistance in various areas of the language arts curriculum.

MANAGING AND ASSESSING LANGUAGE ARTS LEARNING

Managing and assessing learning in the language arts classroom is not significantly different from other subject areas. Because this content focuses on communication skills, the teacher should provide numerous opportunities to read, share, discuss, and write. Assessment procedures should consider the expressive nature of this content area.

Managing the Language Arts Classroom

The teacher should establish at the beginning of the year the rules and procedures that will govern conduct not only in the classroom in general, but during language arts time in particular. For example, if the teacher provides time at the beginning of the day for a class meeting (in some curricular programs, it is called the "bulletin board" meeting), then rules and procedures governing who speaks, when they speak, and what they speak about should be established. If the purpose of such activity is to develop good speaking and listening skills, then the teacher will want to address the expected student behaviors to accomplish this objective. Establishing rules and procedures is also important for general class meetings, where current events or show-and-share activities are conducted, and for giving and listening to oral book reports or "authors" as they read from their own works or published books.

The teacher may also want to pay particular attention to the classroom's physical arrangement. The space within the classroom should provide an area for the teacher's materials and work area (which is normally off-limits to students), personal work areas for each student, and group work areas. The physical arrangement of the classroom to facilitate management of instruction should be seen as flexible and subject to change, depending on the needs of the teacher and students and the type of learning activity conducted. For example, if students are doing a cooperative learning activity where each group will be producing a printed product (newspaper, book, magazine, etc.), the teacher may want to arrange student desks in clusters according to cooperative learning groups. On the other hand, if the teacher is conducting large group instruction, the students might gather informally by sitting on a rug, while the teacher gives them information or tells them a story. If the teacher is focusing on individual learners, the desks may need to be separated and arranged in a different format.

Beginning teachers should feel free to experiment with different room arrangement patterns that facilitate language arts learning, including reading areas, an author's corner, and library displays. Most importantly, the room should be rich with print materials. There should be many examples of student-made books, newspapers, magazines, scraps of construction paper, software, and shelves of children's literature along with equipment (tape records, video cameras) to capture children reading, role playing, and writing (computers). Figure 10-4 provides an example of an elementary classroom with a language arts area with a reading rug, publisher's corner, and an author's corner.

FIGURE 10-3 Teaching Resources and Tools for the Language Arts Curriculum

Type/Title	Description	Grade Level(s)	Publisher/ Supplier
I. Children's Literature			
Commodore Perry in the Land of Shogun (1985) Roda Blumberg	This ALA Notable Book (1985), and Newberry Honor Book (1996), is a story of Matthew Perry's expedition to Japan.	3+	Greenwillow, William Morrow & Co. 1350 Avenue of Americas New York, NY 10019 (212)779-0965
Farm Alphabet Book (1981) J. Miller	This colorful book using short sentences describes life on a farm, and the reader learns the letters of the alphabet using animals that live on a farm.	K–1	Scholastic 730 Broadway New York, NY 10003-3999 (212)505-3000
The Midnight Horse (1990) J. Miller	This story is about an orphaned boy who goes to live with his uncle who turns out to be a villain. This ALA Notable Book (1990) includes a magician, the ghost of The Great Chaffalo.	3+	Greenwillow, William Morrow & Co. 1350 Avenue of Americas New York, NY 10019 (212)779-0965
Owen (1993) Kevin Henkes	Fuzzy is Owen's favorite yellow blanket and his parents try to figure out how to get the blanket from Owen when he goes to school. This Caldecott Honor Book (1994) is a beautifully told story.	PK–K	Greenwillow, William Morrow & Co. 1350 Avenue of Americas New York, NY 10019 (212)779-0965
Ramona and Her Father (1977) Beverly Cleary	This author has created books that readers have enjoyed for several generations. The topics vary with a special series focusing on Ramona. Ramona responds to her Daddy losing his job and the effect on the family.	2–5	Greenwillow, William Morrow & Co. 1350 Avenue of Americas New York, NY 10019 (212)779-0965

Type/Title	Description	Grade Level(s)	Publisher/Supplier
I. Children's Literature (continued)			
White Snow, Bright Snow (1947) Alvin Tresselt	This 1948 Caldecott Medal Book and ALA 1947 Notable Book captures the mystery of a snowfall.	PK–1	Lothrop, Lee & Shepard William Morrow & Co, Inc. 39 Plymouth St. P.O. Box 1219 Fairfield, NJ 07007 (800)237-0657
II. Teacher Resources			
American Storytelling Resource Center, Inc.	This group provides information and resources for educators if you will send a stamped, self-addressed envelope with a request.	K–6+	American Storytelling Resource Center, Inc. 1471 Chanticleer Ave. Santa Cruz, CA 95062
Arco-Iris	A collection of books translated into Spanish, including several Caldecott Medal winners.	K–3	Celebration Press 1900 E. Lake Ave. Glenview, IL 60025
Author's Toolkit Scottish Council for Educational Technology (Macintosh Family)	A computer program that helps students conceptualize and outline their ideas for a story and then provides illustrations using graphics from outside sources.	4–8	Sunburst Communications 101 Castleton St. P.O. Box 100 Pleasantville, NY 10570
A Zillion Kajillion Rhymes EccentricSoftware (Macintosh Family)	A computer program that helps students write poetry using a rhyming dictionary while building vocabulary.	3–8	Sunburst Communications 101 Castleton St. P.O. Box 100 Pleasantville, NY 10570
Easy Book (Macintosh Family)	A computer program that allows young authors to illustrate their stories by matching their words with stamps or a built-in paint program.	K–8	Sunburst Communications 101 Castleton St. P.O. Box 100 Pleasantville, NY 10570
Invitations (Reference Book) R. Routman	A description of the transformation of an elementary classroom from a traditional format to a whole-language classroom.	Elem.	Heinemann Publishers 361 Hanover Street Portsmouth, NH 03801 (603)431-7894

FIGURE 10-3, continued

II. Teacher Resources (continued)

Type/Title	Description	Grade Level(s)	Publisher/Supplier
Literacy Packages	Prepackaged literacy materials that emphasize modeled, shared, collaborative, and guided or independent reading and writing.	K–1 (emergent readers/writers) 3–4 (newly fluent readers and writers)	Celebration Press 1900 E. Lake Ave. Glenview, IL 60025
Ready to Read Packages	An alternative to the basals designed for different grade levels. Each package includes children's resources of books, tapes, cards, and teacher resources.	1–6	Richard C. Owen Publishers, Inc. P.O. Box 585 Katonah, NY 10536 (800)336-5588
Teaching with Newbery Books: Strategies for Using Newberrys Across the Curriculum (1994) Christine Broadman Moen	Provides strategies for using and responding to award-winning books/literature such as *Doctor DeSoto: Summer of the Swans, Sounder, Sarah,* and many others.	4–8	Scholastic Professional Books 2937 East McCarty St. Jefferson City, MO 65707 (800)724-6527
Teaching with Caldecott Books: Activities Across the Curriculum (1991) Christine Broadman Moen	Includes activities and ideas for using a variety of Caldecott books across the curriculum. Such Caldecotts are featured: *Strega Nona, Frog and Toad Are Friends, Where the Wild Things Are,* and others.	K–3	Scholastic Professional Books 2937 East McCarty St. Jefferson City, MO 65707 (800)724-6527
The Literacy Dictionary: The Vocabulary of Reading and Writing (1995) Theodore Harris and Richard Hodges (Eds.)	A collection of terms and essays that apply specifically to the teaching of reading and writing.	All	International Reading Association 800 Barksdale Rd. P.O. Box 8139 Newark DE 19714-8139 (800)336-7323

236

Type/Title	Description	Grade Level(s)	Publisher/Supplier
III. Journals			
Journal of Adolescent and Adult Literacy	A journal of the International Reading Association that provides teachers with contemporary articles related to reading for students in middle school or high school.	Middle school–adult	International Reading Association 800 Barksdale Rd. P.O. Box 8139 Newark, DE 19714-8139 (800)336-7323
The Reading Teacher	A journal of the International Reading Association that provides teachers with current articles related to the teaching of reading, including descriptions of new children's books.	Elem.	International Reading Association 800 Barksdale Rd. P.O. Box 8139 Newark, DE 19714-8139 (800)336-7323
IV. Language-Arts Associations			
National Council of Teachers of English 1111 Kenyon Road Urbana, IL 61801 (217)328-3870 National Center for the Study of Writing and Literature School of Education Univ. of Cal.—Berkeley Berkeley, CA 94720 (510)643-7022	Writing to Learn, Council for Basic Education 725 15th St. N.W. Washington, DC 20005 (202)347-4171 National Writing Project 5627 Tolman Hall Univ. of Cal.—Berkeley Berkeley, CA 94720 (510)642-0963 International Reading Association 800 Barksdale Road Newark, DE 19711 (302)731-1600	Illinois Reading Project National Louis University 2840 Sheridan Road Evanston, IL 60201 (708)691-9390, ext. 2136 Whole Language Umbrella Unit 6-846 Marion St. Winnipeg, Manitoba Canada R1J0K4 (204)237-5214	

FIGURE 10-4 Classroom Arrangement: A Language Arts Focus

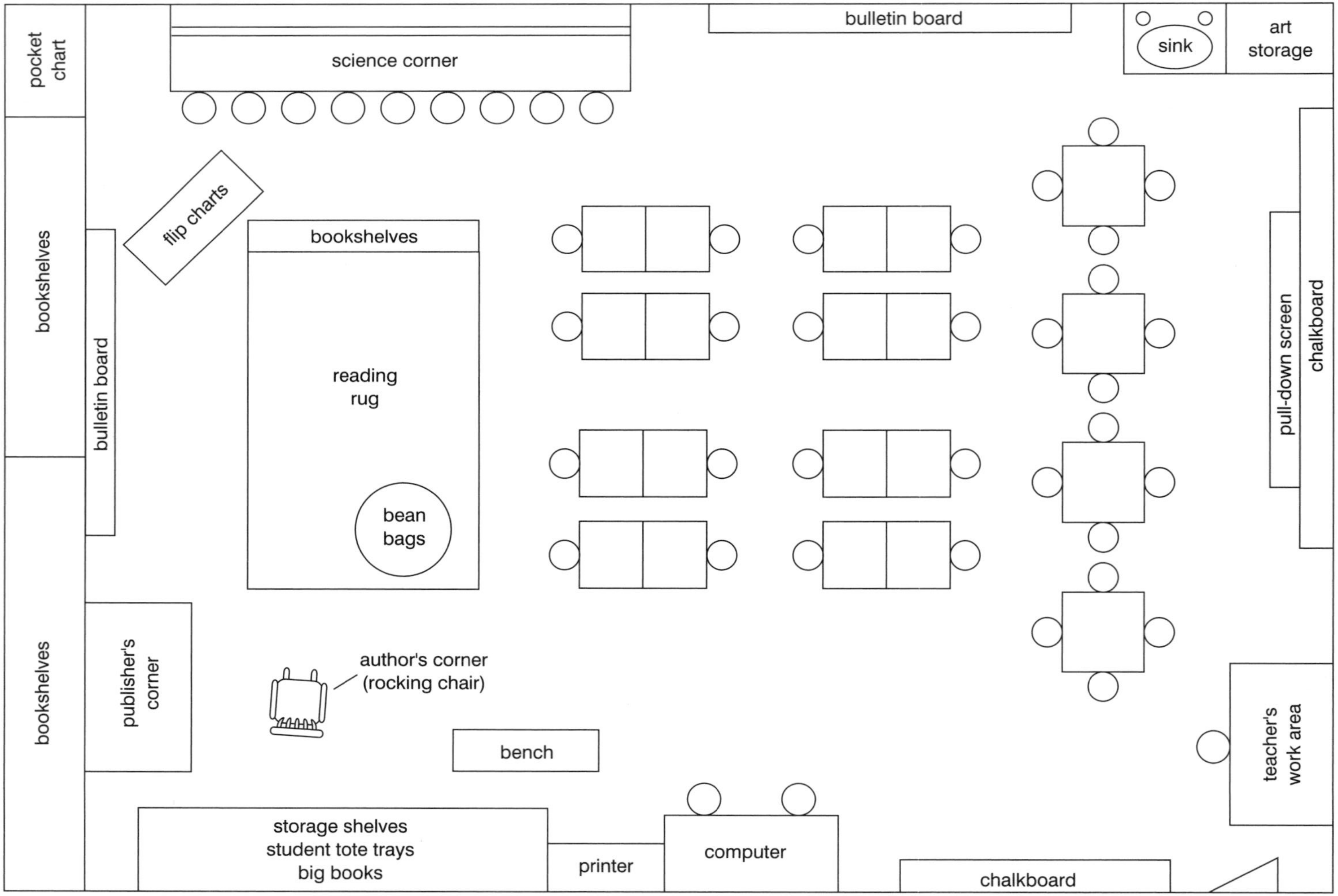

In addition to the physical arrangement of the classroom space, the teacher will want to address the issues of scheduling, tempo and pacing, keeping students engaged in learning, and creating a positive climate for learning (Epanchin, Townsend, & Stoddard, 1994). Included within these areas are routines for distributing paperwork, time lines for assignments, grading or checking procedures, and procedures for notebooks or personal files (portfolios).

An important part of classroom management involves tempo and pacing. The goal is to keep students engaged in language arts learning from "bell to bell." Students engaged in learning are less likely to be off-task or disruptive. Furthermore, children are more likely to be engaged in learning when they are given some choices about things that interest them. Using a constructivist approach gives students ownership of their learning and helps to reduce off-task behavior. Teachers need to make sure that the lesson is neither too easy nor too difficult, in order to keep students engaged.

Finally, it is especially important to establish a positive learning climate where students are willing to take risks, share information, and participate in group activities. Teachers must establish management procedures that provide a sense of respect and worth for each member of the class. It is therefore never appropriate to use sarcasm or put-downs to control student behavior in the classroom, especially in a classroom that works to establish the students' willingness to volunteer and share information through speaking and listening activities.

Assessment of Language Learning

Probably no other content area in the curriculum has received as much attention as assessing learning in the language arts, especially in the areas of reading and writing. Assessment in these two areas is done regularly with the use of standardized tests or criterion-referenced tests to establish reading ability or writing proficiency with regard to peers or some standard of performance. A number of commercially available tests, as well as state-mandated tests, are designed to assess the student's ability in the language arts, but on a day-to-day and week-to-week basis, teachers must be concerned with assessing student performance in their classrooms.

Assessment in a Traditional Language Arts Classroom. Guthrie, Van Meter, and Mitchell (1994) believe that performance assessment in reading and other language arts is (1) instructional as it mimics the teaching environment, (2) realistic as it reflects the regular events of reading, writing, and problem solving, and (3) a public record of specific skills and tasks students have mastered. Performance assessment in a traditional model includes such activities as spelling tests, reading comprehension tests, vocabulary tests, and writing assignments with concern for addressing writing skills (e.g., punctuation, grammar, and capitalization). In a traditional classroom, teachers use a number of daily grades reflecting worksheets to develop understanding of vocabulary and spelling tests to determine mastery of words. In addition, they use reading or language arts workbooks that accompany the basal reader adoption. These workbooks complement the basal reader and are designed to reinforce comprehension skills, as well as to help students with the grammar and syntax of language. Teachers then use a number of workbook pages to compile a grade and maybe even a unit test in the workbook as a major language arts grade.

Assessment in an Integrated Language Arts Classroom. In an integrated language arts classroom, the assessment process is quite different. Teachers often use portfolios as a way of monitoring students' progress as readers and writers. The portfolio provides a way to do several things:

■ Acknowledge individual use of language.

■ Verify that teachers and students have met instructional goals and objectives.

■ Provide an opportunity for students to write and respond to what they have read.

■ Provide for several types of writing to be sampled.

Students conference with their teacher to determine the content of their portfolios. Sample items may include biographies and self-portraits, journals (personal, dialogue, literature response, and issue), "best" pieces of work, original stories, story completions, reading logs, attitude and interest inventories, checklists completed by the teacher during reading conferences, and semantic maps related to reading and writing assignments (Farr & Tone, 1994). As students engage in reading, they write about what they have read. Their writing is edited, revised, resubmitted, and maybe even published. Teachers regularly observe the reading and writing behavior of students and assessment is based on the progress over time.

Often teachers maintain that if work is not graded, students will not do their best. McNergney and Haberman (1990) report that if school writing is contextualized, students do their best work, and researchers in California and Israel found this to be the case; as long as students had an audience, they wrote more effectively. Assessment is more informal when students have a choice about who they write to, so teachers need to consider this aspect when deciding what to teach and what product they will grade when teaching writing. The issue of student interests should be considered when teaching and assessing reading activities. Teachers can use the conferencing process to determine student interests as well as reading and writing skills. If children are not interested in a story or a book, they will not read for comprehension and meaning.

Current views of reading suggest that steps be taken to (1) assess prior knowledge as a way of determining reading comprehension, (2) get students to question and predict before, during, and after reading, (3) get students to construct meaning using metacognitive strategies to monitor and comprehend what is being read, and (4) promote

positive habits and attitudes toward reading (Valencia, Pearson, Peters, & Wixson, 1989). Formal assessment in language arts involves teacher-made tests and standardized tests (Iowa Test of Basic Skills, ITBS; California Achievement Test, CAT; or state developed and administered tests). Informal assessment involves listening to students and keeping running records of miscues or error patterns and conducting interest and attitude inventories. Language arts assessment involves a product, which is comprehension, and a process, which involves the application of specific skills to the reading and writing process.

Whatever assessment strategies are used (portfolios, student conferences, group work, etc.), they must be based on what is known about how children learn and on teaching approaches that facilitate the development of language and literacy learning. Teachers need to be knowledgeable about the most effective ways to promote literacy in their classrooms and move toward that goal using developmentally appropriate approaches in all the areas of the language arts.

MAKING CONNECTIONS

Figure 10-5, a unit on birds, illustrates how other content areas can use literature as a bridge for teaching the content. In this unit, "Birds of a Feather Flock Together," literature books are used (e.g., *Owl Moon, Urban Roosts,* and *Feathers for Lunch*) to teach about birds—their names, physical characteristics, habitats, and their role in the food chain. As part of the unit, the teacher's philosophy about teaching thematically is presented. Next, the instructional goals that were formulated during the planning step (discussed in Chapter 6) are implemented. In addition to including literature resources, this unit utilizes the instructional model (the five Es—Engagement, Exploration, Explanation, Elaboration, and Evaluation) that was presented in Chapter 6.

Figure 10-5 illustrates the value of literature and its role in promoting literacy skills as well as

FIGURE 10-5 Thematic Unit: Birds of a Feather Flock Together

The role of my philosophy in planning and teaching and how I see learning are reflected in how I organized this unit on birds. For me, learning is viewed in terms of wholes and integrating knowledge, and these are the keys to successful teaching and learning by elementary students.

I. Goals of the unit
    A. To use literature to promote interest in science and, in particular, the environment (environmental literacy).
    B. To use literature as a means of promoting science processes as well as literacy skills (literature/environmental studies connection).
    C. To use the 5E model (Engagement, Exploration, Explanation, Elaboration, and Evaluation) as a lesson planning and implementation design which encourages hands-on science experiences.

II. Suggested literature for the topic of birds, food web/chain, interdependence, ecosystems, and adaptations
    A. *Feathers for Lunch*, Lois Ehlert, Harcourt, 1990, fiction, ages 3–8.
    B. *A Visit to the Country*, Herschel Johnson, 1989, fiction, ages 4–8.
    C. *The Tale of the Mandarin Ducks*, Katherine Paterson, 1990, fiction, ages 6–9.
    D. *Urban Roosts*, Barbara Bash, 1990, nonfiction, ages 6–10.
    E. *Saving the Peregrine Falcon*, Caroline Arnold, 1985, nonfiction, ages 8–12.
    F. *Peeping in the Shell: A Whooping Crane is Hatched*, Faith McNulty, 1986, nonfiction, ages 8–12.
    G. *The Whooping Crane: A Comeback Story*, Dorothy Hinshaw Patent, 1988, nonfiction, ages 9–12.

III. Example: In the unit, *Owl Moon* is used to promote interest in environmental studies.
    A. Read *Owl Moon* by Jane Yolen (**Engagement**).
        1. Science topics: birds (use the owl as a case study—nocturnal, survival needs—food, water, shelter)
        2. Environmental topics: food web/chain, interdependence, ecosystems, and adaptations
    B. Hands-on environmental studies activities
        1. Owl pellet dissection (**Exploration**): owls do not digest bones, feathers, and fur, and in a 24-hour period they "cough up" an owl pellet.
        2. In small groups, read the *Young Naturalist* by Ilo Hiller to get more information about owls (**Explanation**)

science skills and knowledge. Using literature in science and other subject areas provides opportunities for students to share ideas and information about the topics being studied and ask real-world questions for discussion and further research. Literature can also present situations that encourage readers to make decisions about issues/dilemmas/concerns, while introducing and applying new ideas, terms, and vocabulary. Finally, literature helps students construct new ideas, recognize both the specific and the big picture, and discuss possible actions to be taken at the local level by constructing practical and meaningful contexts in which students can express their

FIGURE 10-5, *continued*

3. Construct a food chain activity: students pick an animal in their ecosystem and find out the following—what it eats, where it lives, what eats it, and other facts about this animal (**Elaboration**).

4. Draw a picture of a food web/chain with a written script. The criterion for grading is that the visual and the explanation are accurate. Students could use a cartoon format, do a creative writing piece from the animal's point of view, write an autobiography as if they were the animal, use poetry, or a fantasy story to explain the food web/chain (**Evaluation**).

IV. Making connections across the curriculum: Additional environmental science experiences and activities

  A. Fine arts: Birds: Fair Feathered Friends
Feather Fun: Act out the poem about how feathers grow and why birds preen and molt (*Nature Scope*, World Wildlife Federation, Washington, DC, p. 43).

  B. Science: Adaptation of beaks, feet, legs, wings, and coloration
Clothes pins as beaks: "What's for dinner?" (analyzing beaks and sources of food)

Pouch-like	= pelican
Pointed	= woodpecker
Curved	= hawk
Short, stout	= finches
Slender, long	= hummingbird

(*Nature Scope*, World Wildlife Federation, Washington, DC, p. 29)

  C. Social studies: Habitats/shelters ("everyone needs a home") and their role in the ecosystem

    1. House building: To explore what materials birds use to build a few variations using recycled and natural materials

    2. Sponsoring projects to help protect birds

    3. Benefits of birds: Dispersing seeds, role as a predator as well as a prey, food for humans

  D. Mathematics: Flappers—to research types of birds and wingbeats per 10 seconds

Crow	20
Pigeon	30
Chickadee	270
Hummingbird	700

(*Nature Scope*, World Wildlife Federation, Washington, DC, p. 7)

thoughts in journaling, pictures, paintings, poetry, and stories.

In selecting literature for use with children in other subject areas, the teacher should consider the following criteria:

■ accuracy of content

■ facts and points of view clearly delineated and generalizations supported by factual information

■ appropriate reading level

■ text, illustrations, pictures, and format aligned and appropriate for grade-level usage

- drawings, pictures, and illustrations clear, detailed, and captioned
- representations of all groups and both genders

The types of literature used can include picture books, fiction and nonfiction books, biographies, autobiographies, information or how-to books, and poetry. (Refer to Figure 10-1 and its list of literature that focuses on specific skills.) Through these types of literature, students learn and apply literacy skills as they read about birds or any other subject. In addition, they learn writing skills as they examine fiction and nonfiction stories and poems for the plot, character development, use of descriptive words, and the viewpoint of the author.

When students share reports from their reading, they are practicing listening and speaking skills. Through a public forum, students have the opportunity to ask questions, debate ideas, and discuss their point of view. In such a forum, often literature is the catalyst for the discussion, the role play, and/or the debate.

SUMMARY

This chapter has provided an overview of issues that teachers will encounter in the language arts curriculum of the elementary classroom. Language is the vehicle for encoding and decoding content from what is experienced. The language arts curriculum helps children express their thoughts and feelings using language. A literate person is one who can communicate orally and in written form, comprehends what has been spoken and written, can express ideas, and appreciates what has been said and written.

The focus of the chapter has been to provide a framework of literacy with which to structure language learning. In particular, the chapter has examined and described the language-learning process and the characteristics of effective language arts instruction. The chapter has also discussed and provided, through Jesse, a look at a traditional language arts classroom as he reflected on his past experiences as a child and during his first years of teaching. The chapter then presented a more contemporary look at language learning by examining an integrated, holistic, whole-language classroom. Jesse gave us a glimpse of what this kind of approach could accomplish in language learning as he made the transition to a more holistic language arts program. As he emphasized, the transition is slow and takes place over time.

The chapter discusses the content and skills in each area of the language arts curriculum (reading, writing, handwriting, and spelling) that teachers can expect to teach within a traditional language arts program.

The chapter concluded with several suggestions for managing and assessing language arts learning. These management techniques focused on the rules and procedures of conduct as well as the physical arrangement of the room. Assessment strategies mentioned were portfolios, conferences, kidwatching checklists, and other opportunities to measure progress in all areas of the language arts curriculum.

■ YOUR TURN

1. Obtain a copy of the teacher's guide or teacher's edition of a basal reading series.

Look at the kinds of reading skills that are taught in the first four or five lessons. What assumptions does this approach make about knowledge of phonics and word attack skills?

Are the other language arts areas incorporated within this approach?

2. Using what you know about integrated, holistic, whole-language instruction, sketch out a thematic unit you might use in your elementary classroom. What topic would you choose? What subject areas would be included? What literature/story books would you use to teach/reinforce the concepts? What writing activities would you have students engage in?

3. Refer to Figure 9-1, which provides a list of software for the language arts curriculum. Select an item from the list or a similar one from a school, and use the rating sheet in Figure 9-7 to review the program. Then answer the following questions. Did the program emphasize a particular approach to the teaching of language arts content? Did it emphasize skill or process? Did it emphasize isolated content or integrated content? Would you purchase it? Why, or why not?

4. Survey teachers in your class or school to determine what they read (magazines, books, novels, etc.). Also ask how many of them write. Develop a position paper on why "Teachers Should Be Readers and Writers Too." How might you encourage students in your class or teachers in your school to be readers and writers?

5. After reading this chapter, reflect on your own learning experiences in the language arts and visit an elementary classroom. Like Jesse, describe how you learned to read, write, and spell. Once you have described the process for yourself, describe what you observed while visiting a real class. Finally, describe in writing the kind of language arts teacher you want to be.

6. Examine Figure 10-4 carefully; then think about and sketch in your journal the kind of classroom you would like to have.

7. Visit a preschool or kindergarten classroom, and list all of the different language-development activities the students either engage in or have the opportunity to engage in through centers. Then visit a fifth- or sixth-grade classroom, and list all of the language-learning activities the teacher has the students participate in. Compare your lists. How are they alike? How are they different? Do the two classrooms use a different approach to language learning?

8. Write your own definition for *emergent literacy*. Discuss with your classmates and teachers in the school your views of language learning. How are they like others? Different?

■ REFERENCES

Cambourne, B. (1984). *Language, learning and literacy.* Crystal Lake, IL: Rigby.

Cambourne, B. (1988). *The whole story: Natural learning and the acquisition of literacy in the classroom.* Richmond Hill, Ontario, Canada: Scholastic-TAB Publications.

Carbo, M. (1995, September). Continuum of modeling reading methods. *Instructor, 26*(1), 85.

Daly, E. (1991). *Monitoring children's language development.* Portsmouth, NH: Heinemann.

Durkin, D. (1989). *Teaching young children to read* (4th ed.). Boston: Allyn & Bacon.

Epanchin, B. C., Townsend, B., & Stoddard, K. (1994). *Constructive classroom management: Strategies for creating positive learning environments.* Pacific Grove, CA: Brooks/Cole.

Farr, R., & Tone, B. (1994). *Portfolio and performance assessment.* Fort Worth, TX: Harcourt Brace.

Finn, P. (1993). *Helping children learn language arts.* New York: Longman.

Goodman, K. (1986). *What's whole in whole language?* Portsmouth, NH: Heinemann.

Graves, D. H. (1983). *Writing: Teachers and children at work.* Portsmouth, NH: Heinemann.

Graves, M. F., Watts, S., & Graves, B. (1994). *Essentials of classroom teaching elementary reading.* Boston: Allyn & Bacon.

Guthrie, J., Van Meter, P., & Mitchell, A. (1994). Reading assessment. *The Reading Teacher,* *48*(3), 266–271.

Heilman, A. W., Blair, T. R., & Rupley, W. H. (1994). *Principles and practices of teaching reading.* Upper Saddle River, NJ: Merrill/Prentice Hall.

Helms, D. B., & Turner, J. S. (1986). *Exploring child behavior* (3rd ed.). Pacific Grove, CA: Brooks/Cole.

Holdaway, D. (1979). *The foundations of literacy.* Portsmouth, NH: Heinemann.

Lemlech, J. (1994). *Curriculum and instructional methods for the elementary and middle school* (3rd ed.). Upper Saddle River, NJ: Merrill/Prentice Hall.

Literacy and human empowerment. (1994). *Texas Journal, 16*(2), 4.

Lucas, J. (1993). Teaching writing: Emphasis swings to process, writing as tool for learning. *Curriculum Update.* Alexandria, VA: Association for Supervision and Curriculum Development, 1–8.

Maimon, E. P. (1988). Cultivating the prose garden. *Phi Delta Kappan, 69*(10), 734–739.

McClaran, N. (1996, January). Breakthroughs: Truth about spelling. *The Leader of Learners,* p. 7. Austin, TX: Texas Association for Supervision and Curriculum Development.

McIntyre, E. (1993). Decoding skill and successful beginning reading in different instructional settings. *Reading Horizons, 34*(2), 122–136.

McNergney, R., & Haberman, M. (1990). To improve kids' writing, make the topics real. *NEA Today, 8*(7), 28.

Moffett, J., & Wagner, B. J. (1993). What works in play. *Language Arts, 70,* 32–36.

Morrison, G. (1993). *Contemporary curriculum K–8.* Boston: Allyn & Bacon.

Nelson, J. (1989). *Peanut butter and jelly.* Los Angeles: Price Stern Sloan.

Norton, D. (1993). *The effective teaching of language arts* (4th ed.). Upper Saddle River, NJ: Merrill/Prentice Hall.

Norton, D. (1997). *The effective teaching of language arts* (5th ed.). Upper Saddle River, NJ: Merrill/Prentice Hall.

Reutzel, D. R., & Cooter, R. (1992). *Teaching children to read: From basals to books.* Upper Saddle River, NJ: Merrill/Prentice Hall.

Reutzel, D. R., & Cooter, R. (1996). *Teaching children to read: From basals to books* (2nd ed.). Upper Saddle River, NJ: Merrill/Prentice Hall.

Routman, R. (1991). *Invitations: Changing as teachers and learners K–12.* Portsmouth, NH: Heinemann.

Routman, R. (1988). *Transitions: From literature to literacy.* Portsmouth, NH: Heinemann.

Strickland, D. S. (1990). Emergent literacy: How young children learn to read and write. *Educational Leadership, 47*(6), 18–23.

Teale, W. H., & Sulzby, E. (1986). Introduction: Emergent literacy as a perspective for examining how young children become writers and readers. In W. H. Teale & E. Sulzby (Eds.), *Emergent literacy: Writing and reading* (pp. vii–xxv). Norwood, NJ: Ablex.

Vacca, J. A., Vacca, R., & Gove, M. K. (1995). *Reading and learning to read* (3rd ed.). New York: HarperCollins.

Valencia, S. W., Pearson, D. P., Peters, C. W., & Wixson, K. K. (1989). Theory and practice in statewide reading assessment: Closing the gap. *Educational Leadership, 46*(7), 57–63.

Wagner, B. J. (1988). Research currents: Does classroom drama affect the arts of language? *Language Arts, 65*(1), 46–65.

Yonemura, M. (1969). *Developing language programs for young disadvantaged children.* New York: Teachers College Press.

chapter 11

The Mathematics Curriculum

AFTER READING THIS CHAPTER, YOU WILL BE ABLE TO DO THE FOLLOWING:

- Explain the historical role mathematics has played in the elementary curriculum.

- Discuss the issues surrounding the mathematics curriculum in the elementary school.

- Identify and describe the goals of mathematics in the elementary curriculum.

- Identify and give examples of the mathematics concepts for grades K–6.

- Describe at least three ways to connect mathematics concepts with other subject areas.

- Discuss the various ways to assess mathematics learning in the elementary school.

Mathematics has been one of the essential or basic areas of the elementary curriculum from early Colonial days when it was called "ciphering" and "arithmetic." It has consistently been one of the three Rs of the elementary curricular program and will continue to play an important role in the education of children in the twenty-first century. The demands of modern society, particularly in the areas of science and technology, require that individuals have the ability to think and to process data in a meaningful way. In an increasingly technological world, the average person is confronted with the need to utilize the principles of mathematics daily. Mathematics is an integral part of understanding credit and installment buying, taxation formulas or tax tables, cost-of-living data, as well as the everyday procedures of budgeting and running a household or business. Mathematics is more than computation; it is a study of patterns and relationships; a tool to be used in daily life when interpreting data; a way of communicating; a way of thinking as students organize, analyze, and synthesize information; and even an art form with underlying orderliness and consistency (Reyes, Suydam, & Lindquist, 1995).

In learning mathematical concepts, students should be actively involved in doing mathematics, for as Shepherd and Ragan (1992) note, "it is through such participation that clear and functioning conceptual understandings are created upon which increasingly abstract constructs may be derived and supported" (p. 383). The procedures that are used to teach mathematics and the attitudes toward learning mathematics significantly affect the level of understanding achieved by students. Schwartz and Riedesel (1994) suggest that the single most important variable in learning of mathematics is the teacher, for "the way he or she guides the child in thinking and feeling is the crucial ingredient" (p. 2). There is no single best way to teach mathematics. The use of manipulatives and the attitude of the teacher coupled with the guidelines provided by the National Council of Teachers of Mathematics' *Curriculum and Evaluation Standards for School Mathematics* (NCTM, 1991, 1995) offer possibilities for teachers to improve mathematics instruction and learning in elementary classrooms.

This chapter provides a historical account of mathematics education in the United States as well as identifying some of the current issues related to mathematics teaching in the elementary school. It also presents an overview of the content and skills in mathematics that are presented to students as they progress through the elementary grades, along with strategies, resources and tools, and connections to other subject areas. Finally, the implications for teaching mathematics and assessing student achievement will be discussed.

THE HISTORICAL CONTEXT OF MATHEMATICS TEACHING

Just as the language arts curriculum is frequently in a state of flux, the mathematics curriculum in the elementary school is also undergoing change. Although the mathematics curriculum has changed over the past hundred years, the current evolution in the curriculum is designed to make it more responsive to the present needs, as well as the future needs, of students. The mathematics curriculum at the turn of the twentieth century was characterized as being difficult and having little practical value. As children entered school, they began the serious business of memorizing number facts. As Brownell (1954) notes,

> In the first two grades they memorized all the simple number facts. By the time they had finished grade three they were well embarked into computation with whole numbers. In grade four they performed operations with common fractions, many of which are now generally deferred to grade five or six, and others have been eliminated from school arithmetic. In the upper grades they studied square root and even cube root, worked long and difficult examples with decimal fractions, percentage, and ratio and proportion, and solved intricate problems involving many steps. (p. 1)

During the early 1900s, the mathematics curriculum was developed with little concern for students' developmental abilities and therefore contained difficult content that had no apparent application to their lives. Following the view of learning at the time (faculty psychology), which emphasized training of the mind, mathematics became a vehicle for improving the faculties of reasoning and memory. As Sowards and Scobey (1968) point out, research at this time focused on two ways of conceptualizing mathematics; one was in the form of social usage and the other was on the science of numbers. Chantelle, the "Voice of Experience" for this chapter, recalls how her first years of teaching mathematics looked very similar to the practices of this earlier time.

Read this

 **Voice of Experience**

Chantelle reflects on her first years of teaching. She says, "The single most important strategy I employed, as did almost every other teacher in my school, was flash cards coupled with timed math fact sheets. Students had to master their multiplication and division facts. What amazed me was how the kids could recite their math multiplication or division facts and yet not understand the process of multiplication or division." Chantelle says she soon realized that students who were not good at memorizing their math facts seemed to fall further and further behind, and by January they began to believe that they couldn't "do math." As she recalls the situation, "Most of these students were able to 'do math' by using objects, but if they had to memorize, the math became virtually impossible."

The emphasis on mathematics as social usage reached its height during the 1930s when educators were concerned with what mathematics skills the average person would need to function in daily life. In deciding what was to be taught in addition to the basic functions of addition, subtraction, multiplication, and division, much attention was given to fractions, decimals, and compound numbers (Wilson, 1950). Those who favored the science of numbers emphasized analysis of number systems more than usage, and all possible types of number solutions were considered appropriate for the elementary curriculum. This view of mathematics education lasted well into the 1940s.

The school restructuring efforts of the 1950s and 1960s accelerated concern for what should be taught as part of the mathematics curriculum, which ranged from mastering basic facts to understanding fundamental processes. Throughout those two decades, educators were caught in the tug-of-war between mathematics as a process and mathematics as mastering facts; this time period is generally considered to be the era of "new math." The debate concerning the appropriate way to teach mathematics focused on isolated versus integrated instruction. Following much discussion, the Committee on the Teaching of Arithmetic of the National Society for the Study of Education (1951) issued the following statement:

> An especially designed [mathematics] program should include not only provision for systematic and meaningful learning in the arithmetic class but also careful attention to the mathematical needs and contributions of other areas.... Mathematics achievement cannot be obtained either in the arithmetic period alone or in integrated units alone. Both types of instruction are needed. (pp. 18, 21)

The statement issued then might also apply today. Rather than viewing the teaching of mathematics as an isolated event, mathematical concepts should be integrated into other areas of study in the elementary curriculum. Integration makes mathematics more meaningful for elementary students, and they experience greater success.

The decades of the 1970s and 1980s brought change again in the elementary mathematics curriculum, as new math came under attack. Kline (1973) received much attention from his book *Why Johnny Can't Add*, which criticized the new math as being based on false assumptions about teaching mathematics. Kline contended that the reasoning required of the students under new math was not at an appropriate developmental level. The impact of new math on actual classroom practices appears minimal, and the publicity from the criticism may have been more show than substance. Gibney and Karns (1979) found that mathematics instruction was characterized by teachers using a single textbook from which they presented information that was then followed by seatwork focusing on computational skills with whole numbers and fractions.

The debate related to the use of drill and practice procedures continues today, as elementary teachers are faced with the challenge of developing basic computational skills in all students. Teachers are also confronted with the national emphasis on getting students to apply mathematical concepts to solve problems and interpret data using graphs, tables, and charts. Teachers are caught in the bind: teach computation skills or problem-solving strategies. To echo the thoughts of the national committee in 1951, the teaching of mathematics today is not an either/or situation, it is *both*. Both computation skills and problem-solving strategies should be taught as a part of the mathematics curriculum.

ISSUES IN TEACHING ELEMENTARY MATHEMATICS

Mathematics instruction has long been an established component of the elementary school, yet the results from achievement tests in the past two decades have been disappointing. These scores have prompted educators to review and rethink the practices in teaching and assessing mathematics learning in the elementary grades. Driscoll (1988) calls math the "underachieving curriculum" and notes that researchers in both education and cognitive psychology have discovered numerous flaws in the way math is usually presented to students in the classroom: flaws in scope, in sequence of topics, and most importantly in the psychological assumptions about how math is learned. (p. 2)

One issue that continues to plague elementary teachers is the tendency to teach mathematics using programs and materials that promise to produce quick results. These packaged programs do not necessarily translate into improving mathematics achievement. There are numerous reasons for the poor scores on achievement tests, and solutions will not be found overnight. Many teachers feel poorly prepared to teach mathematics, and, lacking confidence in their teaching ability, they tend to use the "tell and show" strategies and have students "copy and do." These teacher-directed lessons emphasize mastering basic computational skills. In addition, many elementary teachers tend to follow the textbook and rely on drill and practice. The end result is lessons that are dull and turn students off to mathematics.

Another issue that concerns elementary teachers about the mathematics curriculum is repetition. Driscoll (1988) points out that there is "persuasive evidence that the curriculum cyclically repeats information . . . with futile revisiting of [difficult] math concepts and skills" (p. 3). According to Flanders (1987), who conducted a detailed analysis of mathematics textbooks, less than 40 percent of new material is presented in each grade level as students progress through the elementary grades. By the time students get to the sixth grade, they have encountered extensive review and repetition and still have not mastered the basic operations.

A third issue in mathematics education involves the way in which mathematics is typically taught through the use of rote memory teaching strategies. Alternative strategies have been proposed that would facilitate mathematics learning among all children. Burns (1994) suggests using cooperative learning strategies, in which students work in groups to learn and practice mathematics concepts and skills. In coopera-

tive groups, students have numerous opportunities to talk about the problem, think aloud, and reason out their answer with the input from others. In cooperative work groups, students have the opportunity to develop, cement, and extend their understanding by spending the bulk of the time in situations in which they build their own understanding of mathematics. Group learning encourages sharing information and exchanging ideas with peers, as well as with the teacher (Good, Reys, Grouws, & Mulryan, 1990; Burns, 1994).

Finally, in an attempt to make math more meaningful and understandable, educators have called for the use of manipulatives. Using manipulatives has made a difference in student learning because they make mathematics concepts and operations more concrete (Merseth, 1993). *Manipulatives* are defined as materials that students use to solve problems and/or construct visuals as they think through a situation. They provide elementary students with the necessary kinesthetic experiences to help them learn specific mathematics concepts. Figure 11-1 provides a list of recommended mathematics manipulatives for the elementary classroom, grades K–6.

Manipulatives, such as interlocking counting cubes, base ten blocks, unifix cubes, geoboards, tangrams, and pattern blocks, encourage students to use them as concrete tools in their learning. For example, manipulatives provide students with opportunities to reason out that a set of two added to a set of two equals four because objects are added to the original set which results in a larger set (the whole). Chantelle's "Voice of Experience" illustrates how she used manipulatives in her classroom.

 Voice of Experience

Today was a good day for Chantelle as she finished her math lesson. She says to her class, "You really worked hard in your cooperative groups, and I saw a lot of sharing of information

FIGURE 11-1   Recommended Mathematics Manipulatives by Grade Level

Kindergarten

Interlocking counting cubes measuring 2-cm or 1-inch square (1000)

Pattern blocks (4 sets with 250 in each with mirrors) of bright colors in various geometric shapes and good for patterning concepts, fractions, and geometry

Attribute blocks (4 sets with 60 in each set) of wood or plastic in various shapes, sizes, and colors for developing sorting, classifying, comparing, and problem-solving skills

Materials such as buttons, shells, keys, etc. to sort, count, sequence, and compare and contrast

Measuring tools such as scales (metric and customary units) to develop concepts in mass, comparing materials—heavier, lighter

First Grade

Interlocking counting cubes (1000)

Cuisinaire rods (one student set per child) to develop number concepts, basic addition and subtraction computations

Attribute blocks (4 sets)

Measuring tools of scales, rulers, meter sticks, tape measures, and trundle wheels with graduated units, measuring cups, spoons, and containers of various shapes, thermometers, and clocks for measuring length, volume, mass, temperature, time, and money

Second Grade

Interlocking counting cubes (1000)

Base ten blocks (a set of ones, tens, and hundreds for each student) color and proportionally coded for each place value—white = ones; orange, longs = tens; orange, flats = hundreds; orange cube = thousand

Attribute blocks

Pattern blocks

Measuring tools

Cuisenaire rods

Two- and three-dimensional geometric models (wooden or plastic) of square, circle, triangle, rectangle, sphere, cube, cone, rectangular solid, and various prisms

Third Grade

Interlocking counting blocks (1000)

Base ten blocks

Pattern blocks

when you constructed the problem with your base ten blocks to solve the problem. I believe each group came up with a logical solution, and tomorrow we will verify the answers each group came up with."

The use of manipulatives is just one suggestion for improving mathematics teaching in the elementary school. This section has focused on the issues that affect the teaching and learning of mathematics. Several of these issues are not new; they have continued to be of concern

FIGURE 11-1, *continued*

Fraction models including circles, squares, bars, and rods that show wholes and parts

Measuring tools

Two- and three-dimensional geometric models

Fourth Grade

Base ten blocks

Decimal models of cardboard or plastic squares and rectangles that are divided into tenths, hundredths, and thousandths

Fraction models

Measuring tools

Interlocking centimeter cubes (2000) of plastic that snap together, have a mass of one gram, and are used for activities in mass, length, and volume

Tangrams (one per student), a set of 7 plastic or wooden pieces which develop concepts in geometry, measurement, and problem solving

Two- and three-dimensional geometric models

Geoboards (one per student and one for demonstration purposes) of square plastic or wooden boards, usually five-inches by five-inches, with an array of pegs or nails to develop concepts in geometry and measurement

Fifth Grade

Base ten blocks

Decimal models

Fraction models

Measuring instruments

Interlocking centimeter cubes

Tangrams

Two- and three-dimensional geometric models

Geoboards

Sixth Grade

Decimal models

Fraction models

Measuring tools

Tangrams

Geoboards

Geometric models

Probability tools including spinners, cubes, other regular geometric solids with colors, numbers, letters, etc. on the faces to develop concepts in probability and statistics to educators and the general public for years. Responses to these issues, as addressed in the *NCTM Standards* (National Council of Teachers of Mathematics, 1991, 1995), may ultimately improve student achievement in mathematics. Figure 11-2 provides an example of how real-world experiences can be used to teach the math concepts and skills described in the *NCTM Standards*. For example, by using edible snacks in the shape of fish, students touch and manipulate real objects as they develop their spatial sense, reason, and learn to estimate, and then make connections with other areas of study.

FIGURE 11-2   Using Fish to Relate Math to Real-world Experiences

Problem solving	■ Examine diet of fish in ponds, streams, lakes, and oceans. ■ Recognize fish as a food product for humans and other aquatic animals. ■ Note number of fish offspring in the classroom aquarium. ■ Study salmon and their return to spawning grounds and survival rate.
Communication	■ Interpret charts, graphs, and tables related to the different types of fish in the ocean (cold/warm water). ■ Read about different types of fish which live near the surface, etc. (body parts, colors, etc.).
Reasoning	■ Use fish crackers as counters for students to reason through different mathematical operations by first estimating. ■ Develop a model of an aquarium to simulate different types of problems.
Connections	■ Read children's book about fish. ■ Explore the endangered fish species locally and around the world. ■ Research the problems related to water pollution and the impact on the fish population. ■ Study different parts of the United States where the economy is dependent upon fish catches, and if these markets are dwindling.
Whole number operations	■ Develop different types of one-, two-digit problems involving addition, subtraction, multiplication, and (partitive and measurement) division.
Geometry and spatial sense	■ Use the geoboards to determine population density of fish populations in a given area.
Measurement	■ Measure the length of different types of fish and calculate the amount of food that is consumed. ■ Determine amount of food fish eat. ■ Estimate weight based on body measurements.

Note: For additional information, see "Thematic Webbing and the Curriculum Standards in the Primary Grades" by J. A. Piazza, M. M. Scott, & E. C. Carver, February 1994, *Arithmetic Teacher, 41*(6), 294–298.

THE NATURE OF ELEMENTARY MATHEMATICS EDUCATION

At times, over the past fifty years in elementary mathematics education, the emphasis was on memorization of skills and specific content; at other times, on the processes used to arrive at the answers or solutions. In 1989, the National Council of Teachers of Mathematics (NCTM) took a leadership role by providing a blueprint for addressing the questions of what mathematics content should be taught and how to teach it. The NCTM took the lead when educators and the public were demanding answers to the lack of mathematics literacy among students.

Goals of Mathematics Education

When the NCTM suggested goals for the mathematics curriculum in grades K–12, it became essential that the elementary-school goals be aligned with those at the secondary level. The general goals for elementary mathematics are few:

■ learning to value mathematics
■ becoming confident in the ability to do mathematics
■ becoming mathematical problem solvers
■ learning to communicate mathematically
■ learning to reason mathematically

These goals are different from those of the past. It is clear from these goals that the learner is important. Helping the learner become empowered to do math is the major objective. The debate over what should be taught continues to be a part of the discussions about mathematics instruction.

Scope and Sequence of Elementary Mathematics

The NCTM has offered not only standards but also a suggested curriculum. In recommending a structuring of the mathematics curriculum, the NCTM has identified in its standards (National Council of Teachers of Mathematics, 1991, 1995) the following conceptual areas that should guide mathematics instruction in the elementary school:

■ problem solving
■ communication
■ reasoning
■ connections
■ estimation
■ number sense and numeration
■ concepts of whole-number operations
■ whole-number computation
■ geometry and spatial sense
■ measurement
■ statistics and probability
■ fractions and decimals
■ patterns and relationships

These conceptual areas are accompanied by student objectives that further define the mathematics content and skills to be taught in the elementary school (see Figure 11-3).

In addition to these concepts and skills, the following paragraphs discuss the mathematical content themes that are typically taught in grades K–6.

In *kindergarten*, children experience mathematics through such activities as number recognition and one-to-one correspondence. Students learn to match numerals with appropriate number representations. In such experiences, they assign numerical symbols to the quantity. They experience mathematics in concrete ways as they learn to count with objects, such as trucks, carpet squares, tongue depressors, and/or clothespins. Kindergartners also learn the concepts of quantity (greater than, less than) by pouring rice or macaroni into cups and other measuring tools. They also learn the basic geometric shapes: circles, squares, rectangles, and triangles.

In *first grade*, students learn the family of numbers ($5 = 4 + 1 = 3 + 2$) by manipulating objects

FIGURE 11-3   Recommended Conceptual Areas of the Mathematics Curriculum and Suggested Student Objectives

1. Mathematics as problem solving: Students will
   - solve problems to investigate and understand mathematical content
   - formulate problems
   - construct and use strategies to solve a wide variety of problems
   - verify and interpret results
   - acquire confidence in using mathematics meaningfully

2. Mathematics as communication: Students will
   - relate physical materials, pictures, and diagrams to mathematical ideas
   - reflect on and clarify their thinking about mathematical ideas and situations
   - relate their everyday language to mathematical language and symbols
   - realize that representing, discussing, reading, writing, and listening to mathematics are a vital part of learning and using mathematics

3. Mathematics as reasoning: Students will
   - draw logical conclusions about mathematics
   - use models, known facts, properties, and relationships to explain their thinking
   - justify their answers and solution processes
   - use patterns and relationships to analyze mathematical situations
   - believe that mathematics makes sense

4. Mathematics as connections: Students will
   - link conceptual and procedural knowledge
   - relate various representations of concepts or procedures to one another
   - recognize relationships among different topics in mathematics
   - use mathematics in other curriculum areas
   - use mathematics in their daily lives

5. Estimation: Students will
   - explore estimation strategies
   - recognize when the estimate is appropriate
   - determine the reasonableness of results
   - apply estimation in working with quantities, measurement, computation, and problem solving

6. Number sense and numeration: Students will
   - construct number meanings through real-world experiences and use of physical materials
   - understand our numeration system by relating counting, grouping, and place-value concepts
   - develop number sense
   - interpret the multiple uses of numbers encountered in the real world

FIGURE 11-3, *continued*

7. Concepts of whole-number operations: Students will
   - develop meaning for the operations by modeling and discussing a rich variety of problem situations
   - relate mathematical language and symbolism of operations to problem situations and informal language
   - recognize that a wide variety of problem structures can be represented by a single operation
   - develop operation sense

8. Whole number computation: Students will
   - model, explain, and develop proficiency with basic facts and algorithms
   - use a variety of mental computation and estimation techniques
   - use calculators in appropriate computational situations
   - select and use computation techniques appropriate to specific problems and determine whether the results are reasonable

9. Geometry and spatial sense: Students will
   - describe, model, draw, and classify shapes
   - investigate and predict the results of combining, subdividing, and changing shapes
   - develop spatial sense
   - relate geometric ideas to number and measurement ideas
   - recognize and appreciate geometry in their world

10. Measurement: Students will
    - understand the attributes of length, capacity, weight, area, volume, time, temperature, and angle
    - develop the process of measuring and concepts related to units of measurement
    - make and use estimates of measurement
    - make and use measurements in problem and everyday situations

11. Statistics and probability: Students will
    - collect, organize, and describe data
    - construct, read, and interpret displays of data
    - formulate and solve problems that involve collecting and analyzing data
    - explore concepts of chance

12. Fractions and decimals: Students will
    - develop concepts of fractions, mixed numbers, and decimals
    - develop number sense for fractions and decimals
    - use models to relate fractions to decimals and to find equivalent fractions
    - use models to explore operations on fractions and decimals
    - apply fractions and decimals to problem situations

13. Patterns and relationships: Students will
    - recognize, describe, extend, and create a wide variety of patterns
    - represent and describe mathematical relationships
    - explore the use of variables and open sentences to express relationships

in the math center, and over time commit the one hundred addition facts to memory. The focus of the curriculum is on addition of one- and two-digit numbers with and without renaming (regrouping). First-graders also continue learning measurement concepts in terms of length, weight, and volume.

Second-graders learn the concept of take away (subtraction), including one- and two-digit numbers with and without renaming (regrouping). They master the one hundred subtraction facts and continue to refine their concepts of problem solving, communicating math using symbols, and measurement as they learn about money and time.

By *third grade*, students are ready for multiplication of one- and two-digit numbers at first, followed by three-digit problems, along with learning the one hundred basic multiplication facts. Students become proficient in measuring volume, weight, length, time, and money not only as they work in groups, but also as they discuss ways to solve problems using reasoning and appropriate communication skills.

By *fourth grade*, students focus on division, which requires proficiency in addition, subtraction, and multiplication. As students use manipulatives, they learn their ninety division facts, and by the end of fourth grade have committed to memory a total of three-hundred-ninety basic mathematics facts involving all whole number operations. Students find division one of the most difficult mathematical concepts to learn; therefore, manipulatives should be used to make the connections between the concrete level of learning and the abstract level of understanding division. Basic problems using simple fractions are also introduced in the fourth grade.

By the time students are in *grade five*, operations that deal with parts less than one are the focus. They explore basic operations with mixed fractions and decimals and perform whole number operations in addition, subtraction, and multiplication involving more than three digits. Students continue to work division problems with remainders.

In *sixth grade*, students develop proficiency in working with integers, geometry, and statistics and probability. Sixth graders refine their basic mathematics skills before moving to higher levels of math. They begin to explore variables and open sentences to express mathematical relationships and refine their understanding of geometry, algebra, and integers. Figure 11-4 provides an overview of the mathematics concepts and skills taught in grades K–6 which were just described. Along the left side are selected conceptual areas recommended by the *NCTM Standards*, which are included at each grade level.

To successfully implement such an overview, mathematics educators suggest that a variety of strategies be used to help students master the concepts. Group problem solving helps students learn essential mathematical skills (Farivar & Webb, 1994). Within the context of group problem solving, students learn basic communication skills, teamwork, and social skills, as well as develop math reasoning abilities. Farivar and Webb (1994) note that research "has shown multiple benefits for students" (p. 524) with regard to solving problems and improving their math achievement. Dorward and Archibald (1994) suggest that teachers draw upon their own interests and backgrounds to connect mathematics with real-world or authentic experiences for their students.

The *NCTM Standards* have served as a framework for mathematical initiatives at the local level (Frye & May, 1991). The following statement summarizes the basic goals that should guide teachers in developing their elementary mathematics curriculum:

> These goals imply that students should be exposed to numerous and interrelated experiences that encourage them to value the mathematical enterprise, to develop mathematical habits of mind, and to understand and appreciate the role of mathematics in human affairs; that they should be encouraged to explore, to guess, and even to make and correct errors so that they gain confidence in their ability to solve complex problems; that they should read, write, and discuss mathematics; and that they should conjecture, test, and build arguments about a conjecture's validity. (Frye & May, 1991, p. 47)

FIGURE 11-4   Overview of Mathematics Content

Measuring	**Kindergarten**	Number concepts, matching, labels with quantity, one-to-one correspondence, number recognition, geometric shapes
Communicating	**First grade**	Family of numbers, addition of one digit (100 basic addition facts) and two-digit numbers without and with renaming (regrouping) and beginning subtraction
Reasoning	**Second grade**	Subtraction of one-digit numbers and two digits (100 basic subtractions facts) without and with renaming (regrouping)
Connections with the real world	**Third grade**	Multiplication of one- and two-digit numbers (100 basic multiplication facts)
	Fourth grade	Division of one- and two-digit numbers (90 basic division facts)
	Fifth grade	Fractions and decimals (less than one concept)
Problem solving	**Sixth grade**	Geometry, integers, statistics and probability

The *NCTM Standards* (National Council of Teachers of Mathematics, 1991, 1995) continue to evolve, and the hope is that teachers will recognize their importance and use them to structure the elementary mathematics curriculum.

Dorward and Archibald (1994) conclude by saying that when planning for mathematics teaching, "viewing one's own life experiences as a resource is an important step" (p. 303). By making connections between mathematical concepts and real-world situations, teachers provide students with a mechanism for understanding math concepts in "an ecology of experience" rather than as "isolated bits of information" (p. 300).

MAKING CONNECTIONS

To provide linkages between mathematics, the real world, and other subject areas, Whitin (1994) advocates using literature to teach mathematics in the primary grades. He says that as children "read math" in story situations and within the context of a story, mathematics makes more sense than an "isolated series of rules to follow or facts to memorize" (p. 4). By using books, teachers can discuss with children such topics as counting, measuring, and/or problem solving concepts. These concepts can then be applied to everyday activities such as the calendar, celebrating birthdays, the daily schedule, taking attendance, and the lunch count.

Such activities help students extend their learning of mathematical concepts and apply them to other areas of the curriculum and school program. For example, in social studies, as students look at distances from their town to other towns in their state and even towns in other countries, they measure distances and use scales of miles or kilometers. As children explore science concepts, they use math skills when they measure the distance different objects move depending on the strength of a magnet. They also use math when they record frequency data from an experiment and plot those data on a bar graph or a line graph. When studying weather concepts, students interpret weather maps and use the legends to determine changes in weather patterns over time. Finally, as a part of the daily schedule, they use math skills in reading the thermometers inside and outside of the classroom. In physical education, they use math skills to determine how far they have run or how large a playing field should be. They also use math skills when they record times for races to determine the winner.

Whitin (1994) further suggests that one thing can lead to another as children move from calendars to place value. By listening to children's spontaneous questions and observing while they read books, teachers can use their questions as ways to motivate students in mathematics. Teachers can also encourage students to tell their own mathematical stories. For example, after reading *Only Six More Days* by Marisabina Russo, about a birthday, the teacher might have the children determine the number of days until their next birthday. This would become the basis for their own mathematical story.

According to Gailey (1993), there are many different types of children's books—counting, number, miscellaneous story, and concept books—that can be used during mathematics teaching. The following books can be used to teach mathematics content in the elementary school (Thrailkill, 1994): "The Lost Button" from *Frog and Toad Are Friends* (Lobel, 1985) focuses on attributes; *The Philharmonic Gets Dressed* (Kuskin, 1986) emphasizes numbers from 1 to 105; the *Round Trip* (Jonas, 1983) addresses spatial relations; and *The Doorbell Rang* (Huchins, 1986) presents beginning division skills. *Math Curse* (Scieszka & Smith, 1995) shows how math is everywhere. Books provide children with an opportunity not only to read, but also to talk math.

Figure 11-5 provides a list of additional children's books that can be used in teaching mathematics content plus resources and tools teachers can use to enrich the teaching-learning process and motivate students.

FIGURE 11-5　Teaching Resources and Tools for Mathematics

I. Children's Literature

Title	Description	Grade Level(s)	Publisher/ Supplier
Buttons, Buttons (1994) Rozanne L. Williams	Story helps children with counting, creating sets, and subsets based on colors and shapes of buttons.	K–2	Creative Teaching Press P.O. Box 6017 Cypress, CA 90630-0017
Joe's Pool (1994) Claire Henley	Counting book depicts each newcomer to the pool in a way that students can follow patterns of 1+1, 2+1, 3+1, etc.	K–3	Hyperion Books for Children 114 Fifth Avenue New York, NY 10011
Math Curse (1995) Jon Scieszka Lane Smith	A day in the life of a student where math is everywhere, and everything becomes a math problem to solve.	4–6	Viking Publishers 375 Hudson Street New York, NY 10014
The Amazing Book of Shapes (1994) Lydia Sharman	Introduction to shapes of objects and folding concentric squares into a pattern, testing for symmetry, and creating patterns for grids.	3–5	Dorling Kindersley 95 Madison Avenue New York, NY 10016
The Crayola Counting Book (1995) Rozanne L. Williams	Counting crayons by fives, twos, ones, colors, and numbers of crayons in boxes.	K–2	Creative Teaching Press P.O. Box 6017 Cypress, CA 90630-0017
The Greedy Triangle (1994) Marilyn Burns	An exploration of shapes and the many ways they appear in our world.	K–3	Scholastic Inc. 730 Broadway New York, NY 10003
Ten Old Pails (1994) Nicholas Heller	A counting book that chronicles the pails a boy uses to feed cows, hold golf balls, etc.	K–4	Greenwillow Books 1350 Avenue of Americas New York, NY 10019
Ten Out of Bed (1994) Penny Dale	A child and nine stuffed animals provide the basis for this counting book with a subtraction pattern of 10-1, 9-1, 8-1, etc.	K–3	Candlewick Press 2067 Massachusetts Avenue Cambridge, MA 02140
Who Took the Cookies from the Cookie Jar? (1995) Rozanne L. Williams	Story helps children count by twos as cookies disappear from the cookie jar.	K–2	Creative Teaching Press P.O. Box 6017 Cypress, CA 90630-0017

II. Teacher Resources: Books

Title	Description	Grade Level(s)	Publisher/ Supplier
Math and Literature (1992) Marilyn Burns	Provides imaginative ideas and suggestions for children's literature to do mathematical problem-solving.	K–3	Math Solutions Publishers Distributed by Cuisenaire Co. P.O. Box 5026 White Plains, NY 10602-5026
Math and Literature (1996) Rusty Bresser	Identifies a sample of children's literature that can be used to complement math lessons. Books included: *Anno Magic Seeds*, *The 329th Friend*, *Postal Rate History*, and others.	All	Heinemann 361 Hanover Street Portsmouth, NH 03801-3912 (800)541-2086
Math and Literature Book One (1992) Marilyn Burns	Books featured are the *Rooster's Off to See the World*, *The Button Box*, *How Many Feet in the Bed*, and many others.	K–3	Heinemann 361 Hanover Street Portsmouth, NH 03801-3912 (800)541-2086
Math and Literature Book Two (1994) Stephanie Sheffield	A sequel to the first book, it features classroom-tested lessons that link math with literature and writing. Twenty book descriptions are provided.	K–3	Heinemann 361 Hanover Street Portsmouth, NH 03801-3912 (800)541-2086
My Travels with Gulliver (1994) Education Development Center	Uses Gulliver's adventures to develop a real sense of size and math skills to problem solve.	4–8	Sunburst Communications 101 Castleton Street P.O. Box 100 Pleasantville, NY 10570-0100
Putting it Together: Middle School Math in Transition (1994) Gary Tsurada	Suggestions for incorporating the constructivist philosophy in classroom instruction.	5–8	Heinemann Educational Books 361 Hanover Street Portsmouth, NH 03801-3959 (800)541-2086
Read Any Good Math Lately: Children's Books for Mathematical Learning (1992) D. Whitin, S. Wilde	Takes each major mathematics concept taught in the elementary school and provides a list of books and a brief discussion for each.	K–4	Heinemann Educational Books 361 Hanover Street Portsmouth, NH 03801-3959 (800)541-2086

FIGURE 11-5, continued

Title	Description	Grade Level(s)	Publisher/Supplier
II. Teacher Resources: Books (continued)			
Sideways Arithmetic from Wayside School (1989) Louis Sachar	At Wayside School, the students have opportunity to solve over fifty mind-boggling puzzles and brainteasers in mathematics. Can you answer this question: Why does elf+elf=fool? Read the book and see.	2–6	Scholastic Inc. 730 Broadway New York, NY 10003
Thinking Like Mathematicians: Putting the K–4 NCTM Standards into Practice (1994) Thomas Rowan Barbara Bourne	Describes ways to implement the NCTM *Standards* in classrooms using classroom vignettes.	K–4	Heinemann Educational Books 361 Hanover Street Portsmouth, NH 03801-3959 (800)541-2086
III. Teacher Resources: Other			
Fraction Mate FX-55 Calculator	Expresses fractions with numerators and denominators.	4–6	Casco Inc. 570 Mt. Pleasant Ave. Dover, NJ 07801
The Flashcards System (1993) Computer program (for IBM-compatible PCs)	Focuses on basic computational skills and illustrates operations with number lines, objects, and number tables.	K–4	You and Me Products P.O. Box 61488 Vancouver, WA 98666
Cuisenaire Rods Cuisenaire Attribute Shapes	Manipulatives using color, shapes, and length to help children learn math concepts.	K–8	Cuisenaire Co. of America, Inc. P.O. Box 5026 White Plains, NY 10602-5026
Teaching Children Mathematics Journal	Includes ideas for improving the teaching of mathematics.	K–6	National Council of Teachers of Mathematics 1906 Association Drive Reston, VA 22091-1593
Manipulative Starter Kit	A collection of 12 different materials to use in teaching math concepts; includes the manipulatives for the teacher and a 92-page resource book in a binder.	K–6	Cuisenaire Co. of America, Inc. P.O. Box 5026 White Plains, NY 10602-5026

Title	Description	Grade Level(s)	Publisher/Supplier
IV. Software			
Race Car'rithmetic	Interactive game to be played by one to four players. The goal is to cross the finish line by solving addition, subtraction, multiplication, and division problems.	1–4	Cambridge Development Laboratory, Inc. 86 West Street Waltham, MA 02154 (800)637-0047
Math Football Set	Series of five packages of activities that focus on various math concepts. Students learn these concepts by playing football.	5–12	Cambridge Development Laboratory, Inc. 86 West Street Waltham, MA 02154 (800)637-0047
Turtle Math (1990) Douglas Clements	Math is presented in a series of measurement and geometry activities using visual and Logo-based investigations.	3–6	Educational Resources 1550 Executive Dr. P.O. Box 1990 Elgin, IL 60121
Math Power and DynaMath Student Periodicals	Builds math skills through the use of fun photos, graphics, humorous illustrations, and hands-on activities.	3–4 or 5–6	Scholastic Inc. P.O. Box 3735 Jefferson City, MO 65102-9962
V. Videotapes			
Mathematics: Assessing Understanding (1993) Marilyn Burns	Three tapes that discuss individual assessments using questions and other strategies.	1–8	Sunburst/Wings for Learning 101 Castleton Street P.O. Box 100 Pleasantville, NY 10570-9963
Mathicas Workshop (1994)	Twenty videotapes that present problem-solving activities that integrate literature and meet NCTM's *Standards*.	K–3	TV Ontario U.S. Office 1140 Kildare Farm Road, Ste. 308 Cary, NC 27511
How Much is a Million? (1985) David M. Schwartz (*If you Made a Million*, 1989, companion book)	ALA Notable Book (1985) focuses on the concept of a million and gets readers to realize what size bowl is needed to hold a million goldfish.	2–6	Lothrop, Lee & Shepard Books William Morrow & Co, Inc. 39 Plymouth St, P.O. Box 1219 Fairfield, NJ 07007 (800)237-0657

ASSESSING MATHEMATICS LEARNING

A critical element in the teaching of mathematics is determining not only what children have learned but also how they think. Assessment is an integral part of the instructional process as teachers ascertain students' level of understanding. Educators need to overcome the habit of using product-oriented mathematics assessment techniques to measure process-oriented mathematics teaching (Costa, 1989). Measuring student achievement in mathematics should be based on the decisions that teachers make on a daily basis and not determined solely by achievement test scores. As indicated in Chapter 8, assessment based on instruction means implementing a wide range of techniques to measure learning results in mathematics. Such techniques are not limited to paper-and-pencil tests but include portfolios of student work, long-term projects, logs and journals, student interviews, writing samples, and videotapes of student performance (Costa, 1989). Gathering a variety of student assessment data means having a more accurate picture of what students know and understand.

The *NCTM Standards* (National Council of Teachers of Mathematics, 1991, 1995) have defined and operationalized the criteria for assessing mathematics learning. These criteria are aligned with the mathematics curriculum goals and the teaching strategies discussed earlier in this chapter. As part of the *NCTM Standards*, these criteria for assessing student learning include the following:

■ examining the thought process as well as what has been learned

■ integrating assessment with teaching

■ viewing mathematics learning holistically and using a broad range of mathematical tasks

■ using problem situations that require the application of several mathematical concepts

■ incorporating a variety of assessment techniques that include written, oral, and demonstration formats

■ incorporating the use of calculators, computers, and manipulatives in the assessment process

When a lesson objective is written and presented to students during instruction, it should be written with an eye toward how it will be measured. Teachers should recognize the connections among planning, teaching, and assessing. Assessment is not something that is tacked on after a lesson is taught; rather it should provide focus for the lesson as well as feedback for reteaching and future instruction.

Determining whether students can solve addition and subtraction problems is only a small part of the assessment process. Assessing understanding is more difficult and time consuming. These NCTM criteria can be implemented as teachers conduct informal and formal assessments, when they listen to students as they interact with each other and with the teacher or as they function in cooperative work groups and use manipulatives to solve problems. If students can explain what they are doing with the manipulatives, they understand the operation or concept under study. Such experiences help to build a strong foundation for future mathematics learning.

Until recently, teaching in mathematics "has rested on the assumption that students must learn lower-order facts and skills before they are able to master higher-order problem-solving and application skills" (Peterson, Fennema, & Carpenter, 1988/1989, p. 43). Research from cognitive psychology suggests that students store knowledge in their heads as a network of concepts (constructs); the metaphor often used is that a child's mind is "like the construction of tinker toys" (Peterson, Fennema, & Carpenter, 1988/1989, p. 43). And it is through this construction process that students make connections between what they already know and what they are learning.

If students construct their own knowledge base, they do not have to be told that two added to seven equals nine; they know it because they have constructed the knowledge base by working with their mental "tinker toys." Through such inventing and constructing, students eventually commit to memory the basic computational skills. Therefore, it is not necessary to teach these skills prior to higher-order mathematical skills; students learn them in relation to and as part of the total problem-solving process (Peterson, Fennema, & Carpenter, 1988/1989).

The six assessment criteria in the *NCTM Standards* remind teachers that assessment and teaching are linked, and that it is important to provide a variety of mathematics situations in which students can demonstrate their level of comprehension and their ability to make connections. When viewing mathematics teaching and assessing as a continuum, teachers look for information about the students' ability to do the following things (National Council of Teachers of Mathematics, 1991, 1995):

■ Use mathematics to solve mathematical problems as well as problems in other areas of study.

■ Communicate ideas using mathematical language.

■ Use mathematics to reason and analyze the situation or problem.

■ Know and understand concepts and procedures.

■ Understand the nature and structure of mathematics.

■ Exhibit an improved attitude toward and confidence in mathematics.

When teachers keep these criteria in mind while planning mathematics experiences, they can observe during instruction how their students approach each math problem, as well as ascertain students' attitudes and levels of confidence. Such observations can help the teacher determine each student's level of mathematical readiness. This readiness can be determined in several areas (Kennedy & Tipps, 1994):

■ pedagogical readiness: the understanding of the instructional materials students use as they learn mathematics

■ maturational or developmental readiness: the student's cognitive level and mental maturity

■ affective readiness: the student's feelings and attitudes about mathematics

■ contextual readiness: the degree to which the student is aware of the uses of mathematics in real life

The following section offers a sampling of assessment techniques that can be implemented to measure student learning in mathematics. Reyes, Suydam, and Lindquist (1995) suggest a variety of ways of gathering information about the students' dispositions, attitudes, and abilities. These ways of obtaining data include observation, interviewing, self-assessments, performance tasks, work samples, portfolios, writings, written tests, and achievement tests.

Observation

Observation is particularly important and helpful when students are working with manipulatives or in groups to solve problems. Suppose that renaming in subtraction is being taught and the teacher uses the base ten blocks. He or she can observe the students as they perform the operations to make sure that they understand the concept and are using the manipulatives to solve the problem. It is also important to listen as the students exchange ideas. Consider the following dialogue between students as they use derived facts to solve this problem:

> Six frogs were sitting on lily pads. Eight more frogs joined them. How many frogs are there then?

Rudy, Denise, Theo, and Sandra each answer *14* almost immediately.

Teacher: How do you know there are 14?

Rudy: Because 6 and 6 is 12, and 2 more is 14.

Denise: Eight and 8 is 16. But this is 8 and 6. That is 2 less, so it's 14.

Theo: Well, I took 1 from the 8 and gave it to the 6. That made 7 and 7, and that's 14.

Sandra: Eight and 2 is 10, and 4 more is 14. (Peterson, Fennema, & Carpenter, 1988/1989, p. 43)

As seen from this example, observation is a natural partner to questioning when the teacher asks, "How do you know there are 14?" As teachers observe students working in cooperative groups, they can call on various members of the group to provide the answer or explain a procedure. This allows the teacher to monitor the learning that is occurring in the group. It also allows for followup on nonverbal expressions of students (such as frowns) to ask why students feel confused.

Interviewing and Self-assessment

A second technique for mathematics assessment, interviewing, combines questioning and observing as the teacher works with individual students to assess their thinking and understanding of mathematical concepts and procedures. Although there is seldom if ever enough time to interview each student each week, over the course of several weeks the interview process provides the opportunity for the teacher to give each student individual attention while the student expresses his/her concerns, fears, and doubts, as well as understanding of mathematical content. Teachers may use inventories for self-assessment purposes; then students reflect on their own abilities in mathematics. Sentence starters such as, "I am a good problem solver because" or "I do not like to try problems that are hard to understand because" encourage students to assess their own ability in mathematics. Students can record their responses in their math logs or journals. These self-assessment inventories also can serve as the basis for an interview.

Performance Tasks and Work Samples

Behaviors that are designed to mirror the real world often involve performance tasks; in Chapter 8 these are referred to as *authentic assessment activities*. These generally require more time for students to grapple with the issues so that they can interpret the information, analyze it, and organize it. Students are engaging in higher-order understandings as they think about models (mathematical structures), systems (mathematics as communication), and real-world applications (mathematical connections).

Performance tasks provide teachers with the opportunity to analyze the strategies students use to solve problems. Work samples are similar to performance tasks but typically require less time and are derived individually. Frequently, work samples include written or daily assignments, projects, and/or other student-generated long-term products.

Portfolios

Along with work samples, students may develop portfolios, as suggested in Chapter 8. Students might include in their mathematics portfolios such items as work samples, problem-solving activities, mathematical writings, projects, and written tests. Portfolios also provide an opportunity to show growth in the areas of using mathematics such as reasoning, communicating, and making connections. By having a collection of mathematics materials that can be revisited over time, students begin to see how much they have learned, and by doing so they become empowered. For many students, "portfolios stimulate thinking and promote independence" (Tierney, 1992, p. 62). Portfolios allow students to engage in self-assessment as they review and reflect on their abilities, strengths, and weaknesses. Because portfolios are personal in nature, students should have the opportunity to select work samples to include. Through this selection process, students develop a greater appreciation of their math ability and of themselves.

Communicating

With the *NCTM Standards* calling for a greater emphasis on communicating in mathematics, student *writing* and *reading* about mathematics are also important assessment strategies. Initially, teachers might have students write about what they understood or did not understand in the lesson. Beyond this beginning effort, students might write letters to friends or parents incorporating something about mathematics; later they might write a poem about mathematics. Writing mathematical stories goes hand in hand with reading stories that have mathematical ideas connected "to the setting, characterization, plot, and the theme of the story—not just a word problem masquerading as a story or a story with some computation problems thrown in" (Borasi, Sheedy, & Siegel, 1990, p. 174). Borasi, Sheedy, and Siegel (1990) recommend stories that require more than one reading and that are a part of the mathematics lesson. From reading, students are in a position to author their own mathematical stories. Such opportunities get students to reason and communicate mathematically, which can then be assessed.

Tests

Finally, two summative procedures provide data for assessing mathematics learning. Teacher-made or textbook-made written tests, when done well, can provide valuable information about students' mathematics ability, not only for grading purposes but also for helping them improve. Most paper-and-pencil tests do not provide teachers with insights as to how students arrived at their solution to problems, but they do provide data as to whether students can perform mathematical operations. Written tests can also be used in combination with calculators and manipulatives to assess student learning. In addition to classroom written tests, there are achievement tests. These tests may be state or nationally developed around a set of objectives (criterion-referenced), or they may be normed at the state or national level to compare student performance against that of other students (norm-referenced), at the same grade level.

Mathematics classrooms in the elementary school are moving away from a testing culture

> where teachers are the sole authority, students work alone, and learning is done for the test—to assessment culture—where teachers and learners collaborate about learning, assessment takes many forms, . . . and distinctions between learning and assessment are blurred. (Seeley, 1994, p. 6)

The challenge for elementary teachers is to design assessment systems in mathematics that are aligned with the district curriculum and the national standards.

SUMMARY

This chapter has described the mathematics curriculum of the elementary school and some of the related issues confronting elementary teachers. Despite the dialogue and reform, teachers are caught in the middle between the focus on memorization and drill of math facts and the more recent emphasis on problem solving and reasoning. Elementary teachers should be aware of the *NCTM Standards* that serve as a framework for guiding and directing elementary mathematics teaching and assessment.

Teachers should focus on the teaching of problem solving, communicating, reasoning, making connections, estimating, number sense and operations, whole-number concepts and operations, whole-number computation, geometry and spatial sense, measurement, statistics and probability, fractions and decimals, and patterns and relationships. These concepts, operations, and skills form the foundation of the elementary mathematics curriculum that helps students make the connections for constructing their own knowledge base. These elements should not be taught in isolation but integrated into other areas of study in the elementary curriculum so that students see the mathematical connections. A list of resources and tools has been provided to assist teachers in planning their elementary mathematics curriculum.

As teachers assess mathematics learning, they should do so within both a formal and an informal context. Informally they can use such procedures as observations, interviews, questioning, performance tasks, and self-assessment inventories. In a more formal way, teachers can use student writing, portfolios, work samples, and tests. The key to assessing students' understanding of mathematics is to use a variety of techniques and procedures to make the best judgment possible about student performance.

Restructuring in mathematics education began in the late 1980s with the publication of the *NCTM Standards*, which served as the beacon for a new approach to and view of mathematics. As technology expands and our world grows more complex, mathematics is critical not only for individual opportunity, but also for our economic well-being as a nation. Elementary teachers need to rethink how they plan, teach, and assess mathematics learning and believe they can make a difference.

> >
< < < < < < < < < < < < < < < < < < < < < < < < < < < < < < < < < < < < < < < < < < < < < < < < < < < < < <

▪ YOUR TURN

1. Obtain a copy of the *NCTM Standards* and become familiar with it. Review the sections that describe the general goals for the elementary curriculum as well as the section on assessment. Make a list of topics to be taught in grades K–6 and the corresponding assessment technique(s).

2. Interview a classroom teacher and discuss the changes that have occurred in the teaching of mathematics during his or her time in teaching. How does he or she personally feel about mathematics in general and teaching the subject? If he or she likes math, why—or why not? How many college courses in math has he or she had?

3. Assess your own feelings about mathematics using the math inventory provided. Use the following rating scale:

    5 = Strongly agree

    4 = Agree

    3 = Not sure/No opinion

    2 = Disagree

    1 = Strongly disagree

1. When working in groups, I am more comfortable when someone else offers to solve the math problem.	5 4 3 2 1
2. I am at ease when asked to solve a problem.	5 4 3 2 1
3. I get excited when given the opportunity to solve a puzzle.	5 4 3 2 1
4. I often feel that I do not have the ability to solve problems, but other people do.	5 4 3 2 1
5. I see the application of math in everyday life.	5 4 3 2 1
6. When asked who is better at math, men or women, I answer men.	5 4 3 2 1
7. I am comfortable when called upon to figure something out.	5 4 3 2 1
8. I panic when the group leader says the dilemma requires math.	5 4 3 2 1
9. I seem to be motivated by getting the right answer.	5 4 3 2 1
10. As a group member, I encourage the group to come up with a variety of ways to solve the problem.	5 4 3 2 1

After responding to these ten items, review your responses. Numbers four and six are stereotypes that people have about math, and teachers should try to dispel these by getting everyone—boys and girls—to be successful in math class. Number nine is another myth about math, always getting the answer right; as much can be learned from engaging in the process as getting the correct answer. Teachers should work at discouraging this stereotype—product and process are both important.

4. Consult the suggested list of math manipulatives and take an inventory of your personal teaching supplies. How many do you already have and which ones do you want to obtain?

■ REFERENCES

Borasi, R., Sheedy, J. R., & Siegel, M. (1990, February). The power of stories in learning mathematics. *Language Arts, 67*(2), 174–184.

Brownell, W. A. (1954, February). The revolution in arithmetic, *The Arithmetic Teacher, 1*(1), 1–5.

Burns, M. (1994, April). Math questions? Ask Marilyn Burns. *Instructor, 103*(8), 39–42.

Costa, A. L. (1989). Re-assessing assessment. Guest Editorial. *Educational Leadership, 46*(7), 2.

Dorward, J., & Archibald, S. (1994, February). Linking teacher interests or backgrounds to real-world experiences for students. *Arithmetic Teacher, 41*(6), 300–303.

Driscoll, M. (1988, January). Transforming the "underachieving" math curriculum. *ASCD Update*, 1–8.

Farivar, S., & Webb, N. M. (1994, May). Group problem solving. *Arithmetic Teacher, 41*(9), 521–525.

Flanders, J. (1987, September). How much of the content in mathematics textbooks is new? *Arithmetic Teacher, 35*(1), 18–23.

Frye, S., & May, L. J. (1991, January). Introducing the mathematics standards in action. *Teaching K–8, 21*(4), 47.

Gailey, S. K. (1993, January). The mathematics children's literature connection. *Arithmetic Teacher, 40*(5), 258–261.

Gibney, T., & Karns, E. (1979, February). Mathematics education—1955–1975: A summary of the findings. *Educational Leadership, 36*(5), 356–359.

Good, T. L., Reys, B. J., Grouws, D. A., & Mulryan, C. M. (1990). Using work-groups in mathematics instruction. *Educational Leadership*, *47*(4), 56–65.

Huchins, P. (1986). *The Doorbell Rang*. New York: Greenwillow.

Jonas, A. (1983). *Round Trip*. New York: Greenwillow.

Kennedy, L. M., & Tipps, S. (1994). *Guiding children's learning of mathematics*. Belmont, CA: Wadsworth.

Kline, M. (1973). *Why Johnny can't add*. New York: St. Martin's Press.

Kuskin, K. (1986). *The Philharmonic Gets Dressed*. New York: HarperCollins.

Lobel, A. (1985). *Frog and Toad Are Friends*. New York: HarperCollins.

Math Curse. (1995). New York: Viking.

Merseth, K. K. (1993). How old is the shepherd? An essay about mathematics education. *Phi Delta Kappan*, *74*(7), 548–554.

National Council of Teachers of Mathematics. (1991). *Curriculum and evaluation standards for school mathematics*. Reston, VA: National Council of Teachers of Mathematics.

National Council of Teachers of Mathematics. (1995). *Curriculum and evaluation standards for school mathematics*. Reston, VA: National Council of Teachers of Mathematics.

National Society for the Study of Education. (1951). *The teaching of arithmetic, Fiftieth Yearbook, Pt. II*. Chicago: University of Chicago Press.

Peterson, L. P., Fennema, E., & Carpenter, T. (1988/1989, December/January). Using knowledge of how students think about mathematics. *Educational Leadership*, *46*(4), 42–46.

Reyes, R. E., Suydam, M. N., & Lindquist, M. M. (1995). *Helping children learn mathematics* (4th ed.). Boston: Allyn & Bacon.

Russo, M. (1992). *Only six more days*. New York: Puffin Books.

Schwartz, J. E., & Riedesel, C. A. (1994). *Essentials of classroom teaching elementary mathematics*. Boston: Allyn & Bacon.

Scieszka, J., & Smith, L. (1995). *Math curse*. New York: Viking.

Seeley, M. M. (1994, October). The mismatch between assessment and grading. *Educational Leadership*, *52*(2), 4–6.

Shepherd, G. D., & Ragan, W. B. (1992). *Modern elementary curriculum* (7th ed.). Fort Worth, TX: Harcourt Brace Jovanovich.

Sowards, G. W., & Scobey, M. (1968). *Curriculum and the elementary teacher*. Belmont, CA: Wadsworth.

Thrailkill, C. (1994, January). Math and literature: A perfect match. *Teaching K–8, 24*(4), 64–65.

Tierney, R. J. (1992, September). Setting a new agenda for assessment. *Learning 92, 21*(2), 62–63.

Whitin, D. J. (1994, January). Literature and mathematics in preschool and primary: The right connection. *Young Children*, *49*(2), 4–11.

Wilson, G. (1950). Arithmetic. *Encyclopedia of educational research* (revised edition). Upper Saddle River, NJ: Merrill/Prentice Hall.

chapter 12

The Social Studies Curriculum

AFTER READING THIS CHAPTER, YOU WILL BE ABLE TO DO THE FOLLOWING:

- Define the terms *social studies* and *social sciences* and explain their implications for curriculum development.

- Discuss the goals of social studies education in the elementary school.

- Identify the various component areas of study in social studies, and describe how connections can be made between and among these areas.

- Describe the various social studies themes for the elementary school curriculum.

- Identify and describe the major issues that influence the teaching of social studies in the elementary school.

- Discuss the use of a thematic integrated approach for teaching social studies.

- Identify major concepts/themes for each of the content areas in social studies.

- Describe management and assessment techniques that are unique to social studies.

- Describe ways of making connections between social studies and other subject areas.

The social studies curriculum provides students in the elementary school with information about cultures, societies, governments, heroes/heroines, villains, revolutions, explorations, and other stories of human interest—both past and present—which tell a compelling story of human civilizations. As people engage in daily activities and interact with each other, common themes for the social studies curriculum emerge and crystallize. Shepherd and Ragan (1992) believe that social studies learning is designed to improve conditions in the classroom, community, state, nation, and the world.

Although the study of people, cultures, and civilizations has traditionally been a part of the elementary social studies curriculum, its importance as an "essential" subject is often questioned. The Report of the National Commission on Social Studies in the Schools (1989) notes that social studies is a part of the elementary curriculum because we expect our children to understand and participate effectively as citizens in a world that is becoming increasingly complex. Teachers recognize the need to teach children about their culture, but when teachers feel pressured to focus on reading, writing, and mathematics, as emphasized on achievement tests, then social studies is frequently pushed to the bottom of the curriculum and remains there until the teacher feels that there is more time.

In addition to the lack of emphasis on the social studies curriculum, another common concern regarding this area is that when it is taught, students encounter a dull and lifeless area of study because most of their learning comes from reading textbooks or other printed material. Such experiences are without personal involvement and devoid of human interest, and, as Hakim (1993) says, rarely do you find a "child sneaking a few more minutes reading a textbook under the covers at night" (p. 6). She is right. Even with the colorful packaging of these textbooks, the social studies curriculum still has the reputation of being boring and often meaningless to students—not because of the information but because of the way it is taught and the ancillary materials that are used. Such an approach needs to change. What elementary students are learning in social studies often seems detached and unlike what they read in the newspaper, see on television, and/or encounter on a daily basis. The social studies curriculum has to better reflect what students experience every day—current events, cultural and gender bias, and political elections, for example.

This curriculum area should be exciting and relevant because it is most of all a story of people—where they live, how they interact with each other, how they make a living, and their customs and religions. With such a story line, the social studies curriculum should be presented in a dynamic way that relates these concepts to the everyday lives of elementary students. As Shepherd and Ragan (1992) note,

> the school . . . not only provides opportunities for students to acquire useful information; it also provides a laboratory for social living in which [students] have opportunities to develop their own potentialities and to contribute their maximum efforts to group living. (p. 408)

This chapter provides an overview of the social studies curriculum in the elementary school, along with a glimpse of how it might be modified. It provides a case for making the social studies curriculum a more viable area of study, as a means of developing critical thinking skills. The chapter begins with a rationale for teaching social studies and a brief definition and description of this curriculum area in the elementary school. The next section discusses contemporary issues related to teaching social studies, such as developing historical, social, and global literacy, and using a thematic integrated approach.

In addition, the general goals for teaching social studies will be presented along with a scope and sequence of key concepts for history, geography, economics, and civics. The chapter includes a section on classroom management and assessment related to teaching social studies in the elementary school and concludes with a section on making connections to other curriculum areas.

RETHINKING THE SOCIAL STUDIES CURRICULUM

The social studies curriculum has been recognized as one of the oldest and most respected disciplines of scholarship and represents a rich array of human activity (Beckner & Cornett, 1972). Beard (1938) describes the social studies curriculum as a creation of rich stories that should help students be "equipped with practical knowledge and inspired by ideals so that they can make their way and fulfill their mission in a changing society which is part of a complex world" (p. 179). This has long been a stated goal of the social studies curriculum, but in reality educators tend to give lip-service to this goal rather than working to fulfill its potential.

The social studies curriculum often lacks continuity and integrity as an area of study, even though the goal(s) may be noble. Even when using the most recently published social studies textbook and infusing current topics into the curriculum, teachers are more likely to include seasonal topics (for example, Thanksgiving in the fall and presidents in February) in isolated and somewhat superficial ways. Moreover, these same seasonal topics are repeated year after year without any effort to teach them in a coherent, spiral fashion. Chris, the "Voice of Experience" for this chapter, describes his social studies teaching experience, which emphasizes a seasonal approach and reflects on how that could be changed.

 ## Voice of Experience

In his first year of teaching, Chris remembers falling into the trap of teaching social studies as he remembered how he was taught—seasonal topics were included and the focus was on state history (flag, bird, flower, motto, heroes/heroines, and so on). Chris tells his intern teacher, "In the fall, for example, rather than using a social studies theme or major concept to organize the names, dates, and places, I interjected topics related to holidays as they came along. For example, for Columbus Day, 'discovery' was the focus along with the three ships. For Thanksgiving, the emphasis was on Indians, Pilgrims, and the first Thanksgiving (reading about Pocahontas was a must), and in December the emphasis was on Christmas Around the World and a study of various cultural traditions. In January, the focus was on Martin Luther King Day and black history. In February, the presidents (Washington and Lincoln) took center stage. I also introduced concepts such as neighborhood, city, state, and nation at other times of the year. Seldom, if ever, did I present a thematic integrated social studies unit."

Now, after gaining confidence along with attending several staff-development sessions on teaching social studies, Chris says he is spending more time developing his social studies curriculum around themes. Just recently, he tells his intern teacher, "I taught a unit on 'Consumerism,' another on 'Taking a Trip to Mexico,' and a third on 'Occupations and Careers.' I couldn't believe how my students worked together toward a common end and developed a product, but most importantly, they saw meaning in what they were doing."

Chris has realized that giving the social studies curriculum continuity and integrity as well as making it relevant does not always mean relating it to a holiday or a special event; it means planning and implementing a series of lessons (units) that have something in common and are of interest to the students, while at the same time using a variety of teaching strategies. When approached from this perspective, social studies takes on a whole new meaning and becomes fun and relevant for both students and teacher.

DEFINITIONS AND GOALS

Participation as a competent member of one's culture is considered essential to functioning in a complex world. Yet, as Lemlech (1994) notes, "Children come to school knowing very little about people in their own society or elsewhere. They are to some degree ignorant of . . . social institutions, customs, and values" (p. 274). Social studies has been responsible for helping children learn about their culture and how to function as a member of society. What is social studies?

The phrase *social studies* is used to describe a broad field of study in the elementary school. Members of the National Commission on Social Studies (1989) describe this area as a multidisciplinary study of humankind that provides a bridge to understanding the values and concerns of society. Barr, Barth, and Shermis (1977) define *social studies* as the "integration of experience and knowledge concerning human relations" (p. 69). Through social studies, students come to understand how a dynamic society is governed and how its affairs are conducted (Bragaw & Hartoonian, 1988). When one hears the phrase *social studies*, often history comes to mind, but social studies is much more than history. It includes geography, economics, government, anthropology, and sociology. Even though there are interrelationships between and among all of these areas, many are taught as discrete subjects or content in the elementary school, and for the most part history or geography is taught during the time scheduled for social studies. For the purpose of this book, content from the areas of history, geography, economics, and civics/government will be presented.

This broad field of study provides a natural framework for integrating these areas of study into a coherent mosaic that connects discrete information. Such a view of curriculum is constructivist in nature; according to Beane (1991), this creates meaning for students and fosters critical thinking. Solomon's research (1987) suggests that social studies can also be used to improve metacognition and intellectual tasks (e.g., comprehension, communication, and decision making).

In addition, the integration of information gives students and teachers an opportunity to plan a program in which the barriers between areas of study begin to dissolve and the possibilities for experiencing real-life situations are greatly increased. Such an approach is knowledge-rich because events, historical figures, and the societal conditions are explained not only in greater depth but in a context that is meaningful in relation to contemporary living.

Figure 12-1 illustrates the areas of study included within the social studies curriculum and shows the common core of understandings and skills that are shared and promoted. Whether the emphasis is on government (civics education), economics, geography, history, anthropology, and/or sociology, literacy skills are stressed, along with critical thinking and research skills. Other common cores of understanding include global awareness, geographic literacy, time and the place within historical contexts, and self and others. All the areas of study in social studies work toward developing and refining a common map of understandings, content, and skills.

Goals and Standards of Social Studies Education

The social studies curriculum has been much maligned over the past several decades. In the late 1980s, the Bradley Commission on History in the Schools (1988) released guidelines that included essential topics, themes, and skills. The Bradley Commission report served as a benchmark for social studies and encouraged teachers to use different approaches in order to better tell the story of people.

More recently, the thematic strands proposed by the National Council for the Social Studies (NCSS) (1994) have been discussed as a way of achieving the desired goals and performance expectations for the K–12 social studies curriculum. The NCSS strands serve as the organizing themes for content and skills at each grade level. The themes include the following areas:

- Culture
- Time, Continuity, & Change
- People, Places, & Environments
- Individual Development & Identity
- Individuals, Groups, & Institutions
- Power, Authority, & Governance
- Production, Distribution, & Consumption
- Science, Technology, & Society
- Global Connections
- Civil Ideals & Practices

These ten themes are shared by areas of study (e.g. history, economics, etc.) in the social studies curriculum and serve to unify the curriculum in a common pursuit of understanding about the world. For example, in discussing the theme "individuals, groups, and institutions," the teacher can include government concepts by talking about political parties and can also include geography by discussing local elections and sociology by identifying various groups that influence elections. As these themes are discussed and

FIGURE 12-1   Social Studies Curriculum: Areas of Study

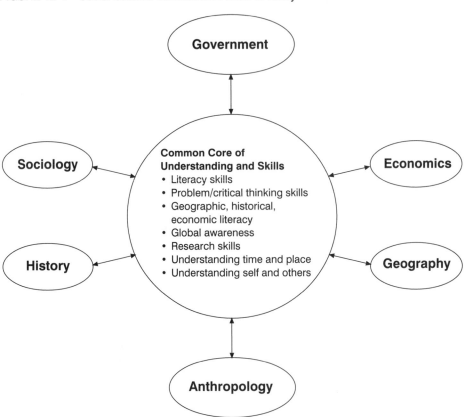

articulated, the goals for the social studies curriculum become more clearly defined.

A variety of goals of the social studies curriculum have been proposed by various groups. The following is a composite list of social studies goals:

■ providing a collective memory of our democratic heritage

■ developing an understanding of the moral value of our nation's social, political, and economic rights as well as obligations

■ studying the themes of continuity and change

■ providing a chronicle of dramatic events in our interdependent world

■ studying causes, issues, and consequences

■ developing an understanding of the complexity of human endeavors

■ taking students on a trip around the world

Depending on state and local mandates, different goals and content are emphasized. Some districts or school campuses place more emphasis on preparing students to be caring and responsible citizens in their community, state, and nation; helping them develop an awareness of their own identity and self-concept; motivating them to learn more about what shapes their world; and helping them become problem solvers and decision makers (Turner, 1994; Schillings, 1994). When adopting the NCSS themes, the goal of the social studies curriculum is to help elementary students develop decision-making skills as they assume their adult roles.

In the elementary school, social studies provides students the opportunity to travel to other places to encounter people of other cultures. It is the trip that can make social studies fascinating and intriguing and take students to different places to meet people they might never otherwise have an opportunity to meet in their lives. Taking students on this journey means getting their attention and helping them develop a global perspective; such a perspective helps them develop a sense of being a citizen of the world.

ISSUES IN THE SOCIAL STUDIES CURRICULUM

As teachers plan and implement the social studies curriculum in the elementary school, they are confronted with several issues that will shape teaching and learning. One of the major issues that social studies educators are addressing involves the tradition from which the social studies curriculum is derived and taught, including the traditions of citizenship training, the social sciences, and reflective inquiry. Another issue is social studies literacy, which incorporates problem-solving and critical-thinking skills within the elementary curriculum. A third issue that social studies educators are focusing on is integration of content using common themes to promote an increased understanding of the interrelatedness that exists within the social studies curriculum.

Traditions

Historically, the first issue in teaching social studies is that it has been taught from one of three main traditions or perspectives: citizenship training, social science content, or reflective inquiry (Barr, Barth, & Shermis, 1977). The tradition of *citizenship* promotes the development of values related to being a good citizen, and citizenship has been the main thrust and justification of the social studies curriculum for a long time. The second tradition, social studies as *social science,* emphasizes a process orientation as the way to understand key concepts and content. For example, students participate in class elections as they learn about the process of democracy. The third tradition, social studies as *reflective inquiry,* portrays social studies as a means of gathering new information and using these data to solve problems. Within this tradition, students research some problem or issue within their community as they seek to address and attempt to solve the problem.

We suggest a fourth perspective or tradition that can be used to teach social studies: *integrated inquiry.* Integrated inquiry promotes the use of thematic teaching coupled with inquiry. By linking a thematic perspective with learning by doing, the collective knowledge of what is being studied from all the areas becomes more apparent. Each of these traditions has a purpose, method, and content (see Figure 12-2).

Integrated inquiry is compatible with the NCSS recommendations, which emphasize teaching social studies using all areas of study and in a way that gets students to be aware of their own humanity (Schillings, 1994).

Social Studies Literacy

A second issue that social studies educators are concerned about is social studies literacy, which emphasizes problem-solving and critical-thinking skills. In his book, *Cultural Literacy*, Hirsch (1987) describes culturally literate students as those who have the basic information about the modern world, the major domains of human activity, and a concept of civilization both modern and ancient. Cultural literacy is broad in scope, goes beyond the proliferation of information, and does not pit one area of study against the other; it attempts to achieve academic and civic competency. Social studies literacy is not confined to specific subjects but is learned within the global

FIGURE 12-2   Four Traditions of the Social Studies Curriculum

	Social Studies as Citizenship	Social Studies as Social Science	Social Studies as Reflective Inquiry	Social Studies as Integrated Inquiry
Purpose	Social studies promoted as a way of developing a values framework for good citizenship	Social studies promoted by mastering social science concepts, processes, and problems	Social studies promoted through the process of inquiry which generates knowledge for decision making and problem solving	Social studies promoted as an interdisciplinary process involving multiple skills and concepts in interactive, integrated ways rather than as isolated, unique areas
Method	Transmission of concepts and values through lecture, recitation, questions, and readings	Discovering, gathering, and verifying information for each of the social sciences	Reflective inquiry—identifying problems and responding to situations in a structured, disciplined way	Cooperative interaction to promote understanding of concepts from multiple perspectives, based on interdisciplinary perspectives
Content	Selected by teacher and other authorities to illustrate the values, beliefs, functions, and attitudes of good citizens	The body of knowledge, the structure of that knowledge, processes, and problems inherent in each social science area	Social problems, dilemmas, or situations that can be analyzed on an individual and collective level using individual needs, interests, and experiences	Interdisciplinary concepts that can be integrated into thematic concerns and involve not only the individual's knowledge and needs, but the collective knowledge of the culture-thematic integrated units

Source: Adapted from *Defining the Social Studies, Bulletin #51* by R. D. Barr, J. L. Barth, & D. S. Shermis, 1977, p. 67, Washington, DC: National Council for the Social Studies; and "Social Sciences Included in the Social Studies," by G. S. Morrison, 1993, in *Contemporary Curriculum K–8*, p. 265, Boston: Allyn & Bacon.

context of thematic integrated studies. Taking students on a trip around the world helps them not only examine their own locale but also address the issue of place in history, as well as the economics of the time, and the benefits and limitations of geography. When geographic literacy skills are increased, students' understanding of history increases as well. There is a cause-and-effect relationship: social studies learning does not take place in isolation.

Thematic Integration of Content

Thematic integrated teaching is a third issue (see Chapter 6). Using such an approach to teaching social studies is like working a jigsaw puzzle; it gives meaning to the individual pieces of the puzzle, whether studying about the resources in the state of Maine, the families in India, the farms in Australia, and/or the exports from Argentina (Beane, 1991). Each of these studies makes sense as part of a greater whole called the social studies curriculum.

The central focus of the NCSS recommendations is a "coordinated, systematic study drawing upon such disciplines as anthropology, archeology, economics, geography, history, law, philosophy, political science, psychology, religion, and sociology, as well as appropriate content from humanities, mathematics, and natural sciences" (Schillings, 1994, p. 199). For example, a unit called "Celebrating Diversity: Immigration to the United States" provides a focus for integrating all areas including history, geography, anthropology, economics, civics, and sociology. Figure 12-3 presents a visual description of how each area of the social studies relates to this theme. By using such an approach, the social studies curriculum becomes more interactive and illustrates the complementary nature of each area. This integrative curriculum design goes beyond the linear and sequential model, which often is associated with the social studies curriculum.

Figure 12-3 identifies the areas of study along with the topics and concepts in each area

that can be integrated into a common social studies theme such as "Celebrating Diversity: Immigration to the United States." Although the areas of sociology, anthropology, and government are often not identified in the elementary social studies curriculum per se, such concepts as the patterns of interaction, culture, ethnicity, and bias can be addressed within this thematic approach. For example, in history, the events related to immigration might include the when, where, why, and who of the people involved. The geographic concepts of time, place, cause and effect of interactions, and movement are nested in the historical context of the theme of immigration. To illustrate this, teachers can have students put a pin on a world map indicating the "home country" of their ancestors and build a composite picture of the world in their classrooms. To help students understand the democratic process and procedures, such topics as choice, human dignity, and diversity can be studied as they relate to the politics of the United States.

By using such an integrated approach, social studies civics education helps students understand what coming to the United States meant to these immigrants. With the reopening of Ellis Island in New York Harbor in 1990, descendants and others have an opportunity to reflect on the experiences of 12 million immigrants when they walked onto American soil between 1892 and 1954. As students revisit this time in our history, they learn that immigrants wore identification tags and moved into the Main Building to be processed. In addition, these newcomers would hear a voice shouting, "Put your luggage here. Men this way. Women this way" (Kinney, 1990, p. 27). America's gateway, now a National Park Service museum, includes pictures of people with their possessions, the Registry Room, and long lines as well as displays to recreate these decades when "we came to America . . . and Ellis Island reopen[ed] and [brought] our history back to life" (Kinney, 1990, p. 26).

Along with showing how people made a living, the unit provides insight into social interac-

FIGURE 12-3   Thematic Integrated Approach to the Social Studies Curriculum

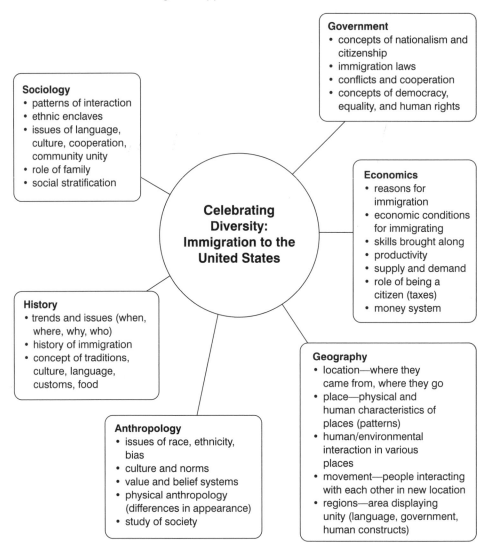

Government
- concepts of nationalism and citizenship
- immigration laws
- conflicts and cooperation
- concepts of democracy, equality, and human rights

Sociology
- patterns of interaction
- ethnic enclaves
- issues of language, culture, cooperation, community unity
- role of family
- social stratification

Celebrating Diversity: Immigration to the United States

Economics
- reasons for immigration
- economic conditions for immigrating
- skills brought along
- productivity
- supply and demand
- role of being a citizen (taxes)
- money system

History
- trends and issues (when, where, why, who)
- history of immigration
- concept of traditions, culture, language, customs, food

Geography
- location—where they came from, where they go
- place—physical and human characteristics of places (patterns)
- human/environmental interaction in various places
- movement—people interacting with each other in new location
- regions—area displaying unity (language, government, human constructs)

Anthropology
- issues of race, ethnicity, bias
- culture and norms
- value and belief systems
- physical anthropology (differences in appearance)
- study of society

tions. Responding to such questions as *What impact did immigrants have on the economy?* and *What was their role in building the local neighborhood businesses?* helps students understand the human dimension of immigration.

To take this theme of "Celebrating Diversity" one step further, the teacher might survey the class and find out what different cultural groups are represented. For example, the Hispanic Amer-

ican students might be interested in where most Hispanics live in the United States, their reasons for coming to America, and the influences they have had on the English language and American food, entertainment, ranching, and the arts. They may also be interested in knowing who the outstanding Hispanic Americans are and in learning more about the origin of their music, games children play, and customs. In addition, students can read biographies about these individuals and do research related to their areas of interest.

By using a thematic integrated approach in social studies, a more complete picture emerges, one more powerful in portraying the current human condition as well as possibilities for the future. By linking all of the areas within the social studies curriculum, this approach serves as a bridge from one island of specific information to the next by linking concepts of culture, people, places, events, and conditions. The major objective of a thematic, integrated approach is to increase social studies literacy—the historical, geographical, economic, political, social, and cultural understanding of each student, as well to model the interrelatedness of the content that students are learning.

Integrating the curriculum using themes completes the social studies portrait in a way that is not possible when each area is studied as an individual jigsaw puzzle piece. Such an approach requires teachers and students to work together (Fredericks, Meinbach, & Rothlein, 1993; Frazee & Rudnitski, 1995). For Beane (1991), integration communicates wholeness and gets students and teachers involved with meaningful experiences and interesting questions. Most importantly, an integrative social studies curriculum is organized around provocative and rich themes that draw from many sources and have the ultimate objective of getting students to examine issues generated from these themes (Beane, 1991; National Council for the Social Studies, 1994). (A sample thematic integrated unit on Antarctica that includes numerous subject areas for the third grade is included in Chapter 6.)

CONTENT AREAS OF THE SOCIAL STUDIES CURRICULUM

Teachers may encounter another term associated with the social studies curriculum. The phrase *social sciences* is often used to describe a perspective that includes several areas of study that critically examine people—their development, behavior, and ways of interacting. Although the term *social sciences* is broader in scope than *social studies* because it may include not only areas of the humanities but also the areas of the natural sciences and mathematics, both views lend themselves to a thematic integrated approach.

Many elementary teachers use what is called the *expanding horizon approach* to teach social studies. This approach begins in the primary grades (K–3) with units that focus on the family and local community and expands to include states in the United States and countries around the world for students in the intermediate grades (4–6). Crabtree (1989) argues that the expanding horizon approach, although popular in the elementary school, is not supported in cognitive psychology and actually may limit the development of thought and feelings in students.

There are other ways to organize the social studies curriculum. The following scope and sequence is one example:

- Historical data about family, community, state, nation, and world
- Geography about the local neighborhood, community, state, nation, and the world
- Economic systems and operations
- Social institutions and political processes of local, state, and national government
- Personal, social, and civic responsibilities
- Sociological, psychological, and cultural factors affecting human behavior
- Social interaction skills

The scope is broad—intentionally so. This scope and sequence along with the proposed NCSS themes serve as the impetus for the elementary social studies curriculum. These topics or themes become important as they help to provide insight about people, social institutions, and/or the culture of a neighborhood, a state, a region, or a nation.

The next section addresses the important concepts of each of the major areas within social studies, describes the contributions of each area as it relates to the totality of the social studies curriculum, and presents various approaches used to teach the concepts and skills. History, geography, economics, and civics (government) are presented in most detail because they generally receive the most attention in the elementary school.

History

Questions related to how events occurred, why they occurred, and how they influenced other events continue to shape the teaching of history. Turner (1994) defines history as the "study of the past, or at least the surviving record of the past" (p. 65). Through simulations, trips across the continent via computer software, and reading biographies, diaries, and other written accounts, students come to examine history from a natural vantage point of human interest.

The National Center for History in the Schools (1994) has published *National Standards for History: Expanding Children's World in Time and Space*, for grades K–4 and *National Standards for United States History: Exploring the American Experience*, for grades 5–12. The K–4 standards include the following topics:

Standard 1: Family life now and in the recent past; family life in various places long ago

Standard 2: History of students' local community and how communities in North America varied long ago

Standard 3: The people, events, problems, and ideas that created the history of their state

Standard 4: How democratic values came to be, and how they have been exemplified by people, events, and symbols

Standard 5: The causes and nature of various movements of large groups of people into and within the United States, now and long ago

Standard 6: Regional folklore and cultural contributions that helped to form our national heritage

Standard 7: Selected attributes and historical developments of various societies in Africa, the Americas, Asia, and Europe

Standard 8: Major discoveries in science and technology, their social and economic effects, scientists and inventors from many groups, and regions responsible for them

The standards for grades 5–12 include the following topics as they relate to the American experience:

Standard 1: Chronological thinking

Standard 2: Historical comprehension

Standard 3: Historical analysis and interpretation

Standard 4: Historical research capabilities

Standard 5: Historical issues—analysis and decision making

These history standards offer a reconceptualized scope and sequence for teaching the social studies in the elementary grades and provide a framework for unifying the history curriculum. Using these standards, elementary students explore their own immediate area and the world beyond.

Currently, the textbook serves as the primary resource for teaching history in the elementary school. Although common, such a practice often neglects contemporary history-making events (Willis, 1990), and according to Tucker (as reported in Willis, 1990), this is a great omission; contemporary issues in social studies provide the opportunity for interest and relevance in the curriculum. However, there are many reasons for omitting contemporary national and world events from the social studies curriculum (Willis, 1990):

■ running out of time before reaching the present

■ covering district-prescribed objectives and content that excludes recent world events

■ teaching current events is a burden on the teacher, who is without time to gather background information

■ teaching contemporary content is controversial

By implementing an integrated thematic approach, teachers can minimize these limitations. It is a matter of reorganizing, not necessarily adding to, the existing social studies curriculum. For example, current events can be integrated where appropriate into topics/themes of study so that students have opportunities to make historical parallels.

Traditionally, direct instruction has been the major instructional strategy used to teach history, focusing on facts such as names, dates, and places. Freire (1983) describes this approach as the "banking" method of teaching social studies—making deposits in the heads of students. Wassermann (1992) offers an alternative, suggesting that the teaching of history can be more effective with the use of case studies. By using cases, teachers can emphasize the major concepts and rely on the strategy of "play-debrief-replay." Students learn to treat thinking as an enjoyable enterprise, and teachers help to make history and "all related issues of the social [studies] meaningful to students" (Wassermann, 1992, p. 801). For example, in learning about Native Americans of the Southwest, students work in groups, and each group is given a "case study," or story, of one of the major pueblos. During the "play" portion of instruction, members of the group read and discuss the printed material provided. The "debriefing" consists of each group reporting to the total class about their pueblo; some may role play what they have read.

Finally, during the "replay," the students individually recall and tell one of the stories studied.

The challenge for elementary teachers is to make events of the past relevant to the events of today. Students in elementary school, particularly those in the primary grades, tend to focus on the present, the now. To make events of the past meaningful, linkages need to be established. Once the "Aha!" takes place, students begin to find those people, events, and/or times fascinating, which helps them understand history better. In conclusion, history plays a key role within the social studies curriculum by providing the context in which events take place—it sets the stage.

Geography

Too often geography has been synonymous with the study of maps and globes; geography is more than finding the location of cities, mountain ranges, and the like. Geography is analysis, problem solving, critical evaluation, decision making, and assessment of data (Collins, 1994). Geography involves problem solving when students are given a situation and they have to analyze the role or impact of the physical environment. For example, when studying westward expansion, students have to consider the effects of the changing environment on the migration of settlers. To help students conceptualize the impact of geography on migration, students can be presented with questions like, "What if the west and east coasts of the United States were reversed?" (Reinhartz & Reinhartz, 1992). "What impact would this reversal have had on the settlers as they moved west?" In order to answer these questions, students have to consider climate, travel conditions, supplies needed, the terrain (maps, drawings), and so on.

Basic to geographic literacy is knowledge about the world, its people, and geographically related problems such as the Ebola virus. Geography provides the "place" for the social studies curriculum. An understanding of the place or geographical setting is key to understanding events that have taken place in a specific location and the conditions that led to decisions that were made.

To help elementary teachers present geographic concepts, a framework has been developed to study geography using five fundamental themes: location, place, human-environment interactions, movement, and regions. These themes form an infrastructure for answering such questions as

■ Where is it?

■ What is it like?

■ What shapes the landscape?

■ How do people and products stay in touch?

■ How do areas within areas develop their uniqueness?

Each of the themes can be expanded to provide for a better understanding of their use in the elementary school.

■ *Location* is a beginning point for responding to the question, Where is something? Where is Canada, the Mississippi River, the Great Lakes, the state of Oregon? According to the *Guidelines for Geographic Education* (1984) and *Geography for Life: National Geography Standards* (1994), the concept of absolute and relative location is a way of describing places and the position of people on Earth's surface. This theme helps to accurately pinpoint the precise place of a country, state, river, or other feature using latitude and longitude on the globe. Using the mathematical grid system of latitude and longitude provides the "global address" for finding a location.

■ *Place* has physical and human characteristics that give it uniqueness. The physical characteristics refer to the geological, atmospheric, and biological processes that result in the type of landforms, rivers, climate, vegetation, and animal life that inhabit the place: "All places on Earth have distinctive tangible and intangible characteristics that give them

meaning and character and distinguish them from other places. Geographers generally describe places by their physical or human characteristics" (Joint Committee on Geographic Education, 1984, p. 4). The human characteristics of place include religion, values, customs, and traditions. There are many places students read about, or experience vicariously or firsthand—desert, wetlands, forest, seashore, or islands. A place has many natural qualities that separate it from other places; these qualities give each place its individual personality.

■ *Human/environment interactions* is defined as the advantages and disadvantages of a place for human settlement. The cultural and physical relationships of a place change over time as the people modify the natural environment. For example, by taking a historical approach to understanding this theme, the Pueblo Indians developed a society that farmed the arid Southwest, Hispanics and Anglo settlers developed the mining industry along with ranching, and today this area is home to a tourist industry because of the big sky and space (Joint Committee on Geographic Education, 1984).

■ *Movement* demonstrates that people move and so do goods and services. Take the apple that is grown in Washington state; it travels or moves several hundred miles to markets in Texas, Louisiana, and Florida. "Geography helps to explain varied patterns in the movement of people, ideas, and materials" (Joint Committee on Geographic Education, 1984, p. 7).

■ *Regions* are the basic units of geographic study because they represent the totality of place, relationships, and movement. A region is defined by its characteristics—language, governmental structure, landforms, and how these interact in a particular place. When focusing on the Northeast, characteristics of this region include deciduous forests with particular animal and plant life, along with four distinct seasons or climatic conditions that include a warm, humid summer; cool, rainy fall; cold winter with some snow; and a cool, crisp spring. This region has particular industries, political views, and language with a regional accent.

In addition to these five fundamental themes, eighteen national geography standards have been drafted and grouped together under a framework of six essential elements (and are currently undergoing modification) (Bednarz, 1994):

- Seeing the world in spatial terms
- Places and regions
- Physical systems
- Human systems
- Environment and society
- Applying geography

According to Bednarz (1994), "the [1994] Standards see the essential elements as going beyond the Five Fundamental Themes" (p. 105). The eighteen geography standards are not intended to serve as an instructional strategy for teaching geography, as are the five themes, though both offer ways to improve the quality of geography instruction in the elementary school. The following major concepts are included in the elementary geography curriculum (Bednarz, 1994):

- Map—thematic, flat, and other types—and globe studies
- Scales on maps to measure area and distance
- Map features—symbols, patterns, relationships—on and across maps
- Relative location
- Reading and interpreting graphs, charts, and tables
- Recognizing that Earth is divided into hemispheres
- Regions are the basic spatial units for geographic analysis

Once thought of as primarily involving memorization of capitals, rivers, oceans, and continents, geography can provide elementary students with a sense of their place on Earth. Geographic literacy is essential if students are to assume their role of citizens, not only at home, but also in the world.

Economics

In the elementary school, the study of economics focuses mostly on consumerism and on goods and services, as well as how goods are produced and how they are distributed in society and the world. This approach to the study of economics is called *economic analysis* (Turner, 1994). In addition to studying how goods and services are produced, students study how different economic systems work and ways to make systems better (Hansen, 1989). Such concepts as scarcity, opportunity cost, productivity, exchange, money, interdependence, supply and demand, banking skills, credit, and the role of government are included. Also, students become aware of economic systems that have social implications and include such terms as *economic growth*, *economic efficiency*, *security*, *stability*, *equity*, and *freedom* (Savage & Armstrong, 1996). Students develop skills in reading and interpreting tables, charts, and graphs.

Learning these concepts and using these skills are best accomplished when themes or topics are integrated into the total social studies curriculum. As students problem solve and make economic decisions, they experience the impact of these decisions on the social and political situation of the time. For example, when students set up a grocery store to purchase food with play money, they are required to make choices regarding purchasing products and staying within their financial means. Students may be asked to make a gift list from various catalogs with a limited amount of money to spend, which requires them to make decisions. Such activities give students an opportunity to experience economics firsthand.

Civics/Government

The study of politics, government, policy, and power is essential for students before they assume their future role as voting citizens. These concepts are part of civics education and are essential components of the governing process (Turner, 1994). "Our day-to-day lives, the quality of our communities, the health, prosperity, and safety of our nation, . . . our very continuation as a species are affected by politics" (Brody, 1989, p. 59). Brody (1989) goes on to say that elementary students should learn about "the realities of political life as well as [being exposed] to the cultural ideals of American democracy" (p. 60). The primary objective of government within the social studies curriculum is to help students learn about democracy and about being active citizens and participating in a free society. As students study the legislative, judicial, and executive branches of government, they learn about political parties, issues related to voting, pressure groups, the courts, and the duties of the president and other elected officials. As part of this study, students use original documents, analyze court cases, and read the laws passed. Turner (1994) notes that throughout the elementary grades, students develop "numerous political concepts including right and wrong, justice, authority, power, security, and politics" (p. 70).

These areas of study (history, geography, economics, and government) form a synergistic relationship in the social studies curriculum. Together they are more powerful and meaningful than each is individually. They form a coherent whole that, when taught thematically, provides a comprehensive picture of the totality of the social studies curriculum.

Resources and Tools for Teaching in the Social Studies Curriculum

Figure 12-4 provides a list of resources and tools that teachers can use to extend the textbook. These materials range from examples of children's literature that focus on different cultures, explorers, and historical biographies to computer programs that reinforce social studies concepts. These resources help students and teachers to extend the walls of their classroom to experience other lands and people.

MANAGING AND ASSESSING STUDENTS IN THE SOCIAL STUDIES CLASSROOM

The way teachers organize and manage the social studies classroom is significant as they consider the placement of materials and movement of students to facilitate the teaching-learning environment. Effective classroom management requires systematic planning by teachers who make conscious decisions regarding how the space, materials, and students are managed (Savage & Armstrong, 1996).

Managing a social studies classroom means establishing an environment that promotes learning and communicates that it is a safe place to be. Savage and Armstrong (1996) say that the physical organization creates a special "ambience." In this context, *ambience* refers to the character of the classroom: it is the general impression a student gets from the classroom. A positive ambience communicates warmth, excitement, a general impression of pleasantness, and safety as students study and learn about historical, geographical, economic, and civic issues using a variety of resources, equipment, software, and materials.

Creating a positive ambience for a unit on Japan means preparing centers that help students learn about that country. For example, the teacher might include one center focusing on language, another on food and customs, and a third on Japan's history and its role in the world economy. As the students walk into the classroom, the teacher gives them an airline ticket to Japan, and as they board the airplane Japanese music is playing to set the "tone" for the unit.

FIGURE 12-4   Teaching Resources and Tools for Social Studies

Type/Title	Description	Grade Level(s)	Publisher/ Supplier
I. Children's Literature			
Abuelita's Paradise (1992) Carmen Nodar with illustrations Diane Paterson	Memorable events of a grandmother and her life in Puerto Rico. Spanish words throughout the story; engages both English and Spanish readers.	K–3	Albert Whitman & Company 6340 Oakton Street Morton Grove, IL 60053 (800)255-7675
Afro-Bets ABC Book (1987) C. W. Hudson	Objects associated with each letter of the alphabet. For letter K, the objects include *kitten, keys,* and Kente cloth.	1–2	Just Us Books 356 Glenwood Avenue East Orange, NJ 07017 Fax (201)677-7570
C is for Curious: An ABC of Feelings (1990) W. Hubbard	Explores feelings in a variety of ways using art and colors to provoke discussions.	1–6	Chronicle 275 Fifth Street San Francisco, CA 94103 (415)777-7240
Celebrate America (1994) N. Panzer	Poems written during a specific time frame or focused on a specific theme. Art work accompanying the poems make a powerful blending of these two forms of art.	3–6	Hyperion Books for Children A Walt Disney Co. 114 Fifth Avenue New York, NY 10016 (800) 343-9204
Chicken Sunday (1992) Patricia Polacco	Series of lessons from generosity and tolerance to sensitivity; involves young children and older members of the community.	Pre-K–3	Philomel Books The Putnam Publ. Group 200 Madison Avenue New York, NY 10016 (800)631-8571
Grandfather's Journey (1993) Allen Say	1994 Caldecott Medal-winner retells the story of the Say's Japanese grandfather and the impact of immigration to the U.S. and his return to Japan. It is a story of love between family members, national pride, and the process of acculturation.	K–3	Houghton Mifflin Company One Beacon Street Boston, MA 02108 (800)225-3362

FIGURE 12-4, *continued*

Type/Title	Description	Grade Level(s)	Publisher/ Supplier
I. Children's Literature (continued)			
Marco Polo (1977) G. P. Ceserani	Adventurous journey of Marco Polo offers an opportunity to experience early forms of transportation and communication. Detailed color drawings add to the interesting travel log.	4–6	G. P. Putnam's Sons 200 Madison Avenue New York, NY 10016 (800)631-8571
Lewis and Clark: Explorers of the American West (1994) Steven Kroll, illustrated by Richard Williams	Good documentary picture book includes detailed paintings illustrating the explorations of Lewis and Clark, 1804–1806.	4–6	Holiday House 18 E. 53rd Street New York, NY 10022
A Passion for Danger: Nansen's Arctic Adventures (1994) Francine Jacobs	Photographs, prints, and maps of the journey of a Norwegian, Fridtj of Nansen, to unexplored locations in the world.	1–6	The Putnam Publ. Group 200 Madison Avenue New York, NY 10016 (800)631-8571
Peace and Bread: The Story of Jane Addams (1993) Stephanie Sammartino McPherson	Story of Jane Addams who lived in the late nineteenth century, a leading voice against war. Especially warm and inspirational.	4+	Carolrhoda Books 241 First Ave. No. Minneapolis, MN 55401 (800)328-4929
Potluck (1991) A. Shelly	Focus on food from various cultures. Presents children in costumes and uses alliteration to join Apho and Betty in their celebration.	1–4	Orchard Books Div. of Franklin Watts, Inc. 95 Madison Ave., 7th Floor New York, NY 10016 (800)621-1115
Talking Walls (1992) M. B. Knight	Unique approach to studing history: walls located around the world. The Great Wall of China is included. Children learn how the Wall affects them.	2–8	Tilbury House 132 Water Street Gardner, ME 04345 (800)582-1899

Type/Title	Grade Level(s)	Description	Publisher/ Supplier
II. Teacher Resources			
Cowboys of the Wild West (1985) Russell Freedman	K–8+	View of life in the West and the role cowboys played in Texas in the nineteenth century. Includes clothes cowboys wore, their equipment, and ranch life.	Clarion Books 215 Park Avenue South New York, NY 10003 Fax: (314)231-7417
Geographunny (1991) M. Gerberg	2–3	Series of riddles about four different areas of the world—United States and Canada; Mexico, South America, and Antarctica; Europe, the Middle East, and Africa; and Asia and the Pacific Islands. A fun way to learn names of countries and other geographic information.	Clarion Books 215 Park Avenue South New York, NY 10003 Fax: (314)231-7417
Group Solutions (1992) Jan Goodman	1–8+	Spiral-bound book includes more than 50 cooperative learning activities, including games, puzzles, and problems. Also has a bilingual section.	GEMS Lawrence Hall of Science University of California Berkeley, CA 94720-5220 (510)642-7771
LIFT 30–40 different titles (1988–1995)	4–8	Newberry award-winning set of novels captures the immigrant experiences of various groups, and the themes of heroism, as well as those that explore the lives of individuals through biographies.	Sundance Publishing P.O. Box 1326 Littleton, MA 01460 (800)343-8204
Literature-Based Geography Activities: An Integrated Approach (1982) T. McCarthy	K–3	Examples of how children can build and apply specific geographic skills and concepts while reading literature.	Scholastic Professional Books 555 Broadway New York, NY 10012
Planning and Organizing Multicultural Instruction (1994) Gwendolyn C. Baker	K–8+	A compendium of tested teaching approaches that can be used to sensitize students to multiculturalism. Divided into chapters focusing on teaching tolerance through various subject areas.	Alternative Publishing Group 200 Middlefield Road Menlo Park, CA 94025 (800)447-2226

FIGURE 12-4, continued

Type/Title	Description	Grade Level(s)	Publisher/ Supplier
II. Teacher Resources (continued)			
The Mailbox Magazine Preschool (3 & 4 yr. olds) Kindergarten Primary (grades 1–3) Intermediate (grades 4–6)	Ideas for literature-based activities, thematic units, bulletin boards, and art activities. In addition, classroom management tips are provided.	PK–6	The Education Center, Inc. 1607 Battleground Ave. Greensboro, NC 27408 (800)334-0298
Social Studies Through Children's Literature: An Integrated Approach (1991)	A series of activities built around 32 books as they relate to seven social studies concepts—self, family, community, city, state, nation, and the world.	K–6+	Teacher Ideas Press P.O. Box 6633 Englewood, CO 80155-6633 (800)237-6124
III. Journals			
Social Education	Focus on strengthening social studies education at all levels. Of particular interest to elementary teachers is *Classroom Teachers' Notebook.*	K–6	National Council for the Social Studies (NCSS) 3501 Newark St. NW Washington, DC 20016 (202)966-7840
Social Studies + The Young Learner	Quarterly journal with creative teaching ideas.	K–16	National Council for the Social Studies (NCSS) 3501 Newark St. NW Washington, DC 20016 (202)966-7840
Theory and Research in Social Education	Quarterly journal of the NCSS. Three general topic areas: international perspectives, features, and book reviews.	K–16	National Council for the Social Studies (NCSS) 3501 Newark St. NW Washington, DC 20016 (202)966-7840

Type/Title	Description	Grade Level(s)	Publisher/Supplier
IV. Software			
Africa Trail	Students plan a cross-continental bike trek across Africa. Students meet people and places in Africa through the use of authentic photos and journal entries from actual treks.	3–8	Educational Resources 1550 Executive Drive P.O. Box 1990 Elgin, IL 60121-1900
All About Me!	Centers around the students' life—home, family, and friends. Promotes writing skills across the curriculum.	2+	Educational Resources 1550 Executive Dr. P.O. Box 1990 Elgin, IL 60121-1900
Dinosaurs Teach Kids Geography Skills	Takes students back to time of the dinosaurs; students learn geography skills as they search for dinosaurs. Challenge upgrade customizes the program.	3+	Mindplay Tucson, AZ (800)221-7911
Music of American History: Apple Pie CD	More than 400 compositions present 350 years of American history. Includes voices of Native Americans, cowboys, and coal miners. Database of historical information provides specific social and political contexts for the music.	4-6	Educational Resources 1550 Executive Dr. P.O. Box 1990 Elgin, IL 60121-1900
National Geographic Kids Network	Uses real-world scientific procedures and connects the classroom with those around the country and the world; expands the students' cultural and social awareness.	4-6	National Geographic Society Kids Network P.O. Box 98018 Washington, DC 20090-8018 (800)733-3000
NCSS Online on World Wide Web	Features information of interest to teachers and students; the home page can be reached at http:\\www.ncss.org\home\ncss		

FIGURE 12-4, continued

Type/Title	Description	Grade Level(s)	Publisher/ Supplier
IV. Software (continued)			
Oregon Trail	An exciting 2,000-mile experience simulates the challenges families encountered as they moved West. Students make decisions that had to be made regarding food, the trail to take, and forging rivers.	5–12	Cambridge Development Laboratory 86 West St. Waltham, MA 02154 (800)637-0047
The Age of Exploration	Students become explorers and get acquainted with new plants, animals, and languages spoken in different lands.	4–9	Educational Resources 1550 Executive Drive P.O. Box 1990 Elgin, IL 60121-1900
V. Other			
Global Art	Ten stencil books from the Ancient and Living Cultures Series include tales, myths, and art projects. The cultures featured include Indians of the Southwest and Yoruba of West Africa. There are punch out stencils to reconstruct actual samurai helmets, totem poles, and a model of the pyramid.	3+	Good Year Books 1900 E. Lake Avenue Glenview, IL 60025 (800)628-4480, ext. 3038
We All Sing Together (video)	The anchormaster discovers we are all different including monsters, but in many ways we are alike. This Sesame Street Home Video depicts how children have different skin colors, family structures, and hairstyles, yet they all share something very special—a common humanity!	K–4	Random House Home Video 201 E. 50th Street New York, NY 10022 (800)733-3000

Space Management

The teacher can minimize student problems by making decisions before instruction begins about the placement of furniture, printed materials and equipment, and stations/learning centers. These space management decisions are based on what the students will be doing. If small group instruction will take place after a short presentation to the entire class, the desks and chairs might be arranged in clusters of four to facilitate cooperative learning activities. If station or center work is the instructional strategy used in the social studies classroom, decisions about where to place each center must ensure that there is enough space to work and for materials.

When considering the placement of the student desks, their relationship to the chalkboard, windows, and lighting is crucial in keeping students on task and engaged. For example, students need enough space as they work together traveling by wagon train to Oregon using the Oregon Trail computer software.

Displaying Student Materials

Walls and bulletin boards should be used to display student work, to recognize individual and group achievement. Also common in social studies classrooms are maps, globes, and other materials to generate interest and provide concrete experiences. Especially effective in social studies is the use of visuals such as inflatable globes showing animals around the world, posters of tropical rain forests, original copies of letters written, reproductions of a typical Western town, and murals of historic leaders and developers of the area. If the teacher wants to display student work, this work should be rotated over a six-week grading period.

A word of caution should be sounded when decorating the room and displaying materials. Having too much material hanging from the ceiling can be distracting for some students and ultimately interfere with their learning. Such a classroom environment often is cluttered. When utilizing the walls in a classroom, teachers should be careful not to provide overstimulation.

Assessing Student Learning

Assessment in the social studies classroom can be described along a continuum from the informal to the formal. At the informal end of the continuum are opportunities to assess student learning, proficiency, and mastery of social studies concepts and skills by observing students as they work individually or in groups. Observations provide information about a student's level of understanding as teachers witness the student's ability to use the legend of a map, for example, as well as the student's ability to address problem situations such as charting a voyage or drawing physical features of a location. Teachers have opportunities to record brief notes as they observe the way the students share ideas and material, and work cooperatively in a group. Other informal evaluation strategies include teacher-student discussions, student-produced questions or tests, and various activities, games, puzzles, and reading assignments (Savage & Armstrong, 1996).

At the formal end of the evaluation continuum, teachers can use rating scales, learning checklists, and attitude inventories to find out about student interest in topics, and a variety of tests (essay, multiple choice, matching, completion) to assess learning. In addition to these formal measures, teachers need to consider using performance assessment. Some examples of performance assessment techniques include having students do oral history projects, oral presentations, surveys, role playing of a particular time period being studied, and portfolios. If "civic competence is highly valued, then students should be able to demonstrate mastery of civic competence through realistic tasks which match the demands and expectations of society" (Nickell, 1994, p. 30)—for example, articulating the importance of a particular law that has been enacted.

The key to performance assessment is getting students to use social studies information, cognitive processes, and/or skills learned, perhaps through posing interesting and thought-provoking questions and demonstrating the use of a tool, software, and/or resource. The purpose of using formal measures is to improve social studies instruction.

As mentioned in Chapter 8, teachers may wish to engage in authentic assessment, which examines student behavior in a natural context. For example, Biener (1993), suggests that for authentic assessment in a social studies unit on the Civil War, students might be asked to find a newspaper clipping about war or conflict today and tell whether and how the war today is like the war of yesterday. Students might also write a news release for their newspaper today about an incident that happened during the Civil War.

Proactive management strategies are essential if students are to learn in a social studies classroom. Teachers who plan how they will manage their students, materials/equipment, and classroom space are more successful in achieving the goals of a social studies lesson/unit. In addition to planning management strategies, teachers need to plan ways they will assess student learning. Managing and assessing student behavior is necessary if teachers are to fully operationalize the goals of the social studies curriculum.

MAKING CONNECTIONS

The beginning of this chapter discussed the need for vertical integration within social studies and the development of a curriculum that includes history, geography, economics, and civics/government into a unified whole. This section focuses on horizontal integration—the teaching of social studies across the curriculum in other subject areas. For example, in art as children learn about other cultures, the role of self-expression through painting, sculpture, weaving, and use of color and design are central to the values and attitudes held by a group of people. In language arts, students have the opportunity to communicate with children in other places by becoming pen pals, using traditional written communication or computers with electronic mail (e-mail). The appreciation of place helps students understand the unique physical and biological differences of flora and fauna from different parts of the world. As they study habitat, biomes, and the environment, students can have a "Creatures in Your Community Party" to study the effects of climate and geography on animals and plants. In addition, during the party, students can develop an awareness of the role of humans in their community and suggest ways to "tread lightly in the great outdoors" (Sheehan, 1992).

When the focus of the science unit is on Earth Day celebrations, the students in social studies can learn about the history and folklore of the Maypole and baskets of different cultures throughout the world. In addition, elementary students can conduct research on their family history and geography by having an "Ancestor Day" and a "Family Map." Students can also role play "100 Years Ago Today" (Sheehan, 1992). Finally, Sheehan (1992) describes an experience in which students learning in social studies class about the interdependence of life (sharing the world with all living things) can help develop an interactive bulletin board with pictures and string illustrating interrelationships between people and animals. With a little construction paper of various colors; pictures of animals, insects, and birds from old magazines; string; and glue, a learning bulletin board is created that reinforces the concepts inherent in science and the content areas in social studies.

SUMMARY

This chapter has provided not only the historical context for the inclusion of social studies within the elementary curriculum but also a call for change in the way the social studies curriculum is taught. Social studies is central to students' understanding of their world and their place in it and should be presented in dynamic ways that stimulate student interest and involvement.

A case for including social studies in the elementary curriculum has been made repeatedly, but its importance continues to be underappreciated. This chapter stressed that the social studies curriculum, one of the oldest disciplines, is a study of people, with a rich and fascinating story to tell. Some of the issues discussed include addressing the traditions from which the social studies curriculum is taught (citizenship, social sciences, reflective inquiry, and integrated inquiry), promoting social studies literacy, and using a thematic, integrated approach. Social studies should be integrated into the elementary curriculum in such a way that students view events, people, and places in a global context. The chapter included a sample unit to show how a teacher can organize a thematic social studies unit; it can be consulted as a model to follow.

Goals for the social studies curriculum were presented as themes that include culture; time, continuity, and change; people, places, and environments; individual development and identity; groups and institutions; power, authority, and governance; production, distribution, and consumption; science, technology, and society; and civic ideals and global connections. The chapter identified the major social studies content areas—history, geography, economics, and civics education—and provided an overview of these areas of study, including suggested goals and topics within each. Learning experiences that integrate these areas were provided, along with a chart of resources and tools for teacher.

The chapter concluded with suggestions for managing students, materials, and the entire classroom environment and for using charts, globes, and other visuals. Approaches for assessing student outcomes (compatible with those presented in Chapter 8) were described, with specific suggestions for authentic assessment. The chapter ended with examples of ways teachers make connections with other subjects in the elementary curriculum.

■ YOUR TURN

1. Obtain a copy of an elementary social studies textbook. Make a list of the topics listed in its table of contents. Review Figure 12-3, the sample unit on celebrating diversity, before proceeding. Now, select one of the topics in the textbook and develop a thematic integrated unit. Try to keep in mind the basic components of a thematic integrated unit; making connections with all areas of social studies is the objective. The more connections that are made and the more opportunities that exist for relating to the common core of understanding and skills (Figure 12-1), the more the students experience the interrelatedness of knowledge and are ready to address problems in their own lives.

2. For students to appreciate the diversity that exists in every classroom, it might be helpful to have students develop a "Me Collage." To understand the impact, construct one for yourself. You will need construction paper, several magazines, scissors, and glue/tape.

Select a minimum of ten pictures, words, and/or phrases that describe something about you—your feelings, likes, dislikes, and so on. When you have selected at least ten items, glue them to the construction paper. Exchange collages with others, and have them try to detect who made the collage. (A variation to try with students is a "Roots" activity in which each student creates a poster using photographs, time lines, or a family tree—some type of visual depiction of the sociocultural forces that have shaped the attitudes and values that students bring to the classroom. Like the "Me Collage," these posters are shared in small groups.)

3. Make a list of social studies concepts and skills appropriate for a particular grade level, and then take some time in the library looking for children's books that could be used to teach them. Biographies are usually interesting: *Just a Few Words, Mr. Lincoln: The Story of the Gettysburg Address* by J. Fritz (1993); *White Lilacs* by C. Meyer (1993); *Long Journey Home* by J. Lester (1993); *Eleanor Roosevelt: A Life of Discovery* by R. Freedman (1993). Scan some library books that describe particular time periods, societies, cultures, and so on.

4. Review several software catalogs and identify those programs that would help to simulate life on the river (The Amazon Trail from MECC is one) and life in ancient cultures (Ancient Empires from The Learning Company is one), as well as to help learn map skills. Where in America's Past is Carmen Sandiego? from Broderbund takes students on Carmen Sandiego's fifth award winning adventure—this time into America's past. Knowing about such programs will be helpful as you consider using technology in your social studies classroom. If possible, review the software using the checklist in the Your Turn section of Chapter 9.

■ REFERENCES

Barr, R. D., Barth, J. L., & Shermis, D. S. (1977). *Defining the social studies. Bulletin #51.* Washington, DC: National Council for the Social Studies.

Beane, J. (1991). The middle school: The natural home of integrated curriculum. *Educational Leadership, 49*(2), 9–13.

Beard, C. (1938). *The nature of the social sciences.* New York: Scribner's Sons.

Beckner, W., & Cornett, J. D. (1972). *The secondary school curriculum: Content and structure.* Scranton, PA: Intext Educational Publishers.

Bednarz, R. S. (1994, March/April). National standards in geography are coming. *Journal of Geography, 93*(2), 105–106.

Biener, L. (1993, May). Authentic assessment. In Trends: Social studies. *Educational Leadership, 50*(8), 81–82.

Bradley Commission on History in the Schools. (1988). *Building a history curriculum: Guidelines for teaching history in schools.* Washington, DC: Educational Excellence Network.

Bragaw, D. H., & Hartoonian, H. M. (1988). *Content of the curriculum: 1988 ASCD yearbook.* Alexandria, VA: Association for Supervision and Curriculum Development.

Brody, R. A. (1989). Why study politics? *Charting a course: Social studies for the 21st century.* Washington, DC: National Commission on Social Studies in the Schools.

Collins, K. (1994, Fall/Winter). Why teach geography with technology? *Texas Alliance for Geographic Education.* San Marcos, TX: Texas Alliance for Geographic Education.

Crabtree, C. (1989, November). Improving history in the schools. *Educational Leadership, 47*(3), 25–28.

Frazee, B., & Rudnitski, R. A. (1995). *Integrating teaching methods.* Albany, NY: Delmar Publishers.

Fredericks, A. D., Meinback, A. M., & Rothlein, L. (1993). *Thematic units: An integrated approach* to teaching science and social studies. New York: HarperCollins.

Freedman, R. (1993). *Eleanor Roosevelt: A life of discovery*. New York: Clarion Books.

Freire, P. (1983). *Pedagogy of the oppressed*. New York: Continuum.

Geography for life: National geography standards. (1994). Washington, DC: National Geographic Research and Exploration.

Fritz, J. (1993). *Just a few words, Mr. Lincoln: The story of the Gettysburg Address*. New York: Grossett and Dunlap.

Hakim, J. (1993). A history of us. *American Educator*, *17*(1), 6–19.

Hansen, W. L. (1989). Economics. *Charting a course: Social studies for the 21st century*. Washington, DC: National Council for the Social Studies.

Hirsch, E. D., Jr. (1987). *Cultural literacy: What every American needs to know*. Boston: Houghton Mifflin.

Joint Committee on Geographic Education. (1984). *Guidelines for geographic education*. Washington, DC: Association of American Geographers.

Kinney, D. G. (1990, September). Reopening the gateway to America. *Life*, *13*(11), 26–38.

Lemlech, J. K. (1994). *Curriculum and instructional methods for the elementary and middle school* (3rd ed.). Upper Saddle River, NJ: Merrill/Prentice Hall.

Lester, J. (1993). *Long journey home*. New York: Dial Books.

Meyer, C. (1993). *White lilacs*. San Diego: Harcourt Brace Jovanovich.

National Center for History in the Schools. (1994). *National standards for history: Expanding children's world in time and space*. Los Angeles, CA: National Center for History in the School.

National Center for History in the Schools. (1994). *National standards for United States history: Exploring the American experience*. Los Angeles, CA: National Center for History in the School.

National Commission on Social Studies in the Schools. (1989). *Charting a course: Social studies for the 21st century*. Washington, DC: National Council for the Social Studies.

National Council for the Social Studies. (1994, October). Ten thematic strands in social studies. *Social Education*, *58*(6), 365–368.

Nickell, P. (1994, Winter). Alternative assessment: Implications for social studies. *ERIC Review*, *3*(1), 29–31.

Reinhartz, D., & Reinhartz, J. (1992). *Geography across the curriculum.* Washington, DC: National Education Association.

Savage, T. V., & Armstrong, D. G. (1996). *Effective teaching in elementary social studies* (3rd ed.). Upper Saddle River, NJ: Merrill/Prentice Hall.

Schillings, D. (1994, April/May). Teaching the human condition through the social studies. *Social Education*, *58*(4), 197–199.

Sheehan, K. (1992). *Earth teacher: A teacher's guide to using Earth Child in the classroom*. Cape Elizabeth, ME: The Earth Child Trust.

Shepherd, G. D., & Ragan, W. B. (1992). *Modern elementary curriculum* (7th ed.). Fort Worth, TX: Harcourt Brace Jovanovich.

Solomon, W. (1987). Improving students' thinking skills through social studies instruction. *Elementary School Journal*, *87*(5), 557–569.

Turner, T. N. (1994). *Essentials of classroom teaching elementary social studies*. Boston: Allyn & Bacon.

Wassermann, S. (1992, June). A case for social studies. *Phi Delta Kappan*, *73*(10), 793–801.

Willis, S. (1990, June). When history happens today. *Update*, *32*(5), 1, 4.

chapter 13

The Science Curriculum

AFTER READING THIS CHAPTER, YOU WILL BE ABLE TO DO THE FOLLOWING:

■ Describe what is meant by the term *scientific literacy*.

■ Explain why science education is important in the elementary curriculum.

■ Identify and describe the factors involved in restructuring the science curriculum.

■ Discuss the various curricular programs and standards recommended for the elementary science curriculum.

■ Identify the unique aspects of managing an elementary science classroom.

■ Describe several ways of assessing science learning.

■ Discuss various ways of making connections between science and other content areas of the elementary school.

Science is not just another subject, it is life and involves the study of rocks, rivers, trees, and animal species on Earth, both present and past (Oehring, 1993). Yet rather than thinking of exciting possibilities for science, many elementary teachers admit they are reluctant to teach this content area. But Mechling and Oliver (1983) suggest that it is through elementary science that students can discover the keys to reading, writing, speaking, and listening, because science promotes thinking, communication, measurement, and process skills and helps to generate an attitude of lifelong learning.

Just as the theme of literacy is presented in other chapters in Part III, a discussion of scientific literacy is a significant aspect of this chapter as well. As reported by McCormick (1989), the National Council on Science and Technology defines scientific literacy as the following:

> being familiar with the natural world and its diversity and unity; understanding key scientific concepts and principles; being aware of how science, math, and technology depend upon one another; knowing that science, math, and technology are human enterprises with strengths and limitations; having a capacity for scientific ways of

thinking; and using scientific knowledge and ways of thinking for individual and social purposes. (p. 3)

A scientifically literate person is knowledgeable about the key concepts and principles of science and can use scientific knowledge and apply scientific ways of thinking to everyday life (*Ed-Talk*, n. d.). Gega (1995) suggests that curiosity, inventiveness, critical thinking, and persistence are also part of scientific literacy. Today, when people have to make difficult choices at a personal level (such as avoiding contracting AIDS) and at the global level (such as understanding the causes and impact of acid rain), a knowledge of scientific principles can be critical. A scientifically literate person understands and is able to apply science principles and make better decisions based on this information.

Perhaps the greatest impetus for developing a scientifically literate populace in the United States came in 1957 when the Soviet Union successfully launched *Sputnik* into orbit. Overnight, the United States entered the space race, and for forty years since then, the United States has been trying to increase scientific literacy. The results of the National Assessment of Educational Progress of Science Achievement between 1969 and 1986 were bleak. When you strip away the rhetoric about scoring low nationally as well as internationally, the real issue is that future citizens are so poorly informed about scientific principles that they will not be able to make informed social and political decisions involving scientific and technological information (McCormick, 1989).

Against this backdrop of years of trying to improve science education, this chapter suggests ways elementary teachers can begin to address this issue. Tolman and Hardy (1995) note that

> For the elementary teacher, science provides some of the greatest opportunities to turn students on about school [as] . . . a place of excitement. . . . Teachers who are not getting students involved with science don't know what they are missing. (p. 5)

This chapter begins with a discussion of why science matters. Then it presents what is known about teaching and learning science, including a discussion of why science education is undergoing change at the national, state, and classroom levels, and why science teaching and learning need to change. The chapter ends with a discussion of the importance of planning and managing science instruction, the trends in assessment currently being implemented in elementary science classrooms, and ways of making connections between science and other content areas.

RATIONALE: WHY SCIENCE EDUCATION IS IMPORTANT

Science is for all students; it is not a curriculum area reserved for just a few—the academically talented—but for all. Studying science is important because it has the potential for improving the quality of life and making the world safer.

When developing a case for science being included in the elementary curriculum, economic reasons often surface first as a justification, but a more fundamental reason is to help students achieve personal success. Science knowledge empowers people, giving them greater control over their lives by providing pathways for finding answers to questions. The ability to generate solutions enhances the quality of life and puts people in the position of making decisions based on data. The ability to make decisions and to act confidently based on those decisions is also a goal of the science curriculum.

Another reason science should be taught in schools is for the betterment of society. For a society to flourish, all of its citizens need to be scientifically knowledgeable as they live and function in an increasingly technological world. Ironically, as the scientific knowledge curve (what is known) increases because of technological advancements, the scientific literacy curve (what people know) flattens and in many instances has dipped. As available technological information expands in business, medicine, transportation, and communication, our ability to apply scientific principles to our daily lives has failed to keep pace (and in some situations has actually decreased). There is concern about students who started school in the late 1980s; with their lack of preparedness in areas of science and mathematics, when they graduate from high school at the beginning of the twenty-first century, they will not fully understand or be able to use scientific knowledge at a time when the need for such knowledge will be even greater.

The American Association for the Advancement of Science (AAAS) has provided a response to answer the question *What does it take to produce a scientifically literate person?* The Association's *Benchmarks for Science Literacy* (1993) identifies standards for guiding teaching and learning in science. These standards suggest that when teaching science, less-is-more and that students should have opportunities not only to do science but also to think scientifically (*NEA Today*, 1993). Figure 13-1 provides an example of science benchmarks for grades 2 and 5 on the specific topic Interdependence of Life. These benchmarks emphasize the theme of interdependency and show how it spirals throughout the elementary grades.

Another reason science is important is economics. The discovery of new technologies and the economic benefit of their application are often the focus for bolstering science education. When coupled with the application of scientific and technological discoveries to national defense, the perceived importance of science education grows. The economic and military reasons for science are often the most compelling for lawmakers who appropriate funds, but the previously discussed reasons for the importance of science are inextricably linked to economics. The linkage of all three reasons—personal empowerment, scientific and technological development, and economic strength—provides a compelling rationale for the science curriculum in the elementary school. The goal is to establish a curriculum that results in students who are scientifically literate and who, because of their grasp of science and technology, have the ability to solve problems and to think critically (*EdTalk*, n. d.).

In spite of the critical need to produce scientifically literate students, the elementary school has been less than successful in achieving this goal. This is due in part to the way science has been taught. The following section describes changes over the past several decades in science education in the elementary grades.

FIGURE 13-1 Science Benchmarks

What does a "benchmark" look like? Here's an example from "The Living Environment," one of the twelve content chapters in *Benchmarks for Science Literacy*. The specific topic here, Interdependence of Life, is from the content chapter, "Living Environment."

By the end of the second grade, students should know that

■ Animals eat plants or other animals for food and may also use plants (or even other animals) for shelter and nesting.

■ Living things are found almost everywhere in the world. There are somewhat different kinds in different places.

By the end of the fifth grade, students should know that

■ For any particular environment, some kinds of plants and animals survive well, some survive less well, and some cannot survive at all.

■ Insects and various other organisms depend on dead plant and animal material for food.

■ Organisms interact with one another in various ways besides providing food. Many plants depend on animals for carrying their pollen to other plants or for dispersing their seeds.

■ Changes in an organism's habitat are sometimes beneficial to it and sometimes harmful.

■ Most microorganisms do not cause disease, and many are beneficial.

Source: Adapted from *Benchmarks for Science Literacy* (p. 116) by the American Association for the Advancement of Science, 1993. New York: Oxford University Press.

ISSUES IN ELEMENTARY SCIENCE EDUCATION: RESTRUCTURING TEACHING AND LEARNING

Some educators view elementary science as a wasteland, a time in the schedule when teachers teach other things, have guest speakers, and/or do a holiday art project. Yet the elementary level is the place where there is most promise for restructuring science education because of the natural curiosity students have in science concepts. As a result of this interest in their world and how it operates, students are more motivated to learn about science concepts. Elementary science does not require teachers to be specialists, just to be interested and knowledgeable.

Despite the reasons for teaching science in the elementary school, the literature reveals that in the elementary school less time is spent on science than on any other contents areas (ACCESS ERIC, n. d.). A national survey found that teachers in the primary grades spend only 19 minutes per day, and those in the intermediate grades only 38 minutes per day, on science. In comparison to the language arts and mathematics, science instruction occupies a very small part of the elementary school day (ACCESS ERIC, n. d.). To complicate the situation, the major instructional strategies being used to teach science are lecture (direct instruction) and some discussion with the textbook serving as the major resource. With the emphasis on teacher-directed instruction, little time is devoted to simple investigations, designing and conducting experiments, and/or engaging in the scientific process skills of observing, measuring, predicting, and hypothesizing (ACCESS ERIC, n. d.).

In some schools and districts, elementary teachers neglect science entirely because reading, writing, and mathematics are considered more important, especially when it comes to district and state achievement testing. Nadine, the "Voice of Experience" for this chapter, is a veteran teacher; she reflects on her journey as a science teacher in the elementary school and the dilemmas she has encountered along the way that have helped her appreciate teaching science.

 Voice of Experience

As Nadine gathered materials and supplies for her science class, she remembered how excited she was when she first enrolled in her science methods class at the university. With each day, she realized how little she knew about science but was always willing to learn. The most surprising part was wanting to see science taught in schools so she could test her ideas, but as a pre-service teacher, she quickly found out that not many teachers liked or even taught science.

During her teaching internship, Nadine confided to her mentor teacher, "It looks to me like many teachers try to find excuses for not teaching science and several have told me that the real reason they prefer not to teach science is that they have not had a science class since they were in high school—and even then it was boring and uninspiring. Others said they also avoided science in college at all cost. It was these experiences that helped to set the stage for their current view and the role of science in their classrooms."

During her first year of teaching, Nadine remembered how eager she had been to teach science. But she soon found that it took a lot of time to prepare student labs, and she had very little time. As she confers with a colleague, she says, "I forgot how much planning beforehand is needed. This was a down-time for me."

Nadine continues to get ready for science and remembers that wonderful Monday when things changed for her and so did her attitude toward teaching science. The students liked science! She could see it and told another teacher, "If you only could have seen the looks on my students' faces, all the questions they asked, the many ideas they had about taking the topic further. It was exhilarating." Nadine acknowledges that if you look only at the preparation time science may not appear to be worth the trouble. But the students' enjoyment of science convinced her that science mattered. The students were thinking, sharing, and learning from each other, researching answers to questions, reading more about things of interest, and they were figuring things out on their own. She asked herself, isn't this what learning is all about?

To restructure science instruction, we must teach science in a way that gets students involved. Most importantly, teachers must realize that the time invested in preparing and teaching science is worth it. Students like to learn by doing. In-service teachers share with us that students in elementary school often rate science as one of their favorite subjects when doing a graphing activity. But their counterparts (secondary teachers) have shared that students are disinterested in science by the time these students reach middle school and high school. What happens as these students move through the grades?

To capture the student's attention in the elementary school and in the upper grades, the science curriculum has to be hands-on and inquiry-based. In addition, it needs to be reality-based; connections need to be made between the science principles the students are learning and the science they encounter in their daily lives. Making these connections builds science literacy. The students begin to see how science fits into their lives; the reasons for learning science become self-evident. As students studied insects in one science class, they read in the newspaper about an elder citizen being stung by hundreds of bees when he disturbed a hive. As students investigated the story, they found that some of the bees were from an African hybrid strain. By learning about insects and specifically about bees, that

current event became more meaningful. With further study, the students learned some geography as they traced the movement of the bees from Africa to South America, Mexico, and then the United States.

A well-coordinated elementary science curriculum does not just happen. It takes time and support from the teachers, the building principal, and parents. The Cheshire Public Schools in Connecticut have made great strides in improving their elementary school science program, and these improvements can be distilled to five elements:

- conducting staff development for teachers
- building time in the school day to teach science
- using a variety of materials and textbooks that provide a balance between content and hands-on experiences
- having materials and equipment to conduct investigations
- having administrative and parental support (ACCESS ERIC, n. d.).

Restructuring the science curriculum in the elementary school requires promoting scientific literacy in elementary classrooms through inquiry and communication skills, attitudes of appreciation, and scientific information. A restructured science curriculum focuses on the world outside the classroom, involves the students in that world through the use of technology, and contains fewer concepts, with greater depth of study for each. In addition, a restructured science curriculum in the elementary school includes concepts that provide a context for other content areas and presents science as a way of solving problems, rather than as the cause of problems. For example, when weather is the science topic, it provides a context for understanding climate and food products (social studies) and provides opportunities for students to graph the number of sunny days versus cloudy days (mathematics).

To establish and maintain high student interest in science, teachers should use a variety of instructional strategies (as discussed in Chapter 7) that include an emphasis on cooperative learning, as students interact with a wide array of objects, equipment, software, and materials. When assessing what students have learned, teachers should use a variety of assessment strategies (as discussed in Chapter 8) so students can demonstrate the skills and information they have learned. As the Cheshire schools discussed earlier found, schools that want to maintain a high-quality science program must emphasize the importance of staff development, including topics such as the integration of the sciences, research on how children learn, the use of varied instructional strategies, and the meaning of scientific literacy.

Finally, the elementary science curriculum should be included in other content areas. According to Hurd (1991), an integrated science curriculum should include the use of science in daily affairs, up-to-date content, higher-level thinking skills, and connections with other subject areas. For example, science can be integrated into the language-arts curriculum by reading literature with a science focus or theme. Books such as *Owl Moon* by Jane Yolen (1987) can be introduced into a reading center to extend the topic on birds. *Where the River Begins* by Thomas Locker (1993) can be used to bring science into the geography classroom by emphasizing the geographic theme of place, which can be discussed in conjunction with the science concept of habitat, which has specific animal and plant life. *Crinkleroot's Book of Animal Tracking* by Jim Arnosky (1979), *The Hidden Life of the Forest* by David M. Schwartz and Dwight Kuhn (1988), and *The Desert Is Theirs* by Byrd Baylor (1973) have science themes, as well, and they can also be used to teach graphing and estimating skills.

Effective elementary science programs capitalize on the interests of students, have personal meaning to students, and are linked to the total elementary curriculum. Such programs do not attempt to have students memorize information,

terms, and definitions; instead, they encourage students to explore the natural world around them through questioning and problem solving. The Mandiville, Louisiana, schools have developed a Science Camp that features hands-on activities. In addition, the district has started hosting family science evenings with such activities as star gazing and "metric olympics" ("Science Curriculum Improvement Program," 1992). Another feature of these promising science programs beyond the use of questions is the development of a science program around the theme of "change." Change takes place in all areas of science—chemistry, physics, geology, and biology—as seen in these examples:

- chemical and physical changes in matter
- metamorphosis in animals
- natural changes in humans—birth, middle age, decline, and death
- changes in rivers and mountains—youth, maturity, and old age

Positive examples of elementary science programs do exist, but more are needed if the goal of science is to include all students. Teachers can become more effective in teaching science if they incorporate these positive characteristics into their classrooms and teaching repertoire.

Restructuring efforts directed toward the elementary science curriculum are based on new perspectives on learning derived from research and have implications for science instruction and how children learn. If we have learned anything about how students learn science, it is that science is interactive and social in context. However, reports indicate that science

> has become a passive pastime, dominated by teacher lecture based on textbooks and measured by standardized tests that show how well students have memorized facts, rather than how well they can apply concepts. (McCormick, 1989, p. 2)

This reality is difficult to accept when both teachers and administrators profess to support hands-on experiences as the way to teach science. From 1977 through 1986, there was a ten-percent decline in activity-oriented science instruction. McCormick (1989) has also found the following: in some states, a percentage of time was required for laboratory activities, but that requirement has been dropped, and nearly 95 percent of science instruction is tied to a textbook and the publisher's materials.

Even if teachers believe that scientific inquiry and activities are essential to science instruction, when it comes time to delivering such science instruction, they fall short. Whether the reasons are lack of preparation time, science background, materials, supplies, or support, or teachers simply feeling uncomfortable with hands-on cooperative learning, the science curriculum in the elementary school is flawed.

VIEWS OF SCIENCE EDUCATION

Historically, beginning with the launching of the space race in the 1950s to the reform report of *A Nation at Risk* (1983) in the early 1980s, science education has received attention. More recently, *Science for All Americans* (1989), *Benchmarks for Science Literacy* (1993), and *NSTA Pathways to the Science Standards* (1996) have created a national dialogue about science. With this attention, the fundamental questions concerning the goals and purposes of science education and ways to achieve scientific literacy are continuing to be addressed. The rhetoric surrounding *America 2000* and *Goals 2000* calls for making the United States first in science and mathematics, but the mechanism for achieving these goals has yet to be defined.

Several promising pathways for redefining science education in the elementary school have been suggested, but barriers to change remain. The first barrier to overcome is dualism: science as a specific discipline or science as an integrative area of study? Traditionalists define *science* as studying the specific science disciplines of chemistry, physics, geology, and biology. Others view *science* as an inquiry-based, integrative area of study (McCormick, 1989).

Promoting the idea of integrative study is a good place to begin when thinking about teaching and learning science. Using a thematic approach to teach science may be a start. Rutherford and Ahlgren (1989) note that "important themes pervade science, . . . whether we are looking at an ancient civilization, the human body, or a comet" (p. 155). They also suggest focusing science teaching and learning on themes such as systems, patterns of change, people in a global ecosystem, and models. Themes provide natural connections for experiencing the interrelatedness of the science content areas.

Trying to determine which view is better or which science is more important is a moot point. All the science areas need to be taught, but the way the goal is accomplished seems to be the significant issue. The key to a comprehensive science curriculum is to include each science area but not teach it as an isolated self-contained entity. Deliberate links should be made between and among all the sciences. No science question, hypothesis, and/or dilemma can be solved with only one science. Chemistry, physics, geology, and biology are part of a larger whole called *science education* that needs to be cultivated if students are going to come away with the idea that scientific knowledge is interrelated. For example, in fourth grade, as students study a pond ecosystem, the sciences of biology, physics, chemistry, and geology can be used to teach about the animal and plant life in the pond, pH of the water, water pressure, stream flow, and rate of erosion. The crossover between and among the sciences is essential to get students to appreciate the interrelatedness of nature and the world around them.

Teaching the science disciplines as separate entities builds artificial barriers between them. When each science area is taught independently of the others, the beauty of nature fades because the cohesiveness that makes science so intriguing is missing. It is the beauty of nature that appeals to students and intrigues them to study it in more depth. When science is taught in an interrelated cohesive manner, students develop a desire to dig deeper.

When the teaching covers less but at a greater depth, students have time to develop an understanding by experimenting with different types of materials, developing new ideas and testing them in a new way, and reflecting on what has been done (Texley & Wild, 1996). Building on students' interest and curiosity about the natural world in the primary grades is crucial because research indicates that by fourth grade students begin to lose interest (Sivertsen, 1993). When studying the topic of flight, for example, students can pursue many facets of this topic such as air pressure, Newton's laws of motion, thrust, drag, the role of oxygen for air-breathing animals, and more.

Research has shown that students learn best when they construct their own knowledge, because children do not absorb knowledge like sponges: they construct their own scientific knowledge base, take this knowledge, and use it in new contexts (Resnick & Chi, 1988). The shift away from giving students the information to having them construct it for themselves is paramount when teaching science and is supported by cognitive learning research. The process of putting students in an active science learning role rather than in a passive one is called *constructivism*, which has been described in earlier chapters. Resnick and Chi (1988) point out that teachers' charge is to help students build scientifically correct interpretations of their world and that teachers must start where the students are and consider their existing conceptions, while helping them alter their scientific misconceptions.

As Nadine, our "Voice of Experience" for this chapter, is speaking to a group of pre-service teachers in a science methods class, she reflects on her role as a science teacher.

 Voice of Experience

"One of the important changes that I have experienced as a teacher is a shift in my approach or the way I teach science. It was hard at first to assume the role of facilitator of learning rather than dispenser of knowledge. I soon realized that my students came to my classroom with prior knowledge about science; often, their views were 'naive,' but they enjoyed investigating and discussing their views and what they found after their investigations. Slowly, I backed away from my role as giver of knowledge to one who became more student directed. I began to see my students not only enjoying science but achieving a greater understanding of the scientific concepts as well.

Sometimes I wanted to teach the way I was taught, which meant telling the students rather than engaging them in problem-solving experiences and using hands-on materials. Maybe I felt this way because telling was easier, and I thought, if I tell my students, they will 'get it' and not miss the key points. But as I began to relax, I felt more comfortable and began to believe that facilitation is as safe as telling.

By teaching science in a way that promoted experimentation and discourse, students were learning communication and measurement skills, not only science skills. When the 'we' idea took hold, teaching science felt more comfortable. I encouraged students to try new things and if they were wrong, it was ok, just try again—figure it out! What a valuable lesson for life—try again!"

Nadine concluded her remarks to the preservice teachers by saying, "As teachers of science, our goal is to link new knowledge with what the students already know in a meaningful way."

What Nadine and other teachers have realized is that they are the key to improving science instruction, not the textbook, not the materials, but her! Through example, teachers model the ability to think, communicate, solve problems, and collaborate by working with others and learning how to master science concepts. Nadine and others have learned that assessment should be aligned with instructional goals by providing many different opportunities to communicate and to demonstrate what her students have learned. Finally, learning science is not confined to a specific lesson and taught during a particular time of day; it is all around—at the zoo, on the playground, watching the sun rise and set, and watering the plants. Science is all around us, and the students need to recognize it as well.

TEACHING RESOURCES AND TOOLS FOR SCIENCE

Learning with materials and hands-on experiences makes science concrete and relevant for students, which in turn allows them to construct meaning by piecing together bits of information (Sivertsen, 1993). Teaching with a variety of materials takes time and is often demanding, but the results are gratifying: students remember what they do (Rosanne Fortnor, cited in Haury & Rillero, 1992). For too long, textbooks have defined the elementary school science curriculum; they certainly should play a role, but only a supportive one. Other resources are needed, such as children's trade books and periodicals, to enrich the science study. In addition, films, videos, and computer software can extend the classroom walls. Figure 13-2 provides a list of periodicals/magazines and trade books that have proven helpful in teaching science. These resources can be helpful when planning science lessons for elementary students.

Another important aspect of science education is consumable materials; everyday materials such as batteries, bulbs, wires, seeds, compasses, plants, planks, alcohol, and baking soda are needed to provide direct observation and experimentation. It is important to recognize that science instruction in the elementary school does not depend on sophisticated equipment and tools; the materials can be as basic as batteries and bulbs. The key element is to have materials for the students to touch, move around, and experiment with, as they test their ideas about a particular concept. By manipulating materials, students generate ideas and exchange them with other students, and these ideas are modified over time. Creating such an environment conveys science learning as interactive and taking place in a social context. Such an environment also helps "students develop understanding from [small and large group] experience[s] with materials [to question, discuss, and reflect] in the classroom as well as from their out-of-school experiences" (Sivertsen, 1993, p. 7).

SCIENCE EDUCATION PROGRAMS AND STANDARDS

In addition to resources and textbooks, commercially available science programs may be helpful when planning science lessons. These science programs, such as the Science—A Process Approach (SAPA), Full Option Science System (FOSS), and others, provide a wide range of options for elementary teachers. Some programs, like SAPA, focus on process skills; others, such as Activities that Integrate Math and Science (AIMS), link science and math learning; while still other programs emphasize hands-on interactive investigations. Figure 13-3 identifies some of these programs and provides a brief description of each.

The scope and sequence of the science curriculum for the elementary school continues to be an issue that science educators, teachers, scientists, and parents address. The National Research Council (1994) prepared a document for discussion only, called the *National Science*

FIGURE 13-2   Teaching Resources and Tools for Science

Title	Description	Grade Level(s)	Publisher/ Supplier
I. Teacher Resources: Periodicals/Magazines			
3-2-1 Contact	General in nature with puzzles, projects, investigations, and questions with answers about the world around us.	3+	Children's Television Workshop One Lincoln Plaza New York, NY 10023
Art-To-Zoo	A topic is featured in each issue (e.g. animal size, using the yellow pages, nineteenth-century portraits). Includes lesson plans, trade books, and suggestions for using community resources.	K-6	Smithsonian Institution Office of Elementary & Secondary Education Arts and Industries Building Washington, DC 20560
Audubon Adventure	Nature newspaper for elementary children that focuses on animals, plants, and current environmental issues.	4-6	National Audubon Society 613 Riversville Road Greenwich, CT 06830
Earth Notes	Quarterly publication designed to provide elementary teachers information about environmental issues. Includes a useful reference list, numerous instructional ideas, and suggested corollary activities.	1-6	Environmental Protection Agency 201 M Street SW Washington, DC 20460
Electric Company	Each issue focuses on one theme. Colorful pictures and intriguing content invite children to explore a variety of subject areas.	1-4	Children's Television Workshop One Lincoln Plaza New York, NY 10023
National Geographic World	Includes excellent photographs, art, and narratives to children as a motivating source of information.	3+	National Geographic Society 17th and M Streets, NW Washington, DC 20036
Owl	Magazine that answers student's questions about nature and science.	2+	Young Naturalist Foundation P.O. Box 11314 Des Moines, IA 50304

Source: National Science Resources Center, 1988.

I. Teacher Resources:
Periodicals/Magazines (continued)

Title	Description	Grade Level(s)	Publisher/Supplier
Ranger Rick	Offers students a way to enjoy nature and appreciate the need for conservation; hands-on activities.	1–6	National Wildlife Federation 1412 16th Street, NW Washington, DC 20036–2266
Science and Children	Provides ideas to teachers for hands-on activities that will engage children in science topics and concepts.	K–6+	1742 Connecticut Avenue, NW Washington, DC 20009
Science Weekly	Each issue focuses on one topic in science, math, and technology with materials for students, along with notes for teachers.	K+	SCIENCE WEEKLY P.O. Box 70154 Washington, DC 20088–0154
Scienceland	Each issue focuses on a single topic and includes lifelike illustrations and color photographs to pique a student's curiosity.	K–6	SCIENCELAND, Inc. 501 Fifth Avenue New York, NY 10017-6165
Your Big Backyard	Photographs and simple text about animals and nature for young children.	PK–1	National Wildlife Federation 1412 16th Street, NW Washington, DC 20036–2266
Zoobooks	Each issue focuses on a specific animal and contains color photographs with brief factual text. Back issues are available.	K–5	Wildlife Education, Ltd. 930 West Washington Street San Diego, CA 92103
Wonderscience	Relates science concepts to technology through physical science investigations. Each issue contains background information, hands-on activities, and ideas for integrating science across the curriculum.	1–6	American Chemical Society P.O. Box 57136 West End Station Washington, DC 20037

FIGURE 13-2, continued

Title	Description	Grade Level(s)	Publisher/ Supplier
II. Teacher Resources: Books			
Always a River (1991)	Includes lesson plans focusing on the Ohio River. The river's geography, its history, and present-day economic uses are discussed. It speaks to the river's changing ecosystems as a result of the chemical, biological, and physical effects of the cities along the river.	3–6	Environmental Protection Agency 201 M Street SW Washington, DC 20460
Deep Down Underground (1989) Oliver Dureau	Fictional book that introduces ten animals that make their homes underground. The reader discovers the very active and fascinating world of the underground.	PK–3	Glencoe/McGraw-Hill School Division 936 Eastwind Drive Westerville, OH 43081 (800)848-1567
Education Goes Outdoors	Guide for developing environmental awareness using the five basic senses. Ideas for outdoor activities and excursions.	K–6	Addison-Wesley Publishing Company 2725 Sand Hill Road Menlo Park, CA 94025 (415)854-0300
Guided Discovery Activities for Elementary School Science (1997)	Includes science activities for incorporating creative problem-solving skills into the existing curriculum.	K–6	Merrill/Prentice Hall One Lake Street Upper Saddle River, NJ 07458 (201) 236-7000
Nature for the Very Young: A Handbook in Indoor and Outdoor Activities (1989)	Activities grouped by seasons, for both classroom and field use. Includes preparatory and followup activities to be used with field and forest environments. Includes songs, stories, poems, and recipes.	K–6	John Wiley & Sons, Inc. 605 Third Avenue New York, NY 10158 (212) 850-6000
Scholastic Environmental Atlas of the United States (1993) M. Mattson	Up-to-date atlas using a visual format. Contains more than 200 color maps and diagrams. Topics covered in the atlas include ecosystems, people, forest, and more.	2–6	Scholastic Inc. 730 Broadway New York, New York 10211–0081 (212) 343-6100
Science Fair (1986) Wendy Saul with Alan R. Newman	Includes activities and ideas for science fairs.	2–6	Harper & Row, Publishers 10 E. 53rd Street New York, NY 10022

Title	Description	Grade Level(s)	Publisher/ Supplier
Science for Children: Resources for Teachers (1988)	Contains many of the resources for hands-on elementary science teaching that are currently available from publishers and distributors. Divided into curriculum materials, supplementary resources, and sources of information and assistance.	K–6	National Science Resources Center National Academy Press 2101 Constitution Ave., NW Washington, DC 20418
The Global Ecology Handbook (1990)	As a resource guide, its primary aim is to increase understanding and awareness of key environmental issues about fresh water sources, tropical rain forests, environmental pollution, and more.	3–6+	Global Tomorrow Coalition Beacon Press 25 Beacon Street Boston, MA 02108–2800
Wow! The Wonders of Wetlands (1995)	Presents the issues associated with wetlands; a hands-on, interdisciplinary approach to wetlands and how to protect them. Includes lesson plans, illustrations, and experiments.	K–6+	Environmental Concern, Inc. P.O. Box P St. Michaels, MD 21663–0480
III. Children's Literature			
The Beginning of the Armadillas (1985) Rudyard Kipling	Story in far-off times on the banks of the Amazon. Beautifully illustrated animals and plants and stickly-prickly.	2–6	Harcourt Brace Jovanovich Publishers 1250 Sixth Avenue San Diego, CA 92101
The Littlest Dinosaur (1989) Bernard Most	Focuses on small dinosaurs compared to familiar objects such as a tub or a teddy bear.	PK–2	Harcourt Brace Jovanovich Publishers 1250 Sixth Avenue San Diego, CA 92101
The Magic School Bus: Inside the Earth (1987) Joanna Cole	Ms. Friggle's students who are studying earth science go on a field trip to the center of Earth through the mouth of a volcano.	1–6	Scholastic Inc. 730 Broadway New York, NY 10003 (212)343-6100
Mighty Tree (1992) Dick Gackenbach	Seeds grow up to be trees, and one tree still stands in the forest today.	K–3	Harcourt Brace Jovanovich Publishers 1250 Sixth Avenue San Diego, CA 92101

FIGURE 13-2, continued

Title	Description	Grade Level(s)	Publisher/ Supplier
Nothing Sticks Like a Shadow (1984) Ann Tompert	Describes how shadows are produced, through animal characters (the rabbit and the groundhog).	K–3	Houghton Mifflin Co. One Beacon Street Boston, MA 02108
A River Ran Wild (1992) Lynne Cherry	Story of the Nashua River that became so polluted it was declared ecologically dead in the 1960s, but a vision of a clean river became a reality.	1–6	Harcourt Brace Jovanovich Publishers 1250 Sixth Avenue San Diego, CA 92101
Two Bad Ants (1988) Chris Van Allsburg	The tale of how a group of ants go out and bring back crystals; but two ants stay behind and have a terrible experience. An interesting view of a kitchen and point of view.	2–6	Houghton Mifflin Co. One Beacon Street Boston, MA 02108
The Very Quiet Cricket (1990) Eric Carle	Chronicles the journey of a young cricket who meets many insects but who cannot greet them until he encounters a female cricket.	K–3	Philomel Books The Putnam Publishing Group 200 Madison Avenue New York, NY 10016 (800) 631-8571
I Want To Be an Astronaut (1988) Byron Barton	Describes what it is like to be an astronaut, from what is eaten to space walks at zero gravity. Illustrations and color engage the reader.	PK–1	HarperCollins Publishers Keystone Industrial Park Scranton, PA 18512 (800) 233-4190
Welcome to the Green House (1993) Jane Yolen	Story welcomes the reader to the green home of the sloth, capuchins, a toucan, coral snake, and others. Beautifully illustrated.	1–4	Scholastic Inc. 555 Broadway New York, NY 10012 (212) 343-6100

FIGURE 13-3 Supplementary Science Programs

Name	Program Description
Science—A Process Approach (SAPA)	Emphasizes the process skills of science in twenty activities for each grade, based on what working scientists do. Actively involves students in doing science.
Science Curriculum Improvement Study (SCIS)	Focuses on twelve units or major concepts throughout the elementary school and emphasizes depth not breadth in science topics; integrates process skills with content using hands-on activities.
Elementary Science Study (ESS)	Includes forty-one self-contained units that cover a wider area of science content and personally involves students with different and interesting materials as they seek answers to questions.
Biological Science Curriculum Study (BSCS)	Organized around a special theme for each grade level, it is more than just biology. Encourages students to construct their own understanding of an integrated world of science, technology, and health.
Full Option Science System (FOSS)	Designed for both regular and special education students, it involves sixteen modules (four at each grade level) and matches activities with ability to think at each grade level; includes extension activities in language arts, mathematics, and computers.
Life Lab Science Program	A comprehensive elementary science program based on garden activities using a planter box or garden space outdoors; incorporates aspects of the natural world as students explore science concepts and processes.
The Science Connection	A mini-museum approach with hands-on activities using unique manipulatives, including fifteen interactive exhibits to construct for each grade level with activity cards and handout masters.
Activities that Integrate Math and Science (AIMS)	A series of books that provides real-life experiences in mathematics and science, with approximately twenty hands-on investigations in each book organized around themes (Fun with Foods) and involving language arts and social studies.
Great Exploration in Math and Science (GEMS)	A flexible, integrated approach to teaching mathematics and science in thirty-three units organized around themes such as "Global Warming." Uses readily available materials to illustrate science and math concepts.

Education Standards, which were then published in 1996. These standards provide criteria for judging the quality of a science curriculum as well as offering a vision for defining scientific literacy. These standards identify what the students should have learned by the end of twelfth grade and work backward to determine what a student should learn regarding science understandings, principles, and skills in the following levels:

■   kindergarten through grade 4

■   grades 5 through 8

■   grades 9 through 12

There are eight content standards for grades K–4 and 5–8, which include Science as Inquiry, Physical Science, Life Science, Earth and Space Science, Science and Technology, Science and Societal Challenges, History and Nature of Science, and Unifying Concepts and Processes. In Figure 13-4, the skills and understandings for standards for grades K–4 are identified.

MANAGING AND ASSESSING STUDENT LEARNING IN SCIENCE

The topics of classroom management and student assessment are as important in science classrooms as in others. Because of the preparation time and the use of equipment and materials, management is essential for conserving valuable time. The process aspect of science presents unique assessment opportunities. It might be helpful for beginning teachers to consider themselves as managers of the classroom who need to take stock—to think about what a teacher does when managing a class. What/who needs to be managed in a science classroom?

Managing a Science Classroom

The management role is not necessarily a difficult one, but it does require that teachers function proactively, which means planning ahead as much as possible. For experienced teachers, being a classroom manager may not be as critical because they have been monitoring student behavior for a long time. But today there are more materials—e.g., computer hardware and software, consumable and nonconsumable materials, trade books, and other literature and resources—as well as more students to manage. This section highlights suggestions for managing a science classroom, and many of the recommendations made in other chapters can be used as well.

For the classroom manager, the first consideration is the design of the classroom: where should materials, equipment, and books be located to create a classroom environment that is stimulating, cooperative, safe, and reflects how one teaches? In science, center work and interactive bulletin boards are common, as are places for microscopes and flat surfaces to conduct experiments. In addition, a water source is desirable, which means the area needs to be protected from spillage, and an abundance of electrical outlets is also helpful (though, of course, they shouldn't be too near the water). In crowded classrooms, the dilemma becomes how to arrange the centers and materials for students to provide easy access and reduce behavior problems. Whatever strategies are implemented, they should be congruent with a teacher's philosophy and goals for student learning. Garcia (cited in Murray, 1994) offers some general advice when designing classrooms:

a.   Move your desk to one side or the back of the room to let kids know that you're a part of their community, not an authority figure presiding over it.

b.   Arrange students' desks to suit the way you teach. Do you want students to work in cooperative groups? Does the arrangement of desks reflect this?

c.   If you have a computer in your room, set it up so that what's on the screen won't distract children who are working on their projects.

FIGURE 13-4   Science Content Standards, Grades K–4

A. **Science as inquiry standards**
   - Abilities necessary to do scientific inquiry
   - Understanding about scientific inquiry

B. **Physical science standards**
   - Properties of objects and materials
   - Position and motion of objects—Light, heat, electricity, and magnetism

C. **Life science standards**
   - Characteristics of organisms
   - Life cycles of organisms
   - Organisms and environments

D. **Earth and space science standards**
   - Properties of earth materials
   - Objects in the sky
   - Changes in earth and sky

E. **Science and technology standards**
   - Abilities to distinguish between natural objects and objects made by humans
   - Abilities of technological design
   - Understanding about science and technology

F. **Science in personal and social perspectives**
   - Personal health
   - Characteristics and changes in populations
   - Types of resources
   - Changes in environments
   - Science and technology in local challenges

G. **History and nature of science standards**
   - Science as a human endeavor

H. **Unifying concepts and processes**
   - Systems, order, and organization
   - Evidence, models, and explanation
   - Change, constancy, and measurement
   - Evolution and equilibrium
   - Form and function

Source: Compiled from *National Science Education Standards*, pp. 105–109, by National Research Council, 1994. Washington, DC: National Research Council.

   d. Be open to adapting your space from time to time. (p. 62)

When designing the physical classroom space for science instruction, it is important to ensure that there are clear paths for traffic flow so that the students do not trip and hurt themselves. For the primary grade students, placing footprints on the floor to show the way to enter and leave an area might be helpful. If there are materials and/or equipment that the students should not handle, place them out of reach and/or in closets for safekeeping. The floor should be free of materials; for example, if extra electrical cords are needed for a science lesson, the cords should be taped down to prevent tripping.

Before moving furniture, sketch out ideas for how the physical space of the science classroom will be used. On the floor plan, identify where the teacher will be presenting, where the students will be investigating, and precisely where materials and equipment belong in the storage area. Animals, plants, and aquariums, which are commonly found in an elementary science classroom, require special considerations; students should receive guidelines for handling and feeding animals and watering plants.

As part of the planning step, consideration must be given to the classroom manager role. When planning science lessons, it would help to identify the activity as well as the facilities and the logistics needed to carry out the activity. As classroom managers, teachers use physical space to communicate expected behavior, security and safety, movement patterns, responsibilities, and warmth. The physical space of the classroom can make the science curriculum in the elementary school work. Figure 13-5 lists a series of questions to ask about the total classroom environment, including three dimensions: the physical environment, the interpersonal environment, and the development of science.

By arranging space (empty, active, and pathways), rearranging furniture (soft areas and establishing physical boundaries), and collecting and "strategically" placing basic furnishings (raw materials, scientific tools, display facilities, and information sources), teachers can create a science learning environment that provides experiences that stimulate both social and intellectual growth. When the physical space carries out the instructional goals, teachers are free from the task of disciplining students and regulating use of materials.

Suppose you were establishing cooperative learning centers for students who have just returned from a field trip to a geology museum. Some of these centers would be located around the room to accommodate three or four students at a time. At each center, all the directions (simply stated) and materials would need to be available. Chapter 6 discussed the roles for each group member; it is essential for each student in the group to have a job. The science centers could include the following:

- *The Measuring Rock Center*: As the students handle/manipulate the rocks, they will be using language to communicate size, shape, weight, and the kinds of rocks they are examining. In addition to learning about the properties/attributes of the rocks, they will learn number concepts of more than and less than, sets of rocks, as well as representing their sets of rocks on a simple bar or line graph.

- *The Rock Garden*: The scientific principles of saturated solutions, evaporation, making crystals, and chemicals are presented. The students will grow and examine crystal growth using the materials at the center, and over the next week they will use a magnifying glass and a microscope to view and then sketch or construct with toothpicks and marshmallows the geometric patterns that developed.

- *The Piedra Book*: The students draw pictures of their visit to the geology museum; some students may decide to draw pictures of the rocks and minerals they saw and handled and others may choose to draw pictures of the students on the bus, having lunch, or looking

FIGURE 13-5   Questions About the Science Classroom Environment

The Physical Environment
1. Where should quiet and noisy science activities be located so as not to disturb one another?
2. Are the materials for science available for students to use when needed and are these materials labeled?
3. Is there a management system in place so that students return science equipment and materials to appropriate areas of the room?
4. Are there clearly defined center areas with easy entrance to and exit from the center?
5. If water is needed, is area surrounding the sink/tub protected?
6. Is the reading/library area equipped with pillows/author's chair/rug for some quiet reading?
7. Do the bulletin boards provide science learning opportunities for students?
8. Is the students' work displayed at their eye level?
9. Are there flat surfaces to conduct experiments/investigations?

The Interpersonal Environment
1. Do students respect the materials and fellow students?
2. Do you (teacher) spend a limited amount of time controlling students' behavior?
3. Is the classroom environment arranged so that students can continue working while others are engaging in group experiences?
4. Do you get opportunities to observe while students are working?
5. Does each student—individual and group—have learning goals in science?
6. Do students feel safe while engaging in science activities?
7. Are there opportunities to engage in individual and group activities?

The Development of Science
1. Are there many opportunities to learn science through reading books, actively investigating, examining materials and equipment, etc.?
2. Is there a variety of science materials, tools, and equipment to use?
3. Are there opportunities for language experience activities—animals, feeling boxes, games, displays of fossils and rocks with magnifying glass, plants, and computers with science software?
3. Are there opportunities and materials to solve problems, puzzles, and so on?
4. Do students suggest ideas for experimentation, and do they have choice of what to investigate?
5. Are the activities/investigations designed so that all students can participate?
6. Is there a range of science experiences?
7. Are there opportunities for students to explore, discover, and problem solve?

at the specimens. They will write something related to their pictures, and the pages will be bound to form a class book, *Our Visit to the Geology Museum,* for all to read and remember about the very special day.

A second consideration when designing a science classroom is safety. Taking a survey of a classroom for potential problems would be helpful. Ensuring that an outlet is not overloaded with electrical equipment, that a fire extinguisher is handy, that a plan is developed in case of an emergency and assistance from the principal is needed, that students wear eye protectors when handling chemicals, and that there are guidelines for handling animals in the classroom to avoid getting bitten and/or scratched is key to a well-organized, inquiry-based science classroom environment.

When considering safety during science class, common sense is important. Discussing the district and school science safety policies with the principal is essential and part of the planning process. These policies, especially valuable in the upper grades, may include information about how to dispose of potentially hazardous or toxic materials, how to smell substances, how to mix chemicals, and how to handle materials properly. In addition, the National Science Teachers Association (NSTA, 1742 Connecticut Avenue, N. W., Washington, DC 20009) offers an excellent checklist of safety suggestions and procedures.

Assessing Student Learning in Science

Like classroom management, assessment has many parts and is a gigantic puzzle that has many separate pieces. Teachers continue to seek answers to the question *How do all these pieces fit together into a coherent assessment system?* A coherent assessment system means having ways to measure progress toward achieving the goals and objectives of science instruction. Many of the general concepts of assessment presented in Chapter 8 can be applied to teaching science.

If science teaching is structured as suggested in this chapter, assessment strategies must be designed to measure the progress toward reaching the general goals and the specific instructional objectives established for promoting scientific literacy. As scientific information grows geometrically, it seems foolhardy to require elementary students to memorize facts and definitions. It becomes more important for students to learn how to access this information, to ask questions and to get answers, than it is to commit facts to memory for a short time to past a test (Loucks-Horsley, 1989). The assessment system in science should revolve around performances, with students being able to do the following things:

- Manipulate laboratory materials and equipment.

- Acquire data through the senses.

- Classify, order, and sequence information/data.

- Measure and use relationships to standards.

- Draw conclusions based on the data, predict outcomes and form generalizations.

- Relate objects and events to other objects and events.

- Apply definitions to terms based on observations.

- Identify and manipulate variables/conditions of investigations.

Once the goals and objectives of a unit or lesson are identified, strategies for measuring levels of achievement need to be determined. For example, how will a teacher "know" if a student uses the microscope properly? One way might be to have the students identify the parts of a microscope on a worksheet and/or respond to a series of questions related to the microscope. Another way might be to have the students use the microscope to demonstrate their level of proficiency; for example, focusing the microscope to see onion cells on the glass slide and then carrying the microscope correctly back to the cabinet. The latter assessment strategy may be more appropriate to achieve the lesson objectives than labeling parts and/or responding to questions. Getting students to "show" what they know is called *performance assessment*; this seems more compatible with the science standards proposed by the National Research Council.

This does not mean that tests with the traditional types of questions are not acceptable; they are, as long as they measure the lesson objectives and provide a variety of ways for students to demonstrate, perform, and/or exhibit what they have learned about the topic/concept under study. Many textbook publishers provide teachers with tests that accompany the textbook chapters and units. Teachers should guard against using these tests without first correlating the items to their objectives for the lesson/unit and the actual concepts that were developed. Just because the test has been provided does not necessarily make it a valid assessment instrument for a particular class. When paper-and-pencil testing is used, teacher-made or teacher-edited tests may provide a more valid assessment of science understanding. In establishing assessment criteria, teachers may want to establish laboratory grades, test grades, homework grades, and/or daily work grades. It is often helpful to develop a set of criteria—grading rubric—for each science unit of study.

There are several assessment options to the traditional paper-and-pencil tests. Brown (1989) calls for a "new concept of testing, one that reflects the active nature of [science] learning" (p. 31). For students to become scientifically literate will require that they do more than comprehend and recall. It will require them to think critically, evaluate data, communicate in a variety of ways, and synthesize information; in short, students need to learn how to learn in a more active way, which in turns calls for greater thoughtfulness (Brown, 1989). By responding to a real situation, students get to experience problem solving and critical thinking in context and in a meaningful way. Such a dilemma provides a

connection to the real world and gets students to see science in their lives.

Other options include the use of portfolio assessment and group assessment. This list is not meant to be exhaustive—only to convey that assessment must go beyond the use of traditional multiple choice, fill in the blank, and matching tests. Portfolio assessment has to be much more than a collection of paper. It should be a collection of many meaningful types of materials that provide tangible proof of a student's progress in science class over the course of one six-week period, one term, and the entire year. Other content areas use logs, folders, files, and portfolios to show work in progress and final products; simply stated, student portfolios contain evidence. The items placed in the portfolio are a sampling of student work. Wolf (1989) describes a portfolio as a biography of work that reveals the geology of different moments that underlie the production of a major project. Collins (1992) provides a series of questions for designing science portfolios, and they include the following:

- Who decides the purpose and contents of the portfolio?

- Is the purpose of the portfolio the same for each student?

- Will there be evidence of proficiency or progress?

- What is the purpose of the portfolio?

- Who will review the portfolio, when and how often?

- Where will the portfolio be housed?

Portfolio assessment is a new and useful tool for science teaching and learning. This new tool is beneficial in managing student work in science as well; not only does it help students be organized, but it helps teachers as well (Swang, 1993).

Another important option is group assessment. Because cooperative learning/center work is an integral part of science learning, group assessment must be too. If these basic elements of cooperative learning are at work, group assessment means making judgments based on individual responsibilities performed toward some group end. All students must be held responsible for their own learning as well as the learning of others, must understand the concepts and complete assignments, demonstrate mastery of assigned work, provide leadership, and assess the progress of the group (Johnson & Johnson, 1987, 1989, 1994; Johnson, Johnson, & Holubec, 1994). To assess the group and its members fairly, a grading rubric needs to be developed for both the entire group and each member.

Well-prepared elementary teachers recognize that the heart of the assessment step is alignment with other aspects of the planning and implementation steps of the curriculum development process. Assessment is a teaching tool (Stiggins, 1994); assessment and teaching are interdependent. Making use of all available assessment tools is essential, to ensure that formative and summative decisions are based on accurate information and lead to quality learning for all students. Finally, effective assessments reveal students' science learning and support investigative science teaching (Loucks-Horsley, 1989).

MAKING CONNECTIONS

To enhance language-arts skills, all students should have opportunities to create a product that demonstrates an understanding of science principles and how to apply them, as well as discussing and writing about the process of how they gained this knowledge. Using the science process skills of questioning, constructing models, hypothesizing, gathering and organizing data, analyzing results, drawing conclusions, and communicating and reporting results, students acquire an understanding of science principles. The use of process skills is "the means by which science content is

learned" (Casteel & Isom, 1994, p. 534) because science principles, facts, and concepts are rooted in inquiry and hands-on experiences. Casteel and Isom (1994) go one step further when they say that process skills in science can be aligned with the literacy skills of purpose setting, predicting, organizing ideas, constructing/composing, evaluating/revising, and comprehending/communicating. Figure 13-6, using the ideas of Casteel and Isom (1994), presents the science concept of deserts to illustrate how science process and literacy skills are parallel and reinforce each other. It further shows how literacy and process skills are applied and developed.

By linking science and literacy process skills, students have an integrated experience that demonstrates that these skills are compatible and complement each other. In addition to language arts and literacy skills, science can also be connected to the fine arts, physical education, and social studies. Making a model of the solar system, with correct proportions to show accurate sizes and distances in the Milky Way requires that students use science and math concepts as they construct a three-dimensional model. For advanced students, scientific notation can be used to express these distances. Mobiles can be constructed to show the parts of an atom, organisms in a food chain, the components of a cell, or a DNA model with the double helix. Finally, students can act out a closed electrical circuit, movement of electrons through an electric wire, and the three parts of Earth (crust, mantle, and core) by holding hands. To illustrate how teeth help with digestion, students can act out how the teeth operate by themselves modeling the teeth in the mouth and passing food along to be "chewed." In social studies, as students study earthquakes, they can locate the Ring of Fire on a world map. Using a map of the United States, students can determine which states are contiguous with major faultlines, to better understand plate tectonics. Students can also do a time line of major earthquakes in the world and can research the cause

FIGURE 13-6   Parallels Between Process and Literacy Experiences

Science Experiences	Literacy-Based Experiences
Questioning Students ask questions about different types of deserts. For example, what is a desert? What conditions contribute to the different animal and plant life in each type of desert?	*Purpose Setting* Students describe the purposes for reading a book about deserts in their science log/journal and read until they find out the conditions that contribute to the variations in animal and plant life in each desert.
Hypothesizing Develop hypotheses about what will occur if there is a 10 percent increase in rainfall. For example, what will an increase in rainfall mean to different types of plants, and in turn, mean to different animal populations?	*Predicting* Predict how an increase in rainfall will influence the plot, setting, and general mood of the various books and stories read.
Gathering/Organizing Data Make a data table to record and categorize the types of plants and animals in each type of desert without the 10 percent increase in rainfall and then with an increase.	*Organizing/Sorting Out Ideas* Develop semantic maps to organize the information gained from the books about deserts. Next, analyze the map and begin to group the information randomly displayed on the map related to science concepts and facts.
Analyzing Results Analyze the data recorded on the data table and identify factors that affected the results. Use graphs, tables, and/or graphic organizer (map) to demonstrate.	*Constructing/Composing* Discuss past experiences students have had when they visited a desert. Using a language experience approach, record the ways the students compare the different types of desert or the types of plant and animal life found there and the impact on people.
Drawing Conclusions In cooperative groups, evaluate the data regarding animal and plant populations with limited rainfall and with increased rainfall in the hypothetical model and state conclusions.	*Evaluating/Revising* Write a story about the desert and its animal and plant life and have students revise by editing on the computer, if available.
Reporting Results Summarize what has been learned and report by making a presentation to the class.	*Comprehending/Communicating* Publish a book about deserts and share individual contributions from the author's chair.

Source: For more information, see "Reciprocal processes in science literacy learning" by C. P. Casteel and B. A. Isom, April 1994, *The Reading Teacher*, 47(7), 538–544.

and the cost of the devastation resulting from each earthquake and compare them in today's costs.

SUMMARY

Chapter 13 began with a discussion of the importance of being scientifically literate. Scientific literacy is the driving force for restructuring the K–12 science curriculum, particularly at the elementary school level. *Scientific literacy* was defined as having the ability to understand key scientific concepts and principles, being aware of how science interfaces with other disciplines, recognizing that science has strengths and limitations, and becoming aware that scientific knowledge and ways of thinking are used for individual and social purposes. The goal of science education at the elementary level is to have students who will develop critical-thinking skills and the ability to make decisions regarding the many technological advancements they read about and encounter in their daily lives.

The chapter provided a glimpse of science teaching in the elementary school; it used a wide lens to get a general picture of why science is important and why there is a need to restructure science education, particularly in grades K–6. The chapter concluded with a discussion of ways to manage a science classroom, along with ways to assess science learning and ways to make connections with other content areas.

As emphasized in the chapter, science is a basic in the elementary curriculum and is for all students. Having such a view means that science is taught and occupies a prominent position in the total elementary instructional program. Science learning requires that students do science, not just read about it. The chapter described several ways this can be done—getting students to work at constructing their own knowledge base as they learn science principles and as they redress misconceptions that they may have, making connections to the world in which they live, and being active learners in an inquiry-oriented classroom environment. The science curriculum in the elementary school will change only when and if teachers acknowledge and implement a philosophy that says that science is interactive and social in nature and requires students to investigate.

■ YOUR TURN

1. In your role as a teacher, as you look at a science textbook, you find that the next topic for study is simple machines. Rather than teach this topic in an isolated, content focused way, you decide to develop an integrated approach to teaching about simple machines. Go to the library and see what resources and trade books are available on the topic of simple machines. Find at least two poems or children's literature books about simple machines. Now plan your instruction so that the theme of simple machines is presented in science, mathematics, language arts, social studies, and art.

2. Review the standards in Figure 13-4. Select one standard and outline ways you would implement it with elementary children. To get started, it may be helpful to refer to the planning chapter and use a semantic map to generate ideas for the unit. It is important to

take this standard and move this concept into the science classroom.

3. Select three science topics (Earth movements, animal and plant life, or atoms and molecules, for example). Review a set of catalogs for materials that you could use to teach these topics in ways other than using direct instruction and the textbook. Review Figure 13-2 for ideas. Check to see if materials—computer software (Chapter 9), literature books, etc.—are available to present the concept. Make a list of the items you would need to purchase to teach this concept. Visit a local elementary school that has a well-developed science program and ask to see the materials they have and determine which specific suppliers they use.

4. Review Nadine's "Voice of Experience" section about being an elementary science teacher who now uses an inquiry-based approach, having moved from being the "giver of knowledge" to a facilitator. Take a few moments and respond to the following questions as you reflect on the kind of science teacher you would like to become.

   a. What role will you play during science class?

   b. Do you feel comfortable about teaching science? If not, why do you feel this way and what can you do about it, to feel more confident?

   c. How will you make the transition from giving students all the science information to letting them construct their own knowledge base?

5. You are interested in how teachers manage children during a science lesson. Where do you begin to plan for such a lesson? You may want to review pp. 314–318 before proceeding, but here are a few ideas:

   a. Visit three or four elementary classrooms where science is taught. (Is science taught in a regular classroom or in a special room? If it is in a special room, is the room spacious, well-equipped, with moveable furniture, and so on?) Describe, using a sketch, the classroom environment that you are observing.

   b. After doing some reading and visiting classrooms, prepare a semantic map. In the middle of a sheet of paper, write "Organizing a Science Classroom." Out from the center, write the major issues/concerns with subheadings where appropriate. Once you have done this, take these ideas and place them in a scale drawing of an elementary science classroom. Compare your sketch developed from the semantic map with the one from the on-site school visits.

6. Use a semantic/spider map to develop a unit on weather. As you think about this science unit, consider the information that has been presented in this chapter as well as the planning and implementation chapters, and develop a series of cooperative learning activities that promote scientific literacy. As a way of determining the effectiveness of these activities in achieving the goal of scientific literacy, develop assessment strategies that will determine the level of student learning and performance. It may be helpful to construct a grading rubric for the center work and products.

■ REFERENCES

ACCESS ERIC. (No Date). *How can elementary science education be improved?* Funding from the Office of Educational Research and Improvement. Washington, DC: U. S. Department of Education.

American Association for the Advancement of Science. (1993). *Benchmarks for science literacy.* New York: Oxford University Press.

Arnosky, J. (1979). *Crinkleroot's book of animal tracking*. New York: Putnam.

Baylor, B. (1973). *The desert is theirs*. Upper Saddle River, NJ: Merrill/Prentice Hall.

Brown, R. (1989). Testing and thoughtfulness. *Educational Leadership, 46*(7), 31–33.

Casteel, C. P., & Isom, B. A. (1994, April). Reciprocal processes in science literacy learning. *The Reading Teacher, 47*(7), 538–544.

Collins, A. (1992, March). Portfolios: Questions for design. *Science Scope, 15*(6), 25–27.

EdTalk: What we know about science teaching and learning. (No Date). Washington, DC: Council for Educational Development and Research.

Gega, P. C. (1995). *Science in Elementary Education* (7th ed.). Upper Saddle River, NJ: Merrill/Prentice Hall.

Haury, D. L., & Rillero, P. (1992). *Hands-on approaches to science teaching*. Columbus, OH: ERIC Clearinghouse for Science, Mathematics, and Environmental Education, 7.

Hurd, P. D. (1991). Why we must transform science education. *Educational Leadership, 49*(2), 33–35.

Johnson, D. J., & Johnson, R. T. (1994). *Learning together and alone: Cooperative, competitive, and individualistic learning* (4th ed.). Boston: Allyn & Bacon.

Johnson, D. J., & Johnson, R. T. (1989). *Cooperation and competition: Theory and research*. Edina, MN: Interaction Book Company.

Johnson, D. J., & Johnson, R. T. (1987). Toward a cooperative effort: A response to Slavin. *Educational Leadership, 46*(7), 80–81.

Johnson, D. W. , Johnson, R. T. , & Holubec, E. J. (1994). *The new circles of learning: Cooperation in the school*. Alexandria, VA: Association for Supervision and Curriculum Development.

Locker, T. (1993). *Where the river begins*. New York: Puffin Pied Piper Books.

Loucks-Horsley, S. (1989). Science. *Educational Leadership, 46*(7), 86–87.

McCormick, K. (1989, June). Battling scientific illiteracy: Educators seek consensus, action on needed reforms. *ASCD Curriculum Update*. Alexandria, VA: Association for Supervision and Curriculum Development.

Mechling, K. R., & Oliver, D. L. (1983). *Science teaches basic skills, Handbook I*. Washington, DC: National Science Teachers Association.

Murray, W. (1994, July/August). Have we got designs for you! *Instructor, 104*(1), 59–62.

National Commission on Excellence in Education. (1983). *A nation at risk: The imperative of educational reform*. Washington, DC: U. S. Department of Education.

National Science Resources Center. (1988). *Science for children: Resources for teachers*. Washington, DC: National Academy Press.

National Research Council. (1994). *National science education standards*. Washington, DC: National Research Council.

What should scientifically literate students know? (1993, December). *NEA Today, 12*(5), 11.

Oehring, S. (1993, March). It's not just science: It's life! *Instructor, 102*(7), 65–66.

Resnick, L. B., & Chi, M. T. H. (1988). Cognitive psychology and science learning. In M. Drugen (Ed.), *Science for the fun of it: A guide to informal science education* (pp. 24–31). Washington, DC: National Science Teachers Association.

Rutherford, J. F., & Ahlgren, A. (1989). *Science for all Americans*. New York: Oxford University Press.

Schwartz, D. M., & Kuhn, D. (1988). *The hidden life of the forest*. New York: Crown.

Science curriculum improvement program. (1992, February). [Profiles in excellence: innovative instruction.] *Executive Educator, 14*(2), A11–A12.

Sivertsen, M. L. (1993). *State of the art: Transforming ideas for teaching and learning science. A Guide for elementary science education*. Washington, DC: Office of Research, U. S. Department of Education.

Stiggins, R. J. (1994). *Student-centered classroom assessment*. Upper Saddle River, NJ: Merrill/ Prentice Hall.

Swang, J. (1993, April/May). Ensuring success in science. *Learning 93, 21*(8), 24–26.

Texley, J., & Wild, A. (Eds.). (1996). *NSTA pathways to the science standards*. Arlington, VA: National Science Teachers Association.

Tolman, M. N., & Hardy, G. R. (1995). *Discovering elementary science: Methods, content, and problem-solving activities*. Boston: Allyn & Bacon.

Wolf, D. P. (1989). Portfolio assessment: Sampling student work. *Educational Leadership, 46*(7), 35–39.

Yolen, J. (1987). *Owl moon*. New York: Philomel.

chapter 14

Physical Education and Fine Arts Programs

AFTER READING THIS CHAPTER, YOU WILL BE ABLE TO DO THE FOLLOWING:

- Discuss the importance of physical education and fine arts to the elementary curriculum.

- Identify and discuss the goals of physical education to the elementary curriculum.

- Discuss the role and importance of adaptive physical education.

- Identify and describe the subjects and goals of the fine arts.

- Describe how teaching art and music in the elementary school has changed over time.

- Discuss ways to link the fine arts to the other subjects in the elementary curriculum.

Previous chapters have described specific subjects of the elementary curriculum that are normally considered the responsibility of the classroom teacher and are frequently thought of as the basics in the core curriculum. The subjects in this chapter are taught as specialized subjects in many elementary schools by teachers who have areas of specializations in physical education or the fine arts (art and music). In many schools, the elementary teacher takes or sends his or her grade-level students to teachers who have specialized knowledge and skills in one or more of these subjects in the curriculum.

Physical education is included as a part of the elementary curriculum because physical activity is a developmental component that adds breadth and depth to student learning and because some form of physical activity or training has historically been an integral part of the elementary school. Elementary schools traditionally have been responsible for helping students understand not only the basics of personal health and hygiene, but the importance of participating in physical activities. Students are expected to be knowledgeable spectators of sports and other

recreational activities as well. Recently, physical education has been viewed as one of the subjects responsible for helping students understand the facts and skills they will need to become and stay healthy as they "navigate through the serious health risks that surround them" (Willis, 1990, p. 1). Physical education activities also engage students in kinesthetic learning, one of the seven avenues of learning (Armstrong, 1994). In order to accomplish this goal, schools should develop comprehensive programs that address students' physical, emotional, mental, and social health (Willis, 1990).

The *fine arts*, which typically include art, music, and sometimes drama, have also been considered an integral part of the elementary curriculum for decades. Educators have provided support for the fine arts by noting that a well-balanced elementary school curriculum should contain such subjects as music, drama, painting, poetry, and sculpture and that these subjects should be included side by side with the traditional subjects of language arts, mathematics, social studies, and science.

The inclusion of the fine arts in the curriculum has not always been the case. These subjects often struggle for identity and have frequently been seen as fringe or "frill" subjects of the curriculum. With the recent preoccupation with test scores and an emphasis on studying the "basics," Fowler (1988) notes that

> The public as well as many teachers and educational administrators view the main business of schooling as essentially developing the mind and the power to reason . . . they see the arts as mindless, nonacademic fare, more related to the hand than the head. (p. 5)

Recently, however, Fowler (1994) has made the case that the arts should be a part of the basic elementary curriculum for all students because they contain unique attributes that make them a valuable resource for other subjects within the instructional program. He continues by saying that elementary schools tend to reward "regimented, convergent thinking," but the arts help students develop divergent thinking; there may be several correct solutions to a problem, which "is far more often the case in the real world, where there are many ways to do something well" (p. 1). Fowler concludes by saying that, unlike science and mathematics, the arts provide "wisdom, not data" and that we "need every possible way to reveal and respond to our world" (p. 7). Within this context, the fine arts are seen as a way of helping students develop an awareness of the aesthetic components in their environment and thereby expand their view of the world.

The subjects of physical education and the fine arts are considered part of a well-balanced elementary curriculum. One or more of these subject areas may be the responsibility of the classroom teacher. Therefore, this chapter presents a brief description of each area. The chapter is organized into two major sections: the first section focuses on physical education and the second on the fine arts (including art, music, and drama). Each section examines the nature of the subject area along with the purposes, goals, typical kinds of activities, assessment procedures utilized, and possible connections with other subjects in the elementary curriculum.

PHYSICAL EDUCATION

Physical education (PE) is a basic curriculum area that contributes to the total education of the individual by emphasizing physical activity to promote body fitness and wellness. Most states (46) require some form of physical education in the elementary grades because it is an opportunity for students to engage in physical activity and movement. PE also gives students an opportunity to engage in kinesthetic intelligence, one of the seven avenues of learning (Armstrong, 1994). Physical education includes but is not limited to fitness, recess, intermural and intramural athletic events, and classroom instruction that may involve "presenting, demonstrating, discussing, and experimenting" (Shepherd & Ragan, 1992, p. 475). Seefeldt and Vogel (1980) suggest that the elementary PE curriculum should provide opportunities for students to learn concepts related to health, improve fundamental motor skills, develop physical and motor fitness, gain body control skills, and participate in activities that develop personal, social, and attitudinal skills.

Schwager and Labate (1993) have suggested that physical education is also a natural subject for teaching students to develop their cognitive skills. Physical education provides an avenue for a developing student's ability to think critically using a variety of teaching models (McBride, Gabbard, & Miller, 1990). By devising solutions to movement problems, students must think about possible actions, try them out, and decide which responses are the most effective. Doolittle and Girard (1991) suggest using games as a means of getting students to reflect on their actions. As students develop their cognitive skills, they also improve their physical skills and fitness. Schwager and Labote (1993) note that

> The advantage of focusing on critical thinking in teaching physical education is that it can heighten students' awareness of their own thinking and the degree to which their thinking skills can be effective in helping them become more skillful, fit, and knowledgeable about physical activity. (p. 25)

Seefeldt and Vogel (1980) agree with others about the benefits of PE, but they also recognize that educators have frequently ignored the fitness needs of students. Recently, the President's Council on Physical Fitness found that elementary students in the U.S. are not in good physical condition and that schools should develop strong physical education programs that promote vigorous physical activity (Greene & Adeyanju, 1991).

In reflecting on the changes that have occurred in the teaching of physical education, Morris, our "Voice of Experience" for this chapter, describes the differences between when he started his teaching career and how the approach seems to him now.

 Voice of Experience

Morris, having just delivered his class to the PE teacher in the gym, takes a few minutes to visit with the teacher. Morris is impressed with the classroom management the teacher has used with the students in PE. As the students arrived, they went to a spot on the floor in the gym where they began with their warm-up exercises. Morris's class is combined with another teacher's for PE, so 50–55 students are in the gym at one time. An aide takes attendance while the PE teacher visits with Morris.

This arrangement for physical education was not like Morris's first year teaching, when he was responsible for PE and recess. He tells the PE teacher, "I really was at a loss for what to do, so I allowed the children to pick teams and play the games they wanted to in PE. At recess, I let them have free time outside on good weather days with no organized activity; students played on various pieces of playground equipment (swings, bars, seesaw, etc.). I really had no idea what I was supposed to do other than let the kids play games, supervise their behavior, and serve as a referee when needed."

Today, Morris brings his students to a gym where the PE teacher takes over; the students learn new skills and practice those skills before they engage in any type of organized competition or group endeavor. Morris notices an emphasis on individual fitness and a sense of well-being rather than an emphasis on competition.

The physical education program that Morris observes is more like what Shepherd and Ragan (1992) refer to as "a balanced program [that] includes the development of skills, achievement of fitness, the understanding of movement, and the extension of perceptual-motor coordination" (p. 475).

Support for including physical education in the curriculum has also come from the literature on multiple intelligences (MI). Armstrong (1994) has applied Howard Gardner's MI theory to classroom teaching. This theory suggests that the broad range of human abilities or capabilities can be grouped into seven comprehensive categories: linguistic, logical-mathematical, spatial, musical, interpersonal, intrapersonal, and bodily-kinesthetic. It is the last intelligence, bodily-kinesthetic, in which students use their entire bodies to communicate and express their ideas and feelings. By using their entire bodies, students can produce things with their hands and increase their coordination, balance, strength, speed, and haptic capacities (Armstrong, 1994). For example, in preschool and primary classrooms, as students engage in block play using large hollow blocks and smaller unit blocks, they "develop creativity as they plan, design, and construct. . . . Block-building requires physical strength, coordination, and balance" (Harris, 1994, p. 23).

Goals of Physical Education

Many educators have been concerned that physical education has had too many objectives with little or no alignment among them as students progress within and between grades. A common complaint is that there is virtually no correlation between achievement and time devoted to teaching the skills or content (Seefeldt & Vogel, 1980). Elementary physical education teachers, in recognizing these difficulties, have attempted to meet the fitness needs of all students by teaching their subject differently and developing a balanced approach to their subject. A good elementary physical education program should include the following:

■ the development and reinforcement of perceptual abilities

■ the development of the functions of the central nervous system

■ the improvement of the proficiency in neuromuscular skills and successful participation in other physical activities

■ the awareness of weight gain (obesity) and improvement in muscle strength, endurance, and tone

■ the enhancement of self-concept and self-esteem, with opportunities for socialization (Seefeldt & Vogel, 1980)

Morris and Keogh (1980) have given direction for the elementary physical education curriculum by providing a comprehensive list of goals that contain five main areas (p. 10):

I. Physical Growth and Development
   A. *Body physiology*: has a high degree of physical fitness as seen in students' efficiently functioning cardiovascular, digestive, and neuromuscular systems.
   B. *Mechanically efficient posture*: exhibits body posture appropriate for the developmental level.
   C. *Symmetrical growth*: has body proportions (muscle, fat, and bone) appropriate for the developmental level.
   D. *Physical attribute development*: has physical attributes of strength, balance, flexibility, and agility appropriate for the developmental level.

II. Psychomotor Behaviors
   A. *Basic body behaviors*: performs mechanically efficient movements in locomotor and nonlocomotor activities as well as reception and propulsion activities.
   B. *Motor control skills*: controls body parts while moving within geographic limits relative to other students.
   C. *Increase movement patterns*: uses the body in a number of ways while maintaining certain body postures.
   D. *Survival skills*: performs efficient movements required within the natural or contrived environment.

III. Intellectual Behaviors
   A. *Knowledge of body physiology*: describes basic body physiology and concepts relating to maintenance and physical activity.
   B. *Strategy/problem solving*: identifies and uses strategies appropriate for the existing movement environ-

ment to solve a variety of movement problems.

C. *Biomechanical concepts*: identifies and uses basic mechanical principles involved in human movement.

D. *Daily living survival strategies*: identifies and selects appropriate programs to participate in and then select the appropriate equipment.

IV. Social Behaviors

A. *Group interaction*: displays appropriate behaviors in successful interaction within a group setting appropriate to their developmental level.

B. *Strategies*: uses both verbal and nonverbal coping strategies in a group setting.

C. *Cooperative and competitive behaviors*: demonstrates the ability to cooperate with other group members while involved in a competitive activity.

V. Recreational Behaviors

A. *Healthy frame of mind*: describes the relationship between recreational participation and the maintenance of a healthy body through their participation in recreational activities.

B. *Positive attitude*: displays a positive attitude toward exercise or movement activities by regular participation in physical activity.

These goals represent a broad range of behaviors that involve not only physical movement and neuromuscular coordination, but also cognitive skills, as students engage in problem-solving strategies. Similar goals are a part of the California physical education framework (California State Department of Education, 1986) which includes physical activity, physical fitness and wellness, movement skills and movement knowledge, social development and interaction, self-image and self-realization, and individual excellence.

Goals for health and physical education in the elementary grades encompass a wide spectrum of learning activities that include, but are not limited to, "body mechanics, movement, rhythms, gymnastics, low-organized games, high-organized games, and exercises" (Shepherd & Ragan, 1992, p. 475). These goals contribute to the total education of students in the elementary school. According to the National Association for Sport and Physical Education (1992), a physically educated person is one who has the skills needed to perform a variety of physical activities, attains and maintains a physically fit body using principles of training and conditioning, knows the benefits and implications of fitness and physical activity in his or her life, and values physical activity as it contributes to general health.

In addition to physical education, health education topics are an integral part of a wellness program, which emphasizes individual responsibility for a personally healthy lifestyle. As Willis (1992) notes

> Students in K-12 physical education classes are learning more than how to kick a soccer ball or field a pop fly. . . . They're also learning how to stay healthy throughout their lives. . . . The overriding goal of P.E. programs today is to help students develop skills and attitudes that will equip them to lead an active, healthy lifestyle. (p. 3)

Health education includes such topics as nutrition, stress management, community health, diseases, alcohol, tobacco and drugs, safety and first aid, and personal and family health/hygiene. In addition, students learn about the relationship of physical activity to health through such topics as aerobics, jogging, and weight training. By incorporating these health topics within the framework of the physical education curriculum, such a program helps students focus on the development and maintenance of total fitness and wellness.

Assessment in Physical Education

Assessment in physical education involves not only evaluating the student's performance for the purpose of reporting achievement and progress or giving a grade, but also determining the overall success of the physical education program in promoting personal responsibility for maintaining a healthy lifestyle. To accomplish these goals, teachers commonly use tests, which are objective in design and measure a certain skill or quality, for example the fifty-yard dash (Thomas, Lee, & Thomas, 1988).

Teachers also use checklists and rating scales, which are more subjective in nature and are based on observations the teacher makes with regard to specific criteria or elements on a rating scale as students practice various skills. Thomas, Lee, and Thomas (1988) advocate that teachers focus on five areas in testing elementary students: "growth, health-related physical fitness, movement skills, related cognitive knowledge, and affective behaviors" (p. 184).

While teachers may give paper-and-pencil tests that assess the students' knowledge of the history, rules, and equipment of a game, this type of assessment should be only be one component in the assessment system. The progress a student has made in physical education also depends on the student's level of performance as measured against his or her own benchmarks. Therefore, assessment in physical education involves the student in a different way from the other subjects in the elementary curriculum.

Adaptive Physical Education

In addition to regular physical education in the elementary school, adaptive physical education has become more common and is designed for learners with special needs. Adaptive physical education uses movement for special education students as a way of reinforcing movement behaviors, especially those linked with the individual's ability to function. Sadler, in Figure 14-1, provides a description of an adaptive physical education program and the emphasis of the program on movement education.

The importance of movement education cannot be overemphasized. As students develop physical skills such as dexterity, flexibility, and strength, they gain confidence in their ability to express themselves in other ways and in other subject areas.

Making Connections

Elementary teachers can incorporate many of the goals of the physical education program within the classroom through thematic integrated units. Movement education lends itself to a variety of classroom applications. For example, a common theme in the primary grades is "Animal Friends." As students find out where certain animals live, they explore geography. As they learn about animal products, they learn economic concepts. In art, students make clay animal figures and put them in a setting to illustrate habitat. As students pick their favorite animal to write about and report on, they use language arts skills. As students give their reports or at the conclusion of their reports, they can demonstrate how the animal they have selected moves. The class can then have an "animal parade," in which the students move like the various animals they have selected. A variation on this theme is to have the students "act out" the way their animal moves and have the class try to guess the name of the animal.

Movement education can be included as students read a "map of movement." As they go through doors, cross the playground, or enter the classroom, they move according to the symbols on their map. As teachers have students role play, act out, or physically demonstrate behaviors, they are linking the cognitive domain of learning with the psychomotor domain and movement reinforces other learning.

There are numerous ways to involve students in motor learning in other subjects: role playing

FIGURE 14-1   Adapted Physical Education

A major step identifying children with special needs and providing early intervention was initiated in the form of federal legislation, specifically Public Law 94–142—the Education for All Handicapped Children Act of 1975 (EHA). This landmark civil rights enactment and subsequent amendments to it have changed the way many school districts provide for the education of students with special needs. This legislation identifies special education as "specially designed instruction, at no cost to the parent, to meet the unique needs of a handicapped child, including classroom instruction in physical education, home instruction, and instruction in hospitals and institutions." An interesting aspect of the mandate is that physical education was identified as the only discipline referred to as a component of special education while being labeled as a direct service. In other words, all special needs children are to be provided the benefits of a properly administered physical education program based on individual needs—not convenience.

Adaptive physical education programs play an essential part in the successful implementation of movement objectives. The physical educator with special education expertise has knowledge about how to structure perceptual-motor learning experiences that serve to support routine daily movement behaviors. Selected practices by the adapted physical education teacher include (1) physical and motor fitness, (2) gross and fine motor development, (3) special athletic/recreational activities, and (4) integration of the child into the least restrictive learning environment.

Motor skills represent initial neuromuscular learning experiences for elementary students. These experiences form the foundation for confronting the multitude of ensuing challenges as students with special needs develop their coordination and gross and fine motor skills. When ample opportunities for sensory stimulation are planned, the central nervous system experiences enhanced viability for perceiving, organizing, and executing neuromuscular responses. Hence, early movement activities are a complementary resource for enhancing cognitive potential.

Sharper conceptual relationships are formed when all learning domains are accommodated and incorporated into learning activities. The table of skills that follows forms the basis of movement education and is the foundation upon which the needs of students who require an adaptive P. E. program are addressed. Each major category has sub-areas for physical educators and teachers to focus on as they plan and implement experiences that promote movement and overall physical development for students with special needs.

Essential Elements of the Movement Education

Health-Related Fitness	Skill-Related Fitness	Movement Awareness	Locomotor Skills	Nonlocomotor Skills	Manipulative Skills
Cardiovascular	Balance	Auditory	Body rolling	Bending	Throwing
Endurance	Coordination Strength	Body Directional	Walking Running	Stretching Twisting	Striking Catching
Flexibility	Agility Power	Spatial Tactile	Jumping Hopping	Turning Swinging	Kicking Bouncing
Muscular Endurance	Speed	Temporal Vestibular Visual	Leaping Galloping Sliding Skipping Climbing Marching	Swaying Dodging Stooping	Dribbling Trapping Volleying Ball rolling Shuffle-boarding

FIGURE 14-1, *continued*

Sensory integration of the nervous and muscular systems makes it possible for rudimentary movements (i.e., rolling over, crawling, creeping, standing, etc.). This phase establishes voluntary control of movement by the individual. As locomotor patterns emerge, the child is afforded new and more diverse sources of sensory information as active exploration of the environment becomes possible so the child not only can see but can touch things as well. Environmental awareness increases as the child learns such concepts as direction, space, timing, and balance. As a result, the processing of information strengthens perceptual-motor tasks and further strengthens the memories that will be used later in higher-order thought.

Intellectual development for the physically challenged child is often associated with limitations in locomotion and the manipulation of objects. These limitations are due in part to a lack of opportunities through the variety of learning modalities (physical, musical, spatial, social, etc.). Children with these limitations do not process information into an integrated neuromuscular movement. They often find themselves in precarious positions when attempting to adapt to everyday behaviors. Locomotion, for example, is of primary concern to all people because simple movement can be laborious and prone to inaccuracies so that walking to the mailbox becomes a complex motor task. Balance and spatial awareness must be mastered to successfully negotiate throughout one's house, on the streets, in school, or in a business. Serious hardships develop when the most routine tasks are responded to in a manner that is incompatible with environmental demands.

Many regular physical educators find themselves ill-prepared for students with special needs and without the necessary base of support from specially trained colleagues. A creative and economical solution may be found in the pooling of resources in the form of cooperatives. School districts may then contract with educational cooperatives for support services for the physically challenged. A co-op will employ an adaptive specialist who consults with the member districts. This is less than ideal, but it serves as a pragmatic alternative for financially strapped school systems. It allows for an adaptive specialist to collaborate with the regular physical educator in creating a learning environment that is consistent with the atypical learner's Individual Education Plan (IEP).

Appropriate education begins with the involvement of the total person. The individual is a movement-oriented, independent thinking, and socially aware being. The needs of exceptional students are no different than those of able-bodied persons. They, like us, desire to be wanted, loved, and respected. Physical education uniquely addresses all of these concerns. Though movement education is the central theme, the psychomotor learning environment is conducive for promoting interaction, cooperation, creativity, and problem solving, along with an element of risk without fear of ridicule. Good physical health and motor development are extremely important to the future success of every child.

Source: Used by permission of Wendell C. Sadler.

or acting out a story in language arts or social studies, physically moving objects to count in math, writing in language arts, and assuming the role of someone else in social studies. Elementary teachers can help maximize learning for all children by involving them in bodily-kinesthetic experiences in each of the other content areas.

FINE ARTS

The fine arts are also sometimes known as the aesthetic or creative arts within the elementary school curriculum and include the visual and performing arts, particularly the areas of art, music, and drama. Music and art are the most common forms of the fine arts found in elementary schools and are generally considered an integral part of a well-balanced elementary curriculum. Increasingly, drama with the use of puppets has become a part of the elementary curriculum. Most educators recognize the value of the fine arts because, as Smith (1994) says, "Studying the arts can inform the study of other subjects, . . . spark creativity, imagination, and critical thinking, . . . [and] raise a person's self-esteem and develop a sense of discipline that carries over into all other areas of life" (p. 427). Students learn about craftsmanship, divergent thinking, presentation skills, attention to detail, empathy and compassion for others, and how to express their fears, struggles, and hopes.

Shepherd and Ragan (1992) suggest several objectives of the aesthetic or fine arts curriculum.

- *Aesthetic awareness*, which includes an appreciation of such areas as music, art, dance, drama, and theater, as products of civilization.

- *Creative awareness*, as students learn to express themselves in experiences that use a wide variety of materials and facilities.

- *Human awareness*, which encourages students to develop their unique personal qualities that serve as vehicles for self-expression.

- *Communication awareness*, as students learn to communicate with each other through various art forms that include (but are not limited to) painting, sculpting, printing, weaving, dancing, singing, composing, reading, and role playing.

- *Selection awareness*, as students assume the role of aesthetic consumers in society and make decisions about personal preferences in art, music, and entertainment.

- *Experience awareness,* as students have direct and indirect involvement in movement, expression, spontaneity, and creativity in each of the fine arts forms.

Morris, the "Voice of Experience" for this chapter, describes the fine arts in his school and contrasts today's approach to earlier approaches.

 Voice of Experience

As Morris takes his students to music class, he remains behind to listen to what they are studying and doing. Morris remarks to a colleague that "I am amazed at what the music teacher is able to accomplish with the students. The music teacher had three classes, half of the grade level, in one big room. My students sat in chairs on risers next to students from other classes. Some of the students were involved with rhythm instruments (tambourines, rhythm sticks, bells, and Orff instruments). As the students studied American folk music, one group sang, while some played the instruments, and others danced to the music in a group activity. I was impressed with how much the students enjoyed the class, and when the activity was over, they returned the instruments to their correct places, went to their assigned seats, and all sang a quiet campfire song to end the class."

In Morris's school, each teacher is responsible for his or her own art activity. Morris has to work constantly to incorporate art activities into his lessons. The subjects that best lend themselves to art are language arts and social studies. However, there are times when Morris has been able to relate mathematics and science to art; sometimes he just teaches a separate art unit. He tells a colleague about a time when he was teaching a unit on "Physics at Play": "I used the state fair as the theme, with all the rides, especially the roller coaster, food, and fun to be had by all, to teach about the role that physics plays at a state fair. I incorporated art by having the students do a mural of what the state fair was like, depicting all the vending and food stands and the many opportunities to have fun. Also, one of my favorite activities is to graph favorite foods eaten, using illustrations, at the fair. Students genuinely enjoy this activity."

As Morris describes his involvement in the fine arts curriculum, he notes how interested the students are in these subject areas. These subjects give students an opportunity to express their musical, dramatic, and visual abilities. The arts promote aesthetic awareness as students develop their sense of self and accomplishment; the arts help students feel good about themselves.

Recently, the arts and humanities have been combined in some schools "to help children better understand the relatedness of all forms of art" (Nelson & Sigmon, 1982, p. 390). Within this combined program, teams of specialists from art, music, and drama contribute activities from each discipline that interrelate these disciplines with others. This approach involves the regular classroom teacher in joint planning with the arts specialists. Using themes like "My World," "Feelings," "Make Believe," and "Hidden Treasures," students engage in activities that help them understand the nature of the humanities and learn something "that brings true joy to life" (Nelson & Sigmon, 1982, p. 391). The goals of each of the fine arts areas (music, art, and drama) are described in the sections that follow.

Goals for Music Education

Calls for greater inclusion of music in the elementary curriculum have increased in recent years as educators have come to recognize its importance in the education of young people. Miller and Coen (1994) have suggested that " a student's education is impaired if it does not also touch the soul, and music can be the key" (p. 461). They further suggest that with the recent focus on cooperative learning strategies in elementary schools, music is a natural subject because it occurs within a cooperative setting.

Musical intelligence is one of Gardner's seven avenues of learning (Armstrong, 1994) and should be an integral part of the elementary curriculum. Armstrong (1994) points out that musical intelligence is the capacity to "perceive (i.e., as a music aficionado), discriminate (i.e., as a music critic), transform (i.e., as a composer), and express (i.e., as a performer) musical forms" (p. 3). He goes on to say that students increase their sensitivity to a musical piece by understanding the role of rhythm, pitch, melody, timbre, and tone. For example, at Cushing Elementary School in Delafield, Wisconsin, students sing their lessons with the help of the Sensational Singing Sponges (*Executive Educator*, 1992). As students sing hits such as "Math Meringue" and "Minute Rock," about telling time; "Recycle It," about conservation; and "The Continents (and Oceans Too)," they retain more of what they have learned by pairing content with rhythm and notes.

To emphasize the importance of music in students' learning, the Music Educators National Conference (1986) recommended the following goals for the elementary music curriculum:

- to develop in students the ability to make music, alone and with others

- to help students understand and use the vocabulary and notation of music

- to help students respond to music aesthetically, intellectually, and emotionally

- to foster and develop in students an appreciation of the value and worth of music in the lives of human beings

- to develop in students the ability to listen critically, make analyses, and make aesthetic judgments

- to foster and promote continued musical learning and support of music within the community

Research (Rauscher, Shaw, & Ky, 1993) further supports the inclusion of music in the curriculum by suggesting that listening to and making music impacts abstract reasoning and intelligence.

Educators must draw upon the concepts of music that range from rhythm to instrument playing, as they implement the goals of the curriculum. Figure 14-2 provides a list of the musical concepts along with the types of activities or content associated with each concept. Teachers can adapt this list to include musical activities in their classroom.

Haines and Gerber (1996) note that musical activities and experiences, such as those listed in Figure 14-2, should be based on the developmental level of the child. McDonald and Simons (1989) also caution that "in musical development, as in all growth processes, each child is unique and each child's musical growth pattern must be understood and respected" (p. 52). In developing

a music program for the elementary grades, Haines and Gerber (1992, 1996) recommend the following kinds of musical learning experiences:

■ *Listening experiences*, because listening is fundamental to all other music skills such as moving, singing, playing, and creating. Although this experience has traditionally been linked to recorded pieces, teachers can provide numerous actual sounds for students to analyze, discriminate among, and respond to.

■ *Movement experiences*, because movement is central to the acquisition of musical concepts as the child uses his or her "whole body to explore and express changes in tempo, dynamics, or pitch, or to express the line of a phrase or the mood of a song" (Haines & Gerber, 1992, p. 11). Movement experiences

FIGURE 14-2   Music Education Concepts

Concept	Typical Activity or Content
Rhythm	clapping, chanting, or moving to beats
Melody	reading and performing notes and recognizing familiar songs
Harmony	distinguishing between harmony and unison and recognizing chords
Form	identifying verse and refrain
Tone color	recognizing and distinguishing voice parts and instrumental parts
Expression	identifying and applying musical terms such as *forte, mezzo piano, allegro*
Science of sound	identifying and describing how sounds are made and what kinds of sounds are made by different instruments
Style	recognizing different types of music (e.g., classical vs. popular)
Singing	reading and singing various tonal patterns and songs
Movement and dance	moving and clapping in beats in various and repeated ways
Instrument playing	playing scales and chords on various instruments

can also be linked with bodily-kinesthetic experiences in physical education.

- *Singing experiences*, because singing can express feelings and emotions and is crucial to vocal development. Rote or unison singing can be used to catch and focus attention, heighten pleasure, and stimulate participation.

- *Playing experiences,* because playing provides opportunities for students to hear and produce many different sounds. As Haines and Gerber (1992) note, "classroom instruments provide opportunities for children to make their own music" (p. 12).

- *Creating experiences*, because as they create, each child uses "a basic vocabulary of musical experiences and skills" (p. 13). Through involvement in listening, moving, singing, and playing, the elementary student learns to create.

Goals for Art Education

Often the inclusion of art in the public school has been viewed as an elitist component of the curriculum, "to be pursued by a privileged or talented few" (Efland, 1990, p. 1). This elitist perspective is often contrasted with art that involves "cutting pieces of orange construction paper to make pumpkins at Halloween, making turkeys at Thanksgiving, [or] so-called holiday art" (O'Neil, 1994, p. 1). O'Neil continues by saying that more recently, elementary schools have incorporated the "disciplines of art history, criticism, production, and aesthetics into their curriculum . . . [and] art is an integral part of many of the units that teachers develop; it's woven into history, literature, and even math" (p. 1). For example, Parks (1995) suggests that art and geometry can be combined to create geometric sculptures whereby students work with angles to construct 3-D sculptures using orange peels and toothpicks.

To help explain the role of art in the elementary curriculum and counteract the elitist view, the National Endowment for the Arts (NEA) (1988) proposed the following goals of the art curriculum in the elementary school:

- to foster and develop within students a sense of civilization from studying many cultures and using great works of art to illustrate the nature and constancy of the human condition

- to foster and develop within students a sense of creativity by studying and emulating master artists, as they experiment with various techniques and media

- to foster and develop in students an extension of communication skills using art forms as the language through which artists speak in the visual and design arts or in combination with other expressive art forms (i.e., music, drama, dance)

- to foster and develop in students the ability of critical analysis so they can make better choices as they recognize the emotional power of the arts to stir, inspire, and move people

Eisner (1987/1988) advocates a more discipline-based art curriculum than does the NEA, one that would provide a

> systematic, sequential teaching of the four things people do with the arts: they make works of art, they appreciate art, they learn to understand art in relation to cultures, and they make judgments about the arts. These four major operations are art production, art criticism, art history, and aesthetics. (p. 7)

Some schools prefer to approach art "up close and personal" by having students work with professional artists and participate in exhibits (*Executive Educator*, 1992). For example, students at Cutler Ridge Middle School in Miami, Florida, have an opportunity to study with a professional artist whereby they are given the opportunity to develop their own skills and shine.

Goals for Drama Education

Although not as visible within the fine arts curriculum, drama or theater education also has a place in the elementary school. According to Corathers (1991), over the past decade educators have come to appreciate and value drama and theater production in schools. Verriour (1986) notes the impact of drama on language development as students assume roles, interact with each other, and communicate the action of this dramatic world to the audience. Verriour (1990) suggests that storytelling in a dramatic context causes students not only to think in a narrative mode, but to think about narration as a way of interpreting and verbalizing experiences. Flynn and Carr (1994) further suggest that drama can provide a vehicle whereby students can more fully explore literature in the classroom as they memorize lines, decide on appropriate actions to match the words, and determine the tone, volume, or pitch with which to deliver the words. Carr and Flynn (1993) also suggest that other subjects, such as science, can be taught through drama by constructing a play about space travel, for example.

The National Endowment for the Arts sponsored a committee to examine the advantages of drama and theater in the curriculum. That committee found that drama or theater contributes to a greater understanding and appreciation of literature and other subjects, has the power to move and change people, provides a way of reframing reality as less threatening, offers a creative and emotional release to academic learning, helps people become better thinkers in other subjects, increases collaborative skills, and creates an exciting, magical, and satisfying experience. The goals for drama and theater education for the elementary curriculum include (National Endowment for the Arts, 1988):

- developing and understanding drama and theater as a metaphor for society
- demonstrating how drama and theater reveal human experience through roles and characters

- recognizing that dramatic performance offers levels of communication through verbal and nonverbal actions
- illustrating the collaborative nature of performance among performers and between the performers and the audience
- recognizing the critical element of expressive behavior of actors or role players
- acknowledging the great care and skill needed to create a performance
- developing lifelong interest in theater and dramatic works

ASSESSMENT IN THE FINE ARTS

The typical form of evaluation in the fine arts program involves observation and feedback from the teacher during the preliminary phase of production or development. In art, this involves providing guidance and information as the students work with different media (paint, clay, and/or charcoal). As one teacher puts it, "I watch the developmental skills growing and provide verbal feedback in the initial stages of a project and then, I hand back projects so they can get feedback about a project" (Barr & Anglin, 1992, p. 25).

Giving feedback about technique, skills, presentation, and/or accuracy is different from making adult judgmental remarks about the students' self-expression. Such judgmental remarks should be avoided, for if a teacher describes a student's art work as "ugly," "strange," or "nothing but junk," the student will tend to become self-conscious and limit involvement in art, which may mean venturing only into areas that are "safe." Similarly, a teacher who describes a student's singing or playing as "hurting their ears," or "an awful sound/racket" destroys the student's self-confidence and negates the objectives of the fine arts program. If a teacher is overly critical of a student's performance in a play or story, the student is likely not to want to participate in any expressive behaviors.

If a grade is required, it should be based on specific characteristics or components the teacher has presented. In art, it is not unusual to have students develop a portfolio (discussed in Chapter 8). The portfolio represents the student's efforts in a variety of media and demonstrates progress that occurs over time as the student masters various art skills and techniques. Auckerman (1992) has suggested a discipline-based art education curriculum that hastens the student's development of such art skills as composition and color range in water color paintings as he or she learns to produce art from art. Such compositions and color range in paintings can be assessed.

As with any aesthetic endeavor, the teacher must walk a fine line between judging and coaching. The teacher's role in inspiring confidence and developing creative ability is to assist students in working on skill, technique, composition, and style.

Making Connections

Of all of the subjects taught in the elementary school, the fine arts are perhaps the easiest to integrate into other areas. Music, art, and drama, because they represent expressive behaviors, lend themselves to being included in a variety of ways. For example, for an integrated unit at the beginning of the year, a second-grade teacher has chosen "We Go to School" as the theme. For their art activity, students draw what they looked like on their first day in that grade. In science, they talk about physical features and hygiene and how important it is to brush teeth and hair, get plenty of rest, and eat healthy foods. The students keep a personal journal for the month recording the number of times they brushed their teeth. In language arts, they read *This Is the Way We Go to School* by Edith Baer (1990) and *Franklin Goes to School* by Paulette Bourgeois and Brenda Clark (1995) and develop a concept map about going to

school from their home. This map becomes the focus for writing about going to school in a class book shaped like a school bus. The teacher also introduces the Magic School Bus series (Cole, 1987) that will be revisited as they take "trips" throughout the year. For mathematics, the teacher has the students count how many are in the class each day, and subtract from the total. The students keep a graph of students present/absent. For physical education, they practice body movements concerning how to walk in school emphasizing posture and how to walk in a (straight) line. The students also develop a fitness profile during the first month which becomes a baseline for their physical development for the year. The teacher also takes a picture of each student to put in their portfolios as an example of what each student looked like at the beginning of the school year. For music, the students learned the song "The Wheels on the Bus Go Round and Round." This becomes their beginning of a school theme song.

Music can be easily integrated into any unit, even traditional topical units, and it makes a great addition to the learning process. For example, in social studies, students can sing pioneer songs for westward expansion, patriotic songs of the founding of the nation, songs of other cultures when students study cultural diversity, and songs about families and feelings when studying home and neighborhood. In science, they sing "Take Out the Trash" or "The Recycle Song" as they study ecology, "Hungry Dinosurs" or "Panda in the Forest" as they learn about endangered species, "Rain, Rain, Go Away" as they learn about the water cycle or states of matter, "Way down Yonder in the Paw Paw Patch" as they learn about seeds and growing plants, and "Johnny Appleseed" as they talk about trees and life cycles. For language arts, students in the early grades love "The Alphabet Song." Perhaps one of the easiest ways to involve music in language arts is choral reading, whereby students learn rhythm and sound variations (loud, soft) as well as staying together. "Grammar Rock" can be sung to help students learn parts of speech and sentence structure. A fun activity to do is to take familiar tunes and have students rewrite the words to fit something they are studying. For example, students might sing "Old McDonald Learned to Read," which would include sounds of letters or parts of speech. For math, students learn to sing about math operations through songs such as "The Ants Come Marching" or variations such as the "Five Speckled Frogs."

Art can be integrated into the curriculum by having students draw or illustrate stories in language arts. They also can make drawings or illustrations in science as they study various topics. For example, in studying the rain forest, one teacher used *The Great Kapok Tree* (1990) by Lynne Cherry as the focus for the unit, then had the students construct a diorama from a box and materials from nature to show what a rain forest looks like. Animal pictures can be cut from magazines or drawn, colored, and placed in the diorama. One teacher has students design a T-shirt to publicize the need to save the rain forest while others create stationery to raise money. In language arts, teachers have students design greeting cards that link illustrations with text or poems. In math, student can illustrate stated or word problems to make the abstract statements more concrete.

In drama, students can use finger puppets and finger plays to act out stories, poems, and songs. They can write their own plays based on books they have read or role play people and events in social studies. Figure 14-3 provides additional resources and tools for elementary teachers to teach or integrate art and music across the curriculum.

SUMMARY

This chapter described those content areas often called the "other subjects" in the elementary curriculum. Physical education and the fine arts provide the finishing touch to the elementary curriculum. Depending on the political and social climate, these areas are sometimes in jeopardy and at other times held in high esteem. Regardless of the climate, these areas have been considered essential to the overall development of elementary students; without them, student capabilities are not nurtured and talents are left unrecognized and untapped. Therefore, physical education and the arts should not only be taught, but valued for their contribution to the total instructional program in the elementary school.

This chapter has examined the nature, goals, activities, and assessment strategies of physical education and the fine arts (art and music) in the elementary curriculum. The classroom teacher may not have direct responsibility for teaching these subjects because they are often taught by teacher specialists within the elementary school. Physical education has become an important part of the elementary school as a way of promoting fitness and wellness along with providing experiences to develop kinesthetic abilities. The concern for the lack of fitness among America's schoolchildren has created the demand for more vigorous physical activity. Other concerns, including health problems and obesity among school-aged students, have led to the inclusion of health education in the elementary physical education curriculum.

Including the fine arts in the elementary curriculum is important because they provide students avenues for self-expression and allow students to be creative. Musical intelligence is also one of the avenues of learning that teachers can capitalize on. Music serves a social and cooperative function as students work together in ensembles as they "make music" together. The music curriculum encourages students to move, listen, sing, and create.

The art curriculum also encourages elementary students to express themselves using media other than the written or spoken word. While often viewed as an elitist subject in the curriculum or an "artsy, craftsy" activity, when coupled with

FIGURE 14-3   Resources for the Arts

Title	Description	Grade Level(s)	Publisher/Supplier
I. Art Books			
Dorathea Lange: Portraits of Women Artists for Children (1994) Robyn Montana Turner	Compelling biography presents a wonderful series of photographs of life in America. Turner uses the photographs to facilitate social change.	2–8+	Little, Brown Time and Life Bldg. 1271 Ave. of the Americas New York, NY 10020 (800)343-9204
Master of Mahogany: Tom Day, Free Black Cabinetmaker (1994) Mary E. Lyons	Biography of a black man who is a talented artisan at the height of slavery and includes first-rate photographs. This is his personal story.	1–8+	Scribner's Simon & Schuster Children's Ordering Dept. 200 Old Tappan Road Tappan, NJ 07675 (800)223-2336
The Piñata Maker: El Piñatero (1994) George Ancona	Spanish-English photo-essay describing how Don Ricardo constructs piñatas for "fiestas." The color photographs are very detailed and provide valuable information regarding the art and craft of piñata making.		Harcourt Brace 8277 Sea Harbor Drive Orlando, FL 32887 (800)831-7799
What Makes a Cassatt a Cassatt? (1994) Richard Muhlberger	Highlights an American-born female artist, Mary Cassatt. Her biography is in one of the series from the Metropolitan Museum of Art, and provides information about ways to identify her work.	1–8+	Viking Publishing Division of Penguin USA 375 Hudson Street New York, NY 10014-3657 (212)366-2000
II. Music Books			
A Moving Experience: Dance for Lovers of Children and the Child Within (1987) Teresa Benzwie	Includes more than 100 activities to help children to discover the qualities of space, time, rhythm, their bodies, and numbers as well as learn the principles of mathematics and physics.	PK–6	Zephyr Press 3316 North Chapel Avenue P. O. Box 66006-C Tucson, AZ 85728-6006 (520)322-5090

II. Music Books (continued)

Title	Description	Grade Level(s)	Publisher/Supplier
Lives of the Musicians (1993) Kathleen Krull	Discusses composers including Verdi, Bach, and Puccini, Gutherie, Foster, and others. Bluebonnet nominee.	4–6	Harcourt Brace Jovanovich 465 S. Lincoln Drive Troy, MO 63379 (800)543-1918
Sing and Shine On! The Teacher's Guide to Multicultural Song Leading (1995) Nick Page	Uses music to promote a desire to sing; step-by-step approach supported by new research in the field proving music's many powers in shaping the body. Provides ways to integrate singing into the curriculum.	1–6	Heinemann 361 Hanover Street Portsmouth, NH 03801-3912 (800)541-2086

III. Drama Books

Title	Description	Grade Level(s)	Publisher/Supplier
Artists: Exploring Art Through the Study of Five Great Lives (1992) Chris Brewer	Introduces students to the basics of design, color, and the creative process by focusing on five world master artists including Van Gogh, Escher, da Vinci, Homer, and Rembrandt.	2–6	Zephyr Press 3316 North Chapel Avenue P.O. Box 66006-C Tucson, AZ 85728-6006 (520) 322-5090
101 Dance Games for Children: Fun and Creativity with Movement (1995) and *101 Music Games for Children* (1995) Paul Rooyackers	Two books that can be used to enhance interpersonal and listening skills. They also illustrate how music and dance helps to develop listening skills and self-expression, as well as ability to concentrate.	K–6+	Hunter House 2200 Central Avenue Suite 202 Alameda, CA 94501 (415) 865-4295
Dramathemes: A Practical Guide for Teaching Drama (1995) Larry Swartz	Best-selling book of games and activities for linking drama to other areas of the curriculum through such themes as fantasy, animals, and folklore.	2–6	Heinemann 361 Hanover Street Portsmouth, NH 03801-3912 (800)541-2086
Dramatic Play in Childhood: Rehearsal for Life (1995) V. Glasgow Koste	This new edition of Koste's book focuses on dramatic play and the role it plays in developing a sensitivity to art as well as to developing skills for life.	PK–6	Heinemann 361 Hanover Street Portsmouth, NH 03801-3912 (800)541-2086

FIGURE 14-3, continued

Title	Description	Grade Level(s)	Publisher/ Supplier
IV. Software			
Art Gallery CD	Students learn about each artist's technique. Includes more than 2,000 masterpieces, plus biographies about the artists.	4+	Educational Resources 1550 Executive Drive P.O. Box 1900 Elgin, IL 60121-1900 (800)624-2926
Kid Works Deluxe CD	Opportunities to be creative and imaginative through painting and writing. Bilingual version available.	PK–4	Davidson and Associates P.O. Box 2961 Torrance, CA 90509 (800)624-2926
Making Music CD: Voyager	This CD provides aspects of music that appeal to a variety of senses. Students paint notes and can modify the volume of the music, instrumentation, and tempo.	2+	Educational Resources 1550 Executive Drive P.O. Box 1900 Elgin, IL 60121-1900 (800)624-2926
Music of American History: Apple Pie CD	Almost 350 years of compositions are provided and students learn about the history of American music. The social and political contexts are presented for each time period.	4+	Educational Resources 1550 Executive Drive P.O. Box 1900 Elgin, IL 60121-1900 (800)624-2926

other disciplines, art can provide greater depth and meaning to concepts by providing a visual dimension to concepts studied. The art curriculum is designed to help students create art, analyze or critique art, understand historical aspects of art, and finally, appreciate and consume art.

The physical education and the fine arts curriculum help to complete the elementary school program. They provide a balance between the abstract learning of mathematics and language arts by providing hands-on physical education, music, and art experiences—participating in mime, making crafts, engaging in creative movements, singing, humming, whistling, playing an instrument, and linking tunes with concepts. What would learning be like without all of these encounters? Students always take their bodies with them as they enter elementary classrooms, and students can use their bodies to express themselves.

>>
<<<<<<<<<<<<<<<<<<<<<<<<<<<<<<<<<<<<<<<<<<<<<<<<<<<<<<<<<<<<<<<<<<<<<<<<<<<<

■ YOUR TURN

1. Working with elementary children of differing ages (e.g. 7, 9, and 11), conduct several activities to determine their level of neuromuscular coordination. You may want to throw a ball to each and observe how the child catches it, with what degree of accuracy and dexterity. You might have them hop on one foot, skip, jump rope, and run a short distance, while you note the efficiency of each child and each age group. If you work with boys and girls of the same age, try to determine if there are any neuromuscular differences.

2. Visit an elementary music class and observe what the students are doing. Make a list of the kinds of activities in which the students are engaged. Interview the teacher and discuss the reasons why he or she included these specific musical activities. What opportunities are there for listening, movement, singing, playing, and creating? What system does the teacher use to assess the students' progress/growth?

3. Visit several elementary school classrooms and observe the kinds of student art work

that are displayed. Does the art work fit the "holiday art" category, or are the students engaged in a variety of activities that address different media, perspective, form, line, composition, personal interest, and other art concepts? After you decide which category the art fits into, talk with the teacher to confirm your opinion. (What are the goals of the art program? What role does art play in the elementary school?)

4. Ask students in at least three different grade levels to draw a person. Such drawings can be used to identify the cognitive development of children. Such information can be helpful as teachers plan units for language arts, social studies, science, and mathematics. The younger the child, the less detail will be provided (kindergarten and first grade); older elementary students provide more specific detail.

5. Obtain a copy of the "Checklist for Assessing Students' Multiple Intelligences" from *Multiple Intelligences in the Classroom* by T. Armstrong (1994, p. 35), and administer it to several children.

6. Select one of the following thematic unit titles, and identify and describe an art, music,

and physical activity you could have students do to help them learn and understand the concepts of the unit:

"Back to the Future in History"

"The Lights of the Holiday Season"

"Rivers, Rocks, and Ridges"

"Talk to the Animals"

■ REFERENCES

Armstrong, T. (1994). *Multiple intelligences in the classroom*. Alexandria, VA: Association for Supervision and Curriculum Development.

Auckerman, R. (1992, April). Children's art from fine art. *SchoolArts, 91*(8), 30-32.

Baer, E. (1990). *This is the way we go to school*. New York: Scholastic.

Barr, D., & Anglin, J. (1992, September). Reflections of a first year teacher. *SchoolArts, 92*(1), 24-26.

Bourgeois, P., & Clark, B. (1995). *Franklin goes to school*. New York: Scholastic.

California State Department of Education. (1986). *Handbook for physical education: Framework for developing a curriculum for California public schools K-12*. Sacramento: California State Department of Education.

Carr, G. A., & Flynn, R. M. (1993). Science through drama. *Science Activities, 30*(3), 23-24.

Cherry, L. (1990). *The great kapok tree*. San Diego, CA: Gulliver Books, Harcourt Brace Jovanovich.

Cole, J. (1987). *The magic school bus inside the earth*. New York: Scholastic.

Corathers, D. (1991, November). Theater education: Seeking a balance between stage and classroom. *ASCD Curriculum Update*, pp. 1-7.

Doolittle, S. A., & Girard, K. T. (1991). A dynamic approach to teaching games in elementary PE. *JOPERD, 62*(4), 57-62.

Efland, A. D. (1990). *A history of art education*. New York: Teachers College Press.

Eisner, E. (1987/1988). On discipline-based art education: A conversation with Elliott Eisner [Interviewed by Ron Brandt]. *Educational Leadership, 45*(4), 7.

Executive Educator. (1992, February). Sensational singing sponges. *Profiles in Excellence: Innovative Instruction, 14*(2), A19-A20.

Flynn, R. M., & Carr, G. A. (1994). Exploring classroom literature through drama: A specialist and a teacher collaborate. *Language Arts, 71*, 38-43.

Fowler, C. (1988). *Can we rescue the arts for America's children?* New York: American Council for the Arts.

Fowler, C. (1994). The arts teach vital lessons. *ASCD Update, 36*(4), 17.

Greene, L., & Adeyanju, M. (1991). Exercise and fitness guidelines for elementary and middle school children. *The Elementary School Journal, 91*(5), 437-444.

Haines, B. J. E., & Gerber, L. (1996). *Leading young children to music* (5th ed.). Upper Saddle River, NJ: Merrill/Prentice Hall.

Haines, B. J. E., & Gerber, L. (1992). *Leading young children to music* (4th ed.). Upper Saddle River, NJ: Merrill/Prentice Hall.

Harris, T. (1994, September). The snack shop: Block play in a primary classroom. *Dimensions of Early Childhood, 22*(4), 22–23.

McBride, R., Gabbard, C., & Miller, G. (1990). Teaching critical thinking skills in the psychomotor domains. *The Clearing House, 63*, 197-201.

McDonald, D., & Simons, G. M. (1989). *Musical growth and development: Birth through six*. New York: Schirmer.

Miller, A., & Coen, D. (1994). The case for music in the schools. *Phi Delta Kappan, 75*(6), 459-461.

Morris, G. S. D., & Keogh, J. (1980). *Elementary physical education: Toward inclusion*. Salt Lake City: Brighton Publishing Company.

Music Educators National Conference. (1986). *The school music program: Description and standards* (2nd ed.). Reston, VA: Music Educators National Conference.

National Association for Sport and Physical Education. (1992). *Outcomes of quality physical education programs*. Reston, VA: National Association for Sport and Physical Education.

National Endowment for the Arts. (1988). *Toward civilization: A report on arts education*. Washington, DC: National Endowment for the Arts.

Nelson, D. S., & Sigmon, B. L. (1982, February). Combining the arts and humanities. *Educational Leadership, 39*(5), 390-391.

O'Neil, J. (1994, January). Looking at art through new eyes. *ASCD Curriculum Update*, pp. 1, 8.

Parks, M. (1995, April). Get an angle on art. *Instructor, 104*(7), 37.

Rauscher, F. H., Shaw, G. L., & Ky, K. N. (1993, October). Music and spatial task performance. *Nature, 365*(6447), 611.

Schwager, S., & Labate, C. (1993). Teaching for critical thinking in physical education. *JOPERD, 64*(5), 24-26.

Seefeldt, V., & Vogel, P. (1980). What can we do about physical education? *Principal, 70*(2), 12-14.

Shepherd, G. D., & Ragan, W. B. (1992). *Modern elementary curriculum* (7th ed.). Fort Worth, TX: Harcourt Brace Jovanovich.

Smith, B. M. (1994). The art of being human. *Phi Delta Kappan, 75*(6), 427.

Thomas, J. R., Lee, A. M., & Thomas, K. T. (1988). *Physical education for children*. Champaign, IL: Human Kinetics Books.

Verriour, P. (1990). Storying and storytelling in drama. *Language Arts, 67*(2), 144-150.

Verriour, P. (1986). Creating worlds of dramatic discourse. *Language Arts, 63*, 253-263.

Willis, S. (December, 1992). Physical education: Promoting lifelong fitness for all students. *ASCD Curriculum Update*, pp. 3.

Willis, S. (November, 1990). Health education: A crisis-driven field seeks coherence. *ASCD Curriculum Update*, pp. 1-2, 8.

Epilogue: Teachers Do Make a Difference

The epilogue brings the curriculum development process to a close. In bringing this book to an end, we will take a more personal and direct style of discussing the issues that confront teachers as they seek to do the best job they can in promoting teaching and learning in their classrooms. From the beginning of the book, we have stressed that teachers are one of the most critical elements in the curriculum development process. Teachers do make a difference. But how?

First, they make a difference because of the philosophy they have about teaching and learning, which profoundly affects the way teachers interact with students, structure their classrooms, and promote learning. As Berliner (1996) notes, teaching is a moral profession, and the intent of this book is to foster the professional understanding of teachers so that they practice their profession with integrity. In Chapter 1, the curriculum development model was presented, with the steps of planning, implementing, and assessing. In each step, the teacher has direct influence on the teaching and learning that occur in the classroom by deciding what will be taught, when it will be taught, how it will be taught, and who has learned.

The following feature is part of a speech given by Dr. George Wright, Provost at The University of Texas at Arlington, to students completing their teacher certification program. Dr. Wright discusses the important lessons about life that he learned from his teachers and describes how teachers make a difference in both positive and negative ways.

 ## Reflections of a Student

Lessons I Learned from My Teachers

What I am about to say would be trite if it were not so significant: *The most important component of education in the 1700s, the 1800s, the 1900s, and I suspect in the beginning of the year two thousand, is the interaction between student and teacher.* Issues like the value of multicultural education and test taking will come and go; schools will even adapt to new and changing technology, *but it is the dedication that the teacher brings to his/her job that will still make the most significant impact on students in grades K through 12.*

Several years ago, I published a book entitled *Pursuit of Equality: A History of Blacks in Kentucky, 1890–1990*. In that book, I made a point about school teachers that is relevant to what I want to say to you today. In a chapter on "Black Education," I pointed out that the physical plant of the segregated black schools most surely was inferior to that of the white schools. Then I said, "Schools, however, are far more than brick and mortar. Schools are places where the young learn, grow, and are encouraged to set high goals and then strive to reach them. Therefore, the most crucial aspect of the entire education experience is the teacher–student encounter in the classroom. With their highly trained and dedicated teachers, who often served as surrogate parents, counselors, and friends, the black schools in the state of

Kentucky definitely were the equal to white schools."

I was born in Lexington, Kentucky in 1950. In the formative years of my life, there were many, many restrictions on what people like me could do or even aspire to. Racial segregation and discrimination were rampant; black people were prohibited from the free use of downtown accommodations. We could not try on clothes or shoes before purchasing them, nor use the restrooms in the department stores. We could not eat in the restaurants nor be buried in the same cemeteries as whites. We attended segregated schools. I do not say these things out of a sense of bitterness but to point out the reality of American society of that day and that the color of one's skin greatly determined one's options.

It would be my elementary and junior high school teachers—women and men who were dedicated to their profession—who gave me the vision to dream, prodded me to work hard, and told me that I could make something of my life in spite of the racial discrimination that was an obvious barrier to black Americans.

One of the most important lessons that was reinforced every year that I attended all-black schools was that I must be responsible for my own actions. My Afro-American teachers said to me repeatedly that just because another student got away with doing something wrong, and I was called to task over the same thing, did not excuse my misbehavior.

My teachers even challenged me on issues related to race. "Being black," they said, "could never be used as a crutch for poor performance." For teachers, one of the things that so troubles me today is that far too often we do not really challenge and educate our students. This is especially true of teachers dealing with minority students; these teachers often "cave in" to their poor, lame excuses, instead of saying because you are a minority, you might have to work twice as hard to prove yourself to members of the majority group.

It was when I was in the eighth grade that one of my teachers said some things that have held me in good stead throughout my life. Back then, I was always in trouble at school, and thanks to my teachers, who were constantly calling my mother and telling her about the latest thing I had done, I seemed to always be on a punishment of some type. One day, while feeling really low, I asked my teacher, "Why do all of my teachers dislike me so?" She said that they realized I had potential, and that I could make something of my life, and that on the few occasions when I was not being disruptive but actually taking part in class activities, I exhibited real ability. The only thing stopping me from being something, she said emphatically, was me. That teacher told me that beginning the very next school year, I would be attending an all-white school and I would need to be prepared for what I would encounter, namely that some of my teachers might not demand the very best of me.

Subsequently, I had a conversation with my history teacher when I was in the eleventh grade that made me at first question my self-worth, but fortunately I then remembered what my teacher and the other black teachers had said to me years earlier. By the time I was in the eleventh grade, I had acquired a love for reading, especially about history. One day, I stayed after class so that I could talk privately to my teacher. I told him that after much thought, I had decided on a career, something other than being a professional basketball player. I wanted to be a history teacher just like him. I will never forget his reply. He said I lacked the intelligence to graduate from college and become a teacher. I should join the Army or get a job on the assembly line at the local plant.

Please do not misunderstand me, enlisting in the Army or working at a manufacturing plant can, in fact, lead to very meaningful lives. But, my history teacher's comments in telling me to go to the Army or to go to work in a factory were intended as a "put-down," to remind me that I had a place in life from which I really could not expect to grow. *Though shocked, dismayed, and even angry at what he said, I refused to buy into his negative assessment of me. Why? Because the words of my earlier teacher were still in my mind and thoughts: that I could be anything I wanted to be. She and the other black teachers at the supposedly "inferior" black school, most definitely had planted a seed in me that I had begun to reap.*

For many years after completing my education, I wondered how many other young people had been given such negative feedback, and who, unlike me, did not have former teachers who had given them confidence in their ability. On several occasions while teaching at the University of Kentucky, I thought about going over to my high school and reminding my history teacher about his comments to me.

Then, the perfect occasion came: in 1990 as part of its 100th Anniversary Celebration, the high school decided to start a Hall of Fame to honor a few of its more than 25,000 graduates. The second year, I was one of the four people chosen for induction. When I was first informed that I had been selected, I told them that I would decline the offer. Then, upon being approached a second time, I told them that I would accept but that I would have some rather frank comments to make at the induction. By that time, however, I decided that it would be unbecoming of me to be mean-spirited, because too many good things had worked out for me in my life. When accepting the award, I simply said that my induction, though it might be considered by some as an individual honor, was really in recognition of all of the Afro-American students who attended the high school during the early days of school integration.

In retrospect, I have lost all bitterness over the incident, but I do believe that the history teacher committed a "sin" within his profession. I want to believe that there simply have to be some sacred values that go with certain occupations: a doctor saves lives, an airplane pilot flies planes safely, and *a teacher motivates students, inspires them to reach beyond what seems to be within their grasp.* For whatever reasons, my history teacher could not relate to me and chose not to try to motivate me to "make something of my life."

In closing, I want to challenge you to do like my earlier teacher did and plant some seeds in the students you come in contact with, so that someday they will benefit from having known you. Each and every one of you can make a tremendous difference in the life of another person. We can all plant something for someone else to harvest. When I look throughout history, the people I most admire are not often labeled as "great" or praised by the larger society but are people who are committed to "truth" and who in their own ways believe that their little part of the world would be better because they had come that way. At the very least, all of us as teachers can serve as models for the young. *Those of you who will be teachers are going into the most important job in the world.* Those of you who teach in elementary schools truly make a difference at the crucial point in the lives of our children. Because of that, you have the unique opportunity to help shape our society and world.

Source: This speech was given on November 29, 1995, at the Teacher Certification Recognition Ceremony at The University of Texas at Arlington by Dr. George Wright, Provost, UT Arlington.

As Dr. Wright's remarks demonstrate, teachers are the critical elements in teaching and learning because of the potential they have to impact the lives of children through interactions and the curriculum development process. If the elementary teacher does not take the concept of a moral profession seriously, great damage can be done by creating a situation in which nothing is taught, students are bored or disinterested, and/or students are not encouraged or motivated to "make something out of their lives." Elementary teachers should bring to the curriculum development process a personal integrity that is geared to instructing children within the framework of what is educationally best for them.

Throughout this book, various teachers have spoken as "Voices of Experience," to illustrate the constant stream of decisions that teachers make daily as they become reflective professionals and think about what and how they plan for teaching and carry out those plans. It should be clear to you after reading the previous chapters that teaching in the elementary school is a challenging endeavor. Elementary teachers are called upon to perform many roles, ranging from comforter and counselor to enforcer or manager. Teaching in the elementary school ultimately means sharing, as teachers give not only academically but emotionally to their students. This epilogue examines some of the ways teachers can create a nurturing curriculum and classroom environment through change and reflective practice.

Linda, the "Voice of Experience" for this section, describes her life as a teacher and expresses the joys and some of the frustrations that accompany teaching and learning in the elementary school.

 Voice of Experience

It is near the end of the year, and Linda visits with several of her colleagues to reflect on the year that they have had. As the school year comes to an end, they are all tired, but they feel a sense of satisfaction for a job well done. As one teacher says, "Most people do not realize how physically demanding teaching is and how teaching 25-30 students during the year takes a physical as well as emotional toll on us." Linda responds by saying, "There are so many more kids each year who come to school with serious emotional problems, and they seem to demand more and more attention from me." Another teacher responds by saying, "It's not so much that parents don't care; they do, but they just

don't want additional hassles because they are so busy with their own lives!"

Although Linda sometimes finds herself feeling that she has to continually give, she loves what she does and thrives on watching kids learn to read and begin to make sense of their world. She comments, "When I am attentive, loving, compassionate, and supportive with my students, they repay me in so many ways by turning on to learning. When that happens, I know I do make a difference in the lives of my students. When they come back one, two, or three years later, they tell me what a special teacher I was to them, or they say that because of me they went on to do something they didn't think they could do. These are special moments and are what keep me trying new things every year to help kids learn." Linda and her colleagues treasure these times that make teaching truly special, and they encourage others to teach because they love seeing the impact good teachers have on the lives of children.

As Linda and her colleagues note, teaching can be rewarding, and each year they strive to develop a curriculum that matches content to needs and activities to interests. They try year after year to create a positive place for teaching and learning. The world of the elementary classroom as described by Fulghum (1988) in *All I Really Need to Know I Learned in Kindergarten* seems timeless in many ways. In such an environment, it is essential to have fun (Fulghum, 1988). Glasser (1984) reminds us to "think back to a teacher whose lessons you still vividly remember and you will almost always recall that, whatever she [he] taught, her [his] class was fun" (p. 14). From the first year, teaching is a continuous learning experience, and each subsequent year provides opportunities to learn and try new things. Kronowitz (1996) suggests that teachers guard against the urge to be the perfect "superteacher" by reciting the following ten times each day:

I will be as forgiving of myself as I am of my students. I will be realistic and won't dwell on mistakes. This too shall pass. Everything is a learning experience. It seemed like the best thing to do at the time. Mistakes are learning opportunities. I'll do my best every day; then I won't worry. (p. 156)

In addition to creating a professional environment for teaching and learning, elementary teachers must also be willing to engage in continuous learning and make changes to be more effective and more responsive to their students' needs. As teachers seek to be more effective and responsive, they can consider implementing mentoring programs, thematic integrated curricula, literature-based reading, and/or hands-on, minds-on science programs. A common thread runs through all these programs, and that common thread is change. In order to grow professionally and to implement any program successfully, change is required—a change in attitudes and philosophy about what is taught and how, in using different materials and equipment (computers and laser discs), in teaching children from diverse backgrounds; a change in the way things are taught and when; a change in how decisions are made and by whom; and a change in expectations. The list is endless because as society changes so does its children—and with them the school curriculum and the teachers who implement it.

Covey (1990) says that change requires new thinking, thinking not steeped in the past and not used as a straitjacket when implementing new programs, experiences, equipment, and/or teaching strategies. Covey (1990) believes that "our paradigms . . . are sources of our attitudes and behaviors, and ultimately our relationships with others" (p. 30). As a result of a shift in thinking, you see things differently, you think differently, feel differently, and behave differently. Perhaps if Dr. Wright's history teacher had been able to think differently, he would have responded differently. Change, then, is the common denominator of curriculum development because it requires us to rethink our goals, objectives, priorities, and values for teaching and learning.

For the skeptics of change, the cup is half empty, and for the risk-takers who dare to change, the cup is half full. In either case, the members of the educational community need to reorder their priorities and be committed to meeting the needs of all children. According to Levin (1992), living the dream of making schools good for both children and adults means thinking of an educational environment in which all are successful. For this to take place requires unity of purpose, empowerment with responsibility, and building on strengths. The seeds of change need to be planted today if they are to bear fruit tomorrow. To make a difference in the professional life of each teacher, the seeds of change need time to grow and be nurtured so they can continue to make a difference in the lives of all children.

In addition to embracing change, teachers are called upon to be vision builders. As indicated earlier, Berliner (1996) and Fullan (1993), as well as others, see teaching as a moral profession with a moral purpose. It is *moral* in the sense of making a difference and having a concern for bringing about change. Fullan (1993) goes on to say that this "moral purpose keeps teachers close to the needs of children and youth; change agentry causes them to develop better strategies for accomplishing their moral goals" (p. 12). Teachers are vision builders, and creating a personal vision involves the process of examining and reexamining the reasons we came to be teachers (Fullan, 1993). For the majority of teachers, the whys for entering the teaching profession are many, and the roots of those reasons run deep. When someone asks why we choose to teach, our responses reveal the moral side of teaching, as we articulate what teaching means to us and why we teach.

As teachers reflect on their role, they are empowered to be not only settlers but pioneers. They come to understand why they wanted to be teachers in the first place and why helping others—students, colleagues, and parents—is fundamental to professional growth and continuous improvement. It is through such introspection that a renewed commitment to students and their learning is developed. By engaging in the process of interpreting one's own classroom events from the very beginning, teachers improve as their experiences become more varied, situation-specific, and dilemma-ridden (Sparks-Langer & Colton, 1991). Such experiences provide deeper and richer opportunities for making curriculum decisions.

With time and reflective practice, teachers can connect with their mental designs and improvise. Improvisation appears natural for experienced teachers because the routines, content, and strategies are readily available in their memory, and they can access this data quickly when the environment calls for it: "schemata do not automatically appear in a teacher's mind; they are constructed through experience" (Sparks-Langer & Colton, 1991, p. 38). Such a constructivist view reaches back to Piaget (1978) who described learning as a process of assimilation and accommodation. Reflective teachers monitor their actions, the decisions and inferences made, and outcomes, and become better at self-regulation (Sparks-Langer & Colton, 1991). The strat-

egy of teachers' reflective thinking may provide them with guideposts for developing appropriate growth experiences on their journey to becoming the best elementary teachers possible.

Each year, as you begin teaching, be sure to notice how you make a difference in your students' lives. Throughout the year, take time to embrace change as you learn more about yourself. As you change, you will begin to live what you value, take responsibility for your actions, and be positive in your outlook (Krupp, 1993).

As vision builders, elementary teachers are proud of what they do as they help students succeed. When students succeed, teachers succeed. Teachers take their job seriously, and they are entrusted with the most important thing—helping young children learn.

We are still teaching after more than fifty (combined) years because we continue to have a dream! We still believe we make a difference in the lives of others preparing to be teachers and in their students' lives. Best wishes in pursuing your dreams!

■ REFERENCES

Berliner, D. (1996, February 27). *Research and social justice.* Paper presented at the 76th Annual Meeting of the Association of Teacher Educators, St. Louis, MO.

Covey, S. (1990). *The 7 habits of highly effective people.* New York: Fireside.

Fulghum, R. (1988). *All I really need to know I learned in kindergarten.* New York: Ivy Books.

Fullan, M. G. (1993, March). Why teachers must become change agents. *Educational Leadership, 50*(6), 12-17.

Glasser, W. (1984). *Control theory: A new explanation of how we control our lives.* New York: Harper & Row.

Kronowitz, E. (1996). *Your first year of teaching and beyond* (2nd ed.). White Plains, NY: Longman.

Krupp, J. A. (1993, August/September). Self-trust in a distrusting environment. *PreK-8, 24*(1), 56-57.

Levin, H. (1992, May). *Accelerating the education of all students.* Santa Rosa, CA: Redwood Region Consortium for Professional Development.

Piaget, J. (1978). *Success and understanding.* Cambridge, MA: Harvard University Press.

Sparks-Langer, G. M., & Colton, A. B. (1991, March). Synthesis of research on teachers' reflective thinking. *Educational Leadership, 48,* 37-44.

Subject Index

Name Index

Adeyanju, M., 329, 346
Ahlgren, A., 305, 324
Alexander, W. M., 20, 24, 102, 117, 122, 173, 193
Allen, D., 202, 203, 216
Allen, J., 43, 46
American Association for the Advancement of Science, 300, 301, 323
American Association of University Women, 53, 66
American Association on Mental Deficiencies, 80, 93
Anderson, R. H., 38, 46
Anglin, J., 339, 346
Anrig, G. R., 33, 46
Appleton, N., 11, 23
Archambault, J., 202, 216
Archibald, S., 257, 259, 269
Arends, R., 127, 147
Aristotle, 104, 121
Armstrong, D. G., 103, 121, 285, 286, 293, 297
Armstrong, T., 78, 82, 93, 143, 147, 327, 328, 329, 330, 336, 345, 346
Arnosky, J., 304, 324
Attanucci, J., 90, 94
Auckerman, R., 340, 346
Ayala, L., 202, 216

Baer, E., 340, 346
Bagley, W. C., 104, 121
Baker, E., 20, 24, 70, 95, 112, 122, 184, 185, 193
Baker, M. B., 43, 46
Ballard, E., 79, 93
Barbour, N., 13, 25
Barr, R. D., 274, 277, 278, 296, 339, 346
Barth, J. L., 274, 277, 278, 296
Baxter, G. P., 171, 193
Baylor, B., 304, 324
Beach. D. M., 101, 103, 116, 117, 118, 121, 122, 151, 156, 161, 167

Beane, J., 132, 133, 135, 147, 275, 279, 281, 296
Beard, C., 273, 296
Beauchamp, G. A., 113, 121
Beckner, W., 273, 296
Bednarz, R. S., 285, 296
Bell, C., 54, 66
Bennett, W. J., 28, 46
Berk, L., 91, 93
Berliner, D., 31, 46, 100, 103, 121, 140, 147, 349, 353, 354
Biehler, R. F., 85, 93
Bierlein, L. A., 43, 46
Biener, L., 294, 296
Bixler, K., 203, 216
Blair, T. R., 225, 245
Bloom, B. S., 140, 147, 148, 161, 167
Bobbitt, F., 19, 23
Bode, B. H., 15, 23, 115, 121
Bondi, J., 19, 25
Borasi, R., 267, 269
Bourgeois, P., 340, 346
Boyer, E. L., 43, 46
Bradley Commission on History in the Schools, 275, 296
Bradsher, M., 203, 216
Bragaw, D. H., 274, 296
Brennan, S., 40, 46
Brody, R. A., 286, 296
Brooks, J. G., 86, 87, 88, 93
Brooks, M. G., 86, 87, 88, 93
Brophy, J., 163, 167
Brown, R., 319, 324
Brownell, W. A., 248, 269
Bruder, I., 201, 216
Bruner, J. S., 20, 23, 73, 74, 78, 94, 96, 118, 121
Burton, V., 143, 147
Buckleitner, W., 202, 208, 216